A Note from the Authors

Congratulations on your decision to take the AP Economics exams! Whether or not you're completing an AP economics course, this book can help you prepare for both the Macroeconomics and Microeconomics exams. Inside, you'll find information about the exams as well as Kaplan's test-taking strategies, targeted reviews of both macro- and microeconomics that highlight the most frequently tested concepts, and a diagnostic and a practice test for both disciplines. Don't miss the strategies for answering the free-response questions: You'll learn how to cover the key points AP graders will want to see.

By studying college-level economics in high school, you've placed yourself a step ahead of other students. You've developed your critical-thinking and time-management skills, as well as your understanding of the practice of economic research. Now it's time for you to show off what you've learned by acing the exams.

Best of luck,

Sangeeta K. Bishop

Christine Parrott

Chuck Martie

Raymond Miller

RELATED TITLES

AP Biology

AP Calculus AB & BC

AP Chemistry

AP English Language & Composition

AP English Literature & Composition

AP Environmental Science

AP European History

AP Human Geography

AP Physics B & C

AP Psychology

AP Statistics

AP U.S. Government & Politics

AP U.S. History

AP World History

SAT Subject Test: Biology E/M

SAT Subject Test: Chemistry

SAT Subject Test: Literature

SAT Subject Test: Mathematics Level 1

SAT Subject Test: Mathematics Level 2

SAT Subject Test: Physics

SAT Subject Test: Spanish

SAT Subject Test: U.S. History

SAT Subject Test: World History

AP® Macroeconomics/ Microeconomics

2008 Edition

Sangeeta K. Bishop

Christine Parrott

Chuck Martie

Raymond Miller

New York

Vice President and Publisher: Maureen McMahon
Editorial Director: Jennifer Farthing
Development Editor: Sheryl Gordon
Production Editor: Dominique Polfliet
Production Designers: Parameshwaran and Sivakumar
Cover Designer: Carly Schnur

Published by Kaplan Publishing, a division of Kaplan, Inc.
1 Liberty Plaza, 24th Floor
New York, NY 10006

Printed in the United States of America

January 2008
10 9 8 7 6 5 4 3 2

ISBN-13: 978-1-4195-5169-7

Table of Contents

About the Authors ix

Kaplan Panel of AP Experts xi

PART ONE: The Basics

Chapter 1: Inside the AP Economics Exams 3

Overview of the Exam Structure 5

How the Exams Are Scored 7

Registration and Fees 8

Additional Resources 8

Chapter 2: Strategies for Success: It's Not Always How Much You Know 15

Strategies for the AP Economics Exams 16

Section I: Multiple-Choice Questions 17

Ten-Minute Reading Period 22

Section II: Free-Response Questions 22

Stress Management 25

Countdown to the Tests 27

PART TWO: Diagnostic Tests

AP Macroeconomics Diagnostic Test 33

How to Compute Your Score 34

Answers and Explanations 44

AP Microeconomics Diagnostic Test 51

How to Compute Your Score 52

Answers and Explanations 60

PART THREE: AP Macroeconomics Review

Chapter 3: Basic Economic Concepts 67

Scarcity, Choice, and Opportunity Costs 67

Production Possibilities Curve 70

Comparative Advantage, Specialization, and Exchange 72
Demand, Supply, and Market Equilibrium.... 73
Review Questions 78
Answers and Explanations 79

Chapter 4: Measurement of Economic Performance 81
National Income Accounts 81
GDP 82
Business Cycles, Unemployment, and Growth 83
Inflation Measurement 84
Unemployment 84
Review Questions 88
Answers and Explanations 91

Chapter 5: National Income and Price Determination 93
Aggregate Demand (AD) 93
Aggregate Supply (AS) 96
Macroeconomic Equilibrium 97
Fiscal Policy and the Multipliers 99
Review Questions 102
Answers and Explanations 105

Chapter 6: Financial Sector 107
Money, Banking, and Financial Markets 107
The Central Bank and Control of the Money Supply 110
Review Questions 115
Answers and Explanations 118

Chapter 7: Inflation, Unemployment, and Stabilization Policies 121
Fiscal and Monetary Policies 121
Inflation and Unemployment 126
Review Questions 128
Answers and Explanations 132

Chapter 8: Economic Growth and Productivity 137
Economic Growth 137
Review Questions 140
Answers and Explanations 142

Chapter 9: Open Economy: International Trade and Finance 145
Balance of Payment Accounts 145
Foreign Exchange Market 147
Trade Restrictions 148
Review Questions 149
Answers and Explanations 152

PART FOUR: AP Microeconomics Review
Chapter 10: Basic Economic Concepts 157
Scarcity, Choice, and Opportunity Cost 157
Production Possibilities Curve 157
Comparative Advantage, Specialization, and Trade 159
Economic Systems 160
Property Rights and Incentives 161
Marginal Analysis 161
Review Questions 162
Answers and Explanations 164

Chapter 11: The Nature and Structure of Product Markets 165
Supply and Demand 165
Theory of Consumer Choice 180
Firm Behavior and Market Structure 184
Review Questions 194
Answers and Explanations 202

Chapter 12: Factor Markets 209

Derived Factor Demand 209

Marginal Revenue Product 209

Labor Market and Firms' Hiring of Labor 211

Review Questions 215

Answers and Explanations 218

Chapter 13: Market Failure and the Role of Government 223

Externalities 223

Public Goods 230

Public Policy to Promote Competition 232

Income Distribution 232

Review Questions 235

Answers and Explanations 239

PART FIVE: Practice Tests

How to Take the Practice Tests 244

How to Compute Your Score 245

AP Macroeconomics Practice Test 249

Answers and Explanations 269

AP Microeconomics Practice Test 281

Answers and Explanations 300

AP ECONOMICS GLOSSARY 311

ABOUT THE AUTHORS

Anaxos Inc. was founded in 1999 by Drew and Cynthia Johnson. Anaxos is a leading provider of educational content for print and electronic media.

Sangeeta K. Bishop is an Assistant Professor of Economics at the Borough of Manhattan Community College, City University of New York. Dr. Bishop has over 10 years of teaching experience and involvement with student advisement and curriculum review.

Christine Parrott is an economics instructor at Austin Community College and holds an MA in economics from the University of Texas at Arlington.

Chuck Martie holds a Ph.D. in Economics from the University of Connecticut and works as an analyst in the Governor's Office for Policy Research in Kentucky.

Raymond Miller holds a Ph.D. in Economics from Tulane University and is an assistant professor of economics at Southern University at New Orleans.

STUDENTS AND TEACHERS—GO ONLINE!

FOR STUDENTS

kaptest.com/booksonline

Get even more AP practice online! Visit kaptest.com/booksonline and take a free 20-question quiz. You'll be asked for a specific password derived from the text in this book, so have your book handy when you log on.

FOR TEACHERS

kaplanclassroom.com

Visit our resource area for teachers. We've provided ideas about how this book can be used effectively in and out of your AP classroom. Easy to implement, these tips are designed to complement your curriculum plans and help you create a classroom full of high-scoring students.

---

kaptest.com/publishing

The material in this book is up-to-date at the time of publication but the College Board may have instituted changes to the test since that date. Be sure to carefully read the materials you receive when you register for the test. If there are any important late-breaking developments—or any changes or corrections to the Kaplan test preparation materials in this book—we will post that information online at kaptest.com/publishing.

kaplansurveys.com/books

If you have comments and suggestions about this book, we invite you to fill out our online survey form at kaplansurveys.com/books. Your feedback is extremely helpful as we continue to develop high-quality resources to meet your needs.

KAPLAN PANEL OF AP EXPERTS

Congratulations—you have chosen Kaplan to help you get a top score on your AP exam.

Kaplan understands your goals, and what you're up against—achieving college credit and conquering a tough test—while participating in everything else that high school has to offer.

You expect realistic practice, authoritative advice and accurate, up-to-the-minute information on the test. And that's exactly what you'll find in this book, as well as every other in the AP series. To help you (and us!) reach these goals, we have sought out leaders in the AP community. Allow us to introduce our experts:

AP Macroeconomics/Microeconomics Experts

Linda M. Manning is a visiting professor and researcher in residence at the University of Ottawa in Ontario, Canada. She has worked with the AP Economics program and the Educational Testing Service as a faculty consultant for almost 15 years, and has served on the test development committee from 1997-2000.

Bill McCormick has been teaching AP Economics at Spring Valley High School and Richland Northeast High School in Columbia, South Carolina, for the past 26 years. He has served as a reader of AP Macroeconomics and Microeconomics exams for the past 8 years.

Sally Meek is an AP Microeconomics and AP Macroeconomics teacher at Plano West Senior High School in Plano, Texas. She has been an AP Economics reader since 1998 and was recently appointed to the AP Economics Test Development Committee. Sally is also a member of the NAEP Economics Steering Committee and was the recipient of the Southwest College Board Advanced Placement Special Recognition Award in 2004. In 2005, she served as the President of the Global Association of Teachers of Economics (GATE).

Peggy Pride has taught AP Economics at St. Louis University High School in St. Louis, Missouri for 15 years. She served for 5 years on the AP Economics Test Development Committee, and was the primary author for the new AP Economics Teacher's Guide published by College Board in the spring of 2005.

AP Biology Experts

Franklin Bell has taught AP Biology since 1994, most recently at Saint Mary's Hall in San Antonio, Texas where he is science dept co chair. He has been an AP Biology reader for 6 years and table leader for 2 years. In addition, he has been an AP Biology consultant at College Board workshops, and he also received the Southwestern Region's College Board Special Recognition Award.

Larry Calabrese has taught biology for 36 years, and AP Biology for 19 years at Palos Verdes Peninsula High School in CA. He also teaches Anatomy and Physiology at Los Angeles Harbor College in Wilmington, CA. He has been an AP Biology reader since 1986, and a table leader since 1993. For the past 10 years, he has taught College Board workshops.

Cheryl G. Callahan has been teaching biology for over 20 years, first at the college level and now at the high school level at Savannah Country Day School, Savannah, Georgia. She has been an AP Biology reader and table leader since 1993. She also moderates the AP Biology Electronic Discussion Group.

AP Calculus Expert

William Fox has been teaching calculus at the university level for over 20 years. He has been at Francis Marion University in Florence, South Carolina since 1998. He has been a reader and table leader for the AP Calculus AB and BC exams since 1992.

AP Chemistry Experts

Lenore Hoyt teaches chemistry at Idaho State University. She has done post-doctoral studies at Yale University and holds a PhD from the University of Tennessee. She has been a reader for the AP Chemistry exam for 5 years.

Jason Just has been teaching AP, IB, and general chemistry for 15 years at suburban high schools around St. Paul, Minnesota. He has contributed to science curriculum and teacher training through St. Mary's University, the Science Museum of Minnesota, and Lakeville Area, South St. Paul, and North St. Paul public schools.

Lisa Zuraw has been a professor in the Chemistry Department at The Citadel in Charleston, South Carolina, for 13 years. She has served as a faculty reader for the AP Chemistry exam and as a member of the AP Chemistry Test Development Committee.

AP English Language & Composition Experts

Natalie Goldberg recently retired from St. Ignatius College Prep in Chicago, Illinois, where she helped develop a program to prepare juniors for the AP English Language and Composition exam and taught AP English Literature. She was a reader for the AP English Language and Composition exam for 6 years and has been a consultant with the Midwest Region of the College Board since 1997.

Susan Sanchez has taught AP English for 7 years and English for the past 26 years at Mark Keppel High School, a Title I Achieving School and a California Distinguished School, in Alhambra, California. She has been an AP reader for 7 years and a table leader for 2. She has been a member of the California State University Reading Institutes for Academic Preparation task force since its inception in 2000. Susan has also been a presenter at the Title I High Achieving Conference and at the Greater Los Angeles Advanced Placement Summer Institute.

Ronald Sudol has been a reader of AP English Language and Composition for 21 years, a table leader for 12, and a workshop consultant for 13. He is Professor of Rhetoric at Oakland University in MI, where he is also Acting Dean of the College of Arts and Sciences.

AP English Literature & Composition Experts

Mitchell S. Billings has taught for over 35 years and began the AP program at Catholic High School in Baton Rouge, LA over 12 years ago. He has taught AP Summer Institutes at Western Kentucky University in Bowling Green, KY, for 5 years, Milsaps University in Jackson, MS for 2 years, and Xavier University in New Orleans, LA for 2 years. He has been an endorsed College Board Consultant for over 12 years and has conducted College Board workshops for English Literature and Composition throughout the Southeast region of the US for over 10 years. He has also been a reader for the AP exam for 10 years and for the alternate AP exam for over 2 years.

William H. Pell has taught AP English for 30 years and chairs the Language Arts Department at Spartanburg High School in Spartanburg, SC where he also serves as the schoolwide Curriculum Facilitator. He has been an adjunct instructor of English at the University of South Carolina Upstate, and has been active in many programs for the College Board, including the reading, workshops, institutes, conferences, and vertical teams.

AP Environmental Science Expert

Dora Barlaz teaches at the Horace Mann School, an independent school in Riverdale, New York. She has taught AP Environmental Science since the inception of the course, and has been a reader for 4 years.

AP European History Expert

Jerry Hurd has been teaching AP European History for 16 years at Olympic High School in Silverdale, Washington. He has been a consultant to the College Board and an AP reader for 9 years and a table leader for the past 5 years. He regularly attends the AP Premier Summer Institute and leads workshops in AP European History. In 2002, he was voted "Most Outstanding Table Leader."

AP Human Geography Expert

Michael Bolsoni has been teaching AP Human Geography since its inception in 2001 and has been an AP exam reader for 3 years. He has just completed his 11th year as a faculty member at the School of Environmental Studies in Apple Valley, Minnesota where he teaches a variety of social and environmental studies courses.

AP Physics Experts

Jeff Funkhouser has taught high school physics since 1988. Since 2001, he has taught AP Physics B and C at Northwest High School in Justin, TX. He has been a reader and a table leader since 2001.

Dolores Gende has an undergraduate degree in Chemical Engineering from the Iberoamericana University in Mexico City. She has 13 years of experience teaching college level introductory physics courses and presently teaches at the Parish Episcopal School in Dallas, Texas. Dolores serves as an AP Physics table leader, an AP Physics Workshop Consultant, and as the College Board Advisor for the AP Physics Development Committee. She received the Excellence in Physics Teaching Award by the Texas section of the American Association of Physics Teachers in March 2006.

Martin Kirby has taught AP Physics B and tutored students for Physics C at Hart High School in Newhall, California for the last 18 years. He has been a reader for the AP Physics B & C exams and a workshop presenter for the College Board for the past 10 years.

AP Psychology Experts

Ruth Ault has taught psychology for the past 25 years at Davidson College in Davidson, North Carolina. She was a reader for the AP Psychology exam and has been a table leader since 2001.

Nancy Homb has taught AP Psychology for the past 7 years at Cypress Falls High School in Houston, Texas. She has been a reader for the AP Psychology exam since 2000 and began consulting for the College Board in 2005.

Barbara Loverich has taught psychology for the past 18 years at Hobart High School in Valparaiso, Indiana. She has been an AP reader for 9 years and a table leader for 6 years. From 1996–2000, she was a board member of Teachers of Psychology in Secondary Schools and was on the state of Indiana committee to write state psychology standards. Among her distinguished awards are the Outstanding Science Educator Award and Sigma XI, Scientific Research Society in 2002.

AP Statistics Experts

Lee Kucera has been teaching Statistics at Capistrano Valley High School in Mission Viejo, California, for 12 years where she has been a teacher for 26 years. She has also been a reader for the AP Statistics exam since its inception in 1997.

Jodie Miller has been a mathematics teacher at the secondary and college levels for the past ten years. As a participant in the AP Statistics program, she has served as an exam reader, table leader, workshop consultant, and multiple choice item writer for the College Board since 1999.

Mary Mortlock has been teaching statistics since 1996, beginning at Thomas Jefferson High School for Science & Technology in Alexandria, Virginia and continuing on to her current position at Cal Poly State University in California, where she has taught since 2001. Mary has also been a reader for the AP Statistics exam since 2000.

Dr. Murray Siegel has been teaching statistics at the high school level since 1976 and at the college level since 1977. He has been a College Board AP Statistics consultant since 1995 and served as an exam reader in 1998 and 2002, and has been an exam table leader from 2003–2005. He currently teaches AP Statistics at the South Carolina Governor's School for Science & Mathematics.

AP U.S. Government and Politics Expert

Chuck Brownson teaches AP U.S. Government and Politics at Stephen F. Austin High School in Sugar Land, Texas. He is currently a graduate student working on his Master's Degree in Political Science at the University of Houston. He has been teaching AP U.S. Government and Politics and AP Economics classes for four years. He has been a reader for the AP U.S. Government and Politics exam for one year.

AP U.S. History Experts

Gwen Cash is a Lead Consultant for the College Board, and has served on the AP Advisory Council, the Teacher Advocacy Committee, and the conference planning committee in the Southwest region. She also helped to write the AP Social Studies Vertical Teams guide. Ms. Cash holds a BA and an MD from The University of Texas at Austin, Texas as she teaches on-level and AP U.S. History courses at Clear Creek High School in League City, Texas. She is currently serving as a member of the College Readiness Vertical Team for the state of Texas.

Steven Mercado has taught AP U.S. History and AP European History at Chaffey High School in Ontario, California for the past 14 years. He has been a reader for the AP U.S. History exam. He has also served as a member of the AP European History Test Development Committee, and as a reader and table leader for the AP European History exam.

AP World History Experts

Jay Harmon has taught world history for the past 24 years in Houston, Texas and Baton Rouge, Louisiana. He has been a table leader for the AP World History exam since its inception in 2002 and has served on its test development committee.

Lenore Schneider has taught AP World History for 4 years and AP European History for 16 years at New Canaan High School in New Canaan, Connecticut. She has been a Reader for 13 years, served as Table Leader for 10 years, helped to set benchmarks, and served on the Test Development Committee for 3 years. She has taught numerous workshops and institutes as a College Board consultant in 8 states, and received the New England region's Special Recognition award.

| PART ONE |

The Basics

Chapter 1:
Inside the AP Economics Exams

- **Overview of the Exam Structure**
- **How the Exams Are Scored**
- **Registration and Fees**
- **Additional Resources**

If you are reading this, chances are that you're already in (or thinking about taking) an Advanced Placement (AP) Economics course. If you score high enough on the exams, many universities will give you three hours of credit (one class) in a related introductory economics course (you can get three hours of credit for each AP exam—three for Microeconomics and three for Macroeconomics).

Depending on the college, a score of 4 or 5 on one or both of the AP Economics exams will allow you to leap over the freshman intro course and jump right into more advanced classes. These classes are usually smaller in size, better focused, more intellectually stimulating, and simply put, more interesting than a basic course. If you are solely concerned about fulfilling your social science requirement so you can get on with your study of Elizabethan music or French literature, AP exams can help you there, too. Ace one or both of the AP Economics exams and, depending on the requirements of the college you choose, you may never have to take a social science class again.

If you're currently taking an AP Economics course, chances are that your teacher has spent the year cramming your head full of the economics know-how you will need for the exams. But there is more to the AP Economics exams than know-how. If you want your score to reflect your abilities, you will have to be able to work around the challenges and pitfalls of the tests. Studying economics and preparing for the AP Economics exams are not the same thing. Rereading your textbook is always helpful, but it's not enough.

That's where this book comes in. We'll show you how to marshal your knowledge of economics and put it to brilliant use on Test Day. We'll explain the ins and outs of the test structure and question format so you won't experience any nasty surprises. We'll even give you answering strategies designed specifically for the AP Economics exams.

Preparing yourself effectively for the AP Economics exams means doing some extra work. You need to review your text *and* master the material in this book. Is the extra push worth it? If you have any doubts, think of all the interesting things you could be doing in college instead of taking an intro course filled with facts you already know.

Advanced Placement exams have been around for a half of a century. While the format and content have changed over the years, the basic goal of the AP Program remains the same: to give high school students a chance to earn college credit or placement in more advanced college courses. To do this, a student needs to do two things:

1. Find a college that accepts AP scores
2. Do well enough on the exams to place out of required subjects

The first part is easy, since a majority of colleges accept AP scores in some form or another. The second part requires a little more effort. If you have worked diligently all year in your coursework, you've laid the groundwork. The next step is familiarizing yourself with the test itself.

As you may know, there are actually two AP Economics exams: AP Macroeconomics and AP Microeconomics. Each exam is 2 hours and 10 minutes long, each exam is graded separately, and each is worth a one-semester college introductory course. A single fee covers both exams, which are administered consecutively on the assigned examination day. You are not required to take both exams. One exam is usually given in the morning and one in the afternoon, so you won't have to sit through the exam you are not taking. Choose the exam for which you have prepared and studied.

OVERVIEW OF THE EXAM STRUCTURE

The Educational Testing Service (ETS)—the company that creates the AP exams—releases a list of the topics covered on each exam. They even provide the percentage amount that each topic appears on a given exam. Check out the breakdown of topics of the AP Macroeconomics and Microeconomics exams below.

MACROECONOMICS

I. Basic Macroeconomics Concepts (8–12%)
   A. Scarcity, choice, and opportunity costs
   B. Production possibilities curve
   C. Comparative advantage, specialization, and exchange
   D. Supply, demand, and market equilibrium
   E. Macroeconomic issues: business cycle, unemployment, inflation, growth

II. Measurement of Economic Performance (12–16%)
   A. National income accounts
   B. Inflation measurement and adjustment
   C. Unemployment

III. National Income and Price Determination (10–15%)
   A. Aggregate demand
   B. Aggregate supply
   C. Macroeconomic equilibrium

IV. Financial Sector (15–20%)
   A. Money, banking, and financial markets
   B. Central bank and control of the money supply

V. Inflation, Unemployment, and Stabilization Policies (20–30%)
   A. Fiscal and monetary policies
   B. Inflation and unemployment

VI. Economic Growth and Productivity (5–10%)
   A. Investment in human capital
   B. Investment in physical capital
   C. Research and development, and technological progress
   D. Growth policy

VII. Open Economy: International Trade and Finance (10–15%)
  A. Balance of payments accounts
  B. Foreign exchange markets
  C. Net exports and capital flows
  D. Links to financial and goods markets

MICROECONOMICS

I. Basic Microeconomics Concepts (8–14%)
  A. Scarcity, choice, and opportunity cost
  B. Production possibilities curve
  C. Comparative advantage, specialization, and trade
  D. Economic systems
  E. Property rights and the role of incentives
  F. Marginal analysis

II. The Nature and Functions of Product Markets (50–70%)
  A. Supply and demand
  B. Theory of consumer choice
  C. Production and costs
  D. Firm behavior and market structure

III. Factor Markets (10–18%)
  A. Derived factor demand
  B. Marginal revenue product
  C. Labor market and firms' hiring of labor
  D. Market distribution of income

IV. Market Failure and the Role of Government (12–18%)
  A. Externalities
  B. Public goods
  C. Public policy to promote competition
  D. Income distribution

HOW THE EXAMS ARE SCORED

Each AP Economics exam is 2 hours and 10 minutes long and consists of two parts: a multiple-choice section and a free-response section. In Section I, you have 70 minutes to answer 60 multiple-choice questions, each of which has five possible answers. This section is worth 67% of your total score.

After this section is completed, you get a 10-minute "reading period." This is not a break or a chance to brush up on your economics knowledge. Instead, you get 10 minutes to pore over Section II of the exam, which consists of three "free-response" questions that are worth 33% of your grade. The term "free-response" means roughly the same thing as "large, multi-step, and involved," since you will spend 50 minutes of Section II answering these three problems. Although these free-response problems are long and often broken down into multiple parts, they are not trying to trip you up or confuse you. Instead they take a fairly basic economic concept and ask you a set of related questions about it. These questions frequently test your ability to see relationships and linkages among different economic processes, costs, and principles.

The first free-response question will require you to connect diverse topic categories and is the longest of the three. You will want to use about half the allotted time (25 minutes) on this question. The remaining two problems usually only relate to one topic or category and should be split evenly with the remaining time of about 12 minutes each.

When your 130 minutes of testing are up, your exam is sent away for grading. The multiple-choice part is handled by a machine, while qualified graders—called "readers"—grade your responses to Section II. The group of readers is made up of current AP economics teachers and college professors of principles-level economics. After a seemingly interminable wait, your composite score will arrive. Your results will be placed into one of the following categories, reported on a five-point scale.

5 Extremely well qualified (to receive college credit or advanced placement)
4 Well qualified
3 Qualified
2 Possibly qualified
1 No recommendation

Some colleges will give you college credit for a score of 3 or higher, but it's much safer to score a 4 or a 5. If you have an idea of which colleges you might attend, check out their websites or call their admissions offices to find out their particular criteria regarding AP scores.

REGISTRATION AND FEES

You can register for the exams by contacting your guidance counselor or AP coordinator. If your school doesn't administer the exam, contact AP Services for a listing of schools in your area that do. At the time of printing, the fee for each AP exam is $82. For students with financial need, a $22 reduction is available. To learn about other sources of financial aid, contact your AP coordinator.

For more information on all things AP, visit **collegeboard.com** or contact AP Services:

AP Services
P.O. Box 6671
Princeton, NJ 08541-6671
Phone: 609-771-7300 or 888-225-5427 (toll-free in the U.S. and Canada)
Email: apexams@info.collegeboard.org

ADDITIONAL RESOURCES

Basic Economic Concepts (Chapters 3 and 10)

Books

Principles of Macroeconomics, 3rd Edition
N. Gregory Mankiw
South-Western
ISBN 0324171897

Macroeconomics: Explore and Apply
Ronald M. Ayers and Robert A. Collinge
Prentice Hall
ISBN 0131463918

Opportunity Cost in Finance and Accounting
H.G. Heymann, Robert Bloom
Quorum Books
ISBN 0899304001

Trade and Market in the Early Empires
Edited by K. Polanyi, C. Arensberg, and H. Pearson
Free Press
ASIN B0007FE9ZU

Property Rights: Cooperation, Conflict, and Law
Edited by Terry L. Anderson and Fred S. McChesney
Princeton University Press
ISBN 0691099987

The Competitive Advantage of Nations
Michael E. Porter
Free Press
ISBN 0684841479

Comparative Advantage in International Trade: A Historical Perspective
Andrea Maneschi
Edward Elgar Publishing
ISBN 1858983002

Websites

Glossary of Economics Terms
economics.about.com/library/glossary/blindex.htm

Economics Basics
oswego.edu/~economic/eco101/chap3/chap3.htm

U.S. Economic Calendar
bloomberg.com/markets/ecalendar/

Economics at the Open Directory Project
http://dmoz.org/Science/Social_Sciences/Economics/

Economics textbooks on Wikibooks
http://en.wikibooks.org/wiki/Economics

The Economist's Economics A-Z
economist.com/research/Economics/

A guide to several online economics textbooks
oswego.edu/%7Eeconomic/newbooks.htm

History of Economics
http://etext.lib.virginia.edu/cgi-local/DHI/dhi.cgi?id=dv2-06

An index of all theories and theoreticians throughout the economic history of thought
economyprofessor.com/

Introduction to Economics
eco.nm.ru/

Comparison of various economic schools of thought on particular issues
http://homepage.newschool.edu/het/thought.htm

A set of economics resources for students
http://economics.about.com/

Measurement of Economic Performance (Chapter 4)

Books

Principles of Macroeconomics, 7th Edition
Karl E. Case and Ray C. Fair
Prentice Hall
ISBN 0131442341

Websites

Economic Report of the President
http://www.gpoaccess.gov/eop/

Bureau of Labor Statistics
http://www.bls.gov/

National Income and Price Determination (Chapter 5)

Books

Principles of Macroeconomics, 3rd Edition
N. Gregory Mankiw
South-Western
ISBN 0324171897

Websites

Say's Law and Supply-side Economics
friesian.com/sayslaw.htm

Business Cycle, Aggregate Demand and Aggregate Supply
http://www.colorado.edu/Economics/courses/econ2020/section7/section7-main.html

Financial Sector (Chapter 6)

Books

Principles of Macroeconomics, 7th Edition
Karl E. Case and Ray C. Fair
Prentice Hall
ISBN 0131442341

Websites

Federal Reserve
federalreserve.gov/

Federal Deposit Insurance Corporation
fdic.gov/index.html

Inflation, Unemployment, and Stabilization Policies (Chapter 7)

Books

Principles of Macroeconomics, 3rd Edition
N. Gregory Mankiw
South-Western
ISBN 0324171897

Macroeconomics: Explore and Apply
Ronald M. Ayers and Robert A. Collinge
Pearson/Prentice Hall, Enhanced Edition
ISBN 0131463918

Principles of Macroeconomics, 7th Edition
Karl E. Case and Ray C. Fair
Prentice Hall
ISBN 0131442341

Websites

Keynesian Economics
econlib.org/library/Enc/KeynesianEconomics.html

Monetary policy
econlib.org/library/Enc/MonetaryPolicy.html

AmosWeb
amosweb.com/cgi-bin/pdg.pl?fcd=dsp&term=Fighting+Business+Cycles+With+STABILIZATION+POLICIES

Economic Growth and Productivity (Chapter 8)

Books

Principles of Macroeconomics, 3rd Edition
N. Gregory Mankiw
South-Western
ISBN 0324171897

Websites

Economic Growth resources
bris.ac.uk/Depts/Economics/Growth/index.htm

Economic Growth
stanford.edu/~promer/Econgro.htm

Open Economy: International Trade and Finance (Chapter 9)

Books

Money, Banking, and the Economy, 6th Edition
Thomas Mayer, James Duesenberry, and Robert Aliber
W.W. Norton & Company
ISBN 0393968480

Websites

Sugar: The Political Economy of Protection
facsnet.org/tools/nbgs/p_thru_%20z/s/sugar.php3

Gold Standard
http://en.wikipedia.org/wiki/Gold_standard

Exchange Rates and Macroeconomics Policy
personal.psu.edu/faculty/d/x/dxl31/ec201/lecture22.html

The Nature and Structure of Product Markets (Chapter 11)

Books

Consumer Choice Behavior: A Cognitive Theory
Flemming Hansen
Free Press
ASIN B0006C5HTG

International Trade Policies, Incentives, and Firm Behavior (Foreign Economic Policy of the United States)
Thomas John Prusa
Taylor & Francis
ISBN 0824074734

New Developments in the Analysis of Market Structure
Edited by Joseph E. Stiglitz and G. Frank Mathewson
The MIT Press
ISBN 0262690934

Websites

Supply and Demand
Hubert D. Henderson at Project Gutenberg
gutenberg.org/dirs/1/0/6/1/10612/10612-h/10612-h.htm

Factor Markets (Chapter 12)

Books

Economics, 16th Edition
Campbell R. McConnell and Stanley L. Brue
McGraw-Hill Irwin
ISBN 0072819359

Microeconomics, 6th Edition
Roger A. Arnold
South-Western
ISBN 0324163568

Principles of Microeconomics, 3rd Edition
N. Gregory Mankiw
South-Western
ISBN 0324171889

Websites

"Factor Demand in the Short Run"
sussex.ac.uk/Units/economics/micro1/lectures/factor1.doc

"Characteristics and Behavior of African Factor Markets and Market Institutions and Their Consequences for Economic Growth" by Adeola F. Adenikiuj and Olugboyeza Oyeranti
http://ideas.repec.org/p/wop/cidhav/31.html

"The Impact of Ageing on Demand, Factor Markets, and Growth" by selected authors
http://papers.ssrn.com/sol3/papers.cfm?abstract_id=700064

Market Failure and the Role of Government (Chapter 13)

Books

Economics: Principles, Problems, and Policies, 16th Edition
Campbell R. McConnell and Stanley L. Brue
McGraw-Hill Irwin
ISBN 0072819359

Microeconomics, 6th Edition
Roger A. Arnold
South-Western
ISBN 0324163568

Principles of Microeconomics, 3rd Edition
N. Gregory Mankiw
South-Western
ISBN 0324171889

Websites

"Global Public Goods: A New Way to Balance the World's Books"
by Inge Kaul for *LeMonde Diplomatique*
http://mondediplo.com/2000/06/15publicgood

"Public Goods and Externalities" by Tyler Cowen
econlib.org/library/Enc/PublicGoodsandExternalities.html

"Inequality of Wealth and Income Distribution" (selected articles for the Global Policy Forum)
globalpolicy.org/socecon/inequal/indexinq.htm

"Income Inequality" from the U.S. Census Bureau, 1996
census.gov/hhes/www/p60191.html

Chapter 2: **Strategies for Success: It's Not Always How Much You Know**

- Strategies for the AP Economics Exams
- Section I: Multiple-Choice Questions
- Ten-Minute Reading Period
- Section II: Free-Response Questions
- Stress Management
- Countdown to the Tests

This book has been split up into two parts, one for each test. Feel free to focus only on the exam that you plan to take. **However, the test structure and question format are the same for both exams. Therefore, the testing strategies outlined in the first part of this book apply to both exams and should be read over and studied carefully, regardless of which exam you plan to take.**

We have scrutinized and analyzed the AP Economics exams to learn everything we can about them so we could then pass on this information to you. This book contains precisely the information you will need to ace the tests. There's nothing extra in here to waste your time—no pointless review material that won't be tested, no rah-rah speeches. Just the most potent test preparation tools available: **strategies**, **review**, and **practice**.

1. **Strategies**
   We're going to talk about Process of Elimination as it applies to the AP Economics exams, and only as it applies to those exams. There are several skills and general strategies that work for these particular tests, which will be covered in the next chapter.

2. **Review**
   The best test-taking strategies in the world won't get you a good score if you can't tell the difference between a marginal revenue product and an anti-trust policy. At its core, the AP Economics exams cover a wide range of economics topics, and learning these topics is **absolutely** necessary. However, chances are you're already familiar with these subjects, so we don't need to start from scratch. This is not an economics textbook; we've tailored our review section to focus

on the most relevant topics and how they typically appear on the exams. We also cover the things you should know to answer the questions correctly and the connections between the concepts that will help you think through the questions.

3. **Practice**

   Few things are better than experience when it comes to standardized testing. Taking a practice test gives you an idea of what it is like to answer economics questions for two-plus hours. It's definitely not a fun experience, but it is a helpful one. Practice tests give you the opportunity to find out which areas are your strongest, and what topics you should spend some additional time studying. And the best part is that it doesn't count—the mistakes you make on our practice tests are mistakes you won't make on the real tests.

The preceding three points describe the general outline of this book. Now let's look at some specific strategies you can use on the AP Economics exams.

STRATEGIES FOR THE AP ECONOMICS EXAMS

Sixty years ago, there was only one standardized test, administered by the U.S. Army to determine which enlistees were qualified for officer training. The idea behind the U.S. Army officer's exam has adapted and flourished in both the public and private sectors. Nowadays, you can't get through a semester of school without taking some letter jumble-exam like the PSAT, SAT, ACT, ASVAB, BLAM, ZORK, or FWOOSH (some of those tests are fake, some aren't). As you may already know, developing certain test-taking strategies is the best way to help prepare yourself for these exams. Since everyone reading this has already taken a standardized test of some sort, you are probably familiar with some of the general strategies that help students increase their scores on this kind of test. Some of these general strategies are:

1. **Pacing**

   Since many tests are timed, proper pacing allows you to attempt every question in the time allotted. Poor pacing causes you to spend too much time on some questions to the point where you may run out of time before attempting every problem.

2. **Process of Elimination**

   On every multiple-choice tests you ever take, the answer is given to you. The only difficulty resides in the fact that the correct answer is hidden among incorrect choices. Even so, the multiple-choice format means you don't have to pluck the answer out of thin air. Instead, if you can eliminate answer choices you know are incorrect and only one choice remains, then it must be the correct answer.

3. **Patterns and Trends**

   Standardized is the key word in "standardized testing." Standardized tests don't change greatly from year to year. Sure, each question won't be the same, and different topics will be covered from one administration to the next, but there will also be a lot of overlap from one year to the next. That's the nature of *standardized* testing: If the test changed wildly each time it came out, it would be useless as a tool for comparison. Because of this, certain patterns can be uncovered about any standardized test. Learning about a test's patterns and trends can help students taking the test for the first time.

4. **The Right Approach**

   Having the right mindset plays a large part in how well you will do on a test. If you're nervous about the exam and hesitant to make guesses, you'll fare much worse than students with an aggressive, confident attitude. Students who start with question 1 and plod on from there don't score as well as students who pick and choose the easy questions first before tackling the harder ones. People who take a test cold have more problems than those who take the time learning about the test beforehand. In the end, factors like these create people who are good test-takers and those who struggle even when they know the material.

These points are valid for every standardized test, but they are quite broad in scope. The rest of this chapter will discuss how these general ideas can be modified to apply specifically to the AP Economics exams. These test-specific strategies—combined with the factual information covered in your course and in this book's review section and practice tests—are the one-two punch that will help you succeed on Test Day.

SECTION I: MULTIPLE-CHOICE QUESTIONS

The worst thing that can be said about AP Economics multiple-choice questions is that they count for 67% of your total score. Although you might not like multiple-choice questions, there's no denying the fact that it's easier to guess on a multiple-choice question than on an open-ended question. On a multiple-choice problem, the answer is always there in front you; the trick is to find it among the incorrect answers.

All 60 questions in Section I of the AP Economics exams are multiple-choice, and there are two distinct question types.

1. **Stand-Alones**

   These questions make up the majority of the multiple-choice section. Each Stand-alone question covers a specific topic, and then the next Stand-alone hits a different topic. Usually there are 5–40 words in the question stem, and the stem provides you with the information you need to answer the question. Stop at the end of the stem and think about what you know; make a prediction about the shape of the correct answer that can guide you through the answer choices. If the question involves a graph or diagram, make yourself a sketch after reading the stem. In short, don't just plow ahead to the answer choices. Stop to make sure that you understand the question and take a few moments to think about the information in the stem. Here's a typical Stand-alone:

   The supply curve for bicycles will shift to the right in response to

   (A) a decrease in the efficiency of robot technology
   (B) a decrease in wages in the bicycle industry
   (C) an increase in the number of consumers purchasing bicycles
   (D) an increase in the interest rates for bicycle loans
   (E) an increase in consumer's income

You get some information, a supply curve shift, and then you're expected to answer the question based on that information. Where this question appears on the exam makes no difference because there's no order of difficulty on the AP Economics Exams. Tough questions are scattered between easy and medium questions.

2. **Graph or Table Questions**

   As their name implies, Graph or Table questions are questions that use graphs and tables to present information graphically. On the AP Economics exams, these graphics are usually accompanied by one or two questions, which will require you to analyze and interpret the information provided in order to answer the question correctly. You might think that because multiple questions concern the same set of data, you have an advantage. However, the time it takes you to analyze and interpret the information in a graph or table is time you are NOT using answering other questions.

Increase Your Profit Margin on Multiple-Choice Questions

There are two factors that you can use on the multiple-choice section of the AP Economics exams to help increase your score: **time** and **knowledge**.

Time

Most standardized test-takers start with question 1 and work consecutively through the exam until they get to the end or run out of time, whichever comes first. Students run out of time because they get stuck on some problems that are more difficult, and thus time-consuming. Then, they not only miss the difficult questions, but by running out of time, don't get a chance to answer the easier questions that may follow the question that stumped them. The result is a lower score.

You know that you have just 70 minutes to answer 60 multiple-choice questions, so make sure you don't spend too much time on any one question. **Answer the questions that take the least amount of time first**; this way, you won't get bogged down on one question and miss the opportunity to answer three or four other questions.

Be careful when you are using this strategy. It is difficult to estimate how much time a particular question might take. Make sure that you sort through the test in an organized way. Jumping haphazardly all over the section just wastes time and you are likely to omit questions. There is nothing wrong with skipping questions and going back to them later, but your final score depends on the number of questions you answer correctly. They all need to be answered at some point.

Knowledge

What students fail to realize is that they don't need to get every multiple-choice question right to score well on the AP Economics exams. You should strive to do as well as you can, but very few people will get perfect scores on AP exams. All you need is a 4 or 5, and that means you need to get a large portion, but not all, of the multiple-choice problems right. Struggling for perfection may lead you to waste time on less valuable questions, or to panic and freeze up if you feel that the exam is not going well.

If you feel like you are not going to have enough time to get to all the questions, make sure that you get to all the questions that you *know*. This means you should not answer the questions in consecutive order, but rather in order of your ability. Take a minute and look over the list of topics covered on the AP Economics exams on pages 5–6 of chapter 1. Divide these topics into two separate lists: "Rock-Solid Economics" and "Economics I Have Trouble With." Keep this list in mind when you begin a multiple-choice section. On your first pass through the questions, answer all the questions that deal with the concepts in the "Rock-Solid Economics" list. Save all the questions dealing with "Economics I Have Trouble With" list for the second pass. The idea here is *not* that you will classify each question on the test before beginning to work on the exam, but for you to develop a clear sense of topics and key words that help you determine whether you should deal with a particular question first, or save it for later in the section. **Remember: You want to correctly answer as many questions as possible, so be sure to answer all the ones you *know* in the given amount of time.**

You can tailor your approach to the exams, so that it addresses your own strengths and weaknesses. No matter what your approach, you should follow the three basic steps to answering AP Economics questions:

1. First pass: Find and answer all the multiple-choice questions that are fast for you to answer and in your "Rock-Solid Economics" list.
2. Second pass: Find and answer the questions that are a little more time-consuming for you to answer and still in the "Rock-Solid Economics" list. This is the time to answer any and all Graph or Table questions.
3. Third pass: In the remaining questions, it is up to you to determine which topics you feel more comfortable with and attack those questions first. Be aware of the time limit and focus on eliminating incorrect answers rather than finding the one correct answer.

For the difficult questions, you should always take a stab at eliminating some answer choices and then make an educated guess. Admittedly, the AP Economics exams are tests of specific knowledge, so picking the right answer from the bad answer choices is harder to do than it is in other standardized tests. Still, it can be done, so it's worth a try.

Comprehensive, Not Sneaky

Some tests are sneakier than others. Sneaky tests feature convoluted writing, questions that are designed to trip you up mentally, and a host of other little tricks. You can take a sneaky test armed with the proper facts, but can get questions wrong because of sneaky traps in the questions themselves.

The AP Economics exams are *not* sneaky tests. Their objective is to see how much economics knowledge you have stored in that brain of yours. To do this, you are presented with a wide range of questions from an even wider range of economics topics. The exams try to cover as many different economics facts as they can, which is why the problems jump around from market equilibrium to derived factor demand. The tests work hard to be as comprehensive as they can be, so that students who only know one or two economics topics will soon find themselves struggling.

Understanding how the tests are designed can help you answer questions correctly. The AP Economics Exams are comprehensive; the hard questions are difficult because they ask about hard subjects, not because they are trick questions.

That said, trust your instincts when guessing. If you think you know the right answer, chances are you dimly remember the topic being discussed in your AP course. The test is about knowledge, not traps, so trusting your instincts will help more often than not. Be aware that on the multiple-choice section of the AP Economics Exams, one-quarter of a point is deducted for an incorrect response from the number correct to determine the raw score. In other words—guessing can be risky.

You don't have time to ponder every tough question, so trusting your instincts can prevent you from getting bogged down and wasting time on a problem. You might not get every educated guess correct, but again, the point is not to get a perfect score. It's about getting a good score, and surviving hard questions by trusting your gut feelings is a good way to achieve this.

On some problems, though, you might have no inkling of what the correct answer should be. In that case, turn to the following key idea: "good economics."

Think "Good Economics"

The AP Economics exams reward good economists. The tests want to foster future economists by covering fundamental topics. What they do not want is bad economics. They do *not* want answers that are **factually incorrect**, **too extreme to be true**, or **irrelevant to the topic at hand**.

Yet bad economics answers invariably appear on the exams, because they're multiple-choice tests and you have to have four incorrect answer choices around the one right answer. So if you don't know how to answer a problem, look at the answer choices and think "good economics." This will lead you to find some poor answer choices that can be eliminated. Look at the Stand-alone question from earlier in the chapter to see if you can spot bad economics in the answer choices.

The supply curve for bicycles will shift to the right in response to

(A) a decrease in the efficiency of robot technology

(B) a decrease in wages in the bicycle industry

(C) an increase in the number of consumers purchasing bicycles

(D) an increase in the interest rates for bicycle loans

(E) an increase in consumer's income

How did you do? Even if you forgot what "shift to the right" means in the question stem, focus on the one topic of the question that any economics student must recognize: "supply curve." Since the supply curve is independent of the other market factor "demand curve," you can eliminate any answer that involves a change in the demand curve. Thinking "good economics," you know that demand deals with consumers, and therefore answers (C), (D), and (E) must be wrong. You now have a fifty-fifty shot at answering correctly, so take a guess.

You would be surprised how many times the correct answer to a multiple-choice question is a simple, blandly worded fact like "Economics is the study of distributing limited resources to unlimited wants." No breaking news there, but it is "good economics": a carefully worded statement that is factually accurate.

Thinking "good economics" can help you in two ways:

1. It helps you cross out extreme answer choices or choices that are untrue or out of place.
2. It can occasionally point you toward the correct answer, since the correct answer will be a factual, sensibly worded piece of information.

That's all that can be said for the multiple-choice section of the AP Economics exams. Make sure to practice these strategies on the practice tests in this book so that you'll actually use them on the real tests. Once you implement these techniques, your mindset, approach, and score should benefit.

Remember:

- There is no order of difficulty. Questions are mixed together, both in terms of difficulty and in terms of the subject matter they cover.
- Other than the Graph or Table Questions that explicitly state that multiple questions concern the same information, no two questions are connected to each other in any way.
- There's no system that can be used to predict where certain economics concepts appear on the exam or the types of questions in which they are likely to appear.

Of course, the multiple-choice questions only account for 67% of your total score. To get the other 33%, you have to tackle Section II. Before jumping into that section, take about 10 minutes to read about the 10-minute reading period.

TEN-MINUTE READING PERIOD

There is a 10-minute reading period sandwiched between the multiple-choice section and the free-response (essay) portion of the AP Economics exams. Note that this is a *reading* period, not a break. Ten minutes isn't much time, but it gives you an opportunity to read the essay questions ahead of time. You can sketch an answer in the test booklet (this is the page with the question), but you cannot open your answer book (blank pages for your answer) and write the answer.

On the AP Economics exams, you will be required to answer three free-response questions. The first will count for 50% of your entire free-response score and the remaining two will each count for 25% of the remaining free-response score. This means you should spend five minutes reading and planning your response to the first question and about two minutes reading and planning your response for each of the remaining questions.

Make sure you understand what is being asked and jot down any thoughts you have about the answer as well as key terms you want to mention. Sketch any graphs that may be required. You have probably brainstormed ideas before in English class. This is exactly what you want to do here as well: brainstorm ideas about the best way to answer each free-response question.

After your brainstorming session, make a quick outline of how you would answer each question (you don't need to write complete sentences here, though you will in your final answer). Jot down notes that you can understand and use to guide you to a detailed, complete answer.

SECTION II: FREE-RESPONSE QUESTIONS

In Section II, you have 50 minutes to write down answers to three free-response questions. As stated before, the first question is worth half of your free-response score and therefore it should require half of your time, or 25 minutes, to answer. The two remaining questions are each worth one-quarter of your free-response score and should require about 12 minutes a piece to answer. You might finish some questions faster than others, but you shouldn't have too much time left over. Take the time to make your answers as precise and detailed as possible.

The first question (the longer and more important question) will require you to connect and synthesize different economics topics across the sequential parts of the question. The second and third questions will generally ask you to discuss one particular topic in detail, as it relates to the question.

These questions do not require an essay such as you might write in a history or English class. Think of them more like problems. For example, you do not need a general introduction to the topic here any more than you would if you were solving a math problem. Many will require you to draw graphs then amend the graphs to show changes. Some free-response questions will show a graph and the sub-questions will require you to analyze the graph and discuss the concepts involved.

There's a bit of a risk in Section II because there are only three questions. If you get a question on a subject that you find difficult, things might look pretty grim for that problem. Still, take heart. Quite often, you'll earn some points on every question because there will be some sub-questions with which you are familiar. Remember, the goal is not perfection. If you can ace the longer question and slug your way to partial credit on the shorter ones, or vice versa, you will put yourself in position to get a good score on the entire test. The total test score is the big picture; don't lose sight of it just because you don't know the answer to one sub-question on Section II.

Free-response questions can come in any shape or size, but there are some important points to remember about free-response questions:

1. **Most questions contain smaller questions.**

   Usually, you won't get one broad question like, "Discuss the impact of economics in our world." Instead, you'll get an initial set-up followed by sub-questions labeled (a), (b), (c), and so on. It's best to clearly label the part you are answering (e.g., (a) or (part a)) and to use each page of your test booklet completely before moving to the next. Putting each part on a single page is not a good idea, because a harried reader might see the end of your part (a) with half a blank page beneath it and think that's the end of your whole answer—you definitely do not want that to happen.

2. **Writing smart things earns you points.**

   For each sub-question on a free-response question, you receive points for writing a correct response to the prompt. The more points you score, the better off you are on that question. The complete details about how points are scored would make your head spin, but in general, the free-response readers use a rubric that acts as a blueprint for a good answer. Every sub-section of a question has two to five key ideas attached to it. If you write about one of those ideas, you earn yourself a point. Readers always use the same rubric for a question, and all questions must be evaluated using this rubric. Every reader who reads your exam should, in theory, award you the same number of points. Readers check and crosscheck each other to ensure that each answer is evaluated in the same way. Two readers rarely differ on a score.

There's an array of other complex rules regarding free-response scoring—e.g., there is a limit to how many points you can earn on a single sub-question—but it basically boils down to this: Writing smart things about each question will earn you points toward that question. Remember that a smart answer is not witty; it is a concise, informed, and intelligent response that demonstrates your mastery of economics.

Free-response questions frequently include key words or phrases that are clues pointing you toward the shape and content of a good answer. Take a look at the most common of these key words and phrases.

- *Identify* prompts an assertion based on the data or other information. Make sure to support your assertions with evidence (e.g., *We know that X, because Y*).
  Example: *Given the facts above, identify the change in price.*
- *List* prompts a bulleted list of items.
  Example: *List the conditions needed for a firm to price discriminate.*
- *Define* prompts you to write out the definition of a term.
  Example: *Define the Law of Diminishing Marginal Utility.*
- *Draw a correctly labeled graph* prompts you to draw the proper graph, using correct labels and correct curves (slope and position). Changes in graphs should be clearly noted with notations like D to D_1 or directional arrows. *Show* is the key word meaning that new equilibriums should be clearly noted and labeled on the graph.
- *Explain* always means that an assertion alone will not be enough—you are required to offer a clear account of the reasoning behind your assertions. For example, a question might ask you to identify and explain the way a certain set of conditions affects price. A sample answer would have the following basic shape: *In this case, the price increases* (assertion). *The supply curve shifted left because the costs of production increased. This resulted in an increase in price and a decrease in quantity* (explanation).

When constructing your answer to the free-response questions, don't rush or leave your thoughts incomplete. The readers will not fill in the ideas or connections that you omit. Do your best to write complete sentences and always strive to express your ideas clearly. You can use well-known economic abbreviations (e.g., it would be fine to label a supply curve with the letter *S*), but otherwise you should make every effort to spell things out.

Be sure to use all the strategies discussed in this chapter when taking the practice tests. Practicing these strategies will help you become comfortable with them so you are able to put them to good use on Test Day.

STRESS MANAGEMENT

You can beat anxiety the same way you can beat the AP Economics exams—by knowing what to expect beforehand and developing strategies to deal with it.

SOURCES OF STRESS

In the space provided, write down your sources of test-related stress. The idea is to pin down any sources of anxiety so you can deal with them one by one. We have provided common examples—feel free to use them and any others you think of.

- I always freeze up on tests.
- I'm nervous about the elasticity questions (or the monetary policy questions, the perfect competition questions, etc.).
- I need a good/great score to get into my first choice college.
- My older brother/sister/best friend/girlfriend/boyfriend did really well. I must match their scores or do better.
- My parents, who are paying for school, will be quite disappointed if I don't do well.
- I'm afraid of losing my focus and concentration.
- I'm afraid I'm not spending enough time preparing.
- I study like crazy but nothing seems to stick in my mind.
- I always run out of time and get panicky.
- The simple act of thinking, for me, is like wading through refrigerated honey.

My Sources of Stress

____

____

____

____

____

____

Read through the list. Cross out things or add things. Now rewrite the list in order of most disturbing to least disturbing.

My Sources of Stress, in Order

____

____

____

____

____

____

Chances are, the top of the list is a fairly accurate description of exactly how you react to test anxiety, both physically and mentally. The later items usually describe your fears (disappointing mom and dad, looking bad, etc.). Taking care of the major items from the top of the list should go a long way towards relieving overall test anxiety. That's what we'll do next.

How to Deal

Visualize. Sit in a comfortable chair in a quiet setting. If you wear glasses, take them off. Close your eyes and breathe in a deep, satisfying breath of air. Really fill your lungs until your rib cage is fully expanded and you can't take in any more. Then, exhale the air completely. Imagine you're blowing out a candle with your last little puff of air. Do this two or three more times, filling your lungs to their maximum and emptying them totally. Keep your eyes closed, comfortably but not tightly. Let your body sink deeper into the chair as you become even more comfortable.

With your eyes shut you can notice something very interesting. You're no longer dealing with the worrisome stuff going on in the world outside of you. Now you can concentrate on what happens inside you. The more you recognize your own physical reactions to stress and anxiety, the more you can do about them. You may not realize it, but you've begun to regain a sense of being in control.

Let images begin to form on TV screens on the back of your eyelids. Allow the images to come easily and naturally; don't force them. Visualize a relaxing situation. It might be in a special place you've visited before or one you've read about. It can be a fictional location that you create in your imagination, but a real-life memory of a place or situation you know is usually better. Make it as detailed as possible and notice as much as you can.

Stay focused on the images as you sink farther into your chair. Breathe easily and naturally. You might have the sensations of any stress or tension draining from your muscles and flowing downward, out your feet and away from you.

Take a moment to check how you're feeling. Notice how comfortable you've become. Imagine how much easier it would be if you could take the test feeling this relaxed and in this state of ease. You've coupled the images of your special place with sensations of comfort and relaxation. You've also found a way to become relaxed simply by visualizing your own safe, special place.

Close your eyes and start remembering a real-life situation in which you did well on a test. If you can't come up with one, remember a situation in which you did something that you were really proud of—a genuine accomplishment. Make the memory as detailed as possible. Think about the sights, the sounds, the smells, even the tastes associated with this remembered experience. Remember how confident you felt as you accomplished your goal. Now start thinking about the AP Economics exams. Keep your thoughts and feelings in line with that prior, successful experience. Don't make comparisons between them. Just imagine taking the upcoming tests with the same feelings of confidence and relaxed control.

This exercise is a great way to bring the test down to earth. You should practice this exercise often, especially when you feel burned out on test preparation. The more you practice it, the more effective the exercise will be for you.

COUNTDOWN TO THE TESTS

STUDY SCHEDULE

The schedule presented here is the ideal. Compress the schedule to fit your needs. Do keep in mind, though, that research in cognitive psychology has shown that the best way to acquire a great deal of information about a topic is to prepare over a long period of time. Since you have several months to prepare for the AP Economics exams, it makes sense for you to use that time to your advantage. This book, along with your text, should be invaluable in helping you prepare for the tests.

If you have two semesters to prepare, use the following schedule:

September

- ☐ Take the Diagnostic Tests in this book and isolate areas in which you need help. The Diagnostic will serve to familiarize you with the type of material you will be asked about on the AP exams.
- ☐ Begin reading your economics textbooks along with the class outlines.

October—February

- ☐ Continue reading this book and use the summaries at the end of each chapter to help guide you to the most salient information for the exams.

March and April

☐ Take the two Practice Tests and get an idea of your score. Identify the areas in which you need to brush up. Then go back and review those topics in both this book and your economics textbooks.

May

☐ Do a final review and take the exams.

If you only have one semester to prepare, you'll need a more compact schedule:

January

☐ Take the Diagnostic Tests in this book.

February–April

☐ Begin reading this book and identify areas of strengths and weaknesses.

Late April

☐ Take the two Practice Tests and use your performance results to guide you in your preparation.

May

☐ Do a final review and take the exams.

Three Days Before the Exams

It's almost over. Eat a Power Bar, drink some soda—do whatever it takes to keep going. Here are Kaplan's strategies for the three days leading up to the test.

Take a full-length practice test under timed conditions. Use the techniques and strategies you've learned in this book. Approach the test strategically, actively, and confidently.

WARNING: DO NOT take a full-length practice test if you have fewer than 48 hours left before the test. Doing so will probably exhaust you and hurt your score on the actual test. You wouldn't run a marathon the day before the real thing, right?

Two Days Before the Exams

Go over the results of your practice test. Don't worry too much about your score, or about whether you got a specific question right or wrong. The practice test doesn't count. But do examine your performance on specific questions with an eye to how you might get through each one faster and better on the test to come.

The Night Before the Exams

DO NOT STUDY. Get together an "AP Economics Exams Kit" containing the following items:

- A watch
- A few No. 2 pencils (pencils with slightly dull points fill the ovals better), erasers
- Photo ID card
- Your admission ticket from ETS

Know exactly where you're going, exactly how you're getting there, and exactly how long it takes to get there. It's probably a good idea to visit your test center sometime before the day of the test, so that you know what to expect—what the rooms are like, how the desks are set up, and so on.

Relax the night before the tests. Do the relaxation and visualization techniques described earlier in this chapter. Read a good book, take a long hot shower, watch something on the WB. Get a good night's sleep. Go to bed early and leave yourself extra time in the morning.

The Morning of the Exams

First, wake up. After that:

- Eat breakfast. Make it something substantial, but not anything too heavy or greasy.
- Don't drink a lot of coffee if you're not used to it. Bathroom breaks cut into your time, and too much caffeine is a bad idea.
- Dress in layers so that you can adjust to the temperature of the test room.
- Read something. Warm up your brain with a newspaper or a magazine. You shouldn't let the exam be the first thing you read that day.
- Be sure to get there early. Allow yourself extra time for traffic, mass transit delays, and/or detours.

During the Exams

Don't be shaken. If you find your confidence slipping, remind yourself how well you've prepared. You know the structure of the tests; you know the instructions; you've had practice with—and have learned strategies for—every question type.

If something goes really wrong, don't panic. If the test booklet is defective—two pages are stuck together or the ink has run—raise your hand and tell the proctor you need a new book. If you accidentally misgrid your answer page or put the answers in the wrong section, raise your hand and tell the proctor. He or she might be able to arrange for you to regrid your tests after it's over, when it won't cost you any time.

After the Exams

You might walk out of the AP Economics exams thinking that you blew it. This is a normal reaction. Lots of people—even the highest scorers—feel that way. You tend to remember the questions that stumped you, not the ones that you knew. We're positive that you will have performed well and scored your best on the exams because you followed the Kaplan strategies outlined in this section. Be confident in your preparation, and celebrate the fact that the AP Economics exams are soon to be a distant memory.

Now, continue your exam prep by taking the Diagnostic Tests that follow this chapter. These short tests will give you an idea of the format of the actual exams, and will demonstrate the scope of topics covered. After each Diagnostic, you'll find answers with detailed explanations. Be sure to read these explanations carefully, even when you got the question right, as you can pick up bits of knowledge from them. Use your score to learn which topics you need to review more carefully. Of course, all the strategies in the world can't save you if you don't know anything about economics. The chapters following the Diagnostics will help you review the primary concepts and facts that you can expect to encounter on the AP Economics exams.

| PART TWO |

Diagnostic Tests

AP Macroeconomics Diagnostic Test

The chapters that follow in Part Three of this book contain a wealth of information and review questions about all the main topics covered on the Macroeconomics exam. Ideally, you will have the time to go through every chapter and try every review question while working at a steady pace. But one thing often prevents students from following it—the real world. The fact is, many students have schedules that are already chock full of activities. Finding large chunks of time to devote to studying for a test—one that isn't even part of your regular schoolwork—isn't just difficult. It's next to impossible.

If this is the case with you, find a moment to take the following 20-question Diagnostic Test. The questions in this Diagnostic are designed to cover most of the topics you will encounter on the AP Macroeconomics exam. After you take it, you can use the results to give yourself a broad idea of what subjects you are strong in and what topics you need to review more. You can use this information to tailor your approach to the review chapters in this book. Hopefully you'll have time to read all the chapters, but if pressed, you can start with the chapters and subjects you know you need to work on.

Give yourself 25 minutes for the 20 multiple-choice questions and 30 minutes for the free-response question. Time yourself, and take the entire test without interruption—let that call go to voicemail; you can get to it later. Also, no headphones or TV! You won't get to use these things while taking the real AP Economics exams, so you may as well get used to the quiet now.

Be sure to read the explanations for all questions, even those you answered correctly. (This is something you should do on the Macroeconomics Practice Test as well.) Even if you got a problem right, reading another person's answer can give you insights that will prove helpful on the real exam.

Good luck on the Diagnostic!

HOW TO COMPUTE YOUR SCORE

To compute your score for this Diagnostic Test, calculate the number of questions you got incorrect, then deduct $\frac{1}{4}$ of that number from the number of right answers. So, if you got 5 questions incorrect out of 20, subtract $\frac{1}{4}$ of that (1.25) from the number of questions you got right (15). The final score is 13.75. To set this equal to a score out of 100, set up a proportion:

$$\frac{13.75}{20} = \frac{n}{100}$$

$$20n = 1375$$

$$n = 68.75 = 69$$

The approximate score range is as follows:

5 = 90–100 (extremely well qualified)

4 = 80–89 (well qualified)

3 = 70–79 (qualified)

2 = 60–69 (possibly qualified)

1 = 0–59 (no recommendation)

A score of 69 is a 2, so you can definitely do better. If your score is low, keep on studying to improve your chances of getting credit for the AP Macroeconomics exam.

AP Macroeconomics Diagnostic Test
Answer Grid

1. Ⓐ Ⓑ Ⓒ Ⓓ Ⓔ
2. Ⓐ Ⓑ Ⓒ Ⓓ Ⓔ
3. Ⓐ Ⓑ Ⓒ Ⓓ Ⓔ
4. Ⓐ Ⓑ Ⓒ Ⓓ Ⓔ
5. Ⓐ Ⓑ Ⓒ Ⓓ Ⓔ
6. Ⓐ Ⓑ Ⓒ Ⓓ Ⓔ
7. Ⓐ Ⓑ Ⓒ Ⓓ Ⓔ
8. Ⓐ Ⓑ Ⓒ Ⓓ Ⓔ
9. Ⓐ Ⓑ Ⓒ Ⓓ Ⓔ
10. Ⓐ Ⓑ Ⓒ Ⓓ Ⓔ
11. Ⓐ Ⓑ Ⓒ Ⓓ Ⓔ
12. Ⓐ Ⓑ Ⓒ Ⓓ Ⓔ
13. Ⓐ Ⓑ Ⓒ Ⓓ Ⓔ
14. Ⓐ Ⓑ Ⓒ Ⓓ Ⓔ
15. Ⓐ Ⓑ Ⓒ Ⓓ Ⓔ
16. Ⓐ Ⓑ Ⓒ Ⓓ Ⓔ
17. Ⓐ Ⓑ Ⓒ Ⓓ Ⓔ
18. Ⓐ Ⓑ Ⓒ Ⓓ Ⓔ
19. Ⓐ Ⓑ Ⓒ Ⓓ Ⓔ
20. Ⓐ Ⓑ Ⓒ Ⓓ Ⓔ

Section I

Time – 25 minutes
20 Questions

Directions: Each of the questions or incomplete statements below is followed by five suggested answers or completions. Select the best choice in each case.

1. The principal advantage of automatic or built-in stabilizers over discretionary fiscal policy is that they

(A) stimulate economic output and employment regardless of the state of the economy

(B) are private sector initiatives, and so do not expand the size of government

(C) require no additional legislative action for their implementation

(D) are more potent than discretionary fiscal policy

(E) fight recession without increasing the government budget deficit

2. Gross investment refers to

(A) private investment plus public investment

(B) net private investment plus depreciation spending

(C) net private investment after it has been "inflated" for changes in the price level

(D) net private investment plus net exports

(E) publicly funded investment for infrastructure spending

3. Shifts in the aggregate demand can occur when

(A) oil prices change

(B) productivity rates change

(C) price of resources change

(D) consumer wealth changes

(E) price level changes

4. The aggregate supply will shift to the right when

(A) prices of energy inputs increase

(B) gains are made in productivity

(C) prices of raw material inputs increase

(D) investment spending for capital goods decreases

(E) government regulators write new rules for pollution controls

5. In 1973, the Organization of Petroleum Exporting Countries (OPEC) agreed to use their power over the world price-setting mechanism for oil to dramatically increase world oil prices. The price of crude oil and petroleum-based products sold in the U.S. and worldwide increased. This increase was a source of

(A) disinflation

(B) hyperinflation

(C) demand-pull inflation

(D) demand-push inflation

(E) cost-push inflation

GO ON TO THE NEXT PAGE

6. A recent study reveals that in a closed economy, households save 20% of any increase in income. If a new technology advance pushes investment upward by $50 billion, economists would forecast a change in Real GDP of

   (A) $ 10 billion
   (B) $100 billion
   (C) $150 billion
   (D) $250 billion
   (E) $500 billion

7. In the macroeconomic circular flow model, which of the following are considered to be leakages from the spending flow?

   I. Saving
   II. Taxes
   III. Investment

   (A) II only
   (B) I and II only
   (C) II and III only
   (D) I and III only
   (E) I, II, and III

8. Which one of the following is NOT an example of a macroeconomic variable?

   (A) The average price level of all goods and services sold in Sri Lanka in 1975
   (B) The value of all incomes received by Canadians in 1980
   (C) The unemployment rate in the United States in August, 1985
   (D) The average price of cigarettes sold in England in 1990
   (E) Total Japanese exports for the fourth quarter of 1995

9. Assume a fiscal policy of increased Federal government spending is implemented. If the government goes into the financial market to borrow the money to finance the new spending, the most likely result is that

   (A) interest rates will rise, "crowding out" investment spending
   (B) the money supply will increase, leading to a higher rate of inflation
   (C) equilibrium nominal GDP will decrease by the dollar amount of bonds issued
   (D) exports will increase, reducing the size of the trade deficit
   (E) the proportion of disposable income saved by consumers will increase

10. Suppose Economy Z is experiencing "stagflation" (slow economic growth) combined with an undesirably high rate of inflation. A "supply side" economic policy-maker would most likely recommend which one of the following policy actions?

   (A) An increase in Federal government spending
   (B) An increase in the growth rate of the money supply
   (C) A decrease in the growth rate of the money supply
   (D) A decrease in Federal excise taxes and user fees
   (E) A decrease in corporate and personal income tax rates targeted to higher income groups

GO ON TO THE NEXT PAGE

Questions 11 and 12 are based on the graph below.

The curves S1 and S2 represent the supply of money before and after a macroeconomic policy action.

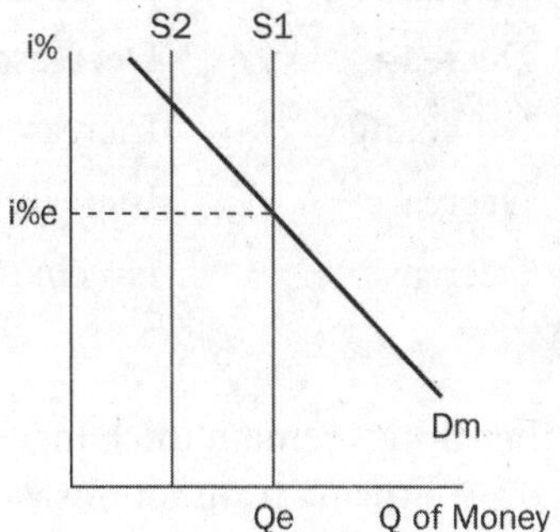

11. A shift in the money supply curve such as that shown in the graph above could have been caused by

    (A) an open market sale of bonds by the Federal Reserve
    (B) an open market purchase of bonds by the Federal Reserve
    (C) an increase in Federal income tax rates
    (D) a decrease in the discount rate
    (E) an increase in Federal government spending

12. The policy action illustrated above would be most appropriate for an economy experiencing

    (A) less than full employment
    (B) a large current account surplus
    (C) a high inflation rate
    (D) declining output
    (E) non-inflationary economic growth

13. In the aggregate demand (AD)/aggregate supply (AS) model, an increase in the foreign exchange value of a country's currency will

    (A) increase both the aggregate demand and aggregate supply
    (B) increase the aggregate demand without affecting aggregate supply
    (C) increase the nation's net exports which increases aggregate demand
    (D) decrease aggregate demand and increase aggregate supply
    (E) decrease the nation's net exports which decrease aggregate supply

14. Which of the following fiscal policy actions would be most effective in combating an inflationary economy?

    (A) Lowering government spending by $100 billion matched with a tax cut that returns $100 billion to the taxpayers
    (B) Lowering government spending by $100 billion matched with tax rate increase that collects an additional $100 billion in tax revenue
    (C) Raising government spending by $100 billion matched with a tax cut that returns $100 billion to the taxpayers
    (D) Raising government spending by $100 billion
    (E) Raising tax rates to collect an additional $100 billion

GO ON TO THE NEXT PAGE

15. Which one of the following combinations of fiscal and monetary policies would have the most expansionary effect on aggregate demand?

(A) an increase in government spending, combined with an increase in the money supply
(B) an increase in corporate tax rates, combined with a decrease in interest rates
(C) a decrease in government spending, combined with an increase in the money supply
(D) a decrease in personal income taxes, combined with a decrease in the money supply
(E) a decrease in personal income taxes, combined with an increase in interest rates

16. Suppose Worker W's pay has increased from $10 to $16 per hour. Over the same time period, the Consumer Price Index has increased from 100 to 200. Which one of the following best describes the effects of these changes on W's nominal and real wages?

(A) W's nominal wage and real wage have increased.
(B) W's nominal wage has increased, but her real wage has decreased.
(C) W's nominal wage has decreased, but her real wage has increased.
(D) W's nominal wage has increased, but her real wage has remained the same.
(E) W's nominal wage and her real wage have decreased.

17. What is the effect of an increase in the short-run aggregate supply on the rate of inflation and the rate of unemployment?

	Rate of Inflation	Unemployment Rate
(A)	Increase	No change
(B)	Decrease	Decrease
(C)	No change	Increase
(D)	Decrease	Increase
(E)	Decrease	No change

18. If all other things remain unchanged, which one of the following transactions would increase the size of the U.S. current account deficit?

(A) A U.S. soldier stationed in West Germany buys a gift box of sausages to ship home to his mother.
(B) A Japanese tourist buys a roll of film at a camera store in Florida.
(C) A U.S. insurance company sells a fire insurance policy to a French manufacturer to cover his Paris factory.
(D) An Australian travel agent buys 12,000 wristbands with his logo on them from a California supplier of athletic equipment to give to American vacationers in Australia.
(E) A Brazilian airplane manufacturer buys titanium rivets from an American manufacturing company.

GO ON TO THE NEXT PAGE

19. If the measured unemployment rate in an economy remains constant at 7%, while the natural rate of unemployment decreases over time from 6% to 5%, which one of the following is most likely to occur?

    (A) The rate of inflation will increase.
    (B) Real GDP will decrease.
    (C) Real GDP will increase.
    (D) The size of the government budget deficit will increase.
    (E) The size of the recessionary GDP gap will increase.

20. Which one of the following best describes the effect of a 1% increase in the expected rate of inflation on interest rates in the long run?

    (A) Both real and nominal interest rates will rise by 1%.
    (B) Real interest rates will rise by 1%, and nominal interest rates will rise by 2%.
    (C) Real interest rates will rise by 1%, with nominal interest rates remaining unchanged.
    (D) Nominal interest rates will rise by 1%, with real interest rates remaining unchanged.
    (E) There will be no change in either real or nominal interest rates.

IF YOU FINISH BEFORE TIME IS UP, YOU MAY CHECK YOUR WORK ON THIS SECTION ONLY. DO NOT TURN TO ANY OTHER SECTION IN THE TEST. **STOP**

Section II

Planning Time – 5 minutes

Writing Time – 25 minutes

Directions: Write out answers to the following question. Where a question asks for an explanation, describe the reasoning used in reaching your answer. Partial credit can be given only if your work is clear and demonstrates an understanding of the question.

Assume that an economy is in recession.

(a) Draw a correctly labeled AD/AS graph and show the position of the economy.

(b) If the government chooses a fiscal policy alternative that lowers taxes on businesses and provides subsidies to businesses to assist with production, show on the graph the effect of this fiscal policy choice. Identify on the graph the change on the Price Level and Output (RGDP).

(c) Explain how this fiscal policy action can contribute to a higher level of economic well-being.

ANSWERS AND EXPLANATIONS

SECTION I

1. C

Automatic or built-in stabilizers are policy features of the economic system, such as unemployment compensation and the progressive income tax, which tend to stabilize national income by restraining aggregate demand during periods of peak economic activity and support spending during periods of weakness. As the name suggests, they are in place and work automatically, without any legislative action required—a big advantage, since discretionary fiscal policy is often slow to respond to changes in economic conditions. Choice (C) is correct. Choice (A) is incorrect since these stabilizers work to lessen recession and thwart inflation. Choice (B) is incorrect since Congress initially set up these programs and determines criteria for enrollment. Choice (D) is incorrect since the automatic stabilizers just cushion the effect of the unstable economy—they cannot correct the situation alone. Choice (E) incorrectly states that budget deficits are not incurred but budget issues are discretionary fiscal policy.

2. B

Gross private domestic investment includes both the investment for new capital goods and depreciation, the spending that maintains the current stock of capital. Choice (B) correctly states that concept. Choices (A) and (E) incorrectly include public investment. Choice (C) incorrectly includes inflation adjustment. Choice (D) errs by including exports.

3. D

Movements to the left and right of the aggregate demand curve are caused by any changes to the consumption, investment, government or export spending. Changes in consumer wealth (D) such as a drop in the stock market will affect consumption spending as more wealth will stimulate spending and a feeling of less wealth will inhibit spending. Choices (A), (B), and (C) will result in changes to aggregate supply.

4. B

Rightward movement of the aggregate supply curve will be caused by lower resource prices and lower cost of production, new technology, and gains in productivity and government subsidies. Choice (B) correctly identifies the gain in productivity which can move the AS curve to the right. Choices (A), (C), (D), and (E) are incorrect since these changes will move the AS curve to the left.

5. E

Inflation caused by increases in costs of production is cost-push inflation. In the case of the 1973 OPEC action, the large, sudden increase in the costs of producing goods and services that use petroleum or its refined products as inputs was sufficient to cause a wave of inflation in the U.S. economy. Choice (E) is correct, but (C) and (D) are not. Demand-pull inflation results from an excess of aggregate demand in the economy, not cost pressures. Choice (A) is incorrect since disinflation is a reduction in the rate of inflation, while (B) is also incorrect. Hyperinflation is a very rapid increase in the price level that often spirals out of control.

6. D

The marginal propensity to save tells one how much of an additional dollar earned will be saved and not spent. The spending multiplier is the reciprocal of the MPS, in this case, $\frac{1}{.20} = 5$. If investment increases by $50 billion, the multiplier effect of that action will add $50B x 5 or $250 billion in RGDP to the economy. Choice (D) is correct while the other choices have miscalculated the amount.

GO ON TO THE NEXT PAGE

7. B

In the circular flow model, leakages occur when spending by households or payments to households are diverted. When household saving occurs (for example, a savings account deposit), spending is reduced, dollar for dollar. When taxes are collected (for example, withholding from income), payments by businesses to households are reduced. Choice (B) is the correct response. Other choices do not reflect these ideas. Further, if the saving referred to in the question stem is "injected" back into the economy, say in the form of a bank loan to a business to finance investment spending, the drag on economic activity created by the leakage can be averted.

8. D

Macroeconomic variables are typically aggregates (sums or averages), reflecting economic activity in the economy as a whole. Choice (D), the price of cigarettes, is a microeconomic variable, indicative of conditions in a single market. Choices (C) and (E) refer to part-year, rather than full-year data; however, they are still measures of aggregate activity.

9. A

When increases in government spending are financed by issuing bonds, this action creates the crowding-out effect. As the government issues bonds to finance the spending, the supply of bonds increases, the (equilibrium) price of bonds decreases, and interest rates rise. Higher interest rates "crowd out" business investment—(A) is the correct response. Choice (B) incorrectly uses the concept called "monetizing the debt" by increasing the money supply. Choice (C) is incorrect since the increased government spending will increase the GDP. Choice (D) is incorrect because higher interest rates will attract foreign buyers and the dollar will appreciate. Exports will fall since American goods are now more expensive to those in foreign countries. Choice (E) is not correct because the proportion of disposable income that is saved is called the marginal propensity to save and is not affected by the government sale of bonds.

10. E

The term "supply-side" economics refers to a school of economic thought which emphasizes the role of aggregate supply in macroeconomic equilibrium, and the tools which government policy-makers can use to influence aggregate supply in an attempt to achieve non-inflationary growth. Chief among such tools are reductions in business and personal taxes, especially income tax changes affect those in upper income brackets, which are viewed as stimulating productivity, increasing aggregate supply while simultaneously reducing inflation and increasing output. Choice (E) is the correct response and all other choices represent policy actions that primarily affect aggregate demand.

11. A

The graph illustrates the money market model of interest rate determination, wherein the supply of and demand for money interact to determine the equilibrium rate of interest. A reduction of the money supply, such as that shown by a shift from S1 to S2, can be accomplished by the Fed using open market operations—specifically, by selling bonds (A) to soak up excess bank reserves, eventually forcing banks to "call in" loans, reducing the deposits component of the money supply. Choices (C) and (E) represent fiscal policy, and (B) and (D) describe expansionary monetary policy actions.

12. C

Reduction of the money supply is a contractionary ("tight money") policy, designed to counteract demand-pull inflationary pressures in the economy. A higher equilibrium rate of nominal interest will reduce investment and interest-sensitive consumption spending, reducing aggregate demand and slow inflation. Choice (C) is correct, but (A) and (D) are incorrect as each states conditions of a recessionary economy. In these choices as well as (E), an expansionary policy is appropriate. Choice (B) is incorrect because a current account surplus essentially means that exports are greater than imports. This condition would not warrant a contractionary monetary action.

13. D

Changes in the foreign exchange value of a currency (appreciation or depreciation) have effects on aggregate demand and sometimes aggregate supply. On the demand side, an appreciating currency increases the prices of domestic goods to foreigners, while making it easier for domestic residents to afford imported goods. Hence, net exports (exports less imports) decrease, and aggregate demand for domestic goods accordingly decreases. It is also easier for domestic firms to afford imported resources. Thus, aggregate supply might increase. Choice (D) is the correct response.

14. B

An inflationary economy needs contractionary policy actions. Contractionary fiscal policies include increases in personal and/or corporate taxes and decreases in government spending. Contractionary monetary ("tight money") policy involves decreases in the supply of money, which are linked to decreases in interest rates. Choice (B) is correct as it lowers spending and increases tax rates. Choices (A), (C), and (D) specify policy combinations that are contradictory or not sufficiently contractionary.

15. A

Expansionary fiscal policy attempts to put more spending power into the economy. Increased government spending and lower personal and business spending will be the effective tools. "Easy money" monetary policy will stimulate investment and consumption. The Fed usually purchases government bonds in the open market, which provides additional bank reserves that can be loaned out. This action increases the money supply, lowering interest rates to encourage investment and consumption. Choice (A) correctly states an increase in government spending and an increase in the money supply. Choice (B) would be contractionary; (C) is incorrect since government spending decreases. Choices (D) and (E) are incorrect since both state that the money supply decreases to raise interest rates.

16. B

The real wage—the wage rate expressed in terms of goods/services which the nominal or money wage can buy—is calculated by dividing the nominal wage by the price level, as noted by the CPI. Prices have doubled using the CPI, while W's nominal wage has not. Therefore, even though W is making more money, her purchasing power, in terms of the goods and services which her wages command, has decreased. Choice (B) is correct, while (C) switches the changes. Choice (A) incorrectly states both have increased, which would mean that W's wages had to increase to $20 per hour. Choice (D) is incorrect since real wages change when price levels change. Choice (E) is obviously incorrect since W's wages increased from $10 to $16 per hour.

17. B

Short-run aggregate supply moves to the right to indicate an increase, causing the price level to decline and the RGDP to increase. When the price level declines, the rate of inflation decreases. When the RGDP increases, more workers are employed so the unemployment rate decreases. Choice (B) is the correct response while the other choices all state incorrect combinations.

18. A

The current account category of the balance of payments includes the trade balance accounts (exports and imports). Choice (A) is the correct response since a gift bought in a foreign country is counted as an import, which would reduce the current account balance. Exports as noted in choices (B), (C), (D), and (E) would increase the current account balance.

GO ON TO THE NEXT PAGE

19. E

The recessionary GDP gap is defined as the difference between the economy's potential (or full-employment) output and its actual output. Potential output, in turn is defined as the output level when unemployment is at the natural rate—that is, when all unemployment is either frictional or structural. A decrease in the natural rate of unemployment increases the difference between the actual and the natural rate of unemployment, and so the size of the shortfall in GDP. Choice (E) correctly states that concept. Other choices are incorrect because the actual rate of unemployment is unchanged, actual output—real GDP—will not change. Without a change in the money supply or in fiscal policy, there is no reason to expect an increase in inflation or the budget deficit.

20. D

In the long run, real interest rates reflect adjustment for the expected rate of inflation. When the expected rate of inflation rises by 1%, the nominal rate rises by 1%, but the real interest rate is unchanged because the real interest rate is the nominal rate—the expected rate of inflation. Choice (D) is the correct response. Choices other than (D) do not reflect the long-run real interest rate adjustment.

SECTION II

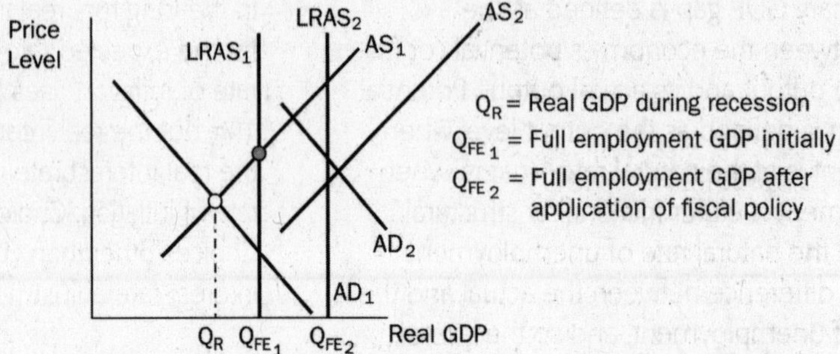

(a) The upward-sloping short-run AS intersects with the downward sloping AD at a point to the left of the long run AS curve at full employment. This diagram shows that the economy is in recession. Answers without the long run AS curve would not show the recessionary state.

(b) The fiscal policy strategy of lower taxes and subsidy payments for businesses will increase the short-run aggregate supply curve. This movement to the right will move the short-run aggregate supply closer to the full employment level of output. Lowering business taxes will also increase investment, which will raise aggregate demand.

(c) Lower tax rates for businesses provide additional funds for capital goods spending. Investment in new equipment linked to more specialized training of workers means long-run changes. The long-run aggregate supply curve will move to the right and the potential GDP will increase. The government subsidy payments also allow for more funds to be allocated to capital formation. When the long-run aggregate supply curve increases, the GDP "pie" grows bigger. This is a way of saying that living standards have risen for people and well-being has been enhanced.

AP Macroeconomics Diagnostic Test Correlation Chart

Use the following table to determine which macroeconomics topics you need to review most. After scoring your test, check to find out the areas of study covered by the questions you answered incorrectly.

Area of Study	Question Numbers
Basic Economic Concepts	6, 8
Measurement of Economic Performance	7, 16, 19
National Income and Price Determination	3, 4, 9
Financial Sector	11, 12, 17, 20
Inflation, Unemployment, and Stabilization Policies	1, 5, 10, 14
Economic Growth and Productivity	2, 15
Open Economy: International Trade and Finance	13, 18

AP Microeconomics Diagnostic Test

The chapters that follow in Part Four of this book contain a wealth of information and review questions about all the main topics covered on the Microeconomics exam. Ideally, you will have the time to go through every chapter and try every review question while working at a steady pace. But one thing often prevents students from following it—the real world. The fact is, many students have schedules that are already chock full of activities. Finding large chunks of time to devote to studying for a test—one that isn't even part of your regular schoolwork—isn't just difficult. It's next to impossible.

If this is the case with you, find a moment to take the following 20-question Diagnostic Test. The questions in this Diagnostic are designed to cover most of the topics you will encounter on the AP Microeconomics exam. After you take it, you can use the results to give yourself a broad idea of what subjects you are strong in and what topics you need to review more. You can use this information to tailor your approach to the review chapters in this book. Hopefully you'll have time to read all the chapters, but if pressed, you can start with the chapters and subjects you know you need to work on.

Give yourself 25 minutes for the 20 multiple-choice questions and 30 minutes for the free-response question. Time yourself, and take the entire test without interruption—let that call go to voicemail; you can get to it later. Also, no headphones or TV! You won't get to use these things while taking the real AP Economics exams, so you may as well get used to the quiet now.

Be sure to read the explanations for all questions, even those you answered correctly. (This is something you should do on the Microeconomics Practice Test as well.) Even if you got a problem right, reading another person's answer can give you insights that will prove helpful on the real exam.

Good luck on the Diagnostic!

HOW TO COMPUTE YOUR SCORE

To compute your score for this Diagnostic Test, calculate the number of questions you got incorrect, then deduct $\frac{1}{4}$ of that number from the number of right answers. So, if you got 5 questions incorrect out of 20, subtract $\frac{1}{4}$ of that (1.25) from the number of questions you got right (15). The final score is 13.75. To set this equal to a score out of 100, set up a proportion:

$$\frac{13.75}{20} = \frac{n}{100}$$

$$20n = 1375$$

$$n = 68.75 = 69$$

The approximate score range is as follows:

5 = 90–100 (extremely well qualified)

4 = 80–89 (well qualified)

3 = 70–79 (qualified)

2 = 60–69 (possibly qualified)

1 = 0–59 (no recommendation)

A score of 69 is a 2, so you can definitely do better. If your score is low, keep on studying to improve your chances of getting credit for the AP Microeconomics exam.

AP Microeconomics Diagnostic Test
Answer Grid

1. Ⓐ Ⓑ Ⓒ Ⓓ Ⓔ	11. Ⓐ Ⓑ Ⓒ Ⓓ Ⓔ
2. Ⓐ Ⓑ Ⓒ Ⓓ Ⓔ	12. Ⓐ Ⓑ Ⓒ Ⓓ Ⓔ
3. Ⓐ Ⓑ Ⓒ Ⓓ Ⓔ	13. Ⓐ Ⓑ Ⓒ Ⓓ Ⓔ
4. Ⓐ Ⓑ Ⓒ Ⓓ Ⓔ	14. Ⓐ Ⓑ Ⓒ Ⓓ Ⓔ
5. Ⓐ Ⓑ Ⓒ Ⓓ Ⓔ	15. Ⓐ Ⓑ Ⓒ Ⓓ Ⓔ
6. Ⓐ Ⓑ Ⓒ Ⓓ Ⓔ	16. Ⓐ Ⓑ Ⓒ Ⓓ Ⓔ
7. Ⓐ Ⓑ Ⓒ Ⓓ Ⓔ	17. Ⓐ Ⓑ Ⓒ Ⓓ Ⓔ
8. Ⓐ Ⓑ Ⓒ Ⓓ Ⓔ	18. Ⓐ Ⓑ Ⓒ Ⓓ Ⓔ
9. Ⓐ Ⓑ Ⓒ Ⓓ Ⓔ	19. Ⓐ Ⓑ Ⓒ Ⓓ Ⓔ
10. Ⓐ Ⓑ Ⓒ Ⓓ Ⓔ	20. Ⓐ Ⓑ Ⓒ Ⓓ Ⓔ

Section I

Time – 25 minutes
20 Questions

Directions: Each of the questions or incomplete statements below is followed by five suggested answers or completions. Select the best choice in each case.

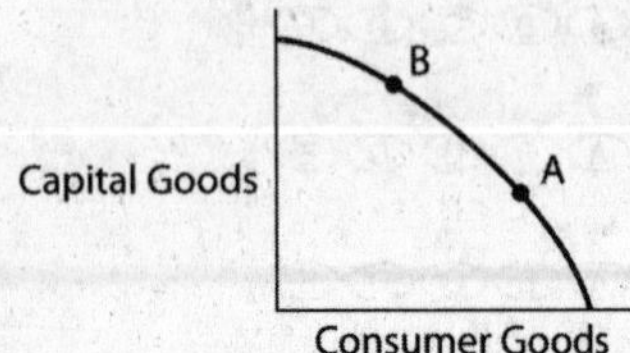

1. As society moves from point A to point B on the production possibilities frontier shown above, which of the following is most likely to occur?
   (A) Capital goods become cheaper.
   (B) Factors of production move from capital goods markets to consumption goods markets.
   (C) Capital goods production increases and future production possibilities increase.
   (D) Capital goods production decreases and future production possibilities increase.
   (E) The opportunity cost of capital is constant.

2. Which of the following would best explain why the demand for bread is less price elastic than the demand for automobiles?
   (A) More people consume bread than automobiles.
   (B) There are more good substitutes for bread than for automobiles.
   (C) Bread is a smaller portion of the consumer's budget than automobiles.
   (D) There are more suppliers of bread.
   (E) Automobiles are a necessity.

3. The market price of MP3 players has fallen lately, while the quantity produced and consumed has increased. Which of the following most likely accounts for this?
   (A) Incomes of consumers have fallen and MP3 players are a normal good.
   (B) Incomes of consumers have fallen and MP3 players are an inferior good.
   (C) An essential input in MP3 player production has gotten cheaper.
   (D) Demand for MP3 players has outpaced supply.
   (E) A price floor has been established for MP3 players.

4. Kentucky, like many other states, has recently raised taxes on cigarettes, alcohol, and gasoline. The result is that
   (A) total expenditures on these goods will rise
   (B) total expenditures on these goods will fall
   (C) tax revenues will grow substantially as personal income rises
   (D) suppliers of these products will bear most of the burden of these tax increases
   (E) the supply curve of these goods will shift to the right

GO ON TO THE NEXT PAGE

5. Which of the following is a short-run production decision?

   (A) Company A doubles the number of plants operating worldwide.
   (B) An elementary school adds new classrooms and teachers.
   (C) Company B closes a textile plant.
   (D) A tax preparation firm hires temporary workers in February to meet increased demand for tax services.
   (E) Three new companies enter the biodiesel market.

6. Several firms are earning economic profits producing and marketing plasma screen TVs in the United States. As a result,

   (A) firms will enter the market, the price will rise, and long-run profits will increase
   (B) firms will enter the market, the price will fall, and long-run profits will decrease
   (C) firms will soon exit the market, the price will fall, and long-run profits will increase
   (D) firms will enter the market, the price will rise, and long-run profits will decrease
   (E) demand for plasma TVs will fall

7. In an hour's time, Caleb can bake more cookies and fold more laundry than Bhanu. To increase the total amount of cookies baked and laundry folded in this household, Caleb should

   (A) bake more cookies only if he has an absolute advantage in baking cookies
   (B) fold more laundry than Bhanu
   (C) fold more laundry if he has an absolute advantage in folding laundry
   (D) fold more laundry if his opportunity cost for doing so is less than Bhanu's
   (E) bake cookies if his opportunity cost for doing so is greater than Bhanu's

8. Miguel quit his $50,000-a-year job and invested his savings (which would have earned $1000 in interest per year) to start his own business. If Miguel earned an accounting profit of $55,000 in the first year, then he also

   (A) earned an economic profit of $5,000
   (B) incurred an economic loss of $5,000
   (C) earned an economic profit of $4,000
   (D) earned a normal profit
   (E) should consider going back to his old job

9. If a rational consumer is in equilibrium, then

   (A) the marginal utility obtained from one product is equal to the marginal utility of another product
   (B) a reallocation of income would increase the consumer's total utility
   (C) the marginal utility per last dollar spent is the same for all good consumed
   (D) marginal utility becomes zero
   (E) total utility is at its greatest point

10. If a firm decides to produce no output in the short run, its costs would be

    (A) limited to the firm's marginal costs
    (B) limited to the firm's fixed costs plus the variable costs
    (C) limited to the firm's fixed costs
    (D) limited to the firm's variable costs
    (E) zero

GO ON TO THE NEXT PAGE

11. What would cause the demand curve for Company Y's MP3 players to shift to the right?

    (A) an increase in the price of Company Q's MP3 encoding software, a complement to Company Y's MP3 players

    (B) an increase in the price of a Company Z's MP3 players, a substitute for Company Y's MP3 players

    (C) an increase in the price of downloadable music files, a complement to Company Y's MP3 players

    (D) a decrease in the price of Company Y's MP3 players

    (E) a decrease in the cost of producing Company Y's MP3 players

12. A single price monopolist having the same cost data as that of a perfect competitor will charge

    (A) the same price and produce the same quantity as the perfectly competitive firm

    (B) a higher price and produce a larger quantity than the perfectly competitive firm

    (C) a higher price and produce a smaller quantity than the perfectly competitive firm

    (D) a lower price and produce a smaller quantity than the perfectly competitive firm

    (E) a lower price and produce a larger quantity than the perfectly competitive firm

13. Manny's Motors produces pine boxcars, which it sells in a competitive market for $20 each. If hiring an additional worker would increase production by five cars per hour, then

    (A) marginal revenue would be $100

    (B) marginal revenue product would be $100

    (C) marginal cost would be zero

    (D) the wage paid must exceed $100 for Manny to earn an economic profit

    (E) the company should hire more workers

14. In a free market, why would consumers buy fewer flu shots than is optimal?

    (A) People are generally irrational about their health.

    (B) The marginal social benefit of a flu shot is zero.

    (C) The marginal social benefit of a flu shot exceeds the marginal private benefit.

    (D) There are no free riders.

    (E) The marginal social benefit is less than the marginal social cost.

15. Which of these is an example of a change in product demand that increases the demand for labor?

    (A) Access to computers increases the productivity of mail order businesses thus increasing demand for their workers.

    (B) Tourism increases in popularity, increasing the demand for workers at tourist resorts.

    (C) A decrease in the price of trucks decreases the cost of transporting goods, thus increasing the demand for truckers.

    (D) A change in work rules increases output per worker in the auto industry, thus increasing the demand for autoworkers.

    (E) A change of preference by consumers for dry cleaning services decreases the number of workers in dry cleaning firms.

GO ON TO THE NEXT PAGE

16. The demand for soybeans is price inelastic and the income elasticity is negative for soybeans. Why is this a problem for farmers?

(A) There will be significant shortages in a prospering economy.
(B) Supply increases will reduce total expenditures on soybeans, while demand for their crop grows slowly.
(C) Price floors will reduce consumption considerably.
(D) As the economy prospers, demand for soybeans declines.
(E) Small changes in demand yield larger changes in market price.

Refer to the table below for questions 17–18.

# of Workers	Total Output of Hats
0	0
1	5
2	11
3	19
4	25
5	30

17. For this firm producing hats in the short run, the marginal product of labor

(A) is constant at 6 hats per worker
(B) diminishes after hiring three workers
(C) diminishes after hiring the first worker
(D) continues to rise as more workers are hired
(E) is negative

18. If the product price is $3 and the firm hires the third worker, what is the maximum wage the firm should pay?

(A) $20
(B) $24
(C) $30
(D) $60
(E) The firm would not hire the third worker at any wage.

19. Firms face U-shaped long-run average cost curves because

(A) diminishing returns set in as they expand output in the long run
(B) capital becomes more expensive in the market as they expand output in the long run
(C) firms face economies of scale, constant returns to scale, and, eventually, diseconomies of scale, as they expand output in the long run
(D) firms can double current production methods by building identical plants as they expand output in the long run
(E) barriers to entry reduce the average costs as they expand output in the long run

20. The market for retail gasoline may be considered monopolistic competition rather than perfect competition because

(A) there are no barriers to entry
(B) consumer information about prices and availability of resources is good
(C) there are a limited number of suppliers in the market
(D) retailers of gasoline can differentiate their products
(E) profits in the long run are excessive

IF YOU FINISH BEFORE TIME IS UP, YOU MAY CHECK YOUR WORK ON THIS SECTION ONLY. DO NOT TURN TO ANY OTHER SECTION IN THE TEST. STOP

Section II

Planning Time – 5 minutes

Writing Time – 25 minutes

Directions: Write out answers to the following question. Clearly label your graphs and show the method used to arrive at your answers. Partial credit can be given only if your work is clear and demonstrates an understanding of the problem.

Assume that baseballs are produced in a competitive market.

(a) Draw a correctly labeled demand and supply graph showing the market equilibrium price and quantity of baseballs. Shade the consumer surplus at this equilibrium.

(b) Explain how the market equilibrium price and quantity is determined.

(c) The government is giving a subsidy to baseball producers. Show the change on the graph in part (a) and indicate the new market equilibrium price and quantity.

(d) Explain how the consumer surplus changes after the government subsidy is given.

(e) Now assume that the government imposes a price ceiling in this market.

(i) Identify the placement of the price ceiling and explain the problem resulting from the-price ceiling.

(ii) Suggest two ways that baseballs can now be distributed.

ANSWERS AND EXPLANATIONS

SECTION I

1. C

The concave shape of the PPF is due to the law of increasing costs. As the economy devotes more resources to capital goods production, the nation can expect more future production. Sacrifice now will mean more goods and services for consumers later. Choice (C) is the correct response, while (D) mixes up the changes. Choice (A) is incorrect since more capital goods means a greater sacrifice of consumer goods due to the law of increasing costs. Choice (B) incorrectly states the movement along the curve. Choice (E) would require a straight line PPC.

2. C

The three common determinants of price elasticity of demand are: the number of available substitutes, the portion of the consumer's budget spent on the good, and time. Here, the largest difference between the two goods, and therefore their elasticities, is that bread is a much smaller portion of the budget. Choice (C) is correct because a 5% increase in the price of bread will have less effect than a 5% increase in the price of a car. Choices (A) and (D) are incorrect since neither are a determinant of elasticity. Choice (B) is incorrect since bread does not have as many substitutes as autos. Choice (E) would mean that autos are inelastic.

3. C

Using supply and demand, in order for the market price to fall and the market quantity to rise, the supply curve must shift to the right. In (C), a fall in the price of an input will increase supply. Eliminate (A) because if incomes fall, demand decreases, causing price and quantity to fall. Choice (B) is incorrect since consumers purchase a lower quantity of a product that is inferior if their income rises. The fallacy in (D) is that a greater demand than supply would raise the price. Choice (E) is incorrect since a price floor is a government action and no mention has been made of such action.

4. A

Because there are few substitutes for cigarettes, demand is highly price inelastic. An excise tax will shift supply to the left and the price of cigarettes will rise more than the quantity demanded will fall, in percentage terms. As a result, total expenditures, calculated as the price times the quantity, will rise—(A). Choice (B) is incorrect as it is the opposite of (A), the correct answer. Eliminate (C) since personal income does not increase with a higher tax rate. Choice (D) is incorrect since the buyer bears most of the burden due to inelastic nature of the demand curve. Choice (E) is incorrect since the supply curve will move to the left with a new tax.

5. D

All choices but (D) involve a firm varying the level of all resources it uses (capital, labor, natural resources, entrepreneurship), which are long-run decisions. Adding temporary workers to a fixed amount of capital (office space, computers, etc.), as tax preparers do in the busy season is an example of a short-run production decision. Choice (D) is correct.

6. B

Because entry into competitive markets is without barriers, firms seeking economic profits will be attracted to the plasma TV industry, which will increase supply, reduce price, and reduce profit. This means (B) is correct. Only when economic profit is zero in the long run will this entry cease. Choice (A) is correct because as firms enter the industry, supply moves to the right and the price falls. Choice (C) is incorrect because economic profits will attract firms and more firms will enter the plasma TV industry. Choice (D) is incorrect because as firms enter the industry, supply moves to the right and the price falls. Eliminate (E) because the demand for plasma TVs will rise since the product price is lower.

7. D

Total output increases when producers specialize in the good where they have a comparative advantage, meaning they can produce with least opportunity cost—(D). In (A), Caleb does hold the absolute advantage, but if he does bake more cookies, he must give up folding more laundry. In (B), if Caleb folds more laundry, he must give up baking more cookies. In (C), Caleb does hold the absolute advantage, but if he folds more laundry, he must give up baking more cookies. Choice (E) is incorrect because specialization of tasks is only a good idea if opportunity costs are least.

8. C

Economic profit equals total revenues minus total costs, including the opportunity cost of capital invested. Choice (C) shows that economic profit = \$55,000 – \$50,000 – \$1,000 = \$4,000. Choice (A) is incorrect because it fails to recognize the opportunity cost of the capital invested. Choice (B) is incorrect since an economic profit is earned, not a loss. Choice (D) is eliminated since the definition of normal profit is not economic profit but rather a break-even position. Choice (E) is incorrect because Miguel does better when he works for himself.

9. C

In consumer equilibrium, the ratio of the marginal utilities to the price of the goods consumed should be equal. Thus, (C) shows that in equilibrium, the marginal utility per dollar must be the same for all goods. Choice (A) is incorrect since it lacks the ratio of MU to P being equal. Choice (B) is incorrect because the rational consumer in equilibrium is using marginal thinking to allocate his income, and total utility would decline under other schemes. Choice (D) is incorrect because what would the consumer gain in satisfaction if marginal utility is zero? Choice (E) is incorrect because when total utility is at its height, the marginal utility is zero.

10. C

Fixed costs do not vary with the level of output so when a firm stops producing in the short run, these fixed costs are still present. Choice (C) is correct. These costs might include the rent or mortgage payment, the cost of the manager's salary. When production started, the firm incurs both fixed and variable costs. Choices (A) and (D) are incorrect because a firm's marginal costs are related to the variable cost. When a firm does not produce in the short run, the variable costs are zero. In (B), it is incorrect to add the two types of costs together, since variable costs are zero when the firm does not produce. Eliminate (E) because of the explanation above that a firm has costs it must cover whether it produces or not.

11. B

One of the determinants of demand is the price of related goods. If the demand curve for Company Y's MP3 players increases (i.e., shifts to the right), either a substitute became more expensive or a complement dropped in price. A higher price for a substitute would cause more people to buy Company Y's MP3 players, and a lower price for complements (accessories) to Company Y's MP3 players would cause people to buy more of their players. Choice (B) is correct for this reason. Choice (A) is incorrect since the encoding software is not a complement to the players; it is a cost. Choice (D) is incorrect because an increase in the price of music files will cause consumers to buy fewer players. A decrease in the price of the players, as in (D), would not be a shift of the demand curve, only movement along the curve to a new quantity demanded. Eliminate (E) because a change in cost will affect the supply curve.

12. C

Because a single price monopoly's marginal revenue curve lies below its demand curve, price will be greater than marginal cost. For the perfect competitor, price equals marginal cost, a measure of allocative efficiency. Price will be higher for the single price monopoly and since marginal cost equals marginal revenue at a position of lower production than perfect competition, its quantity is lower so (C) is correct. Choice (A) is incorrect because competition forces lower prices as sellers compete for sales. Choice (B) is incorrect because a monopoly firm will not be able to offer more at higher prices because of the inelasticity of the demand curve. Eliminate both (D) and (E). The lower price will not be a true statement because the marginal revenue curve lies below the demand curve of a monopolist, and price will be greater than marginal cost.

13. B

Marginal revenue product of labor in a competitive market is equal to the marginal product times the market price of the good, or 5 units of output per worker times \$20 per unit of output, or \$100 per worker. Choice (B) is correct. Choice (A) is incorrect because the marginal revenue is the change in total revenue from the sale of an additional unit; the amount sold is not given to determine the marginal revenue. Choice (C) is incorrect because marginal cost is the additional cost of another worker and since workers do not come for free, marginal cost cannot be zero. Choice (D) is incorrect because paying a wage that is higher than the marginal revenue product, which the new worker can contribute, will mean a loss, not a profit. Eliminate (E) since we do not know the wage to be paid or the marginal product of additional workers.

14. C

When markets fail to include all benefits or costs in the market price, they will produce too much or too little compared to a market which does include them. When consumers value flu shots in the market, they fail to take into account the external social benefit of getting the shot, as they become less likely to spread the illness. Choice (C) is correct. As a result, they demand too few flu shots. Choice (A) is not related to the question. Choice (B) is incorrect because the community in general will benefit when more people have received the flu shot. Choice (D) is incorrect. Free riders are people who benefit from a good or service even though they have not been a part of the market for the good or service. In this case, there are many free riders that will not be exposed to flu since others have gotten the shot. Eliminate (E) since it is the opposite of the correct choice.

15. B

Demand for labor is a derived demand. As goods and services are demanded, labor to produce those products is demanded. Choices (A), (C), (D), and (E) describe changes in supply factors. In (B), when the demand for resort vacations rises, more workers at these resorts are demanded.

16. B

Choice (B) is correct because for goods with price inelastic demand, increases in supply will reduce price, and therefore, total expenditures, as the quantity demanded raises little. Furthermore, an economy with rising incomes will purchase fewer goods that are income inelastic. Choice (A) is incorrect because it cannot be related to the cause given. Choice (C), price floor, helps farmers since it sets a price above the equilibrium and then buys the surplus. This is not a problem but an aid to farmers. Choice (D) is partially correct but does not deal with the inelastic demand factor. Choice (E) is incorrect since small changes in an inelastic demand curve will yield smaller net change.

17. B

Marginal product of labor equals the change in output divided by the change in labor. Marginal product is 20 for the first worker, 30 for the second worker and 10 for the third. Thus, diminishing marginal returns sets in at the third worker, as stated in (B). All other choices incorrectly apply the marginal product of labor calculation.

18. B

Firms will hire workers up to the point where the marginal revenue product (marginal product times price) is equal to the marginal resource cost (wage rate). For this firm, the MRP of the third worker is $24 since MP (8) times P ($3) equals $24. Choice (B) is the correct response. The other choices do not correctly apply the formula for hiring workers.

19. C

Economies of scale reduce long-run costs per unit, or average cost. Constant returns to scale imply constant average costs, and diseconomies of scale result in higher average costs. Choice (C) is correct. A typical firm may find as it expands that is has exhausted opportunities for economies of scale and that the average costs eventually rise as they try to coordinate production among multiple plants. In (A), the diminishing returns create only the downward side of the U-shaped curve. Choice (B) is incorrect since the statement that capital becomes more expensive is not necessarily true. Choice (D) is incorrect since identical plants' sizes will not yield the U-shaped curve. Choice (E) is incorrect because barriers to entry to lead to resource ownership which can lead to higher costs for some firms.

20. D

Monopolistic competition differs from perfect competition in the ability of suppliers to differentiate their product from their competitor's product. In gasoline retailing, firms use advertising, brand recognition, and location advantages to allow them some pricing flexibility that would not arise under perfect competition as noted in (D). Choice (A) is not correct since there are barriers to entry due to the high start-up costs such as licensing, government regulation and liability insurance. Choice (B) is a determinant of demand, though how much information does the average buyer really have? Choice (C) is incorrect because the term "limited number of suppliers" is not clear. Choice (E) is incorrect though some might think there are excessive profits in this industry. The firms do not collude and hence profits are lower than thought.

SECTION II

This question tests your knowledge of supply and demand curves and efficiency concepts. Understanding the theoretical basis of supply and demand is necessary to predict market outcomes and show the efficiency aspects of changes in markets. Here's what a sample response might look like:

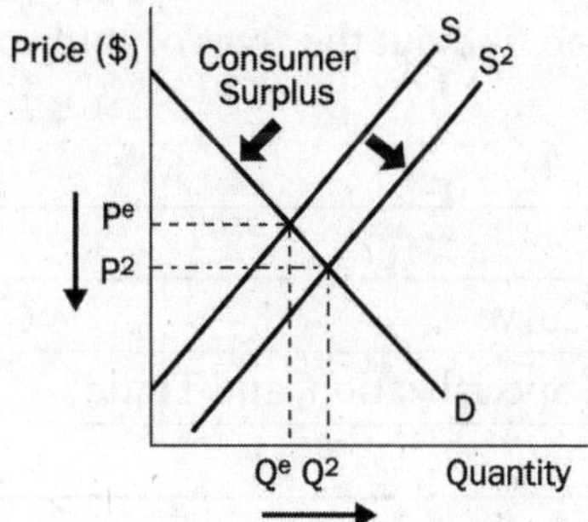

(a) The market price and quantity is an equilibrium position where the quantity demanded exactly equals the quantity supplied, holding all other things constant. Consumers are buying the quantity of baseballs they are willing and able to buy at that price, and sellers are selling the quantity they are willing and able to sell at that price. As such, there is no incentive for demanders to bid the price of baseballs up to acquire more, nor is there an incentive for firms to attempt to cut price to sell more. Consumer surplus is the difference between what consumers are willing to pay for a good, and what they actually pay. The consumer surplus is the triangle determined by the $P_{e,}$ the point where Q_d is equal to Q_s and where demand touches the vertical price axis. This triangle represents the gain in utility earned by buyers who were willing to pay more but only paid the equilibrium price.

(b) The subsidy would induce suppliers to produce more baseballs since their costs are now lower. The supply curve shifts the to the right and the market price of baseballs falls, but the quantity at the new equilibrium would rise.

(c) The new market equilibrium will increase the consumer surplus since the price has fallen.

(d) A price ceiling depresses the price below the market clearing level, increases the quantity demanded and reduces the quantity supplied. A price ceiling is a horizontal line below the market equilibrium. This will create a shortage of baseballs in the market. In the short run, producers will respond to reduced profits by cutting production of baseballs through cutting labor hours and reducing orders for raw materials. In the long run, baseball producers will close plants or shift them to the production of other goods and some firms may exit the baseball industry as they seek a higher profit in other industries. Consumers will wait in line, become more vigilant in discovering where the latest shipment of baseballs can be found, and will offer to pay more, under the table, for baseballs. Over time, as the purchase of baseballs becomes time-consuming or costly in the black market, consumers will begin to substitute other goods for new baseballs, such as used baseballs, tennis balls, etc., until the price reflects the marginal cost of acquiring another baseball.

AP Microeconomics Diagnostic Test Correlation Chart

Use the following table to determine which microeconomics topics you need to review most. After scoring your test, check to find out the areas of study covered by the questions you answered incorrectly.

Area of Study	Question Numbers
Production Possibilities Curve	1
Comparative Advantage, Specialization, and Trade	7
Supply and Demand	2, 3, 4, 11, 16
Theory of Consumer Choice	9
Production and Costs	5, 17, 18, 19
Firm Behavior and Market Structure	6, 8, 10, 12, 15, 20
Marginal Revenue Product	13, 15
Externalities	14

| PART THREE |

AP Macroeconomics Review

HOW TO USE THE MACROECONOMICS REVIEW SECTION

In the following chapters, we will focus on macroeconomics—the factors that affect the behavior and performance of an economy's business, government, and consumer markets as a whole: business cycles, unemployment, inflation, national income, money, banking, financial markets, fiscal and monetary policies, economic growth and productivity, and international trade and finance.

Step 1: Review the concepts.

Each of the following review chapters begins by going over the main concepts that apply to the chapter's topic. The chapters will NOT include loads of factual material, but instead will help you tie all the facts together to understand the concepts and discuss briefly how they fit within the thematic emphases designed by the College Board.

Step 2: Answer the review questions.

In the review chapters you will be given sample questions that will help you learn and review the AP economics course material. Questions from both sections of the AP Macroeconomics exam, multiple-choice and free-response, are included in each review chapter. The quantity and type of multiple-choice and free-response questions in the review chapters do not represent the exact material on the AP Macroeconomics exam, but they are plausible examples of topics covered.

Step 3: Review the answer explanations.

Following these questions are detailed answer explanations that explain how these questions address the course concepts. You will be given the correct answer for each question and be informed of the thought processes you should go through to reach a correct answer. Sometimes you will be given examples of how you might have reached the incorrect answer and how to avoid that problem in the future. Again, the emphasis is not just on repetition, but on effective repetition. It's not only about learning information, but how to apply it to the task at hand—scoring well on the exam.

Chapter 3: **Basic Economic Concepts**

- **Scarcity, Choice, and Opportunity Costs**
- **Economic Systems**
- **Production Possibilities Curve**
- **Comparative Advantage, Specialization, and Exchange**
- **Demand, Supply, and Market Equilibrium**
- **Review Questions**
- **Answers and Explanations**

SCARCITY, CHOICE, AND OPPORTUNITY COSTS

Economics is a powerful and broad field of study. It analyzes much of what goes on in our world. At the simplest level, economics is the study of how people deal with scarcity. It analyzes how society makes choices about the allocation of scarce resources. Scarcity implies that choices must be made.

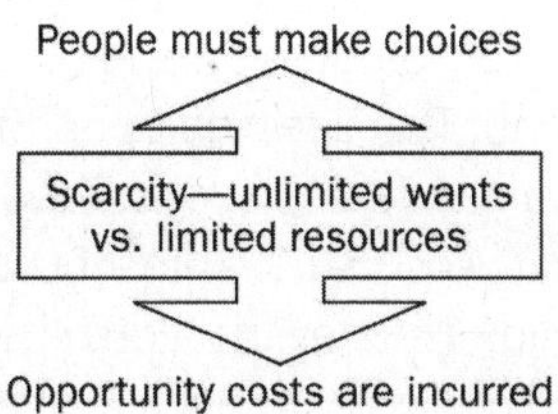

Microeconomics studies how the components of a nation's economy—firms, households, and individual consumers—allocate resources. Macroeconomics analyzes the overall performance of the economy, the big picture that is made up of the individual pieces considered in microeconomics. Across all of economics, there is a fundamental concern: how to get the greatest satisfaction from limited resources. Economists define resources as land, labor, capital, and entrepreneurship. Financial experts often use the word "capital" to refer to money or other assets, but in economics, capital is not money. This term refers only to goods that are used to produce other goods, such as buildings and equipment.

Even though the numerous economic resources are very different from one another, they have something important in common: They are all limited factors of production. The fact that resources are limited while our wants are not forces us to make choices about how those resources will be used. In economics, the production process is simply transforming these scarce resources (or inputs) into output (goods and services) that can be sold to and used by the members of society.

Three Economic Questions

There are three economic questions that any society must answer, regardless of its political form.

1. What goods will be produced?
2. What methods of production are appropriate?
3. Who will be able or permitted to consume the goods and services that are produced?

These questions are answered differently by different societies. Command economies get answers to these questions from a country's government. In many other countries, the market is allowed to answer these questions about resource allocation. Interaction between supply and demand creates prices that send signals to both producers and consumers. However, even in these market-oriented economies, governments still transfer income and supply public goods ranging from national defense and police protection to roads, education, and health care. The level of government transfers and public goods provided varies among nations; for example, there is a lower level of both in the United States relative to many European countries.

Opportunity Cost

In economics, we talk about resources that are scarce. This does not mean that their supply is too low, but it does mean that their supply is limited—too limited to satisfy everyone's needs and desires. As a result, we must choose which resources to use and how much of them to use. Making these choices is how we allocate our resources. As soon as we use a resource in a specific way, it can't be used anywhere else. For example, the time you spend reading this text is time that cannot be used to do anything else. So the allocation of scarce resources requires trade-offs and choices. When we make one choice, we simultaneously choose not to pursue other possible options. We forego other opportunities because we prefer this one. This declined opportunity is a cost that must be considered when making a choice, along with any financial costs associated with it. For example, the choice to attend college often involves opportunity costs such as the income that could be earned from a full-time job, the cost of books and tuition (money that could be spent on something else), and the time committed to studying and attending class (time that could be used differently).

Opportunity cost is also an important factor in trying to hire someone away from another job. It is not enough just to beat the person's current salary; the would-be employer must also match many—if not all—of the other benefits attached to the old job, such as office quality, title, number of people managed, and health insurance. A job that matches one's present salary but provides none of the present job's other benefits is unlikely to be an attractive alternative to one's present job. The value of the benefits that one would give up by quitting is too high. However, we should remember that people's views about what counts as a benefit can vary widely. This means that the attractiveness of various options (and each person's perception of the associated opportunity cost) can be highly subjective.

Opportunity costs can sometimes be figured a bit more objectively, when an individual knows the actual monetary value associated with an array of options. Suppose you are thinking about starting a business that makes and sells computers. Your plan is to make 20 computers and sell them at $1,000 each, making $20,000 in sales. This task will cost you $10,000 in labor costs, in addition to $5,000 worth of materials and other expenses. Your total costs will be $15,000 and you will be making $5,000 in profits. An accountant would say that you should definitely go ahead and start the business.

An economist, on the other hand, will ask you another question: If you were not starting this business what would you be doing instead? Suppose that instead of starting this business, you would be working at a job at which you make $20,000. When you start your business you will have to give up that job. This is your opportunity cost—the value attached to your next best option.

The economist will tell you that your total costs are not just the monetary costs for your labor and other expenses (which in this case are $15,000) but also your opportunity costs of $20,000. So according to the economist, your total costs will be $15,000 + $20,000 = $35,000. With sales of only $20,000, you would be losing money in this business and the economist will tell you not to start it. When economics looks at costs, opportunity costs are *always* included.

ECONOMIC SYSTEMS

All societies must deal with the problem of scarcity. They must make choices about resource allocation because their resources are limited, and they must strive to use their resources as efficiently as possible. In doing so, societies must answer three basic economic questions:

1. What should be produced?
2. How should it be produced?
3. For whom should it be produced?

Different economic systems have different ways of answering these questions. There are three types of economic systems: traditional, command, and market.

Traditional economies are still found in places in South America, Asia, and Africa. In a traditional economy, the economic roles that people fill are the same roles that their ancestors filled. Usually organized at the village level, traditional people plant and harvest the same land their parents and grandparents did and most products are produced as they were in the past. The people follow their traditions to answer the three economic questions.

In a command economy the government is the primary decision-maker. The government designs a central plan to determine what is to be produced, how to allocate resources to produce it, and how (and to whom) the product is to be sold. This means that individual citizens cannot simply choose to open their own private businesses. To a large extent, therefore, the government in a command economy determines how resources are used.

In a market economy the three basic economic questions are answered largely by buyers' and sellers' decisions in the marketplace. Profit acts as the incentive for production. As consumers make product purchases, they are "voting" in the marketplace and helping sellers to make decisions about products to produce for people who are willing and able to pay for them. Resources flow to those industries producing profitable products.

Economic systems also differ with respect to ownership of the means of production—i.e., the physical, non-human resources used in production. These include natural resources, farms, factories, mines, and machinery. In a command economy, the government owns and operates most of the means of production. In a market economy, private citizens and businesses own most of these means.

No country is purely a market economy or a command economy, largely because each system has serious flaws in its pure form. Contemporary economic systems are increasingly a mix of market and command systems. Even though the United States relies heavily on markets to make economic decisions, the government still owns many schools and colleges, as well as the postal service, the military, some bus and train systems, some electric plants, and many housing projects. Government welfare and retirement programs such as Social Security ensure that even citizens with few or no resources to sell get a share of the products produced. In China, which is mainly a command economy, the government is starting to allow more private businesses to operate and to permit markets to make more economic decisions. Other economies, such as Sweden's and Denmark's, have different mixes of market and government control.

PRODUCTION POSSIBILITIES CURVE

The production possibilities curve (PPC; also called the production possibilities frontier, (PPF)) is a tool we can use to answer the basic economic question of what to produce. It is a graphical way to represent the fact that we must give up some of one good to get more of another. The PPC shows us what combinations of goods we can produce when we are using our resources efficiently. By *efficient*, we mean that no resources are unemployed and all of our resources are allocated to the production of the good that they are most suited to produce. The classic example of the PPC illustrates a society's choice between military spending (guns) and consumption spending (butter). A society could be using all of its resources for military spending and producing no consumption goods, or it could focus exclusively on consumption goods while ignoring military production. However, it is more likely that a society would choose some point of production between these extremes, producing some of both goods. During times of war, we are likely to see an increase in military spending, but that is likely to occur at the expense of consumption spending because our resources are scarce. Scarcity is the reason that the PPC slopes downwards. Resources are likely to be specialized (i.e., better suited to the production of one good than another). Because this is so, resources that are transferred from producing guns to producing butter will not be as productive as they were when producing guns. The result is a smaller increase in butter output each time we transfer resources from the production of guns; each additional unit of butter costs more than the previous one, in terms of guns given up to obtain it. This is called the **law of increasing opportunity costs** and gives the PPC its convex shape.

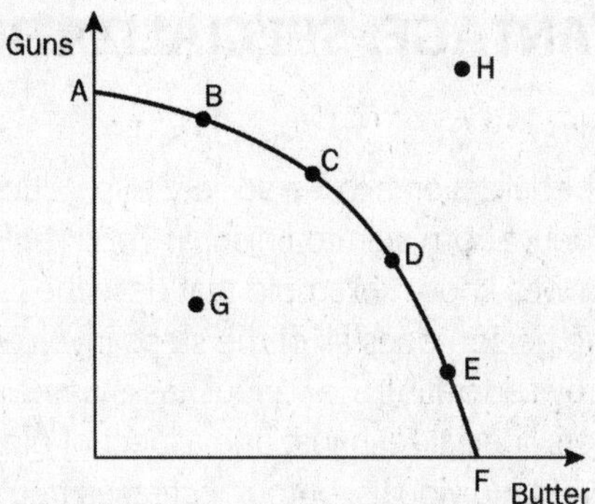

Points that are on the PPC (points A through F) are efficient. At each of these points, resources are being used in an efficient way; the society is producing an allocation of goods that maximizes what can be achieved, given its resources. The only difference between these various points is the amount of each good being produced; none of these points is objectively better than another one. A society must choose among these production combinations.

Points that are *inside* the PPC (such as G) are inefficient, producing less of each good than is possible given the society's resources. The society could produce more of each good without producing less of anything else, and thus it is not currently making the most of its resources. It might be that some of its resources are unemployed, that its technology is inefficient, or both.

Finally, points that are *outside* the PPC (such as H) are unattainable given current resources and technology. Economic growth means an increase in the economy's total output production and is represented by an outward shift of the PPC. This growth brings previously unattainable points within reach of the new PPC.

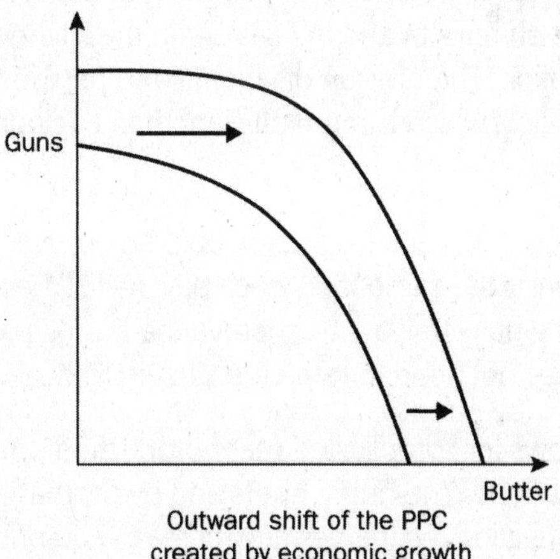

Outward shift of the PPC
created by economic growth

COMPARATIVE ADVANTAGE, SPECIALIZATION, AND EXCHANGE

The division of labor and labor specialization allow a society to produce much more than it could if one individual created each product from start to finish. In *The Wealth of Nations*, economist and philosopher Adam Smith offers a well-known example that describes a pin factory. Smith compares the output possible when a single person does all of the steps involved in making each pin with the output that can be achieved by separating the various tasks associated with pin-making among different individuals. When workers specialize in just one aspect of pin-making, and the steps of the task are divided among different individuals, output increases tremendously. Smith suggests that a worker who must complete each step on her own could make no more than twenty pins a day, while ten people who have specialized and divided the pin-making tasks can make as many as 48,000 pins per day. An individual's proportional output thus increases from 20 pins to 4,800 pins per day. The division of labor and specialization increases output by 240 times.

Specialization allows a person, business, or nation to specialize in those endeavors that they do best, instead of striving for self-sufficiency. This benefits us in two ways: A greater variety of goods and services are available and they are available at a lower cost.

WHY DO SPECIALIZATION AND THE DIVISION OF LABOR LEAD TO INCREASED OUTPUT?

When labor is divided, tasks can be assigned (or chosen) according to what people like and are best at. Imagine a bakery run by only one person. He might be a very good baker who is very bad at handling customers. The demand for his product will increase, and he will have more time to focus on baking, if he hires a more cheerful person to run his cash register. However, it would make no sense to put the baker at the cash register and the cashier in the kitchen; neither of them would be productive in their new location. The division of labor allows people to work according to their individual preferences and abilities, which is more efficient than forcing them to perform tasks they dislike or to which they are unsuited.

Specialization also increases output because it gives people an opportunity to become better at one specific job. As the baker performs the same tasks each day, he will become faster and more skilled at them, and will probably come up with ways to improve the baking process. In addition, the baker can bake more because he does not need to leave the kitchen to deal with customers.

Finally, the division of labor allows for complicated mass-production processes that are far beyond the ability of an individual household. The huge mixers and ovens that are typical in commercial bakeries allow for different production techniques and increased output; these methods would not make sense on a smaller scale.

TRADE AND COMPARATIVE ADVANTAGE

Trade helps to create economic growth because it enables an economy to take advantage of specialization, which increases and improves the various options open to a society. When one individual can produce something at a lower opportunity cost than another individual, the first person is understood to have a comparative advantage over the second.

The law of comparative advantage (set out by the 19th-century British political economist David Ricardo) states that individuals, firms, regions, and nations can gain (increase total output) by *specializing* in tasks at which they are efficient (i.e., which have a low opportunity cost for them) and *trading* for goods which they are inefficient at producing (i.e., that they would pay a high opportunity cost to produce). Even if a country has an absolute advantage (i.e., it is more efficient at producing everything than another country), comparative advantage can still create benefits when that country trades with a comparatively poorer nation. It makes good economic sense to specialize in the activities one can do most cheaply, in terms of opportunity cost.

DEMAND, SUPPLY, AND MARKET EQUILIBRIUM

Demand

A demand curve illustrates how much of a good would be purchased (i.e., the quantity demanded) at each possible price. The **law of demand** states that as prices rise, people are willing and able to buy less of a good and hence the quantity demanded decreases. As prices fall, people are willing and able to buy more and so the quantity demanded increases. Therefore, the demand curve slopes downwards.

When **price** changes, then, there is a change in the **quantity demanded**. This is represented by a movement up or down on a single demand curve. This kind of change is called a **movement along a demand curve**.

We are considering the relationship between price and demand under *ceteris paribus* conditions, or from a perspective in which all other factors that could influence demand are held constant. This is done not to discount the possibility that other changes can affect demand, but instead to focus on identifying the specific effects caused by a change in price.

When we put together the demand curves for each individual consumer in a market (add all the quantities demanded at each price), we get the **market demand** for a product.

Factors that Shift the Market Demand Curve

A change in price changes the quantity demanded. It does not change the demand curve itself. However, other factors can shift the demand curve to the left or to the right. When one of these things changes, it changes how much is quantity demanded at *each* possible price.

There are five broad changes that will lead people to demand more of a good even when there is no change in its price:

1. A change in income
2. A change in tastes or preferences
3. A change in the price of other goods
4. A change in the expected future price of the good
5. A change in consumer information

Income (Normal and Inferior Goods)

If the demand curve for a good shifts to the right (i.e., demand increases) as consumers' income increases, then that good is considered to be a **normal** good. If the demand curve shifts to the left (i.e., demand falls) as consumers' income increases, then that good is considered to be an **inferior** good. Fast food is an example of an inferior good; as income increases, most consumers would prefer to spend their money on a meal at a nicer restaurant. Demand for fast food falls as income increases, while demand for restaurant meals increases.

Tastes and Preferences

As consumers come to know and like a product, demand for it will increase, shifting its demand curve to the right. Consumers will sometimes prefer the new product to whatever they used previously; if enough of them do so, demand for the older product(s) will decrease, shifting its demand curve to the left. Advertising and marketing work to create these widespread changes in consumer tastes and preferences.

Prices of Other Goods (Complements and Substitutes)

Demand for a good can be affected by changes in the price of other products that are used along with that good, or by products that can be used instead of that good. Goods that are used together are called **complements**. An increase in the price of one complement leads to a decline in demand for the other complement. For example, an increase in the price of airline tickets will result in decreased demand for rental cars.

When one good can readily be replaced by another good, they are called **substitutes**. For example, a person who simply wants a caffeinated beverage can pick from coffee, tea, and soda. If all he wants is something tasty that contains caffeine, there is no reason to prefer one of these over the others, and they are substitutes. If the price of one of these goods—let's say coffee—increases, people will choose to purchase tea or soda rather than coffee. Demand for coffee will decrease, and the demand curves for the substitute goods will shift to the right.

Future Expectations about Price

Most people react to expectations about price changes in a predictable way. If a shopper who drinks coffee sees a sign at her local market saying that all coffee will be 50% beginning tomorrow, she will postpone her purchase. Similarly, a sign warning of a 50% increase in the price of coffee beginning tomorrow will lead her to buy more now. In both cases, her desire to get the best price on the good affects demand. Postponed purchases that result from an anticipated price drop shift the demand curve to the left; people buy less at any price, because they expect that price to decrease soon. Larger-than-usual purchases made in anticipation of a price increase shift the demand curve to the right; people buy more than they would previously have at this same price.

Consumer Information

The amount of information available to consumers when they make their purchases is a part of their demand decisions. Today, we can use the Internet to find information about the products we want to buy. There are also publications like *Consumer Reports* and various buyers' guides available. Reliable consumer information helps guide consumers' decisions and can incline them to purchase goods and services that they otherwise might not consider.

SUPPLY

A supply curve illustrates how much of a good would be supplied or produced at each possible price. We might think of a supply curve as a seller's "willingness to supply" curve. As was true of the demand curve, each price is associated with a quantity supplied.

Also similar to the demand curve, a change in price (*ceteris paribus*) creates a change in the quantity supplied, causing movement from one point to another on a single supply curve.

When we add all the quantities of a good supplied by all producers at each price we get the **market supply curve** for that product. The **law of supply** states that as prices increase, sellers are willing and able to sell more of a good so the quantity supplied increases. As prices fall, the sellers are not able or willing to sell as much and the quantity supplied decreases. Therefore the supply curve slopes upwards.

FACTORS THAT SHIFT THE MARKET SUPPLY CURVE

There are six broad changes that will shift the curve itself, changing the quantity supplied at each price:

1. A change in the costs of production
2. A change in technology
3. A change in the number of producers
4. A change in the prices of alternatives using the same resources
5. A change in producers' expectations about price
6. A change in the time period in which to produce

COSTS OF PRODUCTION

The resources that are used to produce a good affect its cost. If, for example, a producer has to pay more in wages or there is an increase in the rent on her factory, she will not be able to afford to produce as much and supply will fall, shifting the supply curve to the left. Similarly, a decrease in the cost of resources will shift the supply curve to the right.

TECHNOLOGICAL CHANGE

Improved technology can make production easier and faster, which means that more can be produced at each price. Technological advances increase supply and shift the supply curve to the right. When technology is destroyed (e.g., during war or after a natural disaster), supply decreases and the supply curve shifts to the left.

Number of Producers

The market supply curve reflects the quantity supplied by all producers at each price. This means that an increase in the number of producers will shift the curve to the right, while a decrease in the number of producers will shift it to the left.

Prices of Alternatives

Producers' resources generally have more than one possible use; the same labor, equipment, and skills could be used to produce different goods. As the price of wheat increases, the opportunity cost of growing corn goes up. As producers shift to the option of growing wheat, the supply curve for corn will shift to the left. A decline in the price of an alternative makes one's current choice more attractive, and can shift the supply curve to the right as more producers pursue this appealing option.

Future Expectations about Prices

If a producer expects that coffee prices are going to rise next year, she will plant more coffee this year. The supply of coffee increases as a result, shifting the supply curve to the right. An anticipated drop in price will lead to decreased production, which shifts the supply curve to the left.

Time Period to Produce

The time frame for production varies. In the market period, once goods are sold, there is a time gap for new production—once his entire crop is sold, a tomato farmer has no more to sell until the next season. In the short run, variable resources can be adjusted as needed; for example, a restaurant at the beach can hire more cooks and waiters when the tourists arrive each summer. All costs are variable in the long run, so capital improvements can be made. The beach restaurant in the example above could expand the dining room in the long run. All of these periods of production will influence the amount of supply available for sale.

Market Equilibrium

Market equilibrium is reached when supply and demand are balanced such that the market price and the **quantity exchanged** (amount actually sold) are under no market pressure to change. The **market equilibrium price** is a price at which the quantity supplied (Q_s) and the quantity demanded (Q_d) are equal, so that there is no shortage or surplus that pushes toward a change in price.

When $Q_d = Q_s$, we have market equilibrium. When $Q_d > Q_s$, consumers want to buy more than is available, causing a shortage. When $Q_d < Q_s$, producers want to sell more than consumers will buy at a given price, creating a surplus. Shortages cause prices to increase, while surpluses cause prices to drop.

Changes in Equilibrium

Market equilibrium changes as a result of a shift in the demand curve or the supply curve. Therefore, the same nine factors that were listed as causes of shifts in supply and demand are also the causes of change in market equilibrium. When the demand curve shifts, market price and market quantity exchanged move in the same direction (both rise or both fall).

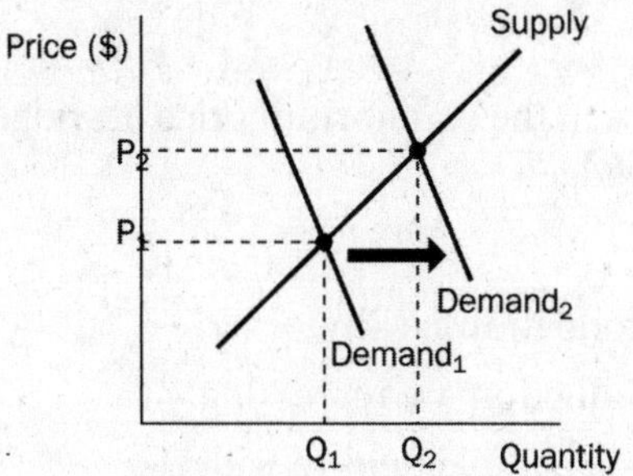

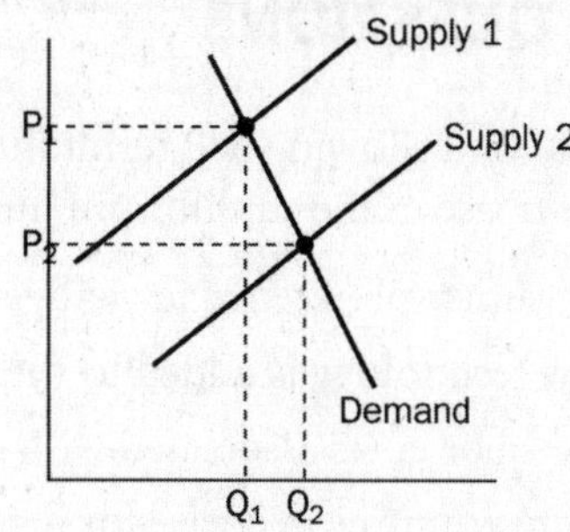

When the supply curve shifts, market price and market quantity exchanged move in opposite directions (one rises while the other falls).

Thus, an increase in demand leads to increase in equilibrium price and quantity, while a decrease in demand leads to a decrease in equilibrium price and quantity. An increase in supply leads to a decrease in equilibrium price and an increase in equilibrium quantity; a decrease in supply leads to an increase in equilibrium price and a decrease in equilibrium quantity.

IF YOU LEARNED ONLY THREE THINGS IN THIS CHAPTER. . .

1. The production possibilities curve (PPC) (also called the production possibilities frontier (PPF)) is a graphical way to illustrate the relationship between spending and consumption.
2. Supply and demand comprise both halves of the market exchange process.
3. Market equilibrium is reached when supply and demand are balanced such that the market price and the quantity exchanged are under no market pressure to change.

REVIEW QUESTIONS

1. Which of the following will result in an increase in the equilibrium price of widgets and a decrease in the equilibrium quantity of widgets?

   (A) Consumer preference for widgets increases.

   (B) New technology is added to the widget production facility.

   (C) The labor costs associated with widget production are increasing.

   (D) There is a price decrease for a good that is a complement to widgets.

   (E) More widget producers enter the market.

2. Which of the following is a macroeconomic statement?

   (A) General Motors can cut its average total costs of production by outsourcing some production functions.

   (B) The anti-pollution devices that are required under the EPA rules will cost the steel industry millions of dollars.

   (C) The unemployment rate reported last month for the nation was 5.4%.

   (D) Monopoly power in the marketplace will result in higher prices.

   (E) Public goods have the characteristics of shared consumption and non-exclusivity.

3. Which of the following is NOT a determinant of demand?

   (A) A change in consumer tastes and preferences

   (B) A change in the price of inputs

   (C) A change in the number of buyers

   (D) A change in the price of a substitute

   (E) A change in the level of consumer information

4. If leather shoes are a normal good and consumers have higher incomes to spend, what is the result?

   (A) As income increases, the quantity demanded increases along the demand curve for leather shoes.

   (B) As income increases, the demand curve for leather shoes shifts rightward.

   (C) As income increases, the demand curve for leather shoes shifts leftward.

   (D) As the price of leather shoes increases, the real income of individuals who demand leather shoes decreases, so the quantity demanded of leather shoes decreases.

   (E) As the price of leather shoes increases, income increases.

5. If the demand for plums increases and the supply of plums decreases, which of the following is true?
   (A) The price and the quantity will both increase.
   (B) The price will increase, but the quantity will decrease.
   (C) The price will rise, but it will be impossible to determine the change in the quantity.
   (D) The price will fall, but it will be impossible to determine the change in the quantity.
   (E) The quantity will rise, but it will be impossible to determine the change in the price.

ANSWERS AND EXPLANATIONS

1. C

Supply must decrease with the supply curve shifting to the left if the price increases and the quantity decreases for widgets. Choice (C) states that labor costs increase; this situation would cause the supply curve to decrease and move to the left. Choice (A) incorrectly uses a demand determinant that would move the demand curve to the right, with a resulting increase in price and quantity of widgets. Choice (B) is incorrect since a technology addition will shift the supply curve to the right, causing price to decrease and quantity to rise. Choice (D) is incorrect because a decrease in the price a complementary good would mean that more widgets would be demanded as more of the other good is purchased at lower prices. Choice (E) incorrectly shifts supply to the right, as in (B).

2. C

Macroeconomics is concerned with the "big picture" of the economy. Macroeconomic topics include the measurement of the economy, the stabilization of the economy through fiscal and monetary policies, economic growth, and international trade. Choice (C) is the only option that states a macroscopic idea. Unemployment is a measure of the number of workers willing and able to work, but unable to find work. It is stated as a percentage of the labor force. The other choices all concern microeconomic concepts such as cost of production, government intervention, monopolistic power, and public goods. Microeconomics studies the agents of the economy—consumers, resource suppliers, businesses, and government.

3. B

Non-price determinants of demand will move the curve to the left (decreased demand) or right (increased demand). All the choices except (B) give reasons not related to the price of the good which can shift the demand curve. In Choice (A), consumers change their buying habits, which is a change in demand. Choice (C) will increase the market and demand will shift right. Choice (D) means that as the price of one good rises, the demand for its substitute will increase. Choice (E) is related to whether the consumer obtains more or less information and how that information relates to a buying decision. Choice (B) is the right answer here because a change in the price of the product will create movement along the same demand curve and change only the quantity demanded.

4. B

When income changes, the demand for normal goods will move in the same direction as the change in income. Inferior goods, on the other hand, move in the opposite direction from income change. Choice (B) correctly states that as the income increases, the demand for leather shoes shifts to the right. Choice (C) mixes up the direction of change. Choice (D) incorrectly states the income effect, which is a reason for the downward sloping demand curve. Choices (A) and (E) are incorrect because they combine ideas and terms in ways that do not accurately reflect the idea of normal and inferior goods.

5. C

When demand and supply both shift, the changes in price and quantity can be somewhat confusing. If we were to draw a graph, it might appear that as we shift the demand to the right (increase) and shift the supply to the left (decrease), we see that the price rises but the quantity falls. However, this graph would be somewhat misleading. What really happens is that we can easily recognize the increase in price, but the change in quantity is said to be indeterminate—it is impossible to determine the change. This is true because we do not know the degree of change in the demand and the supply. Choice (C) is thus the correct response: Price rises but we cannot determine the change in quantity. The other choices fail to accommodate this lack of information about the degree of change and the answers are therefore incorrect.

Chapter 4: Measurement of Economic Performance

- National Income Accounts
- GDP
- Business Cycles, Unemployment, and Growth
- Inflation Measurement
- Unemployment
- Review Questions
- Answers and Explanations

NATIONAL INCOME ACCOUNTS

Macroeconomics is a game of aggregation. It studies the economy as a whole, the ways that all of the smaller pieces and systems of microeconomics interrelate. National income accounts keep track of a country's diverse goods and services. The horizontal (or quantity) measure used in macroeconomics is gross domestic product or **GDP**. GDP is the market value of all the final goods and services produced by a country's economy in a given time period. This time period is generally understood to be a year unless specifically defined otherwise. GDP reflects the total income earned by the suppliers in an economy, because the production of those goods and services is the source of a country's income.

There are two different ways of computing the GDP. Nominal GDP is calculated using current-year prices. The nominal GDP for 2001, then, would calculate the value of production using 2001 prices for goods and services. Nominal GDP can vary widely from year to year because we are counting the current market price of the goods and services. Real GDP can be thought of as nominal GDP corrected for inflation. Real GDP is calculated using prices from a given base year, which may not be the same as the year being measured or the year in which the calculations are made. By focusing on real GDP, we can realistically compare changes in production across years. Real GDP creates a stable price index so that rising prices in general do not increase real GDP.

GDP

The GDP is a specific metric. It aims to include only the total market value of all final goods and services produced within a country's domestic boundaries during a given time period. It does not include the value of non-market activities such as unpaid housework, nor does it include illegal activities. It includes only final goods and services, those that are sold to final or ultimate users (consumers). The GDP does not include intermediate goods and services, those that are used in the process of production or are purchased for resale. A cotton blouse is a final good, but the cotton thread, dye, buttons, and cloth that go into making it are all intermediate goods.

The GDP does not include intermediate goods because to do so would amount to counting their value twice (**double counting**). If a retailer pays $4 for a model car and resells it for $16, there is an intermediate transaction (in which the retailer pays $4) and a final transaction (in which the consumer pays $16). Taken together, these add up to $20, which is more than the final value of the product.

Sometimes you will see references to the **GNP**, or gross national product. What is the difference between GDP and GNP? Until 1992, GNP was the measure that the United States federal government used to evaluate output. GNP measures the market value of all goods and services produced with resources provided by U.S. firms and residents, even if the resources are not located in the United States and the production does not occur there. The GDP does not include income earned abroad; it measures the output produced within the borders of the United States (including the output of foreign-owned labor and capital). Today, most governments count the GDP.

Economic growth is defined as an increase in the real GDP of an economy. So how do we calculate the GDP, and see whether it is increasing or decreasing? There are two approaches—the **expenditure approach** and the **income approach**. Under the expenditure approach, GDP is measured by adding up all spending on final goods and services during a given year. This is an aggregate of all domestic spending on production.

The aggregate expenditure approach includes four types of spending:

1. Consumption: households' purchases of final goods and services during the year
2. Investment: domestic spending on additions to inventories, depreciation (repair of current capital) and new capital goods
3. Government spending: consumption and investment for all government branches
4. Net exports: the value of exports less the value of imports

The expenditure approach determines GDP by adding these four parts.

$$GDP = C + I_g + G + X_n$$

The income approach measures GDP as an aggregate of all of the income derived from that production. Remember that whatever you spend on purchasing goods and services becomes income for the producers of these goods and services. Expenditure and income are thus two sides of the same coin. The economic concept of **circular flow** amounts to the idea that one person's spending is another person's income.

BUSINESS CYCLES, UNEMPLOYMENT, AND GROWTH

The U.S. GDP tends to grow at about 3% per year. Of course, this does not mean that at any one point in time the GDP is increasing at 3%. Sometimes GDP growth is higher than this trend value of 3% and sometimes it is lower. The fluctuations in real GDP around the trend value are called **business cycles** or **economic fluctuations**.

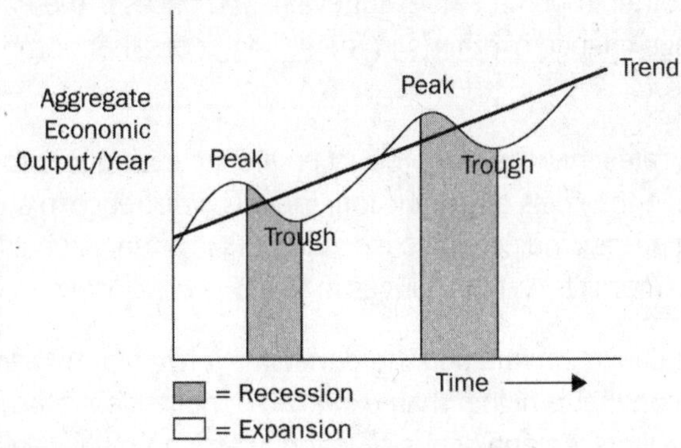

The highest point of a business cycle is called a **peak** and the lowest point is called a **trough**. When the economy moves from a peak to a trough, real GDP is falling and the economy is described as being in a **recession**. When the economy moves from a trough to a peak, real GDP is increasing and this is called an **expansion** or a **boom**. Historically, expansions have often lasted longer than recessions, but the length of the cycle as a whole varies.

A recession usually defined is six consecutive months (two consecutive quarters) of decline in real GDP. When a recession becomes prolonged and deep, involving high unemployment, it is called a **depression**.

When real GDP increases so do investment spending, consumption spending, and stock prices. Because these changes move in the same direction as the real GDP, we call them **procyclical**. Other changes do not move in the same direction as changes in real GDP. When real GDP increases, unemployment falls (because production increases). Unemployment moves in a different direction than real GDP, and it is said to be **countercyclical**.

INFLATION MEASUREMENT

Inflation is a sustained increase in an economy's average price level. There are two kinds of indexes at which we can look to see if the price level has increased. One is called the Consumer Price Index (CPI), which tells us about average changes over time in the prices of a fixed group of goods and services that are bought by consumers. The annual rate of change in the CPI is the annual rate of inflation or deflation. The other important index for evaluation prices is the Producer Price Index (PPI), which reveals average change over time in the selling prices that domestic producers receive for their goods and services.

An increase in the PPI indicates that costs of production are increasing for producers. We know that when there is an increase in the costs of production, there is a decrease in supply, and declining supply leads to increasing prices. Thus an increase in the PPI is often taken as a precursor to an increase in the CPI and economists watch changes in the PPI very closely.

The difference between the inflation rate and the nominal interest rate on a loan is referred to as the real interest rate. Inflation that is higher than expected benefits debtors; inflation that is lower than expected benefits creditors. An analogous situation affects nominal wages and real wages, with higher-than-anticipated inflation benefiting employers and lower-than-expected inflation benefiting workers.

Hyperinflation is a very high rate of inflation. Under hyperinflation, prices go up very rapidly—often more than 1,000% in a single year—and money becomes a poor store of value. **Stagflation** occurs when an economy's output (real GDP) decreases and its price level rises; production stagnates (as during a recession) while prices (and unemployment) go up.

UNEMPLOYMENT

When is a person considered unemployed? To understand what unemployment means, we must first know whom the government considers to be employed. U.S. employment statistics apply to the adult, civilian, non-institutionalized population. This means that we are talking only about people over 16 who are not in the military or in a prison or mental hospital. These are the people who make up the labor force; they can be counted as either employed or unemployed.

The U.S. Bureau of Labor Statistics defines a civilian, non-institutionalized adult as being **employed** when he or she:

- Works for at least one hour per week for wages.
- Works for at least 15 hours per week if not getting paid.
- Is temporarily not working (either with or without pay) but has a job to which he or she can return.

A civilian, non-institutionalized adult is considered to be **unemployed** when he or she does not have a job but is actively looking for one. Only a small percentage of adults who are not working are actually considered to be unemployed. Retirees, students, people who are ill or disabled, and those who do not wish to work are some of the diverse groups that are not considered to be unemployed.

The **labor force** is defined as the group of individuals who are either working or actively looking for work. Therefore, the labor force includes the unemployed: Labor force equals number of individuals who are employed plus number of individuals who are unemployed. The **unemployment rate** measures the percentage of the labor force that is not working; therefore the unemployment rate equals the number of individuals who are unemployed divided by the number of individuals in the labor force (expressed as a percentage). The **labor force participation rate** measures the percentage of the adult population that is part of the labor force, i.e., the labor force participation rate equals the number of individuals in the labor force divided by the number of individuals in the adult population (expressed as a percentage).

Here's a simple example. Imagine a population of 530,000 adults; 300,000 people are employed and 30,000 are unemployed. What is the labor force?

$$\text{Labor force} = 300{,}000 + 30{,}000 = 330{,}000$$

What is the unemployment rate?

$$\text{Unemployment rate} = \frac{30{,}000}{330{,}000} = 9.09\%$$

Given that there are 200,000 people not in the labor force, you can find the labor force participation rate.

$$\text{Labor force participation rate} = \frac{330{,}000}{530{,}000} = 62.26\%$$

When it is difficult to find jobs, some of the unemployed who might otherwise be actively looking for work stop trying to find jobs. These people are appropriately called **discouraged workers**. However, once a person stops actively looking for a job, he or she is no longer considered to be unemployed. These people drop out of the labor force, which can artificially reduce the unemployment rate and give the impression that the economy is doing better than it actually is.

TYPES OF UNEMPLOYMENT

There are three kinds of unemployment: cyclical, frictional, and structural.

Cyclical unemployment reflects changes in the business cycle. In a recession period, firms need less of all resources, including labor. In expansion periods, increased demand reduces cyclical unemployment.

Frictional unemployment is the unemployment associated with the normal workings of an economy. It takes time for workers to find producers who will pay for their labor and it takes producers time to find appropriate workers. A new college graduate looking for her first job must take time to get to know the job market and prospective employers. In the time it takes to find a job that fits her skills, she is considered frictionally unemployed. Seasonal unemployment is considered to be a kind of frictional unemployment. For example, lifeguards and other workers in tourist areas often lose their jobs when the tourist season ends. Employment statistics are adjusted for seasonal unemployment. Because there will always be some people who are frictionally unemployed, frictional unemployment is never equal to zero and there is always some unemployment in the economy.

Structural unemployment is the unemployment that results when there is a mismatch between the kinds of jobs available and the skills of those who are unemployed, or between the location of jobs and the location of unemployed individuals. For example, the U.S. economy is shifting from manufacturing to services. The result is that those who have lost manufacturing jobs do not have the skills to find employment in the service sector. They would need to update their skills before they can find jobs again.

Total unemployment includes all three types of unemployment discussed above.

Total unemployment = cyclical unemployment + frictional unemployment + structural unemployment

When cyclical unemployment is zero, the unemployment rate is called the **natural rate of unemployment**, because it reflects unemployment that arises from natural features of a market society.

Natural rate of unemployment = frictional unemployment + structural unemployment

The natural rate of unemployment is considered to reflect the economy at full employment. For the U.S. economy, this rate is around five; the rate is even higher in many European countries.

Flaws in Accounting for Unemployment

We noted earlier that excluding discouraged workers from the labor force can result in an artificially low unemployment rate. The official unemployment figures are insensitive to other subtle distinctions in employment as well. The most significant of these is **underemployment**, which occurs when people can find only part-time work or can only find jobs that for which they are over-educated or over-trained. These individuals are counted as employed, even though they are at best only partly employed; they are not making the full contribution that would be possible if their labor was being used efficiently. However, it is can be difficult to distinguish between someone who is underemployed and someone who is employed.

These two problems lead many people to believe that official employment figures underestimate the U.S. unemployment rate to some extent. Views differ as to how serious this underestimation may be. Even with these problems, the standard measures of unemployment provide useful information about the condition of the economy.

IF YOU LEARNED ONLY FOUR THINGS IN THIS CHAPTER. . .

1. Gross domestic product (GDP) is the market value of all the final goods and services produced by a country's economy in a given time period; gross national product (GNP) measures the market value of all goods and services produced with resources provided by U.S. firms and residents, even if the resources are not located in the U.S. and the production does not occur there.

2. When the economy moves from a peak to a trough, real GDP is falling and the economy is described as being in a recession; conversely, when the economy moves from a trough to a peak, real GDP is increasing and the economy is described as an expansion, or boom.

3. Inflation is a sustained increase in an economy's average price level.

4. Types of unemployment include cyclical, frictional, and structural unemployment.

REVIEW QUESTIONS

1. A 25-year-old steel worker has not worked for the past two months because her union is on strike against the company for which she works. During these past two months, she has not been paid. She would be classified as

   (A) outside the labor force
   (B) employed
   (C) unemployed
   (D) a discouraged worker
   (E) frictionally unemployed

2. Refer to the table below.

Employed	9,500
Unemployed	500
Not in the labor force	2,000

   The unemployment rate for this population is

   (A) 5%
   (B) 5.25%
   (C) 4%
   (D) 0.4%
   (E) 11%

3. Nancy wants to make a 10% real return on a loan that she is planning to make, and the expected inflation rate during the period of the loan is 12%. She should charge an interest rate of

   (A) 12%
   (B) 22%
   (C) 9%
   (D) –2%
   (E) 10%

4. A firm produced 12 computers in 2005. The firm sold 10 in 2005 and added 2 to inventories. The market value of the computers in 2005 was $600 per unit. What is the value of this firm's output that should be included in the GDP for 2005?

   (A) $7,200
   (B) $6,000
   (C) $1,200
   (D) $13,200
   (E) $600

5. The value of what an American-owned factory produces in Mexico is

   I. Excluded from the U.S. GDP
   II. Included in the U.S. GDP
   III. Included in the Mexican GDP
   IV. Included in the U.S. GNP

   (A) I only
   (B) I and IV
   (C) II and III
   (D) II and IV
   (E) I, III, IV

6. Ayesha graduates from college, but decides to spend a year doing volunteer work before looking for a job. As a result, there is

   (A) an increase in structural unemployment
   (B) a decrease in cyclical unemployment
   (C) a decrease in the labor force
   (D) no change in the unemployment rate
   (E) an increase in seasonal unemployment

7. Discouraged workers are considered to be

   (A) part of the labor force
   (B) a natural result of frictional unemployment
   (C) a natural result of structural unemployment
   (D) unemployed
   (E) outside the labor force

8. Stagflation occurs when

(A) the overall price level increases rapidly during an expansion period
(B) the overall price level falls during a recession period
(C) the overall price level increases rapidly during a recession period
(D) the overall price level and employment are both stable for a long period
(E) the overall price level decreases rapidly during an expansion period

9. Hyperinflation is a

(A) sustained increase in the overall price level
(B) rapid increase in the overall price level
(C) period of high prices and high unemployment
(D) decline in output combined with an increase in the overall price level
(E) rapid decrease in the overall price level

10. Freedonia's economy is in a recession and housing market sales are below average. As a result, a real estate firm lays off half its agents, creating

(A) an increase in the natural rate of unemployment
(B) a decrease in the natural rate of unemployment
(C) an increase in the actual rate of unemployment
(D) a decrease in the actual rate of unemployment
(E) an increase in the rate of frictional unemployment

FREE-RESPONSE QUESTION

Consider the following information for a country:

- Number of employed individuals: 200,000
- Number of unemployed individuals: 50,000
- Number of unemployed individuals outside the labor force: 500,000

Calculate the following and show how you derived the figures.

(a) The size of the labor force
(b) The unemployment rate
(c) The labor force participation rate

ANSWERS AND EXPLANATIONS

1. B

The 25-year-old steel worker is not working and she is not getting paid, but she has a job to which she can return after the strike is over. For this reason, the government views her as being employed. Choices (A) and (C) are both incorrect because she does has a job—to be considered unemployed she has to be out of a job and actively looking for one. This is why (E) is also incorrect. A discouraged worker is one who has quit looking for a job because she is discouraged by the state of the labor market; discouraged workers are outside the labor market. This makes (D) incorrect as well.

2. A

The unemployment rate is calculated as the number of unemployed individuals divided by number of people in the labor force (expressed as a percentage). The number of people in the labor force is the sum of those who are employed and those who are unemployed. In this case it would be 10,000. The unemployment rate is therefore 500 divided by 10,000, or 5%. Make sure that you always convert the answer to a percentage. 500 divided by 10,000 is 0.05, which—when multiplied by 100—gives us 5% (i.e., the answer as a percentage).

3. B

The real interest rate is the nominal rate minus the rate of inflation. Thus, someone who wants to make a real return of 10% when the rate of inflation is 12% should charge an interest rate of 22%.

Real interest rate = nominal interest rate – rate of inflation.

Hence, nominal interest rate = real interest rate + rate of inflation, or 10 + 12 = 22%.

4. A

Twelve computers were produced and their total value at $600 each is $7,200. Even though only 10 were sold, the GDP includes changes in inventories. So the company's sales were 10 times $600, or $6,000. The value of the change in inventories is 2 times $600, or $1,200. Total value of the firm's output is $6,000 + $1,200 = $7,200. GDP is the value of all that is produced within a given year regardless of whether the output is sold or added to inventories.

5. E

The output of a U.S. factory based in Mexico is not produced in the U.S. and so is not included in the U.S. GDP. Because it is produced within the domestic boundaries of Mexico, it is included in the Mexican GDP. The factors of production are owned by a U.S. company, and so its output is a part of the U.S. GNP even though the production is not carried out in the U.S.

6. D

Labor force = employed individuals + unemployed individuals.

Unemployment rate = number of unemployed individuals divided by the total number of individuals in the labor force (expressed as a percentage).

Because Ayesha is a student (i.e., does not have a job) and is not looking for a job, she is neither employed nor unemployed. Choosing to do volunteer work for a year thus leaves the labor force and the unemployment rate unaffected.

7. E

Discouraged workers are not working nor looking for work. So they are neither employed nor unemployed. To be considered part of the unemployed population, a person must be actively looking for a job. Thus discouraged workers are neither part of the labor force nor part of any unemployment rate.

8. C

Stagflation occurs when inflation and unemployment happen at the same time, as during the oil crisis of the 1970s. This requires a period of recession along with an increase in the overall price level. During a recession output is falling and unemployment is rising; if the price level is rising at the same time, we have stagflation.

9. B

Hyperinflation occurs when the overall price level rises rapidly over a short period of time. During this time, the value of money falls rapidly as prices increase. The important point is that prices should be rising rapidly. A slow (though sustained) increase in prices over a long period of time will not be enough to be considered hyperinflation.

10. C

The unemployment in this question is an example of cyclical unemployment. When workers are laid off during a period of declining economic activity, or a recession, this kind of unemployment is called cyclical unemployment. The natural rate of unemployment does not include cyclical unemployment, but the actual rate includes all types of employment: frictional, structural, *and* cyclical. So while the actual rate of unemployment goes up, there is no change in the natural rate.

Free-Response Question

(a) Labor force = employed + unemployed
200,000 + 50,000 = 250,000

(b) $$\text{Unemployment rate} = \frac{\text{unemployed}}{\text{labor force}} \text{ (expressed as a percentage)}$$

$$\text{Unemployment rate} = \frac{50{,}000}{250{,}000} = 20\%$$

(c) Labor force = employed + unemployed
200,000 + 50,000 = 250,000

$$\text{Labor force participation rate} = \frac{\text{labor force}}{\text{population}} \text{ (expressed as a percentage)}$$

Population = labor force + not in the labor force
250,000 + 500,000 =750,000

$$\text{Labor force participation rate} = \frac{250{,}000}{750{,}000} = 33.33\%$$

Chapter 5: National Income and Price Determination

- Aggregate Demand (AD)
- Aggregate Supply (AS)
- Macroeconomic Equilibrium
- Fiscal Policy and the Multipliers
- Review Questions
- Answers and Explanations

AGGREGATE DEMAND (AD)

The macroeconomic analogue to the demand curve is the aggregate demand curve (AD). The demand curve shows demand for a particular product, while the aggregate demand curve depicts the relationship between real GDP demanded and the price level in the economy. The aggregate demand curve slopes downward from left to right.

THREE REASONS WHY THE AD CURVE SLOPES DOWNWARD

Wealth Effect

As the price level increases, the purchasing power of money declines; similarly, purchasing power increases when the price level decreases. There is an inverse relation between real wealth and the price level. Assume that you are holding some of your wealth in the form of cash—let's say $20,000 under your mattress or in the bank. If prices double, the value of your cash decreases by one half; you are worse off and would reduce your spending, a negative wealth effect. If all prices are cut in half, your cash is now worth twice as much. Because lower price levels increase the value of wealth in the form of cash holdings, you spend more when price levels fall because of the positive wealth effect. This contributes to an inverse relationship between the price level and real GDP.

Interest Rate Effect

When the price level rises, interest rates rise too, reducing borrowing and spending. Demand falls as a result and again we have a negative relationship between the price level and real GDP.

The opposite is true when prices fall. Decreasing prices mean decreasing interest rates, and lower interest rates stimulate the economy. Consumers will buy more interest-sensitive goods (such as cars, furniture, and appliances) that require financing. Businesses will increase spending on property, factories, and equipment when interest rates are low. The interest rate effect thus contributes to the downward slope of the AD. The sequence of events is as follows: the price level falls, saving increases, interest rates fall, and real GDP increases. The overall result is an inverse (negative) relation between price and quantity (real GDP).

Exchange Rate Effect

If domestic prices fall, U.S. interest rates will fall. Interest rates are often higher in other countries and this will prompt some U.S. investors to invest abroad. So, for instance, an investor who has U.S. government bonds might sell them to buy German bonds. The result is that this investor will increase her supply of dollars as she tries to convert dollars into euros. Thus the value of the dollar falls (depreciates) relative to the euro. Foreign goods become more expensive compared to domestic goods and people would rather buy U.S. goods because they are now cheaper, causing U.S. exports to increase and imports to fall.

These shifts are not simply—or even usually—the result of individual actions. Imagine a firm such as the UBS (Union Bank of Switzerland), which manages assets in the United States and other countries. The UBS might choose to shift assets from lower-yielding bonds in one country to higher-yielding bonds in another. Hundreds of other investment management firms would do the same thing with their individual investors' assets and this market action would create changes in imports and the value of the dollar.

The overall effect on the GDP is as follows: Americans will buy more domestic products and fewer foreign products (i.e., the value of M [imports] falls). Foreigners will buy more U.S. products (i.e., the value of X [exports] rises) and fewer of their own products. Remember that the net exports figure (X_n, which is X – M) is one of the four main components of aggregate expenditures; all other things being equal, real GDP will expand as net exports increase.

Shifts in the AD Curve

The AD curve will shift when the components of spending change. As we noted earlier, the components of spending are consumption spending (C), firms' investment spending (I_g), government spending on goods and services (G), and net exports (X_n).

$$AD = C + I_g + G + X_n$$

Government Spending (G)

When G goes up, AD does too, and the AD curve shifts to the right. When G goes down AD follows, and the AD curve shifts to the left.

Taxes (T)

When taxes go down, disposable income goes up. People have more money to spend or to save. They will increase their consumption (C) by some percentage of the new disposable income. The result is an increase in AD and the AD curve shifts right. When T increases, disposable income falls; people have less money to spend or save and C falls. AD goes down and the curve shifts left.

Government spending and taxes are in the hands of the president and Congress; changes, adjustments, and strategies here are called **fiscal policy**.

Money Supply

When the money supply increases, there is more money to spend; interest rates fall and consumers can borrow more. The result is that firms and consumers increase their spending (i.e., both C and I go up). There is an increase in AD and the AD curve shifts to the right. The reverse happens if money supply decreases (or interest rates rise).

The money supply is under the control of the Federal Reserve; changes, adjustments, and strategies here are called **monetary policy**.

Classical and Keynesian Approaches to Stabilization

Adam Smith's *Wealth of Nations* instigated the debate over using policy to stabilize an economy. Smith's description of market competition, self-interest and the "invisible hand" prompted another economist, J.B. Say, to formalize what is called the "Classical" view of economics. Say's famous line was "supply creates its own demand," which defined the Classical view that the normal position for an economy was at the full employment RGDP. Aggregate supply is vertical. If aggregate demand is unstable, prices, wages and interest rates adjust to bring the economy back to full employment RGDP. The Classical view about using policy to influence the economy was "Just wait—it will fix itself!"

The length and depth of the Great Depression challenged the Classical approach and led to a 40-year period in which the Classical approach lost favor. A new approach emerged called Keynesian economics (named after British economist John Maynard Keynes). Keynes challenged the self-correcting nature of the market economy. He felt that product prices and wages were downwardly inflexible (i.e., "sticky") and did not shift so easily. He favored active government intervention to stabilize the economy, as he felt the normal position was not where full employment RGDP exists. Many of the relief programs of the New Deal reflect his views. His influence is felt in demand management policies. Some new Classical views have emerged over time: Monetarism, Rational Expectationist, and Supply-Side Economics are hybrids of the original Classical view.

AGGREGATE SUPPLY (AS)

The aggregate supply curve shows the relationship between the price level and the total amount of real output (RGDP) that firms are willing to produce.

The shape of the AS curve depends on whether one is looking at a **long-run AS (LRAS) curve** or a **short-run AS (SRAS) curve**. The LRAS is a vertical line, reflecting the Classical view that wages and prices are flexible, meaning that firms will always produce at the full employment level of output. The Classical AS curve is fixed (vertical) at the full employment level of output. The full employment level itself—which is the same as potential GDP—depends on the availability of labor and capital and the state of technology.

Firms have no incentive to produce more or less than the full employment level. They will produce this amount regardless of market prices. If prices go up, wages will increase as well. The costs of production will increase proportionately and thus there will be no incentive to produce more. Similarly, producers have no incentive to decrease production if prices fall. As prices fall and revenue goes down, wages will also fall and the costs of production will go down by the same amount. The result is no change in profits and no incentive to lower production.

The short-run AS curve is based on the Keynesian belief that prices and wages are sticky (at least in the short run). The result is that firms *do* have an incentive to produce more as prices go up. Many workers are tied into contracts and their wages will not increase at once (if at all) when prices go up. Therefore, the costs of production stay the same and firms increase production to take advantage of the higher revenues offered by increased prices. This AS curve slopes upward from left to right and looks like the familiar, upward sloping supply curve.

Shifts in the AS Curve

What causes the AS curve to shift? Recall that the aggregate supply (AS) curve is a relation between the price level and the RGDP firms produce. This relation will shift as firms' costs of doing business change. The factors that would change how much firms supply at a given price are the same factors that shift the AS curve.

A rightward shift in the AS curve means that the supply of all goods and services is increasing. We refer to this as a **positive supply shock**. It usually occurs when there is economic growth or technological progress. Discoveries of natural resources and changes in the economy that promote production have this effect as well.

The AS can decrease as well. A decline in AS creates a leftward shift of the AS curve and a negative supply shock. For example, a change in the costs of major inputs for firms can create a negative supply shock. Oil, agricultural products, and labor are the most important inputs firms buy. An increase in the price of oil will shift the AS curve to the left. Bad weather that decreases the supply of agricultural products will shift the AS curve to the left as well. Finally, changes in the cost of labor (or any other important input) will alter how profitable firms find it to produce at different price levels. Generally, higher wages will shift the AS curve to the left and lower wages will shift it to the right.

MACROECONOMIC EQUILIBRIUM

The point at which the AS and AD curves meet indicates the equilibrium price level and level of output, or real GDP. It also gives the level of employment and unemployment, because producing GDP requires workers. If real GDP is low, employment will be low and unemployment will be high. If real GDP is high, employment will be high and unemployment low.

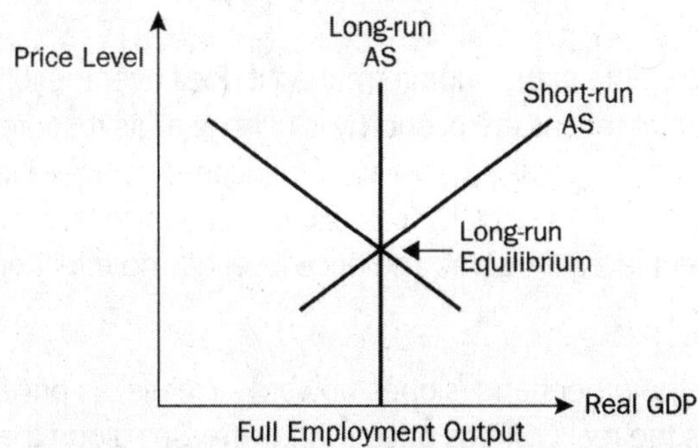

In the figure above, the intersection of the downward sloping AD curve, the short-run AS curve, and the vertical long-run AS is called the **full-employment equilibrium** since it occurs at the full-employment output. As shown on the following page, any price level above the full-employment equilibrium price level, (PL_1) aggregate spending will not be sufficient to support full-employment output. As a result, there will be unemployment and wages will fall as the unemployed workers compete for jobs. This will enable firms to lower prices and the response will be an increase in spending and greater employment. The process continues until the economy reaches equilibrium at the full-employment GDP.

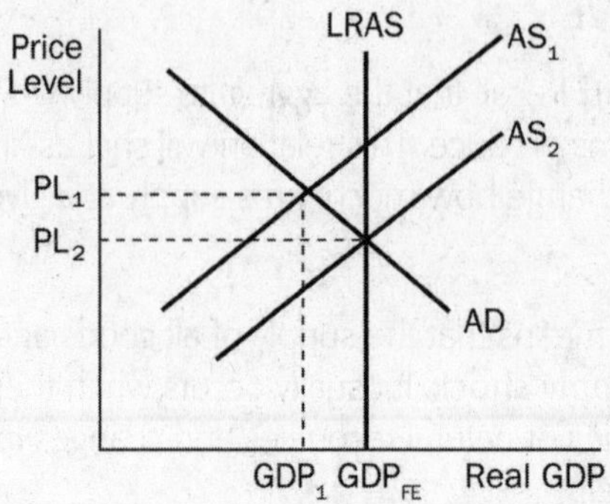

If the actual price level is below the full-employment equilibrium, there will be an increase in aggregate spending above the economy's capacity to produce. Firms will compete for workers and wages will rise. Firms would then pass these higher costs on to consumers in the form of increased prices. This price increase will reduce spending and lead the economy back to its long-run equilibrium.

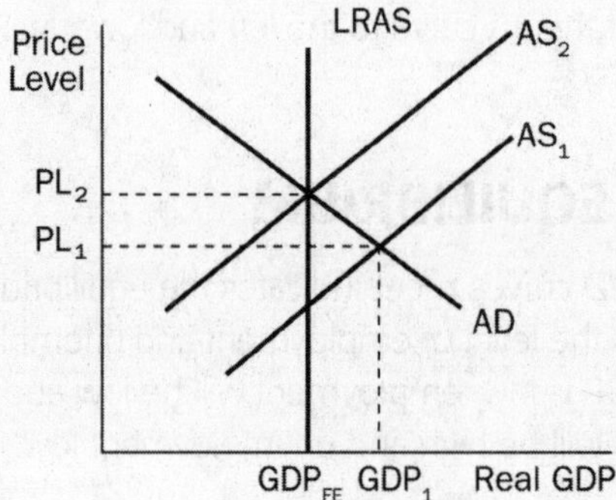

The price level matters much more in the short term than it does over the long term. Full-employment GDP or full-employment output means the economy is utilizing all its resources fully; the economy is *on* the PPC curve. In the long run, people's desire to earn incomes moves the economy towards full-employment output. Full-employment GDP can occur at any price level and the long-run AS curve is vertical at the full-employment level of output. The price level has no effect on the quantity of real GDP in the long run.

The short-run AS curve, on the other hand, slopes upwards. Hence, as price level increases along the short-run AS curve, so does the real GDP; as price level decreases along the short-run AS curve, real GDP declines. In the short run, price level and real GDP are related, but they are not in the long run.

Equilibrium and Shifts in the AD or AS Curve

When AD or short-run AS shifts, changes will occur in the price level and the RGDP.

If an economy had been at full employment RGDP, a decrease in AD (higher unemployment reduces spending) would move the curve to the left. Price level falls and RGDP declines. This is a recessionary gap. If an economy had been at full employment RGDP, a negative supply shock would move the short-run AS curve to the left. Price level would rise and RGDP decline. This is a recessionary gap as well.

If an economy had been at full-employment RGDP, an increase in AD (lower unemployment boosts spending) would move the curve to the right. Price level increases and RGDP increases. This is an inflationary gap. If an economy had been at full employment RGDP, a positive supply shock would move the short-run AS curve to the right. Price level would fall and RGDP increase. This is an inflationary gap as well.

FISCAL POLICY AND THE MULTIPLIERS

How does a change in government spending (G) or taxes (T) result in a change in output or national income (Y)? In other words, how does fiscal policy work?

Multipliers express the ratio of a change in aggregate output to a change in tax or spending policy, and fiscal policy works through the spending multiplier. Let's look at a change in G first. Suppose that the government decides to increase spending. An increase in G means that AD = C + I + G goes up by the same amount; firms increase production by the same amount to satisfy this increase in demand. Y increases by the same amount that G increases. However, the story does not end here. An increase in production also means this new output gets sold and generates income for the producers. They in turn spend this income and C increases. As a result, demand increases again and so does production. This process keeps repeating until the final increase in output is much greater than the initial increase in G. How much greater it is depends on the spending multiplier. It describes increases and decreases in the effectiveness of fiscal policy.

The spending multiplier helps us to determine how a change in G will affect GDP, and it is described by the following equation

$$\text{Government spending multiplier} = \frac{1}{(1-MPC)}$$

$$\Delta \text{ Real GDP} = \delta \text{ G} \times \frac{1}{(1-MPC)}$$

MPC here means "marginal propensity to consume." MPC describes the proportion of each additional dollar of income that will go toward consumption expenditures. **MPS**, the marginal propensity to save, reveals the proportion of the additional dollar that is saved. MPC plus MPS is equal to one. When MPC is high (close to one), this represents a high level of consumption; similarly, the closer MPS is to one, the higher the proportion of savings.

We can now use this information to evaluate the effect of a change in government spending. If, for example, we know that MPC = 0.8, then we can apply the government spending multiplier to find the change in real GDP demanded.

$$\frac{1}{(1-MPC)} = \frac{1}{(1-0.8)} = \frac{1}{(0.2)} = 5$$

$$\Delta \text{ Real GDP} = \Delta \text{ G x } \frac{1}{(0.2)}$$

$$\Delta \text{ Real GDP} = \Delta \text{ G x 5}$$

Thus, we see that if the MPC is 0.8, any increase in government spending (G) will bring about a five times greater increase in output (Y). The same is true of a decrease in G. So if G increases by 100, Y increases by 5(100) = 500. If G decreases by 50, Y decreases by 5(50) = 250 To increase Y, the government must increase spending, and to decrease Y, the government must decrease spending.

This is how the U.S. emerged from the Great Depression. The government increased spending and the Second World War that followed further increased government spending. The result was an increase in AD, an increase in production, and a decrease in unemployment that some economists believe helped the U.S. out of the Great Depression.

If the government wants to increase Y, should it increase or decrease taxes? Suppose the government decreases taxes. When T falls, national disposable income (Y – T, or Y_d) increases. Disposable income is when people pay less in taxes and have more money to spend, creating an increase in C. However, C does not go up by the same amount that income increases. If taxes decrease by $100 million (and income therefore goes up by $100 million), people will not spend all of this extra income. They will spend some of it and save some of it. The ratio of saving to spending depends on the MPS and the MPC.

When T falls, then, Y_d goes up and this results in an increase in C. An increase in C means that AD increases (because AD = C + I + G), and firms produce more to meet this increase in demand. This new output gets sold and generates income for the producers; they then spend this money, causing another increase in C, another increase in AD, and another increase in production. Once again we have an economic effect that goes beyond the amount of the original change. The tax multiplier can help us evaluate the effect of this change in taxes.

$$\text{Tax multiplier} = \frac{-MPC}{(1-MPC)}$$

Notice that this multiplier is negative. This means that if the government aims to increase Y, they should lower taxes. Also, not all tax relief income gets spent; a certain percentage of it will be saved, depending upon the MPC. So, the absolute value of the tax multiplier is smaller than that of the government spending multiplier.

We can see this if we set MPC equal to 0.8, as we did for the government spending multiplier.

$$\frac{-MPC}{(1-MPC)} = \frac{-0.8}{(1-0.8)} = \frac{-0.8}{0.2} = -4$$

$$\delta \text{ Real GDP} = \delta \text{ NT x } \frac{-0.8}{0.2}$$

$$\delta \text{ Real GDP} = \delta \text{ NT x} -4$$

For the same MPC, the absolute value of the tax multiplier is smaller than that of the government spending multiplier. The absolute value of the tax multiplier when the MPC is 0.8 is four, whereas the value of the government spending multiplier was five. This means that to bring about the same increase in Y, the government will need to make a larger change in T (specifically in net taxes, or NT) than it would have needed to make in G.

So if T falls by 100, Y will increase by 400: $-4(-100) = 400$; if T increases by 50, Y will fall by 200: $-4(50) = -200$. The negative sign here indicates a decrease in T or Y, while a positive number indicates that they are rising. The tax multiplier is negative, which means that an increase in net taxes will lead to a decrease in real GDP demanded. The positive value of the government spending multiplier means that an increase in government spending leads to an increase in real GDP demanded.

IF YOU LEARNED ONLY THREE THINGS IN THIS CHAPTER. . .

1. Aggregate demand curve(AD) depicts the relationship between real GDP demanded and the price level in the economy, while the aggregate supply curve (AS) depicts the relationship between the price level and the total amount of real output (RGDP) that firms are willing to produce.
2. Macroeconomic equilibrium for an economy in the short run is established when aggregate demand intersects with short-run aggregate supply.
3. Fiscal policy is defined as the use of the federal government's powers of spending and taxation to stabilize the business cycle.

REVIEW QUESTIONS

1. When a government increases the amount of money spent on infrastructure such as roads and bridges, this is
   (A) a monetary policy
   (B) an incomes policy
   (C) an inflationary policy
   (D) a deflationary policy
   (E) a fiscal policy

2. If the MPC is 0.8 and government spending decreased by $10 billion, how would this affect the nation's income?
   (A) Income would decrease by $62.5 billion.
   (B) Income would decrease by $50 billion.
   (C) Income would decrease by $10 billion.
   (D) Income would decrease by $8 billion.
   (E) Income would decrease by $40 billion.

3. Congressional action to increase funding for space projects will cause short-run price level and RGDP to change in which of the following ways?

	Price Level	RGDP
(A)	Decrease	Increase
(B)	Increase	Increase
(C)	Decrease	Decrease
(D)	No Change	Increase
(E)	No Change	No Change

4. If the tax multiplier is –2 and net taxes are reduced by $300 billion, output will
   (A) increase by $150 billion
   (B) decrease by $150 billion
   (C) increase by $300 billion
   (D) increase by $600 billion
   (E) decrease by $600 billion

5. Which one of the following would shift the aggregate demand curve to the right?
   (A) A higher price level
   (B) An increase in investment spending
   (C) An increase in the interest rate at each possible price level
   (D) An increase in the personal income tax rates
   (E) A decrease in government spending directed to education

6. Assuming that other factors are held constant, nationwide improvements in productivity will
   (A) shift the aggregate demand curve to the left
   (B) shift the aggregate demand curve to the right
   (C) shift the aggregate supply curve to the right
   (D) shift the aggregate supply curve to the left
   (E) increase the price level

7. How does a decrease in the short-run AS affect the price level and the rate of unemployment?

	Price Level	Unemployment
(A)	Increase	No change
(B)	Decrease	Decrease
(C)	No change	Increase
(D)	Increase	Increase
(E)	Decrease	No change

8. A supply shock that increased costs with no change in monetary or fiscal policy would
   (A) shift the aggregate supply curve to the right, increase RGDP, and decrease the price level
   (B) shift the aggregate supply curve to the left, decrease RGDP, and increase the price level
   (C) shift the aggregate demand curve to the left, increase RGDP, and increase the price level
   (D) shift the aggregate demand curve to the right, decrease RGDP, and decrease the price level
   (E) shift the aggregate demand curve to the left, decrease RGDP, and decrease the price level

9. If the MPC is 0.9, then the tax multiplier equals

   (A) –9
   (B) –6
   (C) –3
   (D) –7
   (E) –4

10. When the government sector is included in the circular flow of income, disposable income is exactly equal to

   (A) consumption minus saving
   (B) saving plus taxes
   (C) national income minus net taxes
   (D) net taxes plus total income
   (E) net taxes minus total income

FREE-RESPONSE QUESTION

Assume that the economy has been operating at the full-employment level of output and employment, but has recently experienced a sharp decline in stock market indices that have reduced the wealth of the nation by about 18%.

(a) Use correctly labeled aggregate demand/aggregate supply curves to show the full-employment economy.

(b) Amend the graph to show the short-run effect of the drop in consumer wealth. Identify and explain the effect on the price level and RGDP.

ANSWERS AND EXPLANATIONS

1. E

Government spending and taxes are two tools of fiscal policy. When the government changes its expenditure or changes the level of taxes in the economy, we say that the government is using fiscal policy (E). Monetary policy (A) is when the amount of money circulating in the economy changes. That can only happen when the Federal Reserve changes the money supply. Expenditure by the government does not change the amount of money circulating in the economy and is hence not a monetary policy. Also, monetary policy is only in the hands of the Federal Reserve, just as fiscal policy is only in the hands of the president and the Congress.

2. B

If the MPC is 0.8, the government spending multiplier is $\frac{1}{(1-0.8)} = \frac{1}{(0.2)} = 5$. Change in output equals multiplier times change in government spending. Therefore, a $10 billion decline in government spending results in a $50 billion decline in output, because output falls by the amount of the change in G times the government spending multiplier: 5(10) = $50 billion. Choice (B) is the correct answer.

3. B

If Congress increases the funding for space projects, this signifies an increase in government spending, which is a component of AD. The AD curve will move to the right, resulting in a higher price level and a greater level of RGDP, (B). Other choices show incorrect pairings.

4. D

If taxes go down, then consumers will spend more, AD will increase, and output will increase. In this example, net taxes decrease by $300 billion, and the tax multiplier is –2. Therefore we can determine the change in output by applying the tax multiplier to the change in net taxes: –2(–$300 billion) = $600 billion. Choice (D) is correct.

5. B

The AD curve will shift to the right if any of the components (C, I_g, G, or X_n) increase. When investment increases, new spending for capital goods shifts the AD curve to the right, making (B) the correct answer.

6. C

The AS curve will shift to the right if any of the factors that can move the AS curve change. Lower input prices or lower prices for goods that use the same resources are two of these shift movers. Increases in productivity (the measure of increasing output with the same inputs) will always move the AS curve to the right. Choice (C) is correct.

7. D

As the short-run AS curve moves left indicating a decrease in AS, changes occur in the price level and the RGDP. The price level increases and the RGDP decreases. The lower RGDP means that the unemployment rate rises. There is an inverse relationship between the quantity of RGDP and the level of unemployment. When RGDP rises, the unemployment rate falls. Choice (D) is correct; the other choices show incorrect pairings.

8. B

An increase in the cost of inputs would lower the short-run AS and shift the curve to the left. The price level would increase and the RGDP would decrease. Thus, (B) is the correct answer.

9. A

If MPC = 0.9, the tax multiplier is $\frac{-MPC}{(1-MPC)} = \frac{-0.9}{(1-0.9)} = \frac{-0.9}{0.1} = -9$, choice (A).

10. C

The introduction of the government sector implies that the income left to spend on consumption (or saving) is income after paying taxes (net of transfer payments). Thus, for consumers, the income left to spend on consumption (or saving) is income after paying taxes (net of transfer payments). Hence, disposable income is aggregate income minus net taxes, (C).

FREE-RESPONSE QUESTION

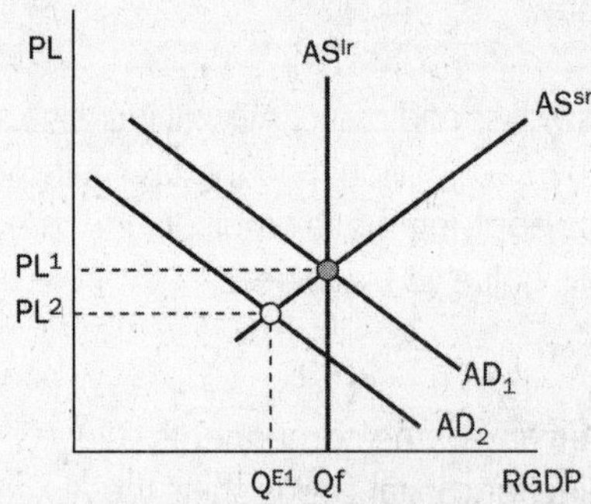

(a) In the graph, the short-run AS and AD curves intersect with the vertical long-run AS curve at the full-employment level of RGDP. This means that this economy is efficiently using available resources.

(b) Note that the AD curve in the graph has shifted to the left to represent the decline in consumer wealth. As wealth declines, consumers tend to reduce spending in an effort to add wealth by saving a greater portion of their disposable income. The decrease in consumer spending has moved the AD curve to the left. The price level falls to PL^2 and the RGDP falls to Q^{E1}, causing a recessionary gap. In a recessionary gap, the economy produces a level of RGDP that is less than full employment: unemployment rises and a spiral of lower incomes and less spending can result.

Chapter 6: **Financial Sector**

- Money, Banking, and Financial Markets
- The Central Bank and Control of the Money Supply
- Review Questions
- Answers and Explanations

MONEY, BANKING, AND FINANCIAL MARKETS

Money's usefulness is displayed all around us. The complexity of our economy means that people are not wholly self-sufficient, which in turn means that they have a need for convenient exchange. As discussed earlier, it makes sense to specialize in ways that reduce one's opportunity costs. Once people are specialists, exchange enters the picture because people must somehow obtain the things they need that they aren't producing for themselves. It is possible to conduct a range of exchanges without money. People can trade their goods and services in a process known as barter. Barter requires that each person who wants to trade be able to find a person who meets two conditions. First, she must want what the trader has to offer. Second, she must be able to offer something in exchange that the trader desires. The more specialized people become, the more difficult it is to find someone who meets these two conditions. As barter becomes more complicated and problematic, money presents itself as a solution to these difficulties.

KINDS OF MONEY

The most basic definition of money is something that is acceptable in exchange for goods and services. Money is meant to appeal to all (or nearly all) traders—that is how it solves the problems of barter. To have this kind of appeal, early monies were often some sort of commodity that traders could either use themselves or trade to someone else. This kind of money is called **commodity money**; items such as corn, tobacco, and salt have all served as commodity money.

However, many desirable commodities have important disadvantages when used as money. Some are perishable and others are not easy to move from place to place. It can be hard to divide a commodity into fractions to exchange for something that is only worth part of the money, and finally, commodities often vary in quality. To be as useful as possible, money should not have any of these drawbacks. It should also have a consistent value and a relatively consistent level of supply. However, value is created by scarcity, so money—like anything else of value—cannot be something that people can easily find or produce for themselves.

The desire to escape the drawbacks of commodity money led to the creation of **token money**. Token money serves as a representation of value; its value is greater than its cost of production would suggest. Coins and paper money are both **token money**, and neither of them possesses the drawbacks associated with commodity money.

Money fulfills three classic roles:

1. It serves as a medium of exchange.
2. It serves as a store of value.
3. It serves as a unit of account or measurement.

Medium of Exchange

As a medium of exchange, money makes it possible to trade without exchanging goods and services directly. Instead, people can trade their goods and services for money. It eliminates the difficulty of finding someone who wants what you are trading and has something desirable of his own to trade as well. Money becomes something that everyone will accept in trade (because they can use it to satisfy their own wants), and exchanges become quicker, simpler, and easier to find.

Store of Value

Money also makes it possible to conduct an exchange without buying something in return. Instead of acquiring a good or service in exchange for her own goods and services, the person who makes a money-based exchange receives stored purchasing power in the form of money. As long as money holds this power over time, it becomes a store of this sort of value.

Unit of Account

When money is used widely, it becomes a measure of goods' and services' worth. When people are bartering, they must use many different standards. A cow might be worth X number of baskets, Y bushels of corn, or Z hours of house painting. Money reduces all of that to a single standard: the cow's monetary value. The common standard allows people to compare and measure values in a way that is not possible in a barter system. For example, there is no simple way to assess GDP in a barter system, or even to determine the value of a single grocery store's inventory.

THE DEMAND FOR MONEY

Liquidity is the ease with which an asset can be converted into spending. Traditionally, currency is the easiest form of money to convert into spending and thus is considered very liquid. Checks are a bit less liquid because they take time to write, many places require identification from the check writer, and some producers cannot or will not accept them. Money in a savings account is generally even more difficult to access; it is thus less apt to be spent and is the least liquid of these three forms of money.

There are three main motives behind the demand for money:

1. The transactions motive
2. The speculative motive
3. The precautionary motive

There is a trade-off between holding cash and holding interest-bearing assets. The demand for money is demand for cash in hand. Money demand can be **transactions demand for money**, i.e., money needed for transactions. The transactions demand for money depends on interest rate and the level of RGDP. As the interest rate goes up, less money will be kept on hand for transactions because there is more to be gained by converting it to a different interest-bearing asset. The **transactions motive** is the desire to hold onto money for cash-based transactions.

There are other reasons for choosing between holding cash and holding other interest-bearing assets. Household expectations and the relationship of interest rates to bond values can lead people to choose cash or other assets, too. This is the **speculative motive**, in which people choose to hold cash because they want to be prepared for cash-based investment opportunities. This idea rests on the theory that market value of most interest-bearing bonds is inversely related to the interest rate. When market interest rates fall, bond values rise; when market interest rates rise, bond values fall.

Both the speculative motive and the transactions motive make the quantity of money demanded a function of the interest rate. Rising interest rates will reduce the quantity of money that firms and households want to hold, and falling interest rates will increase the quantity of money that firms and households want to hold.

The **precautionary motive** describes people's inclination to hold onto money for unexpected cash expenses, such as medical bills or car repairs. These kinds of expenses often need to be paid immediately, and less liquid assets are not much help.

Thus we have a downward sloping demand for money. An increase in the level of output or the price level for a given interest rate increases the demand for money and shifts the money demand curve to the right. A decrease in output or price level for an interest rate shifts the money demand curve to the left.

Private Banks and the Money Supply

The money supply can be defined in terms of two broad categories. M1, or "**narrow money**," consists of coin and currency plus checking accounts plus travelers checks plus other checking deposits. M1 consists of the most liquid forms of money. M2, or "**broad money**," consists of M1 plus savings deposits plus money market funds. Sometimes we call M2 "near money" to denote its slight lack of liquidity.

Every bank has made a promise to its depositors that their demand deposits will be payable immediately. If a bank fails, deposit insurance (provided by the Federal Deposit Insurance Corporation [FDIC]) will repay deposits of less than $100,000 that are lost. However, even a bank in good financial condition (i.e., a bank with assets greater than its liabilities) may be at some risk in terms of its liquidity. A bank's assets are not necessarily liquid because banks are a money-making business and liquid assets generally don't pay a very high rate of return. Therefore, a bank generally invests its depositors' money in a variety of illiquid but potentially profitable investments. Because the money is invested this way, a bank cannot get at its own assets as quickly as depositors might demand to get at theirs. If a depositor comes in and wants to withdraw $100 from her account, her bank better have $100 in its vault or have it on deposit at the local Federal Reserve Bank. If the bank does not have the money, it can hardly offer its depositor some illiquid asset in exchange.

Clearly, banks play an important role in the money supply. This comes as a surprise to many people, especially those who think the government controls the money supply. They are partially right, as we shall see in a moment, but the actions of citizens and their banks can change the size and the composition of the money supply, too.

THE CENTRAL BANK AND CONTROL OF THE MONEY SUPPLY

The Federal Reserve System ("the Fed") is the centralized banking and monetary authority in the United States. It was created in 1913 in response to panic runs on banks, in which many depositors simultaneously demanded their deposits. The effects of such panics ripple through the financial community and can destabilize the economy.

The Fed has three main tools for executing its monetary policy decisions:

1. The required reserve ratio (RRR)
2. The discount rate
3. Open-market operations

The government's role is to create something known as the monetary base, which serves as currency and as bank reserves. Bank reserves are the cash banks keep on hand or on deposit with the **Federal Reserve Bank** in their district. These bank reserves are what a bank that is a member of the Federal Reserve system (i.e., a "member bank") uses to pay depositors when they want to convert their checking or savings account deposits into currency.

The Required Reserve Ratio (RRR)

The Fed sets rules about how much banks must keep in liquid, zero-interest reserves. These required reserves are a fraction of the bank's total deposits. Any excess reserves the bank finds itself holding, it can lend out. In 1992, the Fed lowered the **required reserve ratio** (RRR) from 12% to 10% of checking account deposits. This was an attempt to transform some of the banking system's required reserves into excess reserves, thus increasing potential lending activity and profits for banks.

How does the money supply increase? There are two answers, one for the short run and one for the long run. In the short run, a bank can increase the money supply by the amount of its excess reserves, when it uses these to make loans. In the long run, the money supply can grow through this loan/redeposit process as it happens throughout the banking system until all possible currency and excess reserves are functioning as required reserves.

When excess reserves enter the economy, they create a ripple effect that is greater than the initial amount of money. To determine exactly the amount of the new demand deposits that can be created from an initial deposit (new excess reserves), we use something called the **money multiplier**. The **simple money multiplier** is $\frac{1}{RR}$ where RR is the reserve ratio expressed as a decimal. Thus, if the reserve ratio is 10% (= 0.01), the money multiplier is $\frac{1}{0.1} = 10$. This multiplier is "simple" because it relies on the assumption that borrowers do not want to hold cash or let their money go unused, and no bank holds excess reserves.

Using this simple money multiplier, an initial deposit of $100 will work its way through the banking system, eventually creating a larger change in demand deposits.

$$\text{Multiplier} = \frac{1}{RRR}$$

$$\text{Multiplier} = \frac{1}{0.1} = 10$$

Demand deposits = money multiplier × change in reserves (i.e., the initial deposit, which equals excess reserves)

Demand deposits = 10(100)

Demand deposits = $1000

What is the money multiplier if the reserve ratio increases to 20%? What change in demand deposits will be created by a new deposit of $100 under this new RRR? What if the RRR drops to 5%? What will be the change in demand deposits created by a new deposit of $100 now?

$$20\%\ \text{RRR} = \text{multiplier} = \frac{1}{0.2} = 5$$

100 × 5 = 500 increase in demand deposits

$$5\%\ \text{RRR} = \text{multiplier} = \frac{1}{0.05} = 20$$

100 × 20 = 2000 increase in demand deposits

Changing the RRR, then, is one way that the Federal Reserve can change the money supply in the economy. If the Fed increases the RRR, then banks have to keep more in required reserves, as the examples above show. They make fewer loans and money supply decreases. If the Fed lowers the RRR, banks have to keep less money in reserve; as a result they can make more loans and the money supply increases.

The Discount Rate

Member banks can borrow from the Fed when they have a temporary shortfall; this is the Fed's role as the "lender of last resort." These loans are called **discount loans** and the Fed charges the banks interest. The interest rate is called the **discount rate**. If the Fed increases the discount rate, then the cost of borrowing increases for banks. As a result, they will not borrow as much, they will not be able to make as many loans, and the money supply will decrease. If the Fed lowers the discount rate, this makes it easier for banks to borrow. Thus, they can make more loans and the money supply increases. Lowering and raising the discount rate is thus another tool the Fed can use to control the money supply.

Open-Market Operations

The Fed also controls the money supply through what are called open-market operations (OMOs). The Fed engages in open-market operations when it buys and sells government securities (such as Treasury bills, Treasury bonds, and other federal agency securities) in the open market. OMOs are the Fed's most powerful tool for adjusting bank reserves. The Federal Open Market Committee (FOMC) meets every six weeks to make policy decisions about OMOs. The FOMC targets changes in the Federal Funds Rate and effects those changes through OMOs. The Federal Funds Rate is the inter-bank lending rate. Its rate depends on all the other lending rates in the banking system—the prime lending rate, mortgage rates, and the rates for home equity loans and auto loans.

With respect to OMOs, it is important to distinguish the Federal Reserve from the U.S. Treasury. The U.S. Treasury creates and sells new securities. When the amount of government spending is greater than government revenue, there is a federal deficit. The government then has to find a way to meet this shortfall, usually by borrowing money. In return for these borrowed funds, it issues government securities. If, for example, the government needed to borrow $100,000, the U.S. Treasury would print out new securities for that amount and sell them to banks, citizens, and domestic corporations as well as foreign governments and corporations.

Once these securities are out in the world, they can be bought and sold again. This secondary buying and selling of pre-existing government securities takes place in part through the Fed's open-market operations. The Fed deals only in pre-existing securities.

When the Fed sells securities, the result is a reduction in the money supply. Money is given to the Fed in exchange for government securities; this money comes from banks and checking accounts, therefore bank reserves decrease and the money supply goes down. When the Fed buys securities, it pays money out, increasing deposits and bank reserves. The money supply goes up as a result.

Interest Rate

People generally value present consumption over future consumption. The interest rate (r) is the price of obtaining goods or resources *now* instead of in the future; people are willing to pay more so that they can consume now, rather than later. In other words, the interest rate measures the price of future goods and resources in terms of current ones.

The interest rate is a price determined by the supply of, and demand for, loanable funds. It can also be understood to be determined by the supply of, and demand for, money. For convenience, we assume that the supply of money is fixed at a particular point in time and hence is independent of the interest rate (i.e., we assume that the money supply curve is vertical). The Fed's action to change bank reserves will influence the position of the monetary supply curve. The demand for money varies inversely with the rate of interest, as we discussed earlier with respect to people's motives for demanding cash. The intersection between demand and supply (with respect to loanable funds or money) determines the equilibrium interest rate. As was true for other values discussed earlier, the real interest rate is equal to the nominal interest rate minus the inflation rate; the real value is equal to the nominal value corrected for inflation. The money market graph below shows the nominal interest rate.

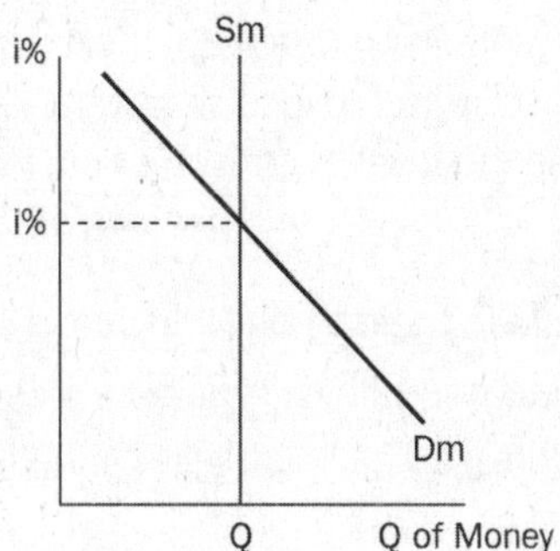

Why do we care about the Fed changing money supply? Because interest rates change when money supply changes, and interest rates are the price of borrowing and lending.

When the money supply increases, interest rates fall and it becomes cheaper for firms and for consumers to borrow. People borrow more and spend more; C and I increase and so does AD. Recall that an increase in AD results in a much greater increase in RGDP through the spending multiplier discussed in chapter 5. When the Fed increases the money supply and lowers interest rates, it creates an increase in output; this is called **expansionary monetary policy**. In pursuit of expansionary policy goals, the Fed can:

- Lower the required reserve ratio
- Lower the discount rate
- Purchase government securities on the open market

When money supply goes down, interest rates go up and it becomes more expensive to borrow. People borrow less, C and I decrease, and so does AD. Output decreases as well, by a much larger amount via the spending multiplier. This is called contractionary monetary policy. To achieve contractionary policy goals, the Fed can:

- Increase the required reserve ratio
- Increase the discount rate
- Sell government securities on the open market

Remember that these are *monetary* policies that depend on changes in money supply and interest rates—they are distinct from the fiscal policies that will be discussed in the next chapter, which use different tools to achieve their goals. Even though fiscal policy and monetary policy are distinct, their aims often converge. An **expansionary monetary policy** has the same aim as an expansionary fiscal policy: increasing output and decreasing unemployment. A **contractionary monetary policy** has the same aim as a contractionary fiscal policy: decreasing output and increasing unemployment.

In economics, investment is understood as additions to capital stock, such as new equipment, new buildings, or additions to inventory. When interest rates fall, firms invest more, and they invest less when interest rates rise. Suppose there is a one dollar increase in investment. What happens?

An increase in investment increases AD. This means that inventories decrease as more spending occurs, prompting increases in new production during the next period. Increased AD increases income, which creates an increase in disposable income. Depending on the MPC, an increase in disposable income may also increase the level of consumption, which would increase AD again and further increase RGDP.

Eventually RGDP increases by more than the one-dollar increase in investment. Once again, the specific amount of the increase is determined by a multiplier: the investment multiplier, $\frac{1}{(1-MPC)}$, is the same spending multiplier we addressed earlier. It tells us that a dollar of investment raises RGDP by more than a dollar.

Quantity Theory of Money

Recall that the new Classical approach, Monetarism, stands in contrast to the Keynesian view. Monetarists focus on the rate at which the money supply grows; they argue that most major economic problems (e.g., recessions and inflation) are caused by the Fed's failure to manage the growth of the money supply appropriately. Monetarists rely on the **quantity theory of money**, which states that the nominal quantity of money determines the level of nominal income. In other words, $MV = QP$, where M is the quantity of money, QP is the level of output and V is velocity, i.e. the number of times a dollar becomes income to someone during a given period.

The quantity theory of money says that velocity is predictable; knowing the nominal supply of money allows one to predict nominal income. Quantity theorists believe that the demand function for money is stable and predictable and that changes in income are primarily explained by the supply of nominal money.

IF YOU LEARNED ONLY THREE THINGS IN THIS CHAPTER. . .

1. Banking is an industry consisting of financial institutions that maintain deposits. and financial markets are markets that trade financial assets.

2. The quantity of money balances that exists in the economy is known as the money supply.

3. Interest rate is the price of funds expressed as a percentage of the total amount loaned or borrowed-the cost of borrowing funds and the payment received for lending.

REVIEW QUESTIONS

1. An item used as money that also has intrinsic value in some other use is
   (A) fiat money
   (B) token money
   (C) commodity money
   (D) legal tender
   (E) barter money

2. Currency and coin held outside banks plus demand deposits plus travelers' checks plus other checkable deposits equals
   (A) M1 money supply
   (B) M2 money supply
   (C) M3 money supply
   (D) L4 money supply
   (E) K1 money supply

3. The Central Bank of the United States is known as the
   (A) Federal Reserve System
   (B) Federal Deposit Insurance Corporation
   (C) Department of the Treasury
   (D) Federal Savings and Loan Insurance Corporation
   (E) Capital Reserve Corporation

4. If the required reserve ratio is 10%, the money multiplier is
   (A) 0.1
   (B) 1
   (C) 9
   (D) 10
   (E) 5

5. Which of the following actions by the Federal Reserve will result in a decrease in the money supply?

    (A) an increase in the required reserve ratio
    (B) a decrease in federal spending
    (C) buying government securities in the open market
    (D) a decrease in the discount rate
    (E) an increase in taxes

6. When the interest rate rises, bond values

    (A) decrease
    (B) increase
    (C) are unchanged because the interest rate paid on a bond is fixed
    (D) can either increase or decrease, depending on the type of bond
    (E) are adjusted by the U.S. Treasury

7. Suppose that the money market is currently in equilibrium, but the Fed wants to reduce the interest rate. The Fed should pursue policies to

    (A) increase the money supply
    (B) decrease the money supply
    (C) increase the demand for money
    (D) make the supply of money more inelastic
    (E) decrease the demand for money

8. As the interest rate increases

    (A) investment decreases, but aggregate demand remains constant
    (B) investment decreases and aggregate demand decreases
    (C) investment increases, but aggregate demand remains constant
    (D) investment increases and aggregate demand increases
    (E) both investment and aggregate demand remain constant

9. When people hold money in the anticipation of future cash-based exchanges, they are acting from the

   (A) speculative motive
   (B) precautionary motive
   (C) transactions motive
   (D) profit motive
   (E) production motive

10. A checking deposit in a bank is considered to be

    (A) one of the bank's liabilities
    (B) one of the bank's assets
    (C) part of the bank's net worth
    (D) part of the bank's capital
    (E) on loan from the bank

FREE-RESPONSE QUESTION

The Fed's required reserve ratio for the banking system is 10%. Currently, the Anytown National Bank—a member bank—has no excess bank reserves. Then Mr. Jones deposits $1,000 in his checking account at Anytown National Bank.

If the bank deducts its RRR amount from the deposit, identify the amount of bank reserve it has available to loan.

(a) Calculate the money multiplier and show your work.

(b) What is the greatest amount by which the banking system can increase the money supply?

(c) Identify the limits the bank system has with its ability to increase the money supply.

ANSWERS AND EXPLANATIONS

1. C

Commodity money is an item that we can use as a medium of exchange and store of value, and we can also use the item as itself. For example, corn is one commodity that has historically been used as money. However, it also serves as food, which makes it commodity money. Dollar bills, on the other hand, can only be used as dollar bills to buy things because they are backed by the U.S. government. They have no inherent value, nor do they serve any other useful purpose. Without the government's support they are just green pieces of paper with no intrinsic value of their own. They are considered fiat or token money.

2. A

M1, or "narrow" money, is the most liquid form of money and consists of cash and other items that are "like" cash or can be converted to cash easily. The most important of these are checking account deposits (or for that matter any checkable deposits) against which you can write a check or withdraw funds with your debit card. Travelers' checks are just as liquid and fall in the same category.

3. A

The Federal Reserve System is the central bank of the U.S. It consists of the seven members of the board of governors located in Washington D.C. The members are appointed by the President and approved by the Senate. This represents the public side of the Fed. The head of this board is the chairman of the Federal Reserve (currently Alan Greenspan). The system also consists of 12 district member banks located in different cities of the United States, such as the Federal Reserve Bank of New York, the Federal Reserve Bank of Chicago, and so forth. The district banks are owned by the member banks in their district. This is the private ownership side of the Fed.

4. D

The money multiplier $\frac{1}{RRR} = \frac{1}{0.1}$ where RRR is the required reserve ratio. To calculate the money multiplier, the RRR must be entered as a decimal (not a percentage) in the formula. In this question, 10% is 0.1. Hence, the money multiplier is 1 divided by $0.1 = 10$, making (D) the correct answer.

5. A

Raising the required reserve ratio increases the amount banks have to keep on reserve. This lowers the monetary base and reduces banks' power to make loans, decreasing the money supply. The Federal Reserve cannot change federal spending or taxes, thus (A) and (E) are incorrect. Decreasing the discount rate or buying government securities on the open market will increase the monetary base as banks borrow more when the discount rate falls, and the Federal Reserve puts more money into circulation as it buys government securities in the open market. Both of these will increase money supply, not decrease it. So (B) and (C) are not correct, either.

6. A

When interest rates rise, bond values fall (A). Consider the following example: Cordell bought a 6% bond a year ago for $100. The market interest rate has increased to 8%. If he offered to sell his bond for $100, no one would buy it because anyone can buy a new bond and earn an 8% interest instead of the 6% interest offered by his bond. He would have to sell his bond at a discount, an indication that the bond's value has decreased as a result of the increase in interest rates.

7. A

The Federal Reserve has no control over money demand; thus, (C) and (E) are incorrect. The Fed only controls money supply. Because interest rates are basically the price of money, interest rates will change as the money supply changes. An increase in the supply of money with no change in money demand (A) will lower the equilibrium rate of interest.

8. B

How much firms plan to invest depends on how much they can borrow. That figure, in turn, depends on the market rate of interest. An increase in interest rates decreases investment (I) and hence decreases $AD = C + I_g + G + X_n$.

An increase in interest rates decreases planned investment and hence decreases $AD = C + I_g + G + X_n$.

9. C

The transactions motive for holding money (or cash) refers to people's demand for cash in order to buy goods and services. This is the main reason we keep our money in the form of cash or checking deposits, both of which earn little, if any, interest. People who are acting from the speculative motive hold cash in anticipation of cash-based investment opportunities, whereas those acting from the precautionary motive hold cash to cover future expenses that will need to be paid quickly (i.e., which cannot be easily paid from less liquid assets).

10. A

A bank's liabilities are sums that it owes. Depositors' accounts are a bank's biggest liability. The bank owes that money to depositors, and must provide it when depositors request it.

FREE-RESPONSE QUESTION

This question requires an understanding of how the banking system works with the Fed to manage the money supply. Banks use their reserves (the "excess," i.e., those remaining after the required ratio amount is deducted) to make loans. Demand deposits (i.e., checking account funds) are given for the loan and new money is created. The process is reversed when a loan is repaid.

The bank reserves will be $900 that are available for loans. A 10% RRR means that $100 of the deposit must be in the vault of the bank or in the Fed's vault in the bank's account.

(a) The money multiplier will be $\frac{1}{RRR}$ or $\frac{1}{0.1} = 10$.

(b) The potential money supply increase will be 10 x $900, or $9,000.

(c) Less than $9,000 will be added to the money supply because this figure assumes that new loans are redeposited in full at other banks in the system. However, some people will borrow money and then take cash out to make purchases or to hold. Further, this potential money supply increase requires that every bank involved in the banking system want to be fully loaned out. This is an unlikely situation, because this puts the bank at risk if loans are not repaid in a timely way.

Chapter 7: Inflation, Unemployment, and Stabilization Policies

- Fiscal and Monetary Policies
- Inflation and Unemployment
- Review Questions
- Answers and Explanations

FISCAL AND MONETARY POLICIES

DISEQUILIBRIUM, RECESSIONARY GAPS, AND INFLATIONARY GAPS

The economy is in equilibrium when AD = AS. When the economy is not in equilibrium, it will either be in a recessionary gap or it will be in an inflationary boom.

When the economy is in a recession or **recessionary gap** and goods are piling up on shelves, inventories accumulate. As a result, firms will cut back on their production and try to sell off those inventories. Eventually, a new equilibrium will emerge at a *lower* level. Production will adjust to that lower-than-expected level of aggregate demand.

When the economy experiences an **inflationary gap**, demand exceeds production. Firms will sell off inventories that they had been planning to sell later. Excess demand for goods will cause the prices of those goods to rise, causing inflation. Firms will expand their production to meet the higher-than-expected demand, and eventually a new equilibrium will emerge at a *higher* level. Excessive demand is not sustainable, but the worry of this situation is stagflation.

In both of these cases, there is debate as to what action to pursue to stabilize the economy: Is it better to use fiscal policy or monetary policy?

FISCAL POLICY AND ITS BROAD EFFECTS

The government has two main tools for managing the economy, fiscal policy and monetary policy. Monetary policy, managed by the Fed, was discussed in the previous chapter.

Fiscal policy centers on the spending and taxing policies with which government influences the state of the economy. Fiscal policy can be complex; there are numerous taxes and many different spending programs. Recall that the spending and tax multipliers differ. For now we will focus on changes in the absolute levels of government purchases (G) and tax revenues (T).

As was true earlier, G represents government spending; G = purchases of goods and services by the government (federal, state, and local). Note that this figure does not include transfer payments (e.g., Social Security, welfare), interest payments on the national debt (to government bond holders), or subsidies to aid production.

T represents total tax receipts, specifically *net* taxes, which are tax revenues minus transfer payments and subsidies. G – T is the government's budget deficit. If $G - T > 0$, we have a deficit; if $G - T < 0$, we have a surplus.

Expansionary Fiscal Policy

Fiscal policy can be either **expansionary** (intended to increase real GDP) or **contractionary** (intended to reduce inflation or reduce the budget deficit). Expansionary fiscal policy is enacted when the government deliberately increases its spending to stimulate the economy. Toward this end, the government increases spending (G+), cuts taxes (T–), or both. Expansionary fiscal policy stimulates the economy by expanding aggregate demand (AD). When the government increases G, it adds directly to AD, because G is part of AD ($AD = C + I_g + G + X_n$). When the government cuts T, it increases people's disposable income (their total income less taxes). People will spend much of that extra income, so consumption (C) increases, even though they will also save some of that income.

In both cases, AD will also increase indirectly through the multiplier effect, as the initial increase in G or C touches off a larger chain of consumption. In both cases, real GDP will increase and so will the price level. Expansionary fiscal policy means the economy is moving to a point of lower unemployment and higher inflation (i.e., the economy is moving northwest along the Phillips curve, which will be discussed later in this chapter). This is an example of **demand-pull inflation**, inflation that follows from an increase in aggregate demand. This will cause equilibrium RGDP (Y) to increase and the equilibrium price level (PL) to increase as well.

Contractionary Fiscal Policy

Contractionary fiscal policy is enacted when the government deliberately reduces its spending to slow the economy down (usually with the goal of reducing inflation or of reducing the deficit for its own sake). In contractionary fiscal policy, the government cuts spending (G–), raises taxes (T+), or both. Contractionary fiscal policy slows the economy by contracting AD.

All other things being equal, the net effect of contractionary fiscal policy is to induce a recession or at least slow down the rate of growth of the economy. This will cause the economy to move to a point of higher unemployment and lower inflation (i.e., southeast along the Phillips curve). As a result, equilibrium RGDP decreases and equilibrium PL decreases.

International Connections

When the government uses expansionary fiscal policy to aid the economy, it often needs to borrow in the market to fund the deficit created. Taking personal savings from the loanable funds market, combined with the fact that the government competes with the business and consumer borrowers in that market, often means that the real interest rate rises temporarily. An increase in the interest rate, all other things being equal, means that the U.S. interest rate increases relative to that in other countries. Foreigners are attracted to the higher interest rate they can now earn on U.S. bank deposits and bonds, which increases the demand for U.S. dollars. With more dollars demanded, the price of the dollar rises on the foreign exchange market. Foreigners must now pay more for U.S.-made goods and services, so U.S. exports decrease. This describes the net export effect, which produces negative net exports, a situation which is counterproductive to expansionary fiscal policy goals. When the government uses contractionary policy to cool the economy, real interest rate falls and foreigners move capital funds to the higher return elsewhere. Net exports shift to a positive number, and the net export effect appears again, opposing the goals of contractionary policy.

Monetary Policy and its Broad Effects

Recall that monetary policy refers to the policies of the Federal Reserve that are designed to influence the money supply and the interest rates. The Fed's actions influence the nominal interest rate. However, it does *not* directly control the nominal interest rate and it has no control over the real interest rate. There are three tools of monetary policy: the required reserve ratio, the discount rate, and open-market operations (OMOs).

Of these, the Fed prefers to use OMOs because they are both discreet and flexible. When the Federal Open Market Committee (FMOC) instructs a district bank to sell securities in the open market, this action decreases bank reserves. Some banks are short of reserves and seek to borrow reserves from other banks; the federal funds interest rate rises as a result. When the FOMC instructs a district bank to buy securities in the open market, this action increases bank reserves. Flush with reserves, banks now seek to lend reserves to other banks and the federal funds interest rate falls.

An increase in the interest rate leads to a decrease in consumption and investment spending. The multiplier effect then results in a larger decrease in aggregate demand. If the Fed conducts an open-market operation that increases the interest rate, the resulting decrease in aggregate demand produces a decrease in real GDP and a decrease in the price level. This is **contractionary** monetary policy.

If the Fed conducts an open-market operation that decreases the interest rate, the resulting increase in aggregate demand produces an increase in real GDP and an increase in the price level.

International Connections

When the Fed increases the nominal interest rate, the real interest rate rises temporarily and investment and expenditure on consumer durables decrease. An increase in the interest rate, all other things being equal, means that the U.S. interest rate increases relative to the interest rate in other countries. Foreigners are attracted to the higher interest rate they can now earn on U.S. bank deposits and bonds, which increases the demand for U.S. dollars. With more dollars demanded, the price of the dollar rises on the foreign exchange market. Foreigners must now pay more for U.S.-made goods and services, so U.S. exports decrease. Here again is the net export effect, which produces a negative level of net exports, but, unlike fiscal policy, in this case the effect reinforces the contractionary monetary policy. When interest rates fall, foreigners shift their capital funds out of the country in search of higher returns and net exports shift to a positive number. The net export effect appears again and reinforces the expansionary policy.

Loanable Funds Market and the Real Interest Rate

In the long run, the supply of loanable funds from personal savings and the demand for investment and consumption funds determine the real interest rate in the global financial market. This model is called the "loanable funds model," and it is depicted in the diagram below:

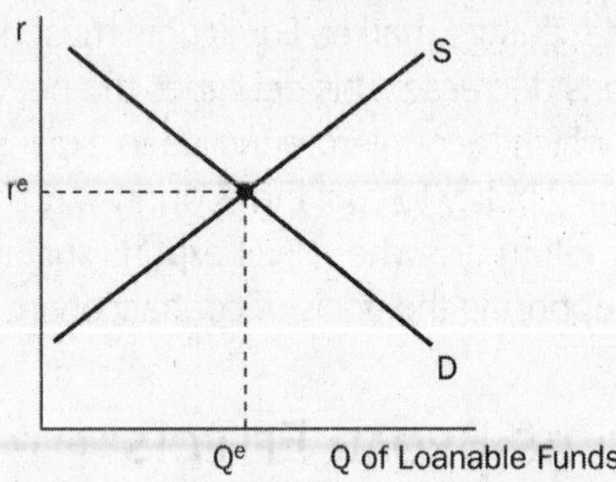

Loanable Funds Market—Real Interest Rates

The loanable funds market is different from the money market in that the real amount supplied and demanded is determined, in part, by what funds earn in real terms. Equilibrium occurs where supply intersects demand. Movement to equilibrium is the process of determining the real interest rate in the economy. Note the use of the label "r" on the vertical axis. This helps to remind us that this graphical model gives us the real interest rate. The supply of loanable funds is all of the income that people have chosen to save and lend out, rather than use for their own consumption. The demand for loanable funds comes from households and firms that want to borrow to make investments.

Stabilization Policy

Stabilization policy refers to the use of monetary and fiscal policy to reduce short-run economic fluctuations. Because both inflation and recession are undesirable, the Fed and Congress can use stabilization policies to reduce short-run fluctuations and move the economy back to the full-employment equilibrium.

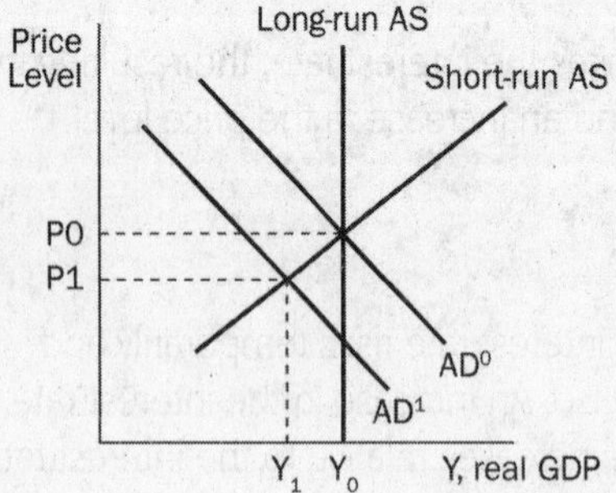

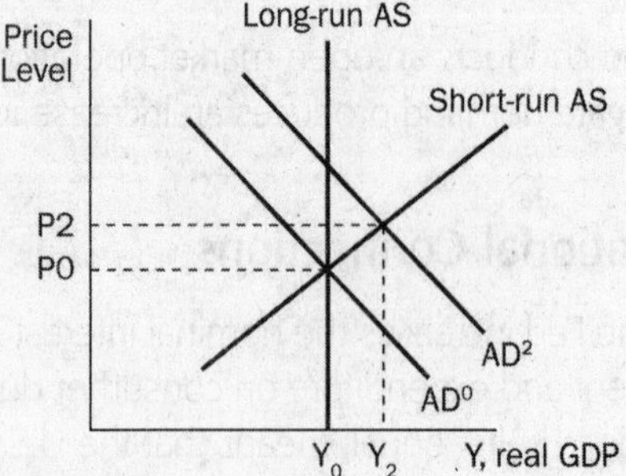

The figures above depict two short-run situations that call for stabilization policy—either AD is insufficient or AD is excessive. In particular, suppose that the AD is less than what is required to produce the "full-employment RGDP" (the full-employment output, given at the long-run AS curve, is Y_0 in *both* figures). In this case, AD = AD_1, and the economy's level of output, Y_1, is less than the natural rate of output, Y_0. This would be the situation if we were in a recession.

There are three possible stabilization policies the Fed might deploy here:

1. The Fed could expand the money supply to shift AD back to AD_0.
2. Congress could reduce taxes to shift AD rightward, back towards AD_0.
3. Congress could increase government spending, shifting back to AD_0.

In terms of the AD-AS model, stabilization policy is what results from using expansionary fiscal or expansionary monetary policy to push the economy back towards the full-employment level of output.

On the other hand, AD might be *more* than what is required for the full-employment level of RGDP as it is in figure 12.2, in which $AD = AD_2$. Output in the economy (Y_2) is more than the full-employment level and unemployment is *lower* than the natural rate of unemployment. This will produce inflationary pressures in the economy.

There are still three appropriate stabilization policies in this situation, all of which reverse the policy actions taken to correct inadequate AD.

1. The Fed could reduce the money supply, raising interest rates and shifting AD to the left, towards AD_0.
2. Congress could increase taxes, which would decrease disposable income and shift AD leftward towards AD_0.
3. Congress could cut spending on goods and services, which would shift AD towards AD_0.

These are contractionary monetary and fiscal policies.

Government Deficits and Debt

When the government spends more than it receives as tax revenue, it incurs a deficit. When the government spends less than it receives as tax revenue, it enjoys a surplus. This is a yearly computation and the accumulated deficits and surpluses that accrue from year to year define the National Debt.

Expansionary fiscal policy is a combination of increased spending and reduced taxes. If the budget was initially balanced, expansionary fiscal policy that increases spending and lowers taxes will create a budget deficit. Budget deficits are not problematic in themselves, though they can have a negative effect. When the economy has many resources that are going unused, higher budget deficits will stimulate the economy, raising GDP and increasing investment demand. This is called "crowding in" investment.

When the economy is close to full employment (potential GDP), higher budget deficits will not increase output by much and will actually decrease investment demand. This effect occurs because the deficit uses up the private sector's supply savings, driving interest rates up and leaving less funding for investment. This is called "crowding out" investment. It can be shown on the loanable funds market model by showing an increase in the demand for funds. The real interest rate rises and "crowds out" other borrowers. Another view holds that the supply of loanable funds is affected by the government financing its deficit—private savings is diverted to bond purchases. The result, however, is the same: a higher real interest rate. The crowding out effect can be reduced somewhat through increases in the money supply. These increases keep the interest rate from getting too high and basically reduce the amount of debt on the market as a result of the change in the money supply. This is known as **monetizing the deficit** and comes at a significant cost: It is apt to cause inflation and lower long-run growth of the GDP.

INFLATION AND UNEMPLOYMENT

DEMAND-PULL AND COST-PUSH INFLATION

Inflation is a sustained and general increase in prices. Inflation may result from either an increase in aggregate demand or a decrease in aggregate supply. **Demand-pull inflation** is an inflationary process that begins with an expansion of aggregate demand. Any factor contributing to increased aggregate demand—such as increases in the money supply, consumer spending, investment, government expenditures, or net exports—can initiate demand-pull inflation. Note, however, that for *sustained* price increases to occur there must be continuing increases in aggregate demand that can only be provided by a continuing increase in the money supply.

The second variety of inflation is **cost-push inflation**. Here, an increase in the costs of production (wages or raw materials) shifts the short-run AS curve to the left, and tends to push prices up while reducing the level of real GDP at the same time (stagflation). As before, this represents only a one-shot change. For a cost-push supply shock to lead to sustained inflation, there again must be continuous increase in the money supply (undertaken as policy to stimulate the economy and increase real GDP). Increased money supply pushes aggregate demand up (this was what happened in the U.S. following the first oil shock in the 1970s).

THE PHILLIPS CURVE

The New Zealand economist A. W. Phillips compared growth in wages against the unemployment rate in the United Kingdom from 1861 to 1913. His data, published in 1958, suggested an inverse relationship between wage growth (percentage change in price level, i.e., inflation) and unemployment. The graphic representation of this relationship is called a **Phillips curve**. Wage growth and inflation move very closely together, so Phillips curves are usually drawn with the inflation rate on the vertical axis and the unemployment rate on the horizontal axis.

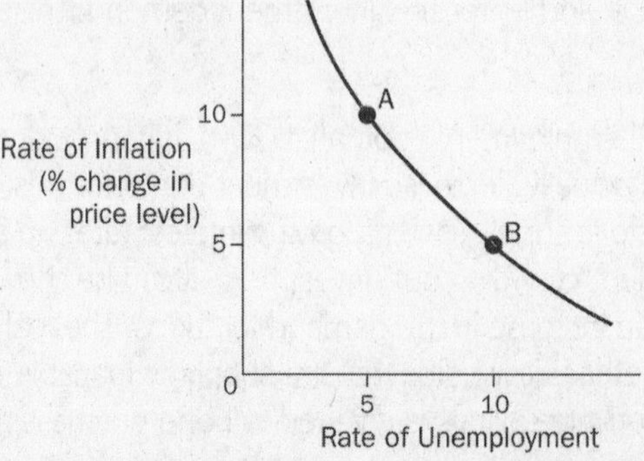

On this curve, points A and B represent possible combinations of unemployment and inflation. Any point that is off the curve, to either the right or the left, is not a viable combination.

Some analysts have used the Phillips curve to predict the inverse relationship between inflation and unemployment when the AD curve moves around full employment. The Phillips curve and its supporting data led many economists and policymakers to believe that higher unemployment was the cost of lower inflation. Given this belief, the government needed to select a point that minimized the sum of those costs. Because it generally seemed more politically urgent to reduce unemployment than inflation, this view helped rationalize a policy of monetary ease that produced waves of double-digit inflation in the 1970s and early 1980s. Controls and guidelines for both wages and prices were adopted to fight inflation, but that simply caused wasteful economic distortions.

It is believed that in the long run, the economy always tends toward full employment–thus there is no long-run trade-off between inflation and unemployment. As AS changes, new dynamics develop between the rate of inflation and the rate of unemployment. New short-run curves are created and as a result, the long-run Phillips curve is a vertical line above full employment. However in the short run, the unemployment rate can differ markedly from full-employment level and this will affect the inflation rate. So in the short run, the Phillips curve is not vertical.

During the 1970s, inflation and unemployment increased at the same time, resulting in stagflation (inflation combined with stagnant production). By 1975, unemployment was at 8.5% with inflation reaching highs in 1974 and 1975. It happened again in the early 1980s with unemployment peaking at 9.7% and inflation hitting highs between 1979 and 1981. It thus became painfully clear that high unemployment did not ensure low inflation, and high inflation did not ensure low unemployment.

IF YOU LEARNED ONLY SIX THINGS IN THIS CHAPTER. . .

1. Disequilibrium in market analysis results in either a shortage, which entices the market price to rise, or a surplus, which entices the market price to fall.

2. The recessionary gap is the difference between the equilibrium real production achieved in the short-run aggregate market and full-employment real production that occurs when short-run equilibrium real production is less than full-employment real production.

3. Inflationary gap is the difference between the equilibrium real production achieved in the short-run aggregate market and full-employment real production that occurs when short-run equilibrium real production is more than full-employment real production.

4. Demand-pull inflation occurs when the four macroeconomic sectors (household, business, government, and foreign) try to purchase more output that the economy is capable of producing.

5. Cost-push inflation occurs when the cost of using any of the four factors of production (labor, capital, land, or entrepreneurship) increases.

6. The Phillips curve depicts the inverse relationship between wage growth and unemployment.

REVIEW QUESTIONS

1. If the economy is operating at potential GDP, an increase in the money supply will lead to
   (A) stagflation
   (B) sustained inflation
   (C) demand-pull inflation
   (D) cost-push inflation
   (E) deflation

2. A government budget deficit occurs when government expenditures are
   (A) greater than government revenue
   (B) less than government revenue
   (C) increasing and government revenue is increasing
   (D) decreasing and government revenue is decreasing
   (E) in balance with government revenue

3. Cost-push inflation is caused by a(n)
   (A) decrease in government regulation
   (B) increase in government spending
   (C) decrease in taxes that stimulates new spending
   (D) increase in wages that go beyond gain in productivity
   (E) increase in investment spending

4. The short-run Phillips curve is a graph showing the relationship between the
   (A) price level and the unemployment rate
   (B) price level and the rate of inflation
   (C) rate of inflation and the unemployment rate
   (D) aggregate output and the price level
   (E) price level and the unemployment rate

5. In the long run, the Phillips curve will be vertical at the natural rate of unemployment if
   (A) the long-run aggregate demand curve is vertical at potential GDP
   (B) the long-run aggregate demand curve is horizontal at the natural rate of inflation
   (C) the long-run supply curve is horizontal at the natural rate of inflation
   (D) the long-run aggregate supply curve is vertical at potential GDP
   (E) the long-run aggregate supply curve is horizontal at potential GDP

6. If the aggregate supply curve is vertical in the long run, then
   (A) fiscal policy has an effect on RGDP in the long run, but monetary policy does not
   (B) monetary policy has an effect on RGDP in the long run, but fiscal policy does not
   (C) contractionary policies have an effect on RGDP in the long run, but expansionary policies do not
   (D) neither monetary nor fiscal policy has any effect on RGDP in the long run
   (E) expansionary policies have an effect on RGDP in the long run, but contractionary policies do not

7. Economists generally agree that for a sustained inflation to occur, the
   (A) government must accommodate it by increasing government spending
   (B) government must accommodate it by decreasing taxes
   (C) Federal Reserve must accommodate it by increasing the money supply
   (D) Federal Reserve must accommodate it by decreasing the money supply
   (E) government must accommodate it by decreasing government spending or increasing taxes

8. The prevailing view of the Phillips curve in the 1960s implied that policies which
   (A) lower the unemployment rate will also tend to lower the inflation rate
   (B) lower the inflation rate will also tend to lower the unemployment rate
   (C) raise the inflation rate will also tend to raise the unemployment rate
   (D) raise the unemployment rate will also tend to raise the inflation rate
   (E) lower the unemployment rate will also tend to raise the inflation rate

9. If the Phillips curve is vertical in the long run, then
   (A) there is a trade-off between inflation and unemployment in the long run
   (B) there is no trade-off between inflation and unemployment in the long run
   (C) the unemployment rate will be zero in the long run
   (D) the inflation rate will always be zero in the long run
   (E) both the inflation rate and the unemployment rate will be zero in the long run

10. If the government does not react to cost-push inflation with any policy actions, then there is likely to be
    (A) an increase in RGDP
    (B) a lower unemployment rate
    (C) an inflation spiral that could become "hyperinflationary"
    (D) a recession
    (E) constant price level

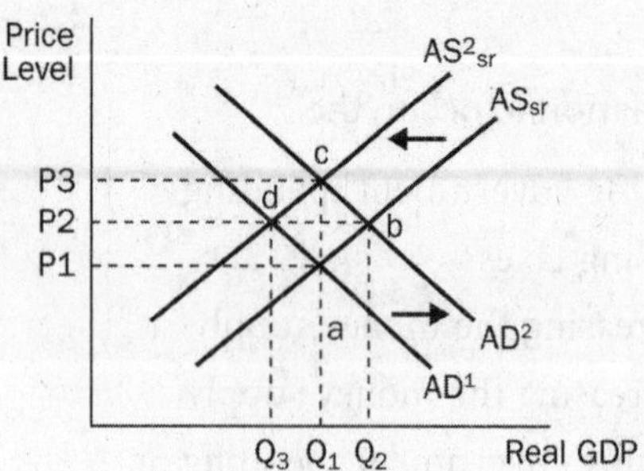

Use the graph above for Questions 11 and 12.

11. Refer to the graph above. Assume that the economy is initially at equilibrium at point (a). If there is demand-pull inflation in the economy such that AD^1 shifts to AD^2, then in the long run, the price level will be
    (A) P2 and RDGP will be Q_3
    (B) P3 and RDGP will be Q_1
    (C) P1 and RGDP will be Q_1
    (D) P2 and RDGP will be Q_2
    (E) P3 and RGDP will be Q_3

12. Refer to the graph above. Assume that the economy is initially at equilibrium at point (a). If there is demand-pull inflation in the economy such that AD^1 shifts to AD^2, the long-run AS curve will be
    (A) AS^2
    (B) AS^1
    (C) Point (c)
    (D) A vertical line at Q_1
    (E) A vertical line at Q_2

13. The phrase "monetizing the deficit" refers to
    (A) inflation reducing the real value of the debt
    (B) the Federal Reserve buying some of the government deficit
    (C) the Treasury repaying the debt
    (D) the Treasury issuing short-term securities in place of long-term securities
    (E) the Federal Reserve issuing government securities

14. An increase in the money supply causes
    (A) a long-run increase in the level of output
    (B) an increase in the level of output over both the long-run and the short-run
    (C) a short-run increase in the level of output
    (D) no change in the level of output
    (E) a short-run increase and a long-run decrease in the level of output

15. "Crowding out" refers to
    (A) an increase in investment caused by an increase in government spending
    (B) a decrease in investment caused by an increase in government spending
    (C) a decrease in government spending caused by a decrease in investment
    (D) an increase in investment caused by a decrease in government spending
    (E) a decrease in government spending caused by an increase in investment

FREE-RESPONSE QUESTION

Assume that an economy is in recession.

(a) Draw a correctly labeled AD/AS graph and show the position of the economy.

(b) Suggest a fiscal policy alternative that can move the economy to full employment.

(c) Amend the graph to show the effect of your policy. Show on the graph the effect of the change on both price level and output (RGDP). Explain how the following will impact the effect of your fiscal policy.

  i. Crowding out

  ii. The net export effect

ANSWERS AND EXPLANATIONS

1. C

The expansionary monetary policy will shift the AD curve to the right, resulting only in increased prices (i.e., inflation). The inflation is caused by an increase in AD, so this is demand-pull inflation. An increase in the money supply is an expansionary monetary policy that increases AD. Because the economy is already operating at potential GDP, firms have no incentive to increase production beyond this point.

There is no fall in output at the same time, so this is not stagflation (A). It is not cost-push inflation (D), because it is not caused by a rise in production costs and the attendant decrease in AS. It is not sustained inflation (B), which requires that prices keep rising; that would only be possible if the Federal Reserve continued to increase the money supply so that AD keeps rising. Because there is no mention here of the Federal Reserve repeatedly increasing the money supply, this cannot be a sustained inflation.

2. A

A budget deficit occurs when government spending rises (usually in response to a recession), but tax revenues are not sufficient to pay for the spending. Expansionary fiscal policy will often create a budget deficit because it tries to create more disposable income. A problem with deficit spending is the "crowding out" effect that tends to produce results that are the opposite of those desired.

3. D

Cost-push inflation is caused by a leftward shift of the short-run AS curve. Because wages are the biggest expense for most business firms, increases in wages must be matched by gains in productivity so that more output is available for sale to pay the addition to costs. Selecting (A) moves the AS to the right. All the other choices available relate to AD.

4. C

A. W. Phillips found a negative relationship between wage growth and unemployment. Wage growth and inflation move very closely together and so Phillips curves are usually drawn with the inflation rate on the vertical axis and the unemployment rate on the horizontal axis. Note that (A) might appear to be correct at first glance, but a Phillips curve depicts the relationship between the *percentage change* in the price level and the unemployment rate; it does not reflect merely the current price level.

5. D

The short-run Phillips curve represents the relationship between the rate of inflation and the unemployment rate. In the long run, the AS curve is vertical at full employment (potential GDP). The economy is said to be at full employment at the natural rate of unemployment. So if the GDP is fixed at full employment, the unemployment rate in the economy is the full employment level and the Phillips curve is vertical at the natural rate of unemployment, (D).

6. D

If the AS is vertical in the long run, input prices react instantaneously to changes in output prices and firms have no incentive to produce more or produce less than the full employment level of output. A fiscal or monetary policy can shift the AD curve, but because the output level is fixed, the result will be only a change in the price level. Expansionary fiscal or monetary policies will increase AD. There will be no change in output in the long run, but the price level will rise. Contractionary fiscal or monetary policies will create the opposite effect.

7. C

Sustained inflation requires a long-term increase in the price level. Prices increase when the government or the Federal Reserve follows expansionary policies that increase AD; they also increase when there is an increase in production costs that lowers AS. Production costs cannot keep increasing continuously and the government cannot continuously keep increasing the budget deficit (by lowering taxes or increasing government spending). Thus, sustained inflation can only be created if the Fed keeps increasing the money supply. The AD curve will then keep shifting to the right and prices will keep increasing. This is why economists believe that sustained inflation is a purely monetary phenomenon.

8. E

The Phillips curve tells us that there is a trade-off between inflation and unemployment rates, at least in the short run. Hence a decrease in unemployment can only be obtained at the cost of a higher rate of inflation.

9. B

In the long run, the AS curve is fixed at full employment or potential GDP. Therefore there is no change in output in the long run and no change in unemployment in the long run. In fact, the level of unemployment is fixed at the natural rate of unemployment and the Phillips curve is vertical at this level. If the Phillips curve is vertical, then at the natural rate of unemployment there is no trade-off between inflation and unemployment.

10. D

When the economy has been driven into an inflationary state, the government's normal plan of action is contractionary fiscal policy, which will move the AD curve to the left and lower the price level but suffer loss of RGDP. Without action, the economy will eventually end up in a recessionary state because inflationary levels of production are not sustainable. Prices cannot go up forever and consumer spending will eventually decrease. Think of the ups and downs of the business cycle to understand this condition. Monetary and fiscal policy tools are used to flatten the ups and downs so that the least harm is done.

11. B

In the short run, excessive demand moves the AD curve to the right at point (b). But in the long run, nominal wages rise as workers realize that their wages are not buying the same level of goods and services at the higher price level (P2). High wage costs force the short-run AS curve to the left and the new long-run price level is at P3.

12. D

Following the logic about how the AD and AS curves move presented in answer 11 above, the long-run equilibrium occurs where AD^2 intersects with short-run AS^2—at P3 and Q_1.

13. B

There are two ways for the government to finance a deficit. One is by borrowing and the other is by asking the Fed to print more money, or effectively buying some of the government debt. This is called "monetization of the deficit" and leads to inflation, sometimes even to hyperinflation. Inflation does not affect the real value of the debt, and the Treasury is responsible for the U.S. government's revenue, not its debts.

14. C

An increase in the money supply is an expansionary monetary policy that results in increased AD. This shifts the AD curve to the right and results in a short-run increase in output and the price level. This increase in output cannot be maintained over the long run, because in the long run the economy is already operating at potential (or full-employment) GDP. Any increase in AD in the long run will only result in increased prices, without changing output.

15. B

When the economy is close to full employment (potential GDP), higher budget deficits (resulting from an increase in government spending or a fall in taxes) will not increase output by much and will actually *decrease* investment demand. This effect occurs because the deficit uses up the private sector's supply of savings, driving interest rates up and leaving less funding for investment. This is the "crowding out" effect.

FREE-RESPONSE QUESTION

This question requires you to draw a recessionary economy, devise a fiscal policy solution, and discuss the changes and the problems associated with that policy choice. See below for a sample response.

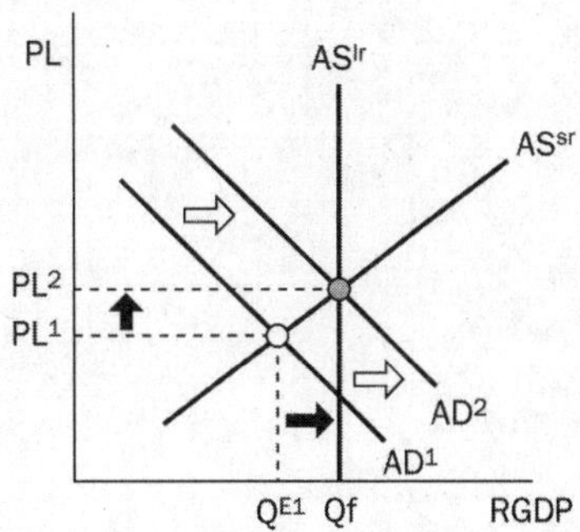

(a) As shown in the graph, the original position of a recessionary gap is found where AD^1 intersects with AS^{sr} (Q^{E1} and PL^1 at less than full employment (Qf)).

(b) Fiscal policy actions include increasing government spending and/or lowering tax rates. Both of these actions have the effect of shifting the AD curve to the right toward full-employment RGDP.

(c) As shown in the graph, the amendment is the shift of the AD curve to AD^2 resulting in the higher price level (PL^2) and a return to the full employment level of RGDP at Qf.

   i. "Crowding out" will have a negative effect if the government policy action increased spending more than the available tax revenue. This deficit would need to be funded and private savings would decline in the loanable funds market because it is diverted to government bond sales. Real interest rates rise, which discourages investment and consumer borrowing. AD decreases at a time when it should be rising. Crowding out causes the AD to fall short of full-employment RGDP.

   ii. The net export effect will also have negative effects. Higher real interest rates will draw capital flows into the economy, increasing the international value of the currency. Net exports are negative as fewer exports are sold and more imports are purchased. Again, AD decreases at a time when it should be rising, so AD falls short of full-employment RGDP.

Chapter 8: Economic Growth and Productivity

- **Economic Growth**
- **Review Questions**
- **Answers and Explanations**

ECONOMIC GROWTH

As we saw in earlier chapters, economic growth can be illustrated by an outward shift in the PPC.

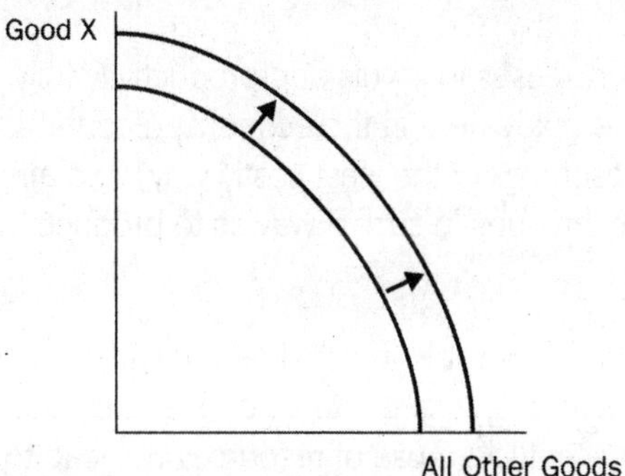

In the simple production possibilities curve diagram above, an increase in production stemming from economic growth can be represented by an outward shift of the curve.

There are two ways to define economic growth, depending upon the final objective. One definition is an *increase in real GDP* over a period of time. The other definition considers economic growth to be an *increase in real per capita GDP* over time. The second definition is superior if the objective of the analysis is a comparison of living standards. An increase in per capita GDP increases real wages and incomes, leading to higher standards of living.

Mathematical approximation—specifically the **rule of 70**—is used to measure the effect of economic growth. This rule tells us the approximate number of years it will take for some measure (real GDP, price level, savings account, etc.) to double, given a known annual percentage increase.

$$\text{Approximate number of years required to double real GDP} = \frac{70}{\text{annual percentage rate of growth}}$$

So if, for instance, an economy has a 3% annual growth rate, dividing 70 by 3 tells us that it will take approximately 23 years for the real GDP to double.

Factors Affecting the Ability to Grow

There are two main ways in which an economy can grow: either by an *increase in inputs* (such as labor and capital) or by *increasing the productivity* of these inputs. Productivity is measured as real output per unit of input. About one-third of U.S. growth comes from increases in inputs; the remaining two-thirds of growth is generated by improvements in productivity.

So we can say that a country's growth rate of output depends on:

- The rate of growth of capital stock
- The rate of growth attributed to technological progress
- The rate of growth of the labor force
- The rate of growth in the skill level of the labor force

All four of these factors will lead to an increase in output or RGDP. However, what is produced must be sold to avoid unplanned increases in inventories. This means that households, businesses, and the government must buy newly produced goods and services, and over time, there must be an increase in total spending.

If the economy is to utilize the increases in inputs and productivity fully, there must be an increase in economic efficiency and full employment in the economy. Economic efficiency refers to both **productive efficiency** (using resources in the least costly way) and **allocative efficiency** (allocating resources among production techniques in such a way as to produce those goods and services that maximize society's well-being).

These factors are related. If there is unemployment due to insufficient spending, investment will decrease and there will be a decrease in expenditures on research and development, both of which result in diminished productivity. Inefficient use of resources will lead to higher production costs, thereby reducing profits. This will, in turn, slow innovation and reduce investment.

Also remember that factors such as the quantity of capital, technological progress, investments in human capital, and allocative efficiency can all lead to increases in labor productivity. Thus another way to analyze the real GDP in an economy in any given year is to look at the amount of labor in the economy (measured in worker hours) and the labor productivity (measured as real output per worker per hour).

Real GDP = labor input × labor productivity

Labor productivity increases when the health, education, training, and motivation of workers improve. Productivity also increases when workers have more and better machines and natural resources to work with, when production is better organized, and when labor is allocated from less efficient to more efficient industries.

We can also look at economic growth from the perspective of the aggregate demand (AD) and aggregate supply (AS) framework discussed in chapter 5. In this model, economic growth can be represented by a rightward shift in the long-run AS curve. This shift indicates the economy's capacity to produce more, as demonstrated by an increase in potential or full-employment GDP. This is shown in the figure below.

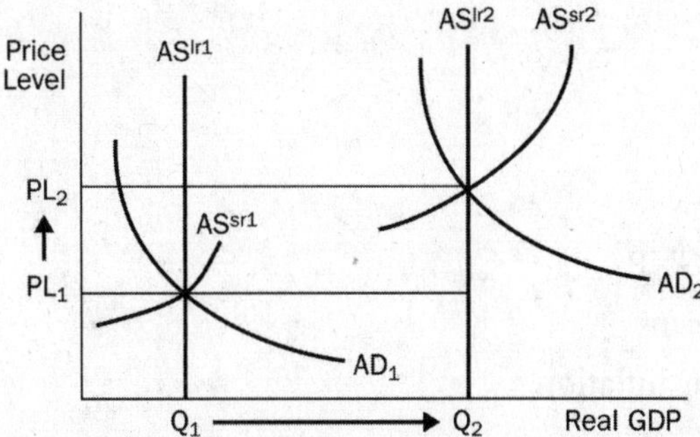

A shift in the long-run AS curve from AS^{lr1} to AS^{lr2} (due to the increase in real GDP from Q_1 to Q_2) is indicative of economic growth. An increase in AD at the same time will enable the economy to take advantage of this increased production.

IF YOU LEARNED ONLY THREE THINGS IN THIS CHAPTER. . .

1. Productive efficiency means that a society uses resources in the least costly way.
2. Allocative efficiency means that a society allocates resources among production techniques in such a way as to produce those good and services that maximize its well being.
3. Increasing inputs and increasing productivity are two main ways in which an economy can grow.

REVIEW QUESTIONS

1. Technological progress occurs when the economy gets more output
   (A) without using any more capital or labor
   (B) by using more capital per worker
   (C) by using more capital but not more workers
   (D) by using more labor but not more capital
   (E) by using more capital but not more labor

2. GDP per capita is
   (A) GDP per person
   (B) GDP in real terms
   (C) the same as the GNP
   (D) GDP nominal terms
   (E) GDP adjusted for inflation

3. Economists compare how rich or poor different nations are by measuring their
   (A) GDP
   (B) debt-to-GDP ratio
   (C) GNP
   (D) GDP per unit of capital
   (E) per capita GDP

4. Increases in the capital stock will lead to
   (A) decreases in wages and GDP
   (B) increases in wages and decreases in GDP
   (C) decreases in wages and increases in GDP
   (D) increases in wages and GDP
   (E) no change in the wages or the GDP

5. To determine the change in the capital stock, the level of gross investment must be adjusted for depreciation because some new investment

   (A) is not used immediately
   (B) replaces existing, but worn out, capital
   (C) replaces existing workers
   (D) is more efficient than existing capital
   (E) is usually unproductive

6. Human capital consists of

   (A) machines that require workers in order to produce most efficiently
   (B) any production technique developed by humans
   (C) workers' education and skills
   (D) workers in factories
   (E) workers who can be used instead of machines

7. A rapid increase in population will result in

   (A) an increase in real GDP and per capita GDP
   (B) an increase in real GDP, but a decrease in per capita GDP
   (C) a decrease in real GDP, but an increase in per capita GDP
   (D) a decrease in both real GDP and per capita GDP
   (E) no change in per capita GDP, but a decrease in real GDP

8. One way that a government can encourage economic growth is by encouraging

   (A) population growth
   (B) consumption
   (C) saving and investment
   (D) imports
   (E) accumulation of wealth

FREE-RESPONSE QUESTION

Economists believe that high budget deficits today will reduce the rate of growth of the economy in the future. Why? Does it matter what causes the high budget deficits?

ANSWERS AND EXPLANATIONS

1. A

Technological progress brings about an increase in productivity without any increases in the factors of production being employed. There is therefore no change in the amount of capital used or numbers of workers employed. However, more is produced as a result of the increased productivity of the factors of production.

2. A

"Per capita" means per person. GDP per capita is calculated as the GDP for the economy in any given year divided by the population of the economy in that year. Real and nominal GDP are GDP values in constant or current prices, but they are an aggregate and thus separate from the per capita figure. GDP adjusted for inflation is real GDP; GNP measures value of production by the residents of a country and is a separate concept from GDP and GDP per capita.

3. E

Rather than using just the GDP to compare different countries, economists prefer to use per capita GDP. Per capita GDP is GDP per person in the economy. Per capita GDP can be used to compare different countries because per capita GDP is taken as a measure of economic growth and allows analysts to compare living standards across nations.

4. D

Increases in quantity of capital are estimated to have contributed 18% to economic growth in the U.S. since 1929. Increases in the capital stock contribute to economic growth, which results in an increase in GDP. As more is produced more workers are hired, unemployment goes down, and there is an increase in wages.

5. B

When new investment replaces old, worn out capital there is no increase in the capital stock–instead, the replacements allow it to stay at the same level. Net investment–i.e., gross investment (including depreciation) minus depreciation–is what results in an increase in capital stock.

6. C

The education of and skills of the work force are human capital. There are four factors that lead to economic growth: increases in the quantity of capital, increases in the labor force, technological progress, and improvement in the quality of labor. An investment in the education and skills of the labor force improves worker quality and is called an investment in human capital.

7. B

Population increase is one factor that leads to economic growth or an increase in real GDP. An increase in the population will result in an increase in the labor force over time and will, hence, increase real GDP. Per capita GDP is GDP divided by population. As the denominator increases rapidly the fraction gets smaller and per capita GDP falls as population increases.

8. C

An increase in saving and investment is a public policy that increases the growth of real output. This is the reasoning behind supply-side policies that give tax breaks to the wealthy and businesses in the hope that this will lead to increased investment and hence an increase in production and economic growth.

FREE-RESPONSE QUESTION

Budget deficits can be caused by increases in government spending or a reduction in taxes. When the budget deficits are financed by borrowing, this reduces private saving that would have increased private investment. If the deficit is used to finance current consumption expenditures it is not contributing to a long-run increase in output. However, if the deficit is generated by increased government spending on infrastructure (such as roads and bridges) or increased human capital through better education and job training, it could offset at least part of the decrease in private investment spending. Whether the net result for output growth is positive or negative depends on whether private capital or public capital has a higher rate of return.

Chapter 9: **Open Economy: International Trade and Finance**

- **Balance of Payment Accounts**
- **Foreign Exchange Market**
- **Trade Restrictions**
- **Review Questions**
- **Answers and Explanations**

BALANCE OF PAYMENT ACCOUNTS

Countries can specialize just like individuals can, and they benefit in similar ways. International trade allows people to buy goods that can be made abroad for less, while specializing in the tasks and goods that they perform better themselves. As discussed in chapter 3, Ricardo's notion of comparative costs describes how countries can benefit from international trade. This idea is now more commonly called **comparative advantage**, and the point is that countries benefit by trading goods they can produce at low opportunity costs for goods that they could produce only at higher opportunity costs. A country that trades for products it can get at a lower cost from another country is better off than it would be if it produced those products domestically.

One of the most significant points to arise from the theory of comparative advantage is the conclusion that even rich, productive countries can gain from free trade. It might be the case, for example, that Country B is better at producing both cloth and wine than Country A (i.e., it has an absolute advantage over Country A in both these goods). However, it will still benefit Country B to specialize in whichever product it is best at producing, and trade with Country A for the product it is less good at producing. If terms of trade are chosen thoughtfully, both countries can end up with more of each good than they had before they started trading. Opportunity costs are the key to comparative advantage—not the labor needed per unit of production or the monetary costs of production.

Balance of Payments

The **balance of payments** (BOP) is a summary record of a country's international economic transactions during a given period of time. The BOP is divided into two accounts: the current account balance (reflecting the trade balance) and the capital account balance or net capital inflows (the difference between foreign purchases of U.S. assets and U.S. purchases of foreign assets).

The trade balance is a sum of debits and credits. U.S merchandise exports create credits, because they reflect amounts that must be paid for the exported goods. U.S. merchandise imports are debits, because they reflect amounts that must be paid out to other countries for the imported goods. A country has a **trade surplus** if the value of its commodity exports exceeds the value of its commodity imports. A country has a **trade deficit** if the value of its commodity imports exceeds the value of its commodity exports.

The level of trade deficit is set by national income changes and the associated changes in AD. A higher level of AD means that people will consume more, pay more in taxes, and spend more on imported goods. A higher level of AD tends to raise imports relative to a given level of exports and so creates a trade deficit. Net capital inflows are essential in financing the U.S. trade deficit.

The current account balance includes all transactions in commodities, together with all transactions in services such as transportation, tourism, royalties and license fees, film rentals, investment income, private remittances such as Social Security payments, and various gifts such as religious charities, UNICEF, and foreign aid. The current account thus tracks income and expenditures from exports, imports, and unilateral transfers.

The characteristic of all international transactions that are *not* included in the current account balance is that they involve transactions in assets or securities with nonresidents, ranging from equities and direct investment to non-interest bearing demand deposits. The capital account records international investment and borrowing, including transactions in monetary gold, government securities, and bonds.

Net BOP is therefore equal to the current account balance plus the capital account balance, or zero. A surplus on the current account generally means that there is a deficit of the same arithmetic value on the capital account. A special account called the **statistical discrepancy** or **reserve account** is used to ensure that the two sides of the BOP actually do balance.

FOREIGN EXCHANGE MARKET

The **exchange rate** is simply the price of a domestic currency in terms of a foreign currency. Like any other price, it is determined by supply (of foreign exchange) and demand (in the foreign exchange market).

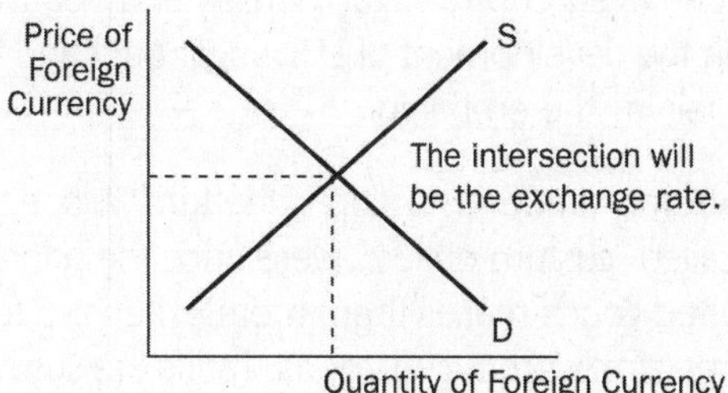

The **demand for dollars** is created by foreign demand for U.S. exports, foreign demand for U.S. investments, and speculation. Some foreign investors also buy U.S. dollars for speculative purposes. When the Russian ruble collapsed, for example, American tourists could get substantial discounts from Russian vendors and restaurants by offering to pay in U.S. dollars. Russians feared that the value of the ruble would drop further and they preferred to hold U.S. dollars as a more stable store of value.

The **supply of dollars** arises from similar sources. On the supply side, it is Americans who are initiating the exchanges. If you take a trip to Mexico, you will need to buy Mexican pesos. When you do, you will be offering to buy pesos by selling dollars. Thus the demand for a foreign currency results in a supply of U.S. dollars. The supply of dollars comes from American demand for imports, American investments in foreign countries, and speculation.

Demand and supply work together to determine the equilibrium price, i.e., the exchange rate. The exchange rate often determines how willing two countries are to trade with one another. When this rate is determined by the market, it is understood to have been freely determined. Such a rate is flexible and largely outside the control of government. **Fixed exchange** rates can be set and maintained by government actions, but this requires continuous fine-tuning by central banks. Monetary officials often must sell foreign exchange to keep the fixed rate in place, increasing their risk of running out of foreign exchange reserves.

When the price of the U.S. dollar falls relative to another currency, we say that the dollar has **depreciated**. When the price of the U.S. dollar rises relative to another currency, we say that the dollar has **appreciated**. Import-competing industries suffer when currency depreciations make imports cheaper. They want to be protected from "unfair" competition. In 1999, the Clinton administration faced mounting anger from Congress and the steel industry over the flood of cheap steel imports.

Although imports typically mean fewer jobs and less income for some domestic industries, exports represent increased jobs and income for other countries. Producers and workers in export industries gain from trade. Thus there are at least some clear winners and losers in international trade. Trade alters the mix of output, but it also redistributes income from import-competing industries to export industries. This potential redistribution is a source of political and economic friction.

TRADE RESTRICTIONS

A sure-fire way to restrict trade is simply to eliminate it. To do so, a country needs to impose an embargo on exports or imports or both. An **embargo** is a prohibition against trading particular goods. The U.S. has maintained an embargo on Cuban goods since 1959, when Fidel Castro took power there. This embargo severely damaged Cuba's sugar industry and deprived American smokers of Havana cigars. It also helped in the development of U.S. sugar beet and tobacco farmers, who now have a vested interest in maintaining the embargo.

A more common—and less extreme—trade restriction is the **tariff**, a special tax imposed on imported goods. Tariffs, also called "custom duties," were once the principal source of revenue for governments. A tariff on imported goods makes them more expensive to domestic consumers, and thus less competitive with domestically produced goods. Tariffs are sometimes invoked to correct for "dumping," which occurs when a firm sells goods for less abroad than it does in its home market. The motives for dumping are diverse, including price discrimination and foreign price subsidies. Critics of this approach argue that tariffs should not be used to prevent consumers from buying goods at the lowest possible prices. Tariffs reduce imports by raising the prices at which imports are sold. **Import quotas** reduce imports by restricting the quantity of a particular good that can be imported. Quotas are a greater threat to competition than tariffs because quotas preclude additional imports at any price.

Imports represent a leakage from the domestic circular flow and a potential loss of jobs at home. From this perspective, curtailing imports looks like an easy solution to the problem of domestic unemployment—just get people to "buy American" and domestic output and employment will expand. Congressman Willis Hawley used this argument to persuade Congress to pass the Smoot-Hawley Tariff Act of 1930, which raised tariffs to about 60% and cut off most imports. Other countries responded by erecting their own trade barriers and cutting off our exports. World trade fell from $60 billion in 1928 to $25 billion in 1938. This trade contraction increased the severity of the Great Depression.

IF YOU LEARNED ONLY FOUR THINGS IN THIS CHAPTER. . .

1. A country has a trade surplus if the value of its commodity exports exceeds the value of its commodity imports; a country has a trade deficit if the value of its commodity imports exceeds the value of its commodity exports.
2. When the price of the U.S. dollar falls relative to another currency, we say that the dollar has depreciated; when the price of the U.S. dollar rises relative to another currency, we say that the dollar has appreciated.
3. An embargo is the restriction of exports destined for sale in another country.
4. A tariff is a tax on imports.

REVIEW QUESTIONS

1. According to the theory of comparative advantage, a country

   (A) imports the goods in which it has a comparative advantage
   (B) exports the goods in which it has a comparative advantage
   (C) exports goods in which it has an absolute advantage
   (D) imports goods in which it has an absolute advantage
   (E) imposes trade restrictions if it does not have a comparative advantage

2. Country X has a comparative advantage over Country Y in the production of Good F, which implies that

   (A) Country X can produce Good F at a lower opportunity cost than Country Y
   (B) Country Y can produce Good F at a lower opportunity cost than Country X
   (C) both countries have the same opportunity costs of production
   (D) Country X has an unfair advantage over Country Y
   (E) Country Y has an absolute advantage in the production of Good F

3. A tariff is

   (A) a limit on the quantity of a good that can be imported into a country
   (B) a tax on imported goods
   (C) a government payment to domestic firms that aims at encouraging exports
   (D) the difference between the price a product sells for in the country in which it is produced and the price at which it is sold in another country
   (E) a trade imbalance created when countries sell large numbers of products on the world market

4. It costs a computer manufacturer $1,000 to produce a personal computer. This manufacturer sells these computers abroad for $750. This is an example of

   (A) a negative tariff
   (B) an export subsidy
   (C) dumping
   (D) a trade-related economy of scale
   (E) a quota

5. The price of one country's currency in terms of another country's currency is the

   (A) balance of trade
   (B) exchange rate
   (C) balance of payments
   (D) currency appreciation
   (E) trade deficit

6. When one currency increases in value relative to another, economists say that the currency that increased in value has

   (A) depreciated
   (B) appreciated
   (C) expanded
   (D) floated
   (E) fixed

7. Which of the following increases the price of the dollar relative to the Mexican peso?

   (A) An increase in the supply of dollars
   (B) An decrease in Mexican demand for American imports
   (C) An increase in the demand for dollars
   (D) A decrease in the supply of pesos
   (E) An increase in American demand for Mexican imports

8. The balance of payments is calculated as the sum of the

   (A) current account and the trade account
   (B) current account and the capital account
   (C) trade account and the capital account
   (D) trade account and the reserve account
   (E) current account and the reserve account

9. Exchange rates that are determined by the unregulated forces of supply and demand are

   (A) fixed exchange rates
   (B) pegged exchange rates
   (C) managed exchange rates
   (D) trade exchange rates
   (E) floating exchange rates

10. If the dollar appreciates relative to the yen, then

    (A) U.S. goods sold in Japan would become more expensive
    (B) U.S. goods sold in Japan would become cheaper
    (C) U.S. goods sold domestically would become cheaper
    (D) Japanese goods sold domestically would become more expensive
    (E) there would be no change in the price of U.S. or Japanese goods

FREE-RESPONSE QUESTION

Assume that interest rates in the United States are currently higher than interest rates in the European Union. Explain how this situation affects:

(a) The international value of the dollar

(b) The international value of the euro

(c) U.S. exports to the member countries of the European Union

(d) European Union exports to the United States

ANSWERS AND EXPLANATIONS

1. B

The theory of comparative advantage argues that each country should specialize in producing the good(s) in which it has a comparative advantage and then trade these goods with other nations. So a country produces and exports those products in which it has a comparative advantage and imports those which other countries are better able to produce. Because a country can produce the products in which it has a comparative advantage more cheaply, comparative advantage implies lower opportunity costs of production. It makes sense to trade these products for those which could only be produced at a higher opportunity cost.

2. A

Comparative advantage implies lower opportunity costs of production (A). If Country X has a comparative advantage in the production of Good F, then it can produce it at a lower opportunity cost than Country Y. There is nothing inherently unfair about comparative advantage; it often arises simply from different distributions of resources and skills. The presence of comparative advantage does not directly entail anything about whether Country X or Country Y has an absolute advantage over the other.

3. B

Trade barriers take many forms. The three most common are tariffs, export subsidies, and quotas. All are forms of protection, shielding some sector of the economy from foreign competition. A tariff is a special tax imposed on imported goods (B).

4. C

Selling below cost in another country is called dumping (C). Here the cost of production is $1,000, while the product is being sold for $750, i.e., $250 below cost. A tariff (A) is a tax on imported goods; a tariff might be imposed in response to dumping, but it is not directly connected to selling goods below cost. Again, export subsidies and other subsidies (B) might enable producers to dump goods in foreign markets, but these subsidies are not explicitly a matter of selling goods more cheaply in foreign markets. Economies of scale (D) will never take costs below the cost of production. Finally, a quota (E) is a restriction on imports and is not directly connected to the price of imported goods; it is more likely to be a reaction to dumping.

5. B

The exchange rate (B) is the ratio at which two currencies are traded for one another, or the price of one country's currency in terms of another country's currency. The direction of trade between any two countries depends heavily on exchange rates. If, for example, the Japanese yen were very expensive (making the dollar cheap), both Japanese and American consumers would buy from U.S. producers. If the yen were very low (making the dollar high and comparatively costly), Japanese and American consumers would both buy from Japanese producers. The balance of trade (A) is a matter of a country's exports (credits) as considered against its imports (debits); this is a separate matter from the exchange rate. A country's balance of payments (C) is equal to its current account balance (income and expenditures from exports, imports, and unilateral transfers) plus its capital account balance (international investment and borrowing, including transactions in monetary gold, government securities, and bonds). Currency appreciation (D) and trade deficits (E) are not directly connected to the exchange rate.

6. B

When the price of the U.S. dollar rises relative to another currency, economists say that the dollar has appreciated (B). *Depreciation* (A) describes what happens when the value of the U.S. dollar decreases relative to another currency.

7. C

The equilibrium exchange rate occurs at the point at which the quantity demanded of a foreign currency equals the quantity supplied. An increase in the demand for dollars will increase the price of the dollar by shifting the demand curve to the right and creating a shortage, or excess demand, for the dollar at the given price. An excess supply of dollars (A) will cause the price of dollars to fall and the peso will appreciate relative to the dollar. A decrease in Mexican demand for American imports (B) translates into a decreased demand for dollars, which will have the same result. A decrease in the supply of pesos (D) will increase their price, with the same result. An increase in American demand for Mexican imports (E) translates into an increase in the supply of dollars, which will lower the dollar's price.

8. B

The balance of payments (BOP) consists of the capital and current accounts. The BOP records a country's transactions in goods, services, and assets with the rest of the world. It also serves as a record of the country's sources (supply) of foreign exchange and its demand for such exchange. The difference between a country's exports and its imports is its balance of trade. The balance on the current account is the total of a country's net exports of goods, net exports of services, net investment income, and net transfer payments. The balance on the capital account (in the U.S.) consists of the sum (measured in a given period) of the change in private U.S. assets abroad, plus the change in foreign private assets in the U.S., plus the change in U.S. government assets abroad, plus the change in foreign government assets in the U.S.

9. E

Floating exchange rates are determined in the foreign exchange market by the forces of supply and demand. Fixed (A), or pegged (B), rates are set by government intervention and policy. In 1971, the U.S. and most other countries abandoned the fixed exchange rate system in favor of floating or market-determined exchange rates. While governments still intervene to ensure that exchange rate movements are "orderly," exchange rates in most nations are largely determined by the unregulated forces of supply and demand.

10. A

To buy U.S.-made goods, Japan needs U.S. dollars just like the U.S. needs Japanese yen to buy Japanese goods. If the dollar appreciates against the yen, the same number of yen would buy fewer dollars. Japan would need more yen to buy the same amount of U.S. goods and U.S. exports to Japan would become more expensive as a result. For U.S. goods to become cheaper in Japan (B), the yen would need to appreciate relative to the dollar. Changes in the exchange rate affect the prices of domestic goods only to the extent that those goods use significant quantities of imported resources.

FREE-RESPONSE QUESTION

(a) The value of the dollar will appreciate because capital will flow into the U.S. as people seek to earn the higher interest rate returns. Individuals in the European Union who want to invest in the U.S. will demand dollars and supply euros to the foreign exchange market.

(b) The value of the euro will depreciate because funds will flow out of the member countries in search of better returns on their investments. The people in the European Union who want to invest in the U.S. will demand dollars and supply euros to the foreign exchange market.

(c) Exports from the U.S. will become more expensive; a depreciated euro means that citizens in the member countries will have to give up more euros to get a dollar for an export good. Exports from the U.S. will decline.

(d) Exports from the European Union are really U.S. imports. We must give up fewer dollars to obtain euros to buy their goods. Exports coming from the European Union will increase; U.S. imports will rise.

| PART FOUR |

AP Microeconomics Review

HOW TO USE THE MICROECONOMICS REVIEW SECTION

In the following chapters, we will look at microeconomics—the factors that concern individual players in an economy. These topics include scarcity, choice, opportunity cost, economic systems, property rights, supply and demand, consumer choice, firm behavior and market structure, labor markets, public policy, and income distribution.

Step 1: Review the concepts.

Each of the following review chapters begins by going over the main concepts that apply to the chapter's topic. The chapters will NOT include loads of factual material, but instead will help you tie all the facts together to understand the concepts and discuss briefly how they fit within the thematic emphases designed by the College Board.

Step 2: Answer the review questions.

In the review chapters you will be given sample questions that will help you learn and review the AP economics course material. Questions from both sections of the AP Microeconomics exam, multiple-choice and free-response, are included in each review chapter. The quantity and type of multiple-choice and free-response questions in the review chapters do not represent the exact material on the AP Microeconomics exam, but they are plausible examples of topics covered.

Step 3: Review the answer explanations.

Following these questions are detailed answer explanations that explain how these questions address the course concepts. You will be given the correct answer for each question and be informed of the thought processes you should go through to reach a correct answer. Sometimes you will be given examples of how you might have reached the incorrect answer and how to avoid that problem in the future. Again, the emphasis is not just on repetition, but on effective repetition. It's not only about learning information, but how to apply it to the task at hand—scoring well on the exam.

Chapter 10: **Basic Economic Concepts**

- Scarcity, Choice, and Opportunity Cost
- Production Possibilities Curve
- Comparative Advantage, Specialization, and Trade
- Economic Systems
- Property Rights and Incentives
- Marginal Analysis
- Review Questions
- Answers and Explanations

SCARCITY, CHOICE, AND OPPORTUNITY COST

Economics is the study of efficiency; economists deal with the problem of **scarcity**. Scarcity requires that people and companies make **choices**. To get one thing, we often must give up another. The cost of what we sacrifice because of the need to choose is our **opportunity cost**.

PRODUCTION POSSIBILITIES CURVE

A production possibilities curve (PPC) shows the various combinations of goods that a society can have given its current level of resources, technology, and trade. For example, if an economy produced only two goods, such as wheat and oranges, its production possibilities curve would look like this:

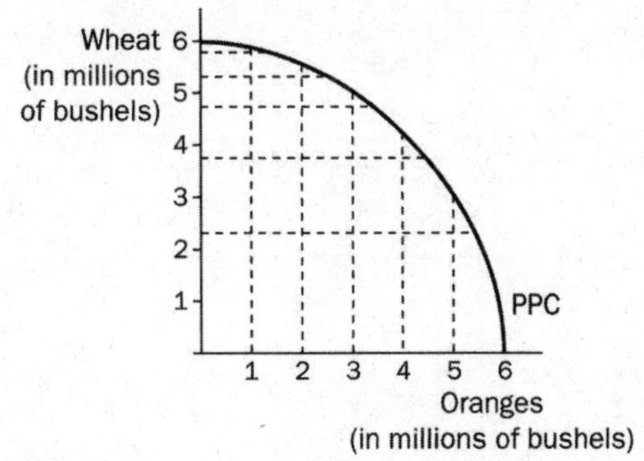

The PPC provides the model of opportunity cost and is bowed outward because in most economies, such as that of the United States, resources are not perfectly interchangeable. Notice in the graph above that as orange production increases, the cost of an additional unit of oranges increases in terms of the wheat given up—recall the definition of opportunity cost.

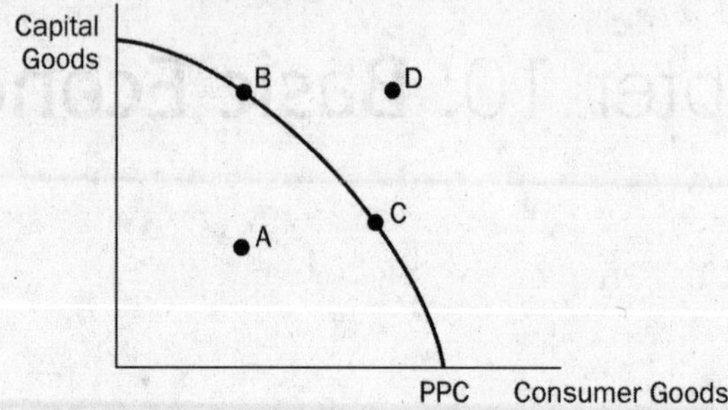

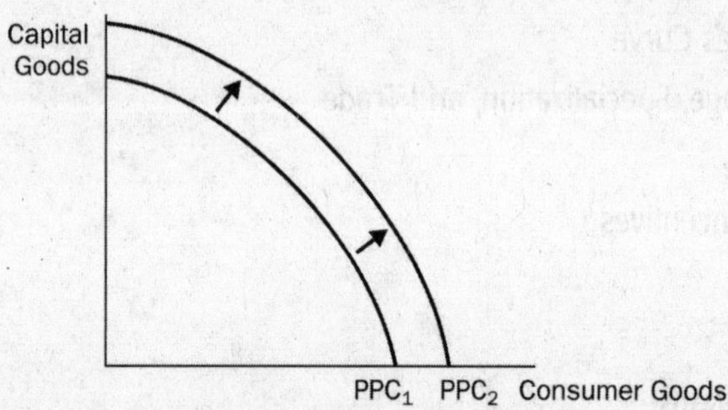

A PPC can be used to illustrate the vast number of choices available to an economy by grouping goods as either capital goods or consumer goods. Capital goods are manufactured goods that are used to produce other goods. At the current level of resources, technology, and trade, any production choice that fits on the production possibilities curve, such as those represented by points B and C, is a viable option for the society. If the society's production choice is represented by a point *inside* the curve, such as point A, then production is inefficient. Resources are not being used as effectively they could be; production of some good or goods could be increased without decreasing the production of anything else. Points *outside* the curve, such as point D, represent production choices that are unattainable. To reach points outside the curve, the society must discover new resources, invent new technology, or engage in more trade. Graphically, any of these three events would shift the curve outward.

COMPARATIVE ADVANTAGE, SPECIALIZATION, AND TRADE

Trade is one mechanism by which we can attain the goods and services we desire; people have been engaging in trade for thousands of years. **Comparative advantage** is the principle that focuses on the cost of producing an item in terms of its opportunity cost.

Suppose that two men, Preston and Daryl, are stranded on a desert island. Together, they make up an economy and have to meet their needs with scarce resources. Assume they face two tasks: collecting coconuts for food and finding logs to build shelter. If Preston works on one of these two tasks all day, he can collect 15 coconuts or he can collect 10 logs. If Daryl works on one task all day, he can collect 12 coconuts or 6 logs.

Preston has the **absolute advantage** in both items, because he can collect more logs or coconuts than Daryl can. That means that at a cost of one day spent working, Preston can obtain more of either item. However, opportunity costs differ between the two men. Because Preston can get either 15 coconuts or 10 logs in one day, he must give up 15 coconuts to get 10 logs, and vice versa. In other words, his opportunity cost for 10 logs is 15 coconuts. We can represent this as: $1 \text{ L} = 1\frac{1}{2} \text{ C}$ and $1 \text{ C} = \frac{2}{3} \text{ L}$. Daryl can get either 12 coconuts or 6 logs in a day, so his opportunity cost is expressed as: $1 \text{ C} = \frac{1}{2} \text{ L}$ or $1 \text{ L} = 2\text{C}$.

Daryl has a comparative advantage in coconuts, because one coconut only costs him one-half of a log whereas one coconut costs Preston two-thirds of a log. That is to say, the opportunity cost of producing a coconut is lower for Daryl than it is for Preston. Preston has a comparative advantage in logs, because one log costs him one and a half coconuts while one log costs Daryl two coconuts. Each man has a comparative advantage in one item, which means he can produce that item at a lower opportunity cost than the other man can. Therefore, they have a basis for trade.

If they trade at a rate of $1\text{C} = \frac{7}{12} \text{ L}$, Daryl will receive $\frac{7}{12}$ of a log by giving up one coconut. This is more than the one-half of a log he could get on his own by giving up one coconut. Preston will only have to give up $\frac{7}{12}$ of a log to get a coconut, whereas on his own he would have to give up $\frac{8}{12}$ or $\frac{2}{3}$ of a log. If they trade with each other, both parties will have more of both goods. This is because both men will be **specializing** in what they do best, and each is doing so at the least opportunity cost. All of the trade in the world takes place because of differing opportunity costs—that is, because of differing comparative advantages.

ECONOMIC SYSTEMS

All societies must deal with the problem of scarcity. They must make choices about resource allocation because their resources are limited, and they must strive to use their resources as efficiently as possible. In doing so, societies must answer three basic economic questions:

1. What should be produced?
2. How should it be produced?
3. For whom should it be produced?

Different economic systems have different ways of answering these questions. There are three types of economic systems: traditional, command, and market.

Traditional economies are still found in places in South America, Asia, and Africa. In a traditional economy, the economic roles that people fill are the same roles that their ancestors filled. Usually organized at the village level, traditional people plant and harvest the same land their parents and grandparents did and most products are produced as they were in the past. The people follow their traditions to answer the three economic questions.

In a command economy the government is the primary decision-maker. The government designs a central plan to determine what is to be produced, how to allocate resources to produce it, and how (and to whom) the product is to be sold. This means that individual citizens cannot simply choose to open their own private businesses. To a large extent, therefore, the government in a command economy determines how resources are used.

In a market economy the three basic economic questions are answered largely by buyers' and sellers' decisions in the marketplace. Profit acts as the incentive for production. As consumers make product purchases, they are "voting" in the marketplace and helping sellers to make decisions about products to produce for people who are willing and able to pay for them. Resources flow to those industries producing profitable products.

Economic systems also differ with respect to ownership of the means of production—i.e., the physical, non-human resources used in production. These include natural resources, farms, factories, mines, and machinery. In a command economy, the government owns and operates most of the means of production. In a market economy, private citizens and businesses own most of these means.

No country is purely a market economy or a command economy, largely because each system has serious flaws in its pure form. Contemporary economic systems are increasingly a mix of market and command systems. Even though the United States relies heavily on markets to make economic decisions, the government still owns many schools and colleges, as well as the postal service, the military, some bus and train systems, some electric plants, and many housing projects. Government welfare and retirement programs such as Social Security ensure that even citizens with few or no resources to sell get a share of the products produced. In China, which is mainly a command economy, the government is starting to allow more private businesses to operate and to permit markets to make more economic decisions. Other economies, such as Sweden's and Denmark's, have different mixes of market and government control.

PROPERTY RIGHTS AND INCENTIVES

One of the problems in a command economy arises from the fact that no one person owns the resources used in production. Because this is true, people have less of a motive to use them as efficiently as possible. Private ownership of these resources provides a self-interested motive to use them wisely—that is, because the resource owner will gain if the resources are used well, she has an incentive to make sure that they are so used. In a market economy, then, the protection of property rights is essential because people respond to these incentives. They weigh the costs and benefits of possible actions and take the actions that offer the greatest benefits for the least cost.

In addition, many people would argue that property rights must be protected to encourage people to use their property in certain ways—in particular, to risk it by opening and funding businesses. People do this because they believe they can gain more for themselves. If property rights are protected, the acquisition of property, or wealth, will be the benefit against which they weigh the risk of losing their property. Secure property rights are thus an important part of the incentive to take risk, and risk-taking is vital to success in a market economy. A market economy therefore requires a legal system that can protect property rights. In addition to the ownership of assets, the American legal system also grants patents and copyrights to reward research and creativity.

MARGINAL ANALYSIS

Most decisions about economic life are made in small increments. Should a restaurant add another dessert to its menu? Should you study one more hour or go to bed? Economic choices—choices about how to allocate resources—are usually about small adjustments, not dramatic shifts. Economists use the term **marginal analysis** to refer to decisions about small, incremental changes to an existing course of action. People make these changes when they expect to benefit from them, and marginal analyses weigh and balance the benefits and costs of alternatives. Microeconomics uses marginal thinking as a primary tool of analysis.

IF YOU LEARNED ONLY THREE THINGS IN THIS CHAPTER. . .

1. Production possibilities curves (PPCs) show the various combinations of goods that a society can have given its current level of resources, technology, and trade.

2. Comparative advantage is the principle that focuses on the cost of producing an item in terms of its opportunity cost; absolute advantage is the ability to produce more goods using fewer resources than another producer.

3. Marginal analysis is a basic technique that analyzes small, incremental changes in key variables.

REVIEW QUESTIONS

1. Which of the following will cause an inward shift of the production possibilities curve?
   (A) Increased funding for training workers and students
   (B) The discovery of a vital natural resource
   (C) An increase in the birth rate that eventually increases the labor force
   (D) The improvement of a society's technological knowledge
   (E) Emigration of skilled workers

2. The term "scarcity" is associated with
   (A) resources that are limited
   (B) a limited set of resources that must meet a limited set of wants and needs
   (C) a limited set of resources that must meet an unlimited set of wants and needs
   (D) rich countries sharing resources so that poor countries can meet some of their wants and needs
   (E) rich countries hoarding resources so they can satisfy all of their own wants and needs

3. A point inside the production possibility curve is
   (A) efficient
   (B) inefficient
   (C) attainable and efficient
   (D) unattainable
   (E) unattainable, but efficient

4. The opportunity cost of a new public library is thc
   (A) money cost of the construction to build the library
   (B) cost of building the library now rather than waiting and building the library in five years
   (C) created by the increase in traffic around the new library that results from the public's desire to use the new resource
   (D) other public goods that now cannot be provided to the community because of the resources used for the library
   (E) result of hiring of new workers to staff the library

5. The effects of specialization and international trade are likely to include all of the following EXCEPT

   (A) elimination of discrimination
   (B) availablity of a greater quantity of goods and services
   (C) moving beyond a nation's current production possibility curve
   (D) improvement in labor productivity
   (E) a more efficient use of resources

ANSWERS AND EXPLANATIONS

1. E

An inward shift of the production possibility curve will generally mean that resources are lost. In (E), the movement of skilled labor out of the country is a loss of labor resources. This will move the PPC inward. All the other choices given will cause an outward shift of the PPC because they all involve an increase in resources or an increase in productivity of the available resources.

2. C

Scarcity is the basic economic problem. Wants and needs are scarce in relation to the quantity of resources. Land, labor, capital and entrepreneurship constitute the factors of production. These are limited, while the wants and needs of society are deemed to be unlimited. Choice (B) mistakenly uses *limited* to describe resources as well as wants and needs. Choice (A) does not provide enough information; resources are scarce, but in relation to the wants and needs. Choices (D) and (E) are incorrect because a country will face scarcity problems regardless of whether it is rich or poor. In general, resources are limited while wants and needs are unlimited for everyone.

3. B

The production possibility curve (PPC) is a model for opportunity costs. The PPC shows the combinations of products that can be produced with the available resources. Outside the curve, we cannot produce—these points are unattainable. Choice (A) is wrong because being on the curve means resources are used efficiently in the allocation that society has set. Inefficiency exists inside the curve, as in (B). Choice (C) is incorrect because this point will not be an efficient use of resources. Choice (E) incorrectly matches efficient with unattainable. Choice (B) is correct.

4. D

Opportunity cost is defined in terms of what is given up when a choice is made. When a new public library is built, resources are allocated to its construction. This means that other public works must be foregone because resources are no longer available. Choice (A) is incorrect because it describes only an actual cost of the library, saying nothing about the cost of what is given up when the library is built. Choice (B) incorrectly uses the future cost of a library, which may have future consequences but says nothing about current opportunity cost. Choice (C) is a cost, but not the opportunity cost. Choice (E)is an addition to the cost of running the library, but not a cost in the sense of a lost opportunity.

5. A

Using the concept of comparative advantage, nations specialize in the production of goods in which they incur the least opportunity cost. All of the choices except (A) are likely results of that specialization. Citizens will have a greater selection of goods and services. Technology and productivity gains will provide the outward shift of the PPC. Only (A) is unlikely to happen as a direct result of specialization—discrimination is a social issue that society must solve by other means.

Chapter 11: **The Nature and Functions of Product Markets**

- **Supply and Demand**
- **Theory of Consumer Choice**
- **Firm Behavior and Market Structure**
- **Review Questions**
- **Answers and Explanations**

SUPPLY AND DEMAND

Two forces make market economies work: supply and demand. Buyers' decisions about the value of a product or service are reflected in demand curves, and sellers' decisions regarding costs are reflected in supply curves. The two forces interact to determine price, and price determines what goods will be produced and what resources will be allocated to producing them.

DEMAND

The quantity demanded of a good or service is the amount of the good that buyers are willing and able to buy at a certain price. Demand is thus created both by the resources buyers have available (e.g., the money they are *able* to spend) and buyers' interest in a product (i.e., their *willingness* to buy it). The law of demand states that, all other things being equal, demand for a good is inversely related to its price. Thus the quantity demanded will fall when the price of a good rises, and vice versa.

The law of demand does not reveal specifically what price will cause people to buy less of a good; this varies relative to the good and the character of people's demand for it. Following the law of demand, we can construct a demand schedule for any good because all goods are subject to this law. The increase in the amount of pizza that the consumer buys when the price falls is the result of two effects.

- The income effect
- The substitution effect

When slices of pizza are cheaper, the consumer's income has more purchasing power and the consumer can buy more slices of pizza. This is the income effect.

However, a decrease in the price of pizza also means that the consumer purchases more slices of pizza rather than spending income on something else. Other goods may now be comparatively more expensive, so the consumer is likely to buy less of those goods and more pizza. This is the substitution effect. The law of diminishing marginal utility is another reason why the law of demand makes sense. This law states that as a consumer buys more of a particular good or service, the marginal utility obtained from each additional unit of that good or service will diminish. All of these concepts explain the downward sloping character of a demand curve.

At any time or price, the market demand is the sum of the amount demanded by each individual who makes up the market. To derive a market demand curve, we would add all the individual demand curves for pizza; graphing this schedule would yield a curve that sloped downward and to the right.

A demand schedule for pizza and the associated demand curve might look like the following table and graph.

Price	Quantity Demanded (in Slices)
$ .50	5
$1.00	4
$1.50	3
$2.00	2
$2.50	1
$3.00	0

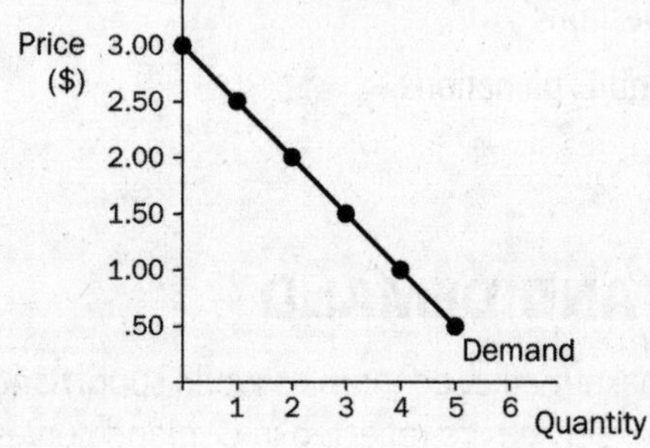

Supply

The supply of a good or service is the amount that sellers are willing and able to sell at a particular price. The law of supply states that, all other things being equal, the quantity supplied is directly related to a good's price. Thus, a rise in a good's price entails an increase in the quantity supplied of a good, and a drop in price entails a decrease in supply. It makes sense that sellers are willing to offer more for sale at high prices than at low prices.

Just as was true of demand, the market supply curve will be the sum of the individual supply curves. To derive a market supply curve, we would add the individual sellers' supply schedules and graph them.

Price	Quantity Supplied (in Slices)
$ .50	1
$1.00	2
$1.50	3
$2.00	4
$2.50	5
$3.00	6

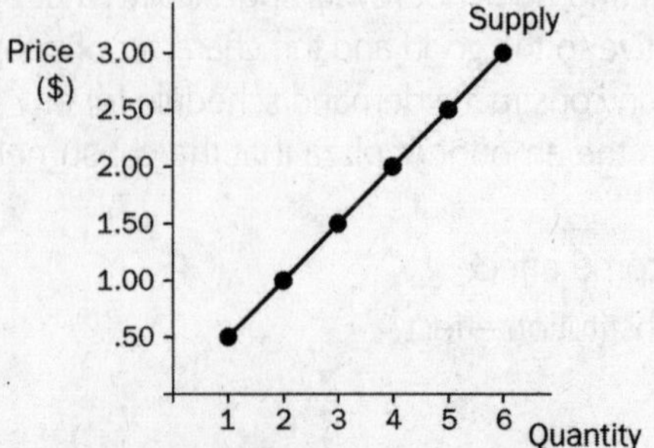

MARKET EQUILIBRIUM

If we compare the market schedules for supply and demand, we can see that there is one price at which the quantity supplied equals the quantity demanded. That price is $1.50, and the quantity demanded is three slices. Above a price of $1.50 per slice, the quantity supplied is greater than the quantity demanded; unsold pizza means wasted resources, so sellers will offer a lower price until they are able to sell all they have. Below the price of $1.50, buyers will not be able to obtain all they want, and they will bid the price up in an effort to obtain more. A buyer can convince a seller to give the pizza to her, rather than to a competing buyer, by offering to pay more. At the price of $1.50, everything offered for sale is purchased, so there is no pressure on the price to move in either direction. This is an **equilibrium price**, created by the independent desires and plans of buyers and sellers. The equilibrium price is also called the **market-clearing price**. Graphically, the equilibrium or market-clearing price occurs where the supply and demand curves intersect. Just as there is an equilibrium price, there is an **equilibrium quantity**, an amount of the good supplied that matches the amount demanded by consumers.

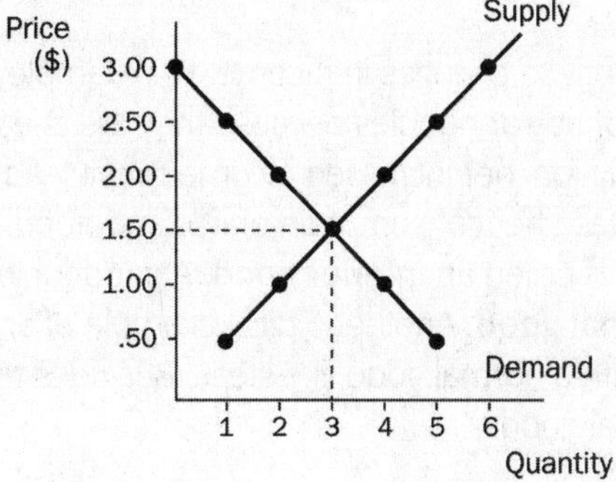

CHANGES IN QUANTITY DEMANDED

Considered together, the law of supply and the law of demand tell us that a change in a good's price will cause a change in the quantity demanded *and* the quantity supplied. This change is represented graphically as a movement along the existing curves; the graphs below show the effect of a price increase.

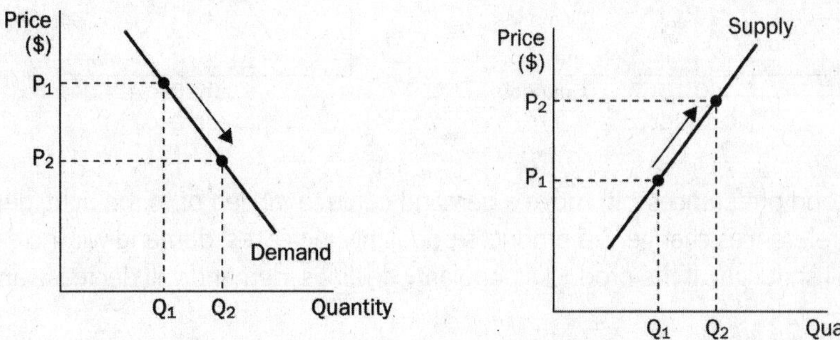

These kinds of changes simply move us along the existing demand and supply curves. So movements along the demand or supply curve are caused by price change only.

Changes in Demand

The demand curve can move to the left or the right of its current location. What causes the curve to change like this? Any factor that causes the quantity demanded or the quantity supplied at all prices to change will relocate the curve. These factors are called the non-price **determinants of demand.** An increase in demand shifts the entire relevant curve to the right, while a decrease shifts the curve to the left.

Determinants of demand include:

- Consumer incomes
- Consumer tastes and preferences
- Prices of related goods
- Number of consumers in the market
- Consumer expectations
- Consumer information

Different goods respond differently to changes in income. For example, a student living on a limited income might eat a lot of rice or noodles because they are cheap and filling. If that student graduates and gets a high-paying job, her increased income might lead her to buy more imported fruits and vegetables, and decrease her consumption of rice and noodles. A good for which there is *less* demand as income rises is called an **inferior good.** A good for which there is *more* demand as income rises is called a **normal good.** Another typical example of an inferior good might be hamburger, when compared with a normal good like steak. Bus rides tend to be inferior goods, whereas automobiles are normal goods.

Graphically, an increase in incomes would cause the following changes to curves for inferior and normal goods.

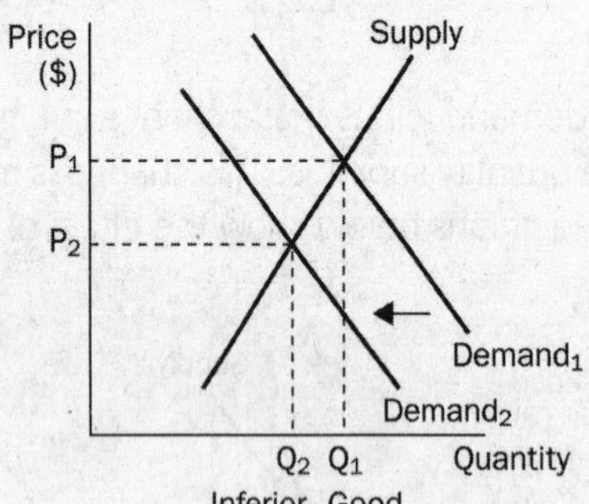

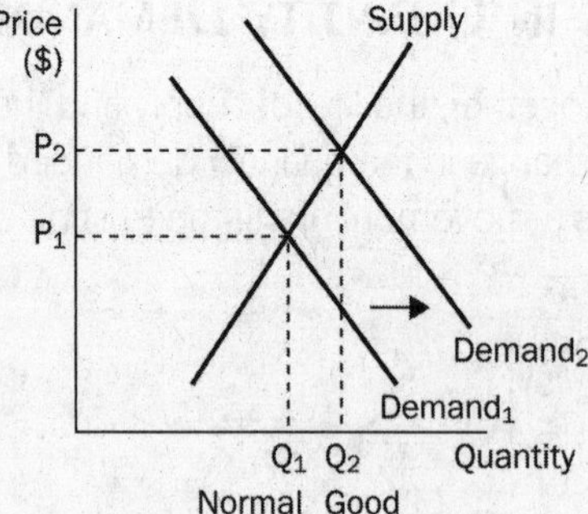

Consumer tastes and preferences can move a demand curve to the left or to the right, depending on how tastes and preferences change. If a product's popularity increases, demand will increase and the demand curve will shift right. If the product's popularity declines, demand will decrease and the curve will shift left.

Many goods are unrelated to each other. Most people's consumption of paper, for example, has nothing to do with their consumption of ice cream. However, some goods are **substitutes** for each other, such as peanut butter and tuna fish (which are both cheap sources of protein), or tea and coffee (which are both caffeinated beverages). Two goods are substitutes if an increase in one good's price increases demand for the other good, or if a decrease in one good's price decreases demand for the other good.

If the price of coffee rises, perhaps as a result of a decrease in supply, the law of demand states that the quantity demand for coffee will decrease. This would be represented graphically by a movement along the demand curve for coffee. However, many people would still want a caffeinated beverage in the morning, so many would switch to drinking tea. The demand for tea would increase, without any change in the price of tea. This is not a movement along the demand curve for tea; it is a rightward shift of the demand curve.

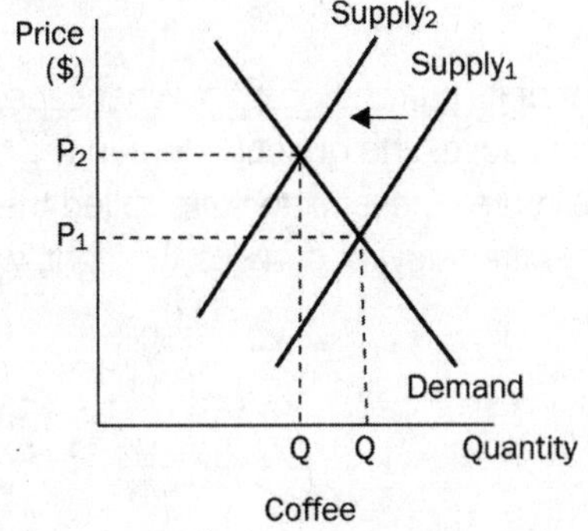

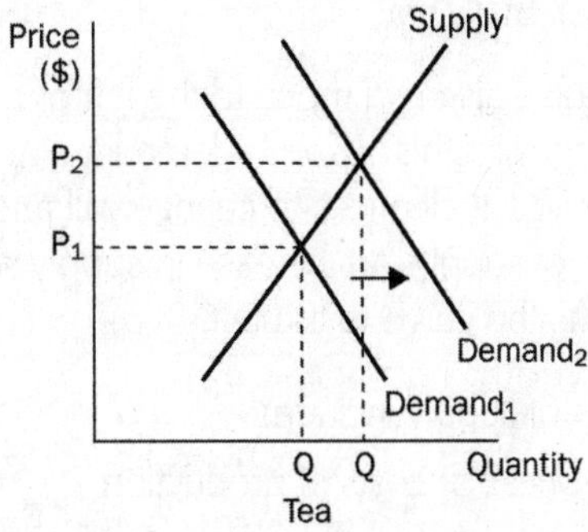

Other goods are what we call **complements**, meaning that they are used together. Examples include peanut butter and jelly, cars and gasoline, and computers and video games. Two goods are complements if a decrease in the price of one good *increases* demand for the other good.

Suppose the price of computers rises. We know that the quantity demand for computers will decrease as a result. Because fewer computers are being purchased, the number of video games purchased will also fall. This will happen without any change in the price of video games. In other words, there will be a decrease in demand for video games, which will shift the demand curve for video games to the left.

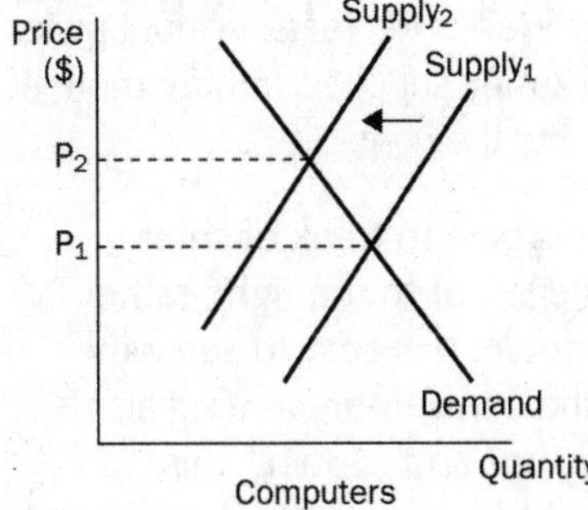

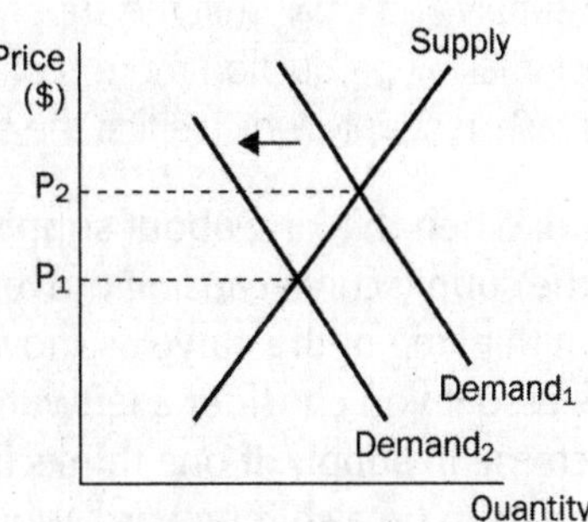

If the number of buyers in a market increases, demand will increase and the demand curve will shift to the right. If the number of buyers decreases, demand will decrease and the demand curve will shift left.

If consumers expect something to happen, their behavior in the marketplace can sometimes cause that event to occur. For example, if consumers expect the price of a good to rise, they will buy the good immediately to get the lower price. Since price has not yet changed, this change in consumer behavior causes an increase in demand. The increase in demand will in turn bring about the very thing that consumers expected: an increase in price. The reverse happens if consumers expect price to fall. In that case they will wait to buy, which will cause a decrease in demand. This decrease will cause price to fall.

If consumers find new information regarding a good or service, the demand for that product may increase or decrease. For example, if consumers hear a news report about a product that has harmful effects or the government announces a recall of a product, then consumers will decrease their demand for that good or service.

Changes in Supply

The supply curve also can move to the left or to the right of its current location. What causes the curve to change like this? As with demand, any factor that causes the quantity demanded or the quantity supplied at all prices to change will relocate the curve. These factors are called the non-price determinants of supply. An increase in supply shifts the entire relevant curve to the right, while a decrease shifts the curve to the left.

Determinants of supply include:

- Input prices or costs of production
- Technology
- Number of sellers in the market
- Supplier expectations
- Taxes and subsidies
- Changes in prices of goods using the same resources

The first determinant of supply is input prices. Inputs (sometimes called "relevant resources") are the resources used to produce a good. For example, bakers need flour, yeast, sugar, milk, eggs, and various other supplies to produce their goods. If the price of any of these resources rises, it will cost the baker more to make her baked goods and she will offer fewer of them at all prices. This is a decrease in supply and it will shift the supply curve to the left. A decrease in input prices has the opposite effect, making production more profitable and causing suppliers to offer more at all prices. This is an increase in supply, which shifts the supply curve to the right.

> **Note: When thinking about supply curves, it is best to think of shifts in the supply curve causing movement to the left or to the right, rather than thinking of the curve as moving up or down. It is easy to see why this is so if you consider a leftward shift of the curve, representing a decrease in supply. If one thinks in terms of "up" and "down," this appears to be a shift upward, which one might incorrectly think means a supply increase.**

Technology also has important effects on supply because many production processes involve some sort of technology. When technology improves or becomes more widely available, it becomes more profitable to produce the goods that rely upon that technology. This causes sellers to offer more at all prices, which is an increase in supply. If technology declines or is reduced, as it can be in the destruction caused by war or natural disasters, then supply would decrease and the supply curve would shift to the left. If the number of sellers rises, supply will rise. If the number of sellers decreases, it will decrease.

Suppliers' expectations influence what happens in the marketplace, though they do so in different ways than consumer expectations do. If suppliers expect price to rise, they will wait to send their goods to market. Because the price is as yet unchanged, this is a decrease in supply, which would in turn cause price to rise. If suppliers expect price to fall, they will rush their goods to market in hopes of getting the present high price. This increases supply, which would cause price to fall.

When a good is taxed, it becomes less profitable to produce and supply will decrease as a result. When a good is subsidized, it becomes more profitable and supply increases.

When prices change on goods or services that use the same resources, there may be a shift in production toward end products that use those resources in order to make a higher-priced good. For example, if the price of gasoline increases in the market, producers of other goods that use crude oil may shift their production and resources to the production of gasoline to increase their profits. This means that the supply of those other goods will decrease.

PRICE AND QUANTITY CONTROLS

Sometimes a country's government believes that the prices determined by the free market are too high or too low. In such cases, price controls are imposed to bring the price into line with what the government believes it should be. These controls are called **price ceilings** or **price floors.**

A price ceiling is set when the market price is deemed to be too high. An example of this is rent control legislation in New York City. Some apartments in New York are rented at prices that are much lower than what could be charged for the apartment if its rent were set by the market. Rent control legislation reflects price controls imposed during World War II to protect people from inflated prices created by a wartime housing shortage. A price ceiling causes a shortage, as shown on the following graph. Effective price ceilings are set below the equilibrium price and quantity.

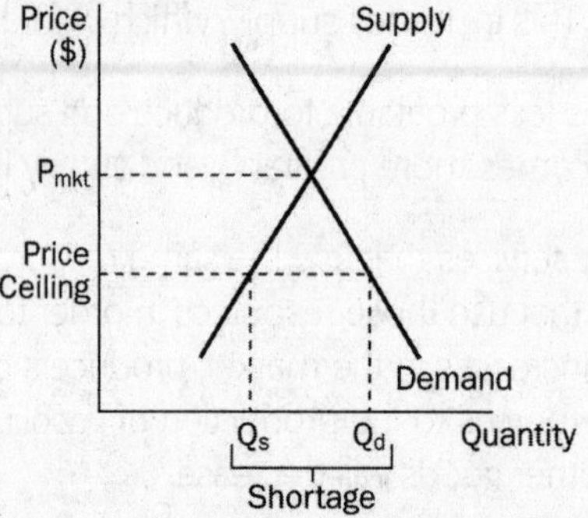

During this shortage, the market price system has been deprived of its **rationing function.** Before the price control was put in place, the market price served to balance the quantity supplied with the quantity demanded. Once these are out of balance, some other mechanism for rationing goods must be put in place. Waiting lists, lines, and cronyism are some of the rationing mechanisms that have been used to replace price.

When a market price is deemed to be too low, a price floor is set. An example of a price floor is the minimum wage. A price floor causes a surplus, as shown below. Effective price floors are set above the equilibrium price and quantity.

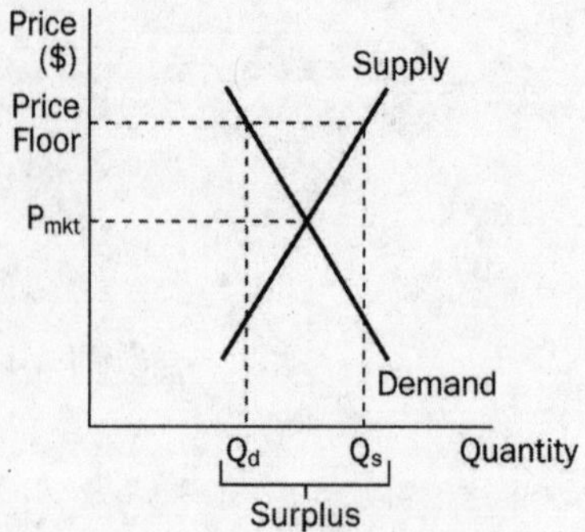

There is much debate about whether the minimum wage is beneficial or not. Studies have shown that the market for teenage labor is the most affected, with an approximate 10% rise in the minimum wage leading to a 1-3% increase in unemployment among teenagers.

ELASTICITY

The law of demand states that if price rises, the quantity demanded falls, and vice versa. However, we need another concept to tell us *how much* the quantity demanded changes. This concept is **price elasticity of demand,** and it measures how responsive demand is to changes in **price**.

Price elasticity of demand is defined by the equation

$$\text{Price elasticity of demand } (E_D) = \frac{\text{Percentage change in quantity demanded}}{\text{Percentage change in price}}$$

Because an increase in price creates a decrease in quantity demanded, this ratio between the changes will be negative. The quantity demanded and the good's price always move in opposite directions; we are interested in the *magnitude* of the changes, not in their direction. Therefore, we use absolute values for the amounts and represent P_E as a positive number. This result of this calculation reflects proportionate changes; it is not reported in units and does not depend on the unit in which price or quantity is expressed.

Thus if a 10% rise in the price of pizza leads to a 20% decrease in the quantity demanded, price elasticity of demand in this case would be calculated like so

$$P_E = \frac{20\%}{10\%} = 2$$

In this example, and for every other case in which the percentage change in demand is greater than the percentage change in price, price elasticity has an absolute value greater than 1. In these situations, demand is said to be **elastic**, or significantly responsive to a change in price.

If, on the other hand, a 10% rise in the price of, say, gasoline, only leads to a 5% decrease in quantity demanded, then

$$P_E = \frac{5\%}{10\%} = 0.5$$

In this example, and for every other case in which the percentage change in demand is *less* than the percentage change in price, price elasticity has an absolute value less than 1. In these situations, demand is said to be **inelastic**, or not very responsive to price changes.

If the absolute value of price elasticity of demand is equal to 1, then the percentage changes in price and demand are the same, which is called **unit elasticity**. When demand is unit elastic, any change in price will create a directly proportional change in demand.

For other kinds of elasticity, demand does not vary along a linear curve. If the absolute value of price elasticity of demand equals infinity, a good is said to be **perfectly elastic**. In this situation, the demand curve is a horizontal line that intersects with the market price. Buyers will buy all that a seller can produce at that price. Sellers in a perfectly competitive market face perfectly elastic demand curves; they can sell all they want at the going price but the quantity demanded will drop to zero at higher prices. Demand is hugely responsive to price change in this case.

Demand is **perfectly inelastic** when the absolute value of price elasticity of demand equals zero. In this case, the demand curve is a vertical line, indicating that demand is unresponsive to price; because demand is price insensitive, any price change will leave the quantity demanded unchanged.

The four factors that determine whether demand for a good is elastic or inelastic with respect to price are:

1. Whether close substitutes are available
2. Whether the good is a necessity or a luxury
3. How much of the consumer's budget is spent on the good
4. The time horizon in which the change is considered

If it is easy to switch to another similar good, consumers will do so in response to even a small price change. This means that the quantity demanded will be very responsive to price changes, or elastic. On the other hand, if there are no close substitutes, consumers will have little choice but to pay the higher price, and the quantity demanded will be unresponsive to price changes, or inelastic. Gasoline is one good that is inelastic with respect to price changes because few substitutes are available.

When a good is a necessity, consumers need the item and must purchase it even if the price rises, so necessities tend to be price inelastic. Luxury goods, however, allow consumers a wide range of choice; consumers tend to respond sharply to price changes in luxury goods. This means that the demand is elastic in response to price. Notice, however, that the judgment about whether a good is a necessity or a luxury varies from consumer to consumer, according to their preferences.

Elasticity to changes in price is also affected by the place of the good in a consumer's budget. When a good represents a large share of a consumer's budget, a price increase importantly reduces the amount of the good that a consumer is able to buy. The amount demanded will decrease significantly as a result. When the good represents a smaller share of the consumer's budget, the consumer's overall income and purchasing power are less effected by an increase in price. Therefore, demand is less price elastic in these cases.

The longer the time span involved, the more price elastic demand tends to be. For example, when the price of gasoline rises, people initially continue to buy close to the same amount because they are in the process of adjusting their habits. However, over time, people buy more fuel-efficient cars, cities develop more public transportation, and consumers modify the amount of driving they must do. As a result, demand becomes more elastic over time.

One important application for the concept of elasticity is its effect on total revenue. Total revenue from selling a product is equal to the price of the product times the quantity sold, or P x Q. Producers with an understanding of price elasticity can therefore predict the effect that a price change will have on total revenue.

A change in price affects both the amount that producers get for their good and the quantity demanded by consumers. These two effects tend to oppose each other. For example, an increase in price means that producers get more for each unit sold, which points toward an increase in total revenue. However, the law of demand tells us that a price increase entails a decrease in demand, which points toward a decrease in total revenue. The overall effect of a change in price depends on the extent to which these two effects balance each other.

If demand for a good is price *elastic*, then a price increase will lead to a decrease in total revenue. The percentage increase in price will be less than the percentage decrease in quantity demanded. If the price rises, total revenue will fall, because quantity demanded has, proportionately, the greatest influence on the outcome.

If demand for a good is price *inelastic*, then a price increase will lead to an increase in total revenue. The percentage change in price is greater than the percent change in quantity for an inelastic good. Total revenue will move with price, because price will have proportionately the greater influence; the decrease in demand (which is small) is offset by the increased price per unit.

The table below shows a summary of the relationship between elasticity and total revenue.

	Elastic $E_D > 1$	Inelastic $E_D < 1$	Unit Elastic $E_D = 1$
Price rises	TR falls	TR rises	TR is constant
Price falls	TR rises	TR falls	TR is constant

Elasticity and Income

It is also useful for producers to know how the demand for a good changes in response to changes in income. Income elasticity of demand ($Y_{E,}$ where Y stands for income) is the measure of this responsiveness, and it is given by the equation

$$Y_E = \frac{\text{Percentage change in quantity demanded}}{\text{Percentage change in income}}$$

Here we are interested in the direction of changes (not just their magnitude) and so do not use absolute values. For a normal good such as fresh vegetables, the change in quantity demanded will move in the same direction as the change in income: Either both will rise or both will fall. Therefore, the income elasticity of a normal good will always be positive. Income elasticities may vary widely even among normal goods, because some normal goods, such as clothing, are necessities, while others, such as steak, are luxuries. A normal good with an income elasticity of less than one is income inelastic, whereas an income elasticity of more than one indicates an income elastic normal good.

For an inferior good such as processed cheese, the change in quantity demanded will move in the opposite direction of the income change, and so the income elasticity will be negative.

Cross-price elasticity of demand measures how responsive the demand for one good is to changes in the price of another good. It is defined by the equation

$$XP_E = \frac{\text{Percentage change in quantity demanded of Good 1}}{\text{Percentage change in price of Good 2}}$$

Because producers often make many different kinds of goods, it is useful to know how changes to one good may affect the others. If two goods are substitutes, then the cross-price elasticity will have a positive value. The price of one will move in the same direction as the price of the other good: Either both will rise or both will fall. For example, an increase in the price of coffee will cause an increase in the demand for tea. Therefore, cross-price elasticity for substitutes will be positive.

In the case of complements, the price of one good and the quantity demanded of another move in opposite directions. If the price of peanut butter rises, consumers eat less peanut butter *and* less jelly, because jelly is a complement for peanut butter. Complements therefore have negative cross-price elasticities.

Price Elasticity of Supply

Price elasticity of supply measures how the quantity supplied responds to changes in price. As with demand, if the quantity supplied is very responsive, then the good is said to be supply **elastic**. If the quantity supplied is not very responsive, then the good is said to be supply **inelastic**. Price elasticity of supply is given by the equation

$$P_ES = \frac{\text{Percentage change in quantity supplied}}{\text{Percentage change in price}}$$

There are two determinants of price elasticity of supply:

1. Flexibility of sellers
2. Time horizon

A seller of beachfront land obviously has little flexibility in supply; there is only a limited amount of this land, so the supply of beachfront land will be inelastic. Sellers of many other goods are more flexible, because they can shift production in response to price changes. These sellers will have elastic supply.

Demand and supply both become more elastic over time, because a longer period of time gives both consumers and producers greater leeway to adjust their behavior. Supply is more elastic in the long run because a longer time period provides enough time for new factories to be built, new land to be cultivated, and new firms to enter an industry. Suppliers cannot usually whimsically change supply dramatically in a short period because they do not have the necessary resources. In six months, however, they can make large changes.

CONSUMER SURPLUS, PRODUCER SURPLUS, AND MARKET EFFICIENCY

Consumer surplus measures the benefit to buyers of participating in a particular market. It is closely related to the demand curve for the product. A market demand curve traces out the maximum prices that different consumers are willing to pay. Therefore, it traces out the value of that good to consumers. The difference between the maximum price a consumer is (or would be) willing to pay and the price she actually has to pay is that consumer's surplus. This is the "extra" value or utility a consumer gets when the good's market price is below what she would be willing to pay for the good.

Because a market demand curve represents an aggregate of values for all of the consumers in the market, consumer surplus is equal to the area under the demand curve and above price.

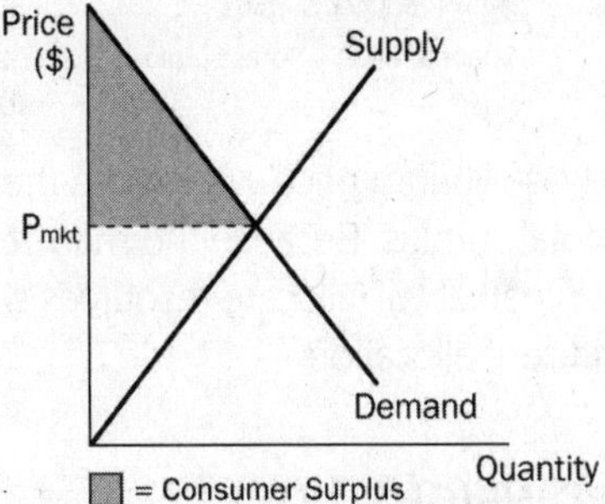

Producer surplus is linked to the supply curve. A market supply curve traces out the minimum prices that various producers are willing to accept for their products. Therefore, it traces out minimum costs. The difference between the price a producer actually gets for her product and the price she is willing to take is her **producer surplus**. Producer surplus for an entire market is the area above the supply curve and below price.

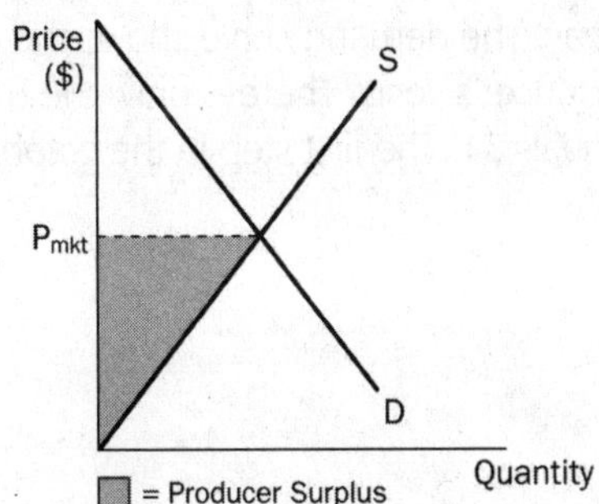

In a market, total surplus is the sum of consumer and producer surplus, as shown below.

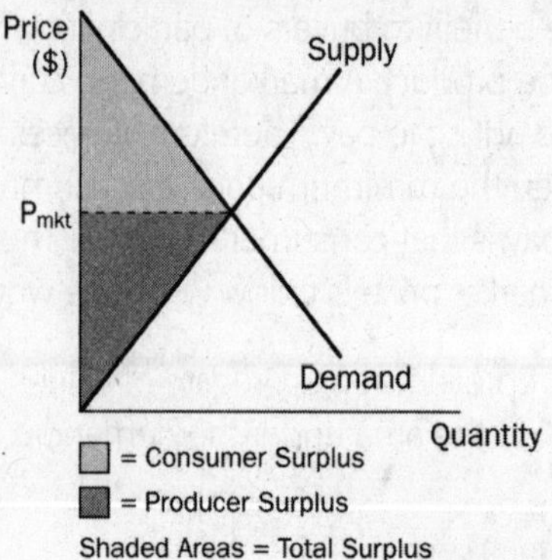

Any price differing from the market equilibrium price will reduce the area between the demand and supply curves, reflecting a drop in total surplus. Because the market will arrive at the equilibrium price if it is allowed to move freely, a free market will allocate resources so as to maximize surplus. In other words, free markets produce an efficient allocation.

TAX INCIDENCE AND DEADWEIGHT LOSS

When the government imposes a tax on a previously free market, it distorts resource allocation and reduces total surplus. To see how this happens, suppose the government imposes a tax of $1 per unit of a product. We can analyze the effects of the tax using a graph as a model.

If the tax must be paid, then the selling price of the product must be high enough to cover the producer's cost *and* the tax. The cost of the tax creates a difference of $1 between the price sellers receive and the price consumers pay. The demand curve shows the prices consumers are willing to pay; the supply curve shows producer's costs. There is only one quantity at which the distance between the two curves exactly equals $1. The first step in the graphical analysis is to find that quantity.

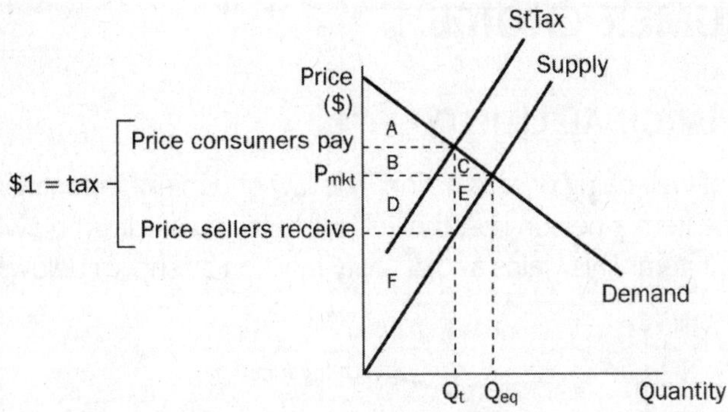

From that quantity, we look to the supply curve to find the price that sellers will receive. We look to the demand curve to find the price consumers will pay. We can now summarize the changes in surplus with the following table.

	Before Tax	After Tax
Consumer Surplus	ABC	A
Producer Surplus	DEF	F
Tax Revenue	0	BD
Deadweight Loss	0	CE

Once the tax is in place, there is another entity (the government) in the market receiving surplus. Area BD on the above graph represents the tax revenue that the government collects. Notice that the quantity exchanged in the market dropped from Q_{eq} to Q_t. The drop represents transactions that no longer take place due to the tax. Areas C and E represent the surplus lost due to this drop in transactions, which is called **deadweight loss** (or "efficiency loss") of the tax.

Where the burden of the tax falls depends on the relative elasticities of the supply and demand curves. In the graph above, demand is more elastic than supply, meaning that consumers can avoid the tax by not buying as much of the product. Therefore, suppliers will bear the greatest burden of the tax in this case. If supply were more elastic than demand, consumers would bear most of the tax.

THEORY OF CONSUMER CHOICE

Total Utility and Marginal Utility

Utility is a person's measure of well-being or satisfaction. The law of diminishing marginal utility states that the more of any one item a person has, the less utility (or satisfaction) he will get from obtaining one more unit of that item. This yields a total utility function as shown below.

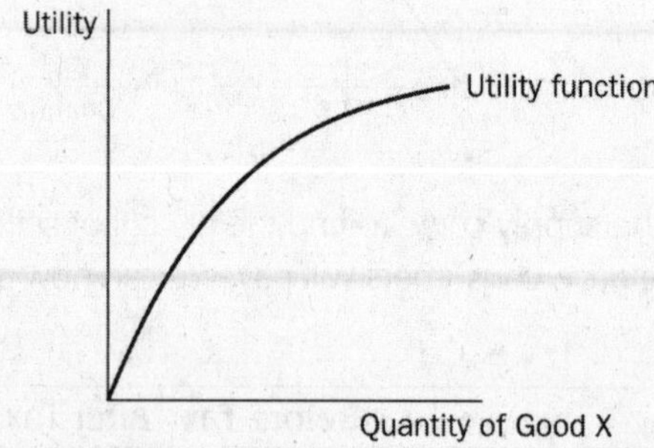

Notice that total utility rises, but at a decreasing rate. The slope of the function at any point is

$$\frac{\text{rise}}{\text{run}} = \frac{\text{the change in utility}}{\text{the change in quantity of Good X}}$$

If the change in quantity equals one, then the slope equals **marginal utility**, which is the change in utility from obtaining one more unit of the good. Marginal utility decreases as more units of Good X are acquired, which is indicated by the decreasing slope.

Utility Maximization: Equalizing Marginal Utility per Dollar

Economists assume that all consumption aims to maximize utility. To maximize utility when acquiring a combination of Goods X and Y, consumers should choose a combination such that the marginal utility from Good X equals the marginal utility from Good Y.

$$MU_X = MU_Y$$

As long as marginal utility from Good X is greater than the marginal utility from Good Y, the consumer can increase total utility by consuming more of Good X and less of Good Y. The reverse is true if the marginal utility of Good Y is greater than the marginal utility of Good X. Once the two marginal utilities are equal, consuming more of one good at the expense of the other will decrease total utility.

Consumers are, of course, subject to budget constraints. Taking account of price, the consumer should choose the combination of goods in which

$$\frac{MU_X}{P_X} = \frac{MU_Y}{P_Y}$$

The utility one receives from a good relative to its price determines how one should allocate one's income. As long as a consumer gets more utility per dollar spent on X than per dollar spent on Y, he should allocate his dollars to the purchase of X, and vice versa if he can get more utility per dollar spent on Y. Once a consumer has balanced marginal utility per dollar (given by the equation $\frac{MU}{P}$) spending more on one good at the expense of the other will reduce total utility.

PRODUCTION AND COSTS

Production Functions: Short-run and Long-run Production

The relationship between the quantity of inputs (resources) a firm uses and the output produced with them is called a **production function**. The **marginal product** of any input used in the production process is the increase in total output obtained from using one more unit of that resource. If fixed inputs are held constant, adding more of one input will initially increase output, but at some point it will increase at a decreasing rate, and will finally decrease. This property is called **diminishing marginal product**.

Think about baking cookies in the kitchen. One worker can produce only so many cookies. Adding a second worker will sharply increase output, because the two workers can then specialize. A third worker will increase output, but probably not by as much as the second worker did. If you continue adding workers, you will get less and less of an increase in production for each one. Eventually, there will be so many workers in the kitchen that they will bump into each other and slow each other down—additional workers will actually decrease output at this point because no one can work efficiently.

In the short run, at least one input (usually factory size or farm size) is constant and not changeable. These constant inputs are called **fixed inputs**. Inputs that can be changed, such as labor, are called **variable inputs**. Adding more variable inputs to a fixed input will eventually result in diminishing marginal product.

Graphically, a production function with an initial increase in marginal product followed by diminishing marginal product looks like the graph below.

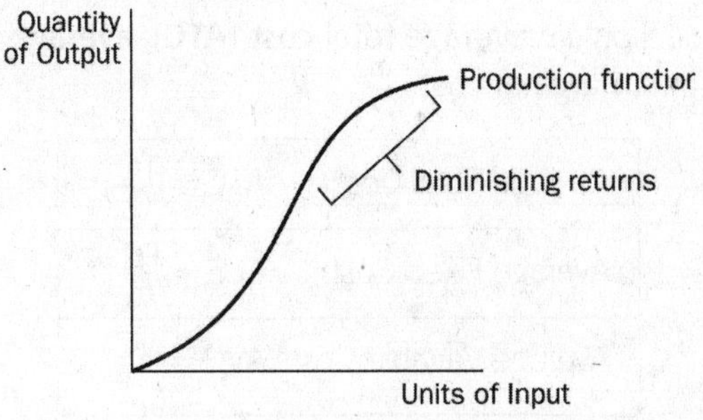

This is a short-run production function. There is no diminishing marginal product in the long run, because all inputs are variable. For example, the cookie bakers described above would have the time and resources to build a larger kitchen over the long run. A long-run production function will slope upward over large amounts of output. However, even a long-run production function will eventually slope downward, as very large businesses run into coordination problems.

Marginal Product and Diminishing Returns

Because marginal product decreases as more units of a variable resource are combined with a fixed resource, returns per unit of input decrease. The property of diminishing marginal product translates to the law of diminishing marginal returns, which states that as more units of an input are used, each additional unit will increase production by a lower amount than previous units. This law has significant impact on short-run production.

Short-Run Costs

In the short run, there are two types of costs: fixed and variable. **Fixed costs** are the costs of those inputs that cannot change in the short run; because these costs are inflexible in this way, they are independent of the amount of output. Costs such as rent on buildings and payments on machinery are fixed costs.

Variable costs are the costs of those inputs that vary with the amount of output produced. To produce ice cream, for example, variable costs would include wages, as well as the cost of raw materials.

As the marginal product gained from additional units of input eventually declines, the cost of output increases, first at a decreasing rate, and then at an increasing rate, as shown in the graph below. Notice that the total cost curve intersects the vertical axis at a positive value. This is the amount of fixed costs.

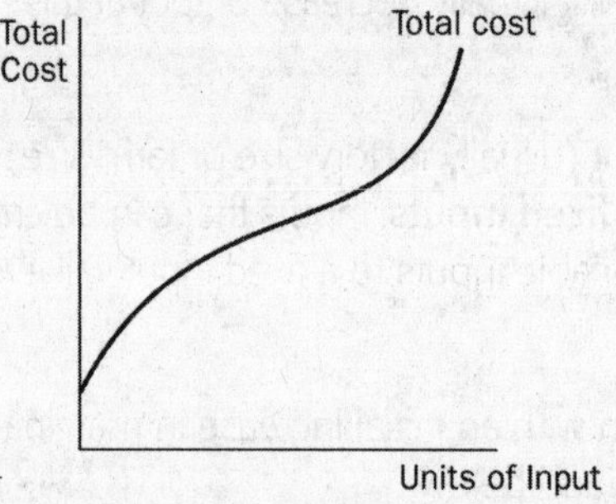

Other costs relevant to production are **average total cost (ATC)**, **average variable cost (AVC)**, **average fixed cost (AFC)**, and **marginal cost**.

Average Total Cost	$ATC = \frac{TC}{Q}$
Average Fixed Cost	$AFC = \frac{FC}{Q}$
Average Variable Cost	$AVC = \frac{VC}{Q}$

Marginal cost is the cost of producing one more unit of output. When marginal product falls, marginal cost rises. It is given by the equation

$$MC = \frac{\text{change in total cost}}{\text{change in output}}$$

These four costs can be represented by curves:

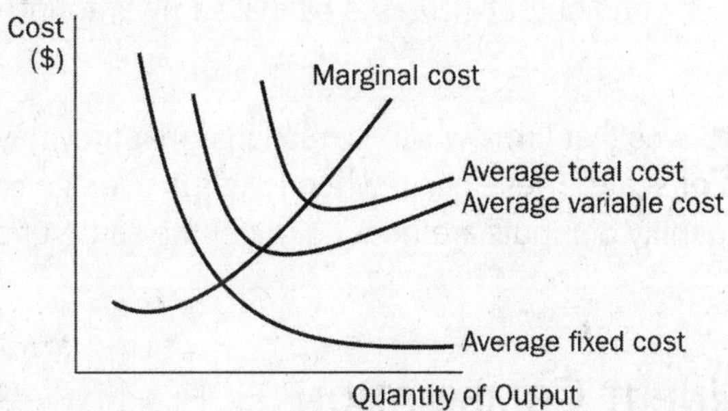

Notice that marginal cost intersects average variable cost and average total cost at their minimums. If a marginal value is less than an average value, it pulls the average down. If a marginal value is more than an average value, it pulls the average up. Also note that the average fixed cost curve approaches the horizontal axis. The average total cost and average variable cost curves are separated by the amount of average fixed cost, and therefore approach each other.

Long-Run Costs and Economies of Scale

The long-run average cost curve (LRAC) is based on the short-run average total cost curves (SRAC) that apply to different levels of fixed resources. If the fixed resource is a factory, the long-run average cost curve would look like this:

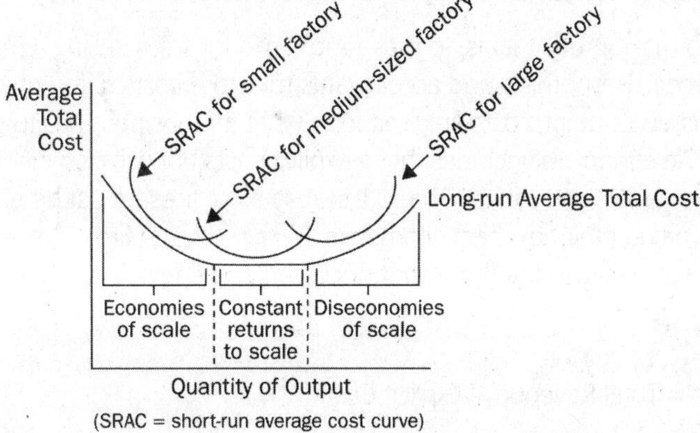

(SRAC = short-run average cost curve)

The LRAC shown above is created by connecting the points on the SRACs that mark the lowest per-unit cost for each rate of output. Notice that at first, long-run average total cost is falling. This is because as the factory is beginning to grow, the firm encounters **economies of scale**. These economies occur because increasing size allows for increasingly specialized equipment and increasingly specialized labor, both of which increase output beyond the level of the increased inputs. That is, economies of scale happen when inputs are increased by a factor of X and output increases by *more* than a factor of X.

Long-run average cost stabilizes relative to output in the range of **constant returns to scale**. When inputs increase by a factor of X and output increases by that same amount, we have constant returns to scale.

Finally, economic theory tells us that firms which get so large that they have coordination problems encounter **diseconomies of scale**. These occur when long-run average cost increases as output increases; an increased quantity of inputs are needed to get the same or smaller changes in level of output.

Cost-Minimizing Input Combination

Costs are minimized when the marginal products of all inputs are equal. Firms almost always operate at output levels at which marginal product is diminishing. Therefore, as long as the marginal product of one input is higher than others, it will benefit the firm to use more of that input and less of others. Once all marginal products are equal, costs will increase if the firm uses more of one input at the expense of others.

FIRM BEHAVIOR AND MARKET STRUCTURE

Profit

Accounting Profits, Normal Profits, and Economic Profits

A business's goal is to make profit, that is, to make more money from selling a product or service than it costs to produce it. Economists and accountants measure costs differently, so they measure profit differently. To an accountant, costs are limited to what the business has to pay out. These are called **explicit costs**. An economist includes these explicit costs but will also include the *opportunity* cost of resources, inventories, and capital. That is because all of these must be earning at least as much as they could earn in their next best alternative to stay with the firm. These opportunity costs are called **implicit costs**, because the firm is not necessarily writing a check to pay for them.

To an accountant:

Accounting Profit = Total Revenue – Explicit Costs

To an economist:

Economic Profit = Total Revenue – (Explicit Costs + Implicit Costs)

If a firm's revenue covers both its explicit and implicit costs, it is said to be making **normal profits**. In a firm that is earning normal profits, the resources are making at least as much money as they could in their next-best alternative, so they will stay in the business. If the firm's revenues cover both implicit and explicit costs with money to spare, that extra revenue is called **economic profit**.

Profit Maximization: MR = MC Rule

As we have stated, marginal cost is the addition to total cost that is (or would be) created by producing an additional unit of output. **Marginal revenue** is the addition to total revenue created by selling one additional unit of output. Profits will be maximized when marginal revenue equals marginal cost. If marginal revenue is greater than marginal cost, then producing an additional unit of output will add more to revenues than to costs, therefore increasing profits. If marginal cost is greater than marginal revenue, the firm is producing too much; additional units are adding more to costs than to revenue, thereby decreasing profits. When MR = MC, profits are maximized, because any other level of output leaves the possibility of increasing profits by raising revenue or decreasing costs.

PERFECT COMPETITION

A competitive market has four characteristics:

1. There are enough buyers and sellers in the market that no single one can influence price.
2. The products of all firms are largely the same.
3. Firms can enter or exit the market freely.
4. Information about prices and products is freely available to all firms.

Because no individual firms in this type of market can influence price, they are called price-takers. They are not large or powerful enough to influence price, which means that all firms must accept the price defined by the market. Each firm thus takes its price from the market. It cannot charge a higher price than the market price because other firms will offer the product at market price and buyers will buy at the lower price. All units are sold for the same price, so each unit adds the same amount to total revenue. Therefore, marginal revenue equals price: MR = P. For all firms, profits are maximized when MC = MR. Because MR = P for the competitive firm, profits are maximized when MC = P.

For goods and services that are sold in the perfectly competitive market, the market is composed of all the sellers and none of them can influence price by acting alone. When the market price moves, the firm's price moves as well. Perfectly competitive firms earn no economic profit in the long run. A graph of the side-by-side relationship between the market and the firm in the long run would look like this:

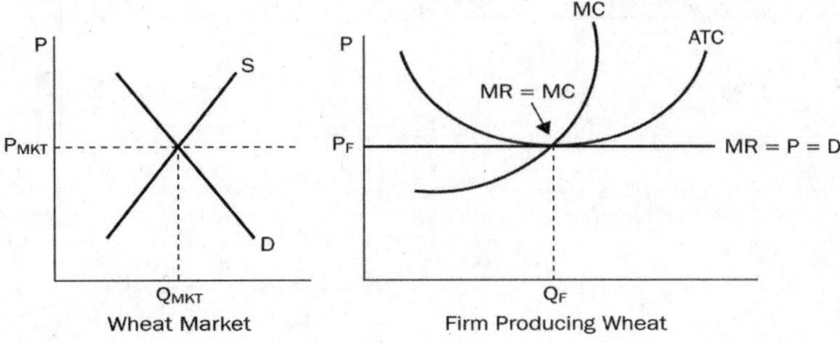

Note here that the price comes directly from the market and gives the firm enough revenue from selling the product at the market price to cover all of its ATC. The quantity in the market is the sum of all the firms' quantities. Here the Q_F shown is determined by MR = MC, which gives us the profit maximizing quantity. At this point, the firm shown is making normal profits—covering its implicit and explicit costs, but no more.

Now, think of what happens when something happens in the market to change the equilibrium. For example, public interest in the good might decline, the income of consumers might rise, or a sudden surge in the number of buyers could move the demand curve. Costs of production may change, new technology could be added to production, or future price expectations may shift. These determinants can move the demand and supply curve. For the firm, this also means change. Examine what happens when the demand curve shifts to the right because one or more of the demand determinants changed. In this new side-by-side graph, the demand curve has moved to the right; market price and quantity have increased, as well. The firm now has the new price from the market and the quantity for the firm is also higher because the MR = MC quantity (Q_{F2}) has moved to the right. If the average total costs do not change, the firm now realizes an economic profit.

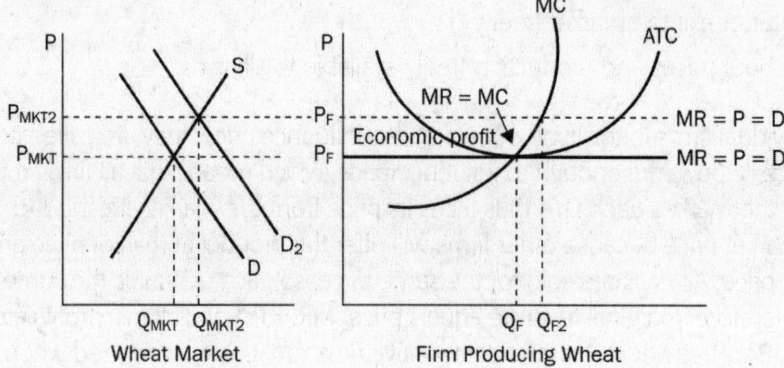

For firms in perfect competition, economic profit attracts new firms. New firms entering the market will cause the supply curve to move to the right and this increase in supply will cause a drop in price. New firms will continue to enter the market until all the economic profits disappear, moving the firm into the long run.

Short-Run Supply and Shutdown Decisions

Starting again from the long-run equilibrium, if market demand decreased, price would fall for the perfectly competitive firm. This price would be below minimum average total cost and the firm would incur a loss. Finding MR = MC would indicate the loss-minimizing level of output.

Economic theory tells us that in the short run, the firm cannot go out of business: it must continue paying its fixed costs. However, it can shut down and avoid paying its variable costs. To find out whether the firm should continue to operate or shut down, we compare marginal revenue to average variable cost. If MR (P) = AVC, or MR > AVC, the firm will continue to operate; as long as MR = AVC the firm is covering its variable costs and only losing its fixed costs, which it would lose anyway if it shut down. If MR > AVC, then the firm will cover its variable costs and have some revenue left over to apply to its fixed costs.

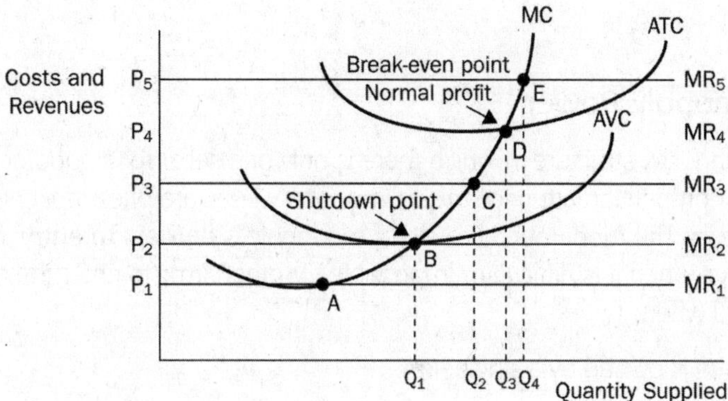

The above graph shows five points on the firm's short-run supply curve—prices and the quantities where those prices equal marginal cost. Point (A) indicates $P = MC_1$ where price is below the AVC. Here the firm should not produce and close. If the price rose, the firm would expand output so that again, price would equal marginal cost. Point (B) where $P = MC_2$ shows the shutdown position, which is the last level of production (Q_1) at which the firm should operate. Here, the firm is only able to cover its variable costs. At point (C), the firm is loss-minimizing where $P = MC_3$. This firm would operate and produce Q_2 in the hopes of doing better in the near future. Cutting its costs or gaining a higher price from the market will move this firm to a better position. Point (D) is the break-even point, where $P = MC_4$ to show that the firm's total costs are paid with the level of output at Q_3. At P = MR_5, price is above the ATC—the firm is earning economic profits. Since this firm will produce at levels above P = MR_2, above minimum average variable cost the firm's short-run supply curve is its marginal cost curve. Below minimum average variable cost, the firm will shut down.

In the long run, then, some firms will exit the market. Firms exiting would cause the market supply curve to shift left, raising price, which benefits the firms remaining in the market. The process would continue until price comes back up to minimum average total cost—the long-run equilibrium position.

Efficiency and Perfect Competition

As we have seen, a perfectly competitive industry will automatically adjust supply to operate until price is equal to minimum average total cost, which means that over time firms will always adjust their output to produce at minimum average total cost. This is why the perfectly competitive industry is the model for efficiency. Perfectly competitive firms are efficient at allocation, producing what society wants or producing where P = MC. Further, these firms are efficient at production, producing at the least cost, or P = minimum ATC. These two measures of efficiency are present in perfect competition but not in the imperfect models that we are about to discuss. This market structure automatically causes output to be produced at the level at which the least amount of inputs are required to achieve a given level of output. Therefore, resources are allocated efficiently under perfect competition.

MONOPOLY

Sources of Monopoly Power

A **monopoly** is an industry structure in which there is only one seller for a good or service. Whereas firms under perfect competition are price *takers*, monopoly firms are price *makers*—they set price to suit the firm's interests. The fundamental cause of monopoly is **barriers to entry**; monopolies are most likely to emerge when it is difficult or impossible for other firms to enter the market. Barriers to entry can be created when:

- A key resource is owned by a single firm.
- The government, through patents, copyrights, or licenses, gives a single firm the exclusive right to produce a product or service.
- Costs of production are such that one large firm can be more efficient than many small firms. We call this a natural monopoly.

Profit Maximization

Because a monopolist is the only firm in an industry, the market demand curve is the same as the firm's. The law of demand says that to increase sales, the firm must lower price. If a firm faced the following (admittedly simple) demand schedule, revenues would follow the pattern shown.

Price	Quantity	Total Revenue	Average Revenue	Marginal Revenue
1	10	10	10	
2	9	18	9	8
3	8	24	8	6
4	7	28	7	4
5	6	30	6	2

Notice that marginal revenue is always below price. This is because the lower price applies to all previous units, as well as the additional units.

The monopolist faces the same types of cost curves as the perfectly competitive firm, so its cost and revenue graph will appear thus:

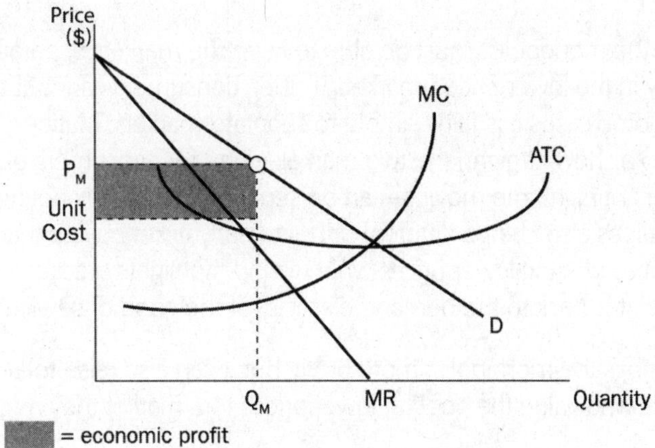

Like the perfectly competitive firm, the monopolist maximizes profits where marginal revenue equals marginal cost. The quantity where this happens is Q_M. From that quantity, we read to the demand curve to find out the price, P_M. Monopoly firms earn economic profit if total average costs are lower than the price. The price in this graph is boxed, with the price as the upper parameter and the unit cost (where the MR = MC quantity intersects with the ATC) as the lower parameter.

Inefficiency of Monopoly

A monopoly will always charge a price greater than marginal cost, because of the difference between the demand and marginal revenue curves. We can use the concepts of consumer surplus to analyze the monopolist's efficiency. As price is greater than marginal cost, not all consumers who value the good above its cost can buy it. Notice that the graph shows fewer transactions being made under monopoly, which produces deadweight loss. The points of the triangle show the P_M the MR = MC output, and P = MC where the perfect competitor would produce. Since P > MC and P > minimum average cost, neither allocative nor productive efficiency is realized.

Price Discrimination

Because a monopolistic firm faces the market demand curve, it faces consumers who value the good at different prices. If the monopolist could sell at a high price to those who value the good highly while selling at a low price to the consumers who value the product less, she could earn more profits. The practice of selling at different prices in different markets is called **price discrimination**.

To price discriminate, the monopolist must be able to keep the markets separate; otherwise all consumers would buy in the lower-priced market. Further, consumers cannot be able to resell the product to others. In some cases it is fairly simple to separate markets. Matinee movie tickets are cheaper than tickets to a show at night; the two markets—one for consumers of afternoon movies and one for consumers of nighttime movies—can be separated simply by noting the time of the show on the ticket. Airlines also charge different prices to early ticket buyers than they do to last-minute buyers, as well as offering lower prices when round-trip flights bracket a weekend. The ability to separate markets relates back to the demand elasticity of the good or service.

Price discrimination brings the monopolist more profit, but it can also raise total surplus, or welfare, by bringing consumers who value the good at lower prices to a market they might otherwise avoid.

Regulated Monopoly

Most natural monopolies are regulated. In certain lines of production, a firm must be a large-scale producer in order to realize the lowest unit costs of production. Because of heavy fixed costs, the demand curve will cut the average cost curve at a point where the average cost is still falling. The relationship between market demand and costs is such that low unit costs usually presume one producer.

If we would allow this single firm to operate without some price regulation, a substantial economic profit would most likely be earned. Further, price exceeds marginal costs, which indicates misallocation of resources.

To achieve allocative efficiency, regulatory agencies would like to mandate a "socially optimum price," a ceiling price where P = MC. Because of the nature of the demand curve, this ceiling price may result in economic losses and eventual shutdown of the firm in the long run. Since many of these natural monopolies such as utilities must be prepared for peak usage times, they incur heavy fixed equipment costs. The market demand curve intersects marginal cost at a point to the left of the MC = AC intersection so that the socially optimal price is below AC.

To compromise, most regulatory agencies establish a "fair return" price. Here P = AC and will allow the monopoly to break even, earning normal profits. Some misallocation of resources is tolerated, because more buyers are served than would be under the single monopoly model.

Oligopoly

Interdependence, Collusion, and Cartels

An **oligopoly** is a market with only a few sellers; each offering a product that is largely the same as the others'. In this type of structure, there is always a conflict between cooperation and competition. If the firms cooperate, they can operate as a monopolist, restricting output to raise price. However, each firm cares the most about its own interests, giving it an incentive to increase output in an effort to get a larger market share. The concentration ratio and the Herfindahl index help one to understand how much market power firms in this market structure have.

Collusion is what happens when several of the firms in an oligopolistically structured industry work together to agree on output and price levels. A group of firms acting in unison like this is called a **cartel**. Collusion is illegal in the United States, but OPEC is an example of a global cartel. The OPEC office in Vienna uses economic models to determine how much to charge for a barrel of oil and thus maximize the profits of the Oil Producing Exporting Countries from the sale of this commodity.

Even when they don't collude, the members of an oligopoly are interdependent. If one of them lowers price, it will attract another firm's customers and that firm will have to lower its price as well if it wants to keep its market share.

Game Theory and Strategic Behavior

Game theory is the study of how people and groups behave in strategic situations. We can use it to analyze the economics of cooperation. Game theory helps us to understand the mutual interdependent nature of oligopoly markets.

Game theory can be used to describe a game when:

- There are rules that govern *actions*.
- There are two or more *players*.
- There are choices of action where *strategy* matters.
- The game has one or more *outcomes*.
- The outcome depends on the strategies chosen by all players, i.e., there is *strategic interaction*.

Players engage in various strategies but the **dominant strategy** is defined as the best strategy for one player regardless of the strategy the other player follows. Here is a payoff matrix that provides an example of how this strategy search takes place.

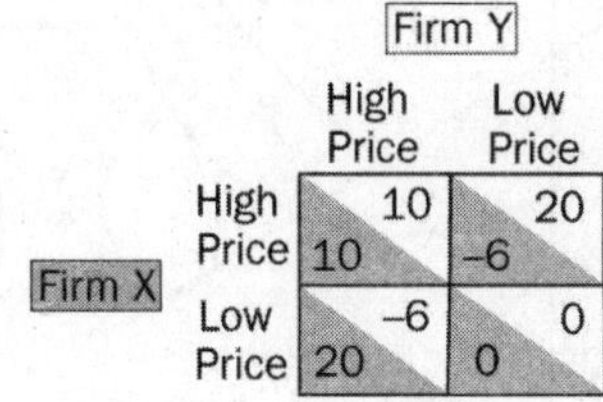

These companies are the only sellers of the same product. The equilibrium of the game—called the Nash equilibrium—occurs when each company takes the best possible action given the action of the other. For each firm, a low price is the dominant strategy because it pays the best reward. So if they compete for customers, both firms set aggressively low prices and both wind up with no profit. However, if they cooperate (collude) they will act like a joint monopoly and set a profit-maximizing price, each earning a profit of $10 million. Collusion would be profitable, but it is difficult to accomplish. If one firm cheats on a collusive agreement by its cutting price, its profit rises to $20 million, and the other firm loses money. There is a great deal of incentive to cheat on these kinds of agreements. Competition forces an outcome that is not the best for each of the firms.

Monopolistic Competition

Product Differentiation and the Role of Advertising

Some producers behave as both monopolists and competitors due to the nature of their products. Think about the market for jeans. All items in the market are jeans, but even jeans of the same size can vary by factors like brand; some fit well while others don't. Often, once a consumer finds a brand that fits well (Brand A) he will stick with that brand, even if it might be more expensive than some others that do not fit as well. Brand A is therefore somewhat like a monopoly, because it faces a downward-sloping demand curve, made up of consumers who like Brand A's fit. Consumer loyalty gives Brand A some ability to control price. The demand curve here is more elastic than the demand curve of a monopoly seller because Brand A can only raise its price so far before consumers start to decide the extra cost isn't worth it. So Brand A is also a competitor.

Sodas are another example of monopolistic competition. All brands are sodas, yet many brands enjoy a high level of brand loyalty, and can change price accordingly. However, a producer cannot price their soda too high or consumers will switch brands, so they do not have total control over price.

The difference between products is called **product differentiation.** Firms in monopolistically competitive industries strive for as much product differentiation as possible, for it is in the differentiation that their monopoly power lies. Many firms use advertising to keep their brand firmly fixed in consumers' minds. Some advertised items truly are different from one another, but some are merely perceived to be different due to the advertising.

The monopolistically competitive firm faces the same pattern of cost and revenue curves as the monopolist. The firm shown is making economic profits, because price is greater than average total cost.

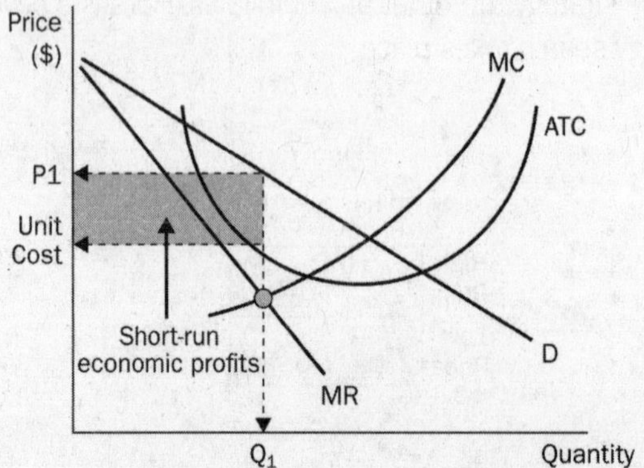

The economic profits that the firm is making will attract new firms into the industry. As new firms enter, consumers are offered more choices, and some of them switch to the new brands. This shifts the original firm's demand curve to the left. New firms will continue to enter until the industry reaches equilibrium. This will occur when all economic profits have been competed away and price equals average total cost. Thus in the long run these firms earn only normal profits.

Excess Capacity and Inefficiency

Monopolistic competition is socially inefficient for a variety of reasons. First, the price at which the product is sold is greater than marginal cost, just like a monopolist. Some consumers who value the good at more than marginal cost but less than price will not be able to purchase the good. Second, because firms are continually striving to increase product differentiation, they do not produce at minimum average total cost. Thus, these firms that reflect imperfect market structures, such as monopolies, do not attain allocative or productive efficiency.

It should be noted here that due to this inefficiency—being able to attain some degree of economic profits—the firm can continue to operate profitably, even if not at lowest cost. Operating above the lowest cost is the source of the inefficiency. A perfectly competitive firm must operate at lowest cost to compete with all of the other firms in the market.

IF YOU LEARNED ONLY FIVE THINGS IN THIS CHAPTER. . .

1. The income effect is produced when consumers' income has more purchasing power; the substitution effect is produced if an increase in the price of one good increases demand for the other good or if a decrease in the price of one good decreases demand for the other good.

2. A good for which there is less demand as income rises is called an inferior good; a good for which there is more demand as income rises is called a normal good.

3. Price controls called price ceilings or price floors can be imposed to bring price into line with what the government believes it should be.

4. The three types of demand elasticity are price elasticity, income elasticity, and cross-price elasticity, while the price elasticity of supply measures how the quantity supplied responds to a change in price.

5. A monopoly is a market structure characterized by a single seller of a unique product with no close substitutes.

REVIEW QUESTIONS

1. Which of the following events will cause the demand curve for a normal good such as steak to shift to the left?

   (A) A decrease in consumer incomes
   (B) An increase in consumer incomes
   (C) A decrease in the price of chicken, a substitute for steak
   (D) The release of a new medical report saying that steak consumption improves health
   (E) A decrease in cattle prices

2. Hamburgers and fries are complements, and Mr. Jones is a potato farmer. Mr. Jones is most likely to sell fewer potatoes at a lower price if

   (A) the price of hamburgers decreases
   (B) the price of hamburgers increases
   (C) farming technology advances
   (D) the wages of farm workers rise
   (E) new legislation requires hamburgers to weigh no more than $\frac{1}{4}$ lb

3. Use the data in the table below to answer the following question.

Units Consumed	Marginal Utility of X	Price of Good X	Marginal Utility of Y	Price of Good Y
1	20	\$5	24	\$6
2	15	\$5	18	\$6
3	10	\$5	13	\$6
4	5	\$5	8	\$6
5	2	\$5	2	\$6

   Given this schedule of prices and marginal utility, which combination of Good X and Good Y should the consumer use to maximize utility?

   (A) 1 unit of X and 3 units of Y
   (B) 3 units of X and 1 unit of Y
   (C) 2 units of X and 3 units of Y
   (D) 3 units of each good
   (E) 2 units of each good

4. Which of the following statements say something true about the firm depicted in the graph below?

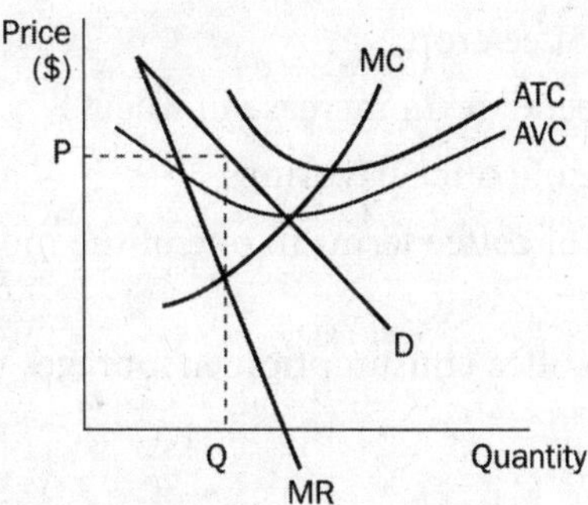

I. The firm may be a monopolistic competitor.
II. The firm is profit maximizing.
III. The firm is making economic profits.
IV. The firm should continue operating in the short run, but should go out of business in the long run.
V. If this firm is typical of other firms in the industry, new firms will enter the industry.

(A) I, II, and III
(B) II, III, and V
(C) I, II, and IV
(D) III and IV
(E) III, IV, and V

5. Economies of scale allow firms to

(A) move upward on the AVC curve and hence reach a lowest cost point
(B) move downward on the AVC curve and hence reach a lowest cost point
(C) enjoy the benefits of small output that will result in the highest revenue
(D) be in a position that affords the greatest flexibility of production
(E) operate such that cost savings makes no difference

6. If Soda A and Soda B are substitutes for each other, which of the following would cause the price of Soda B to rise?

(A) A new study is released showing that consumption of soda leads to diabetes.
(B) The price of aluminum cans decreases.
(C) A new law is passed requiring the recycling of all aluminum cans.
(D) The price of Soda A increases.
(E) The price of Soda A drops.

7. Which of the following will cause the producers of flavored coffee to offer more for sale at all prices?

   (A) A fungus attacks the coffee crop.
   (B) Coffee bean pickers negotiate an increase in wages.
   (C) A decrease in the price of coffee flavorings
   (D) Government takeover of coffee farms in one of the most important coffee-producing countries
   (E) A study showing that coffee consumption encourages weight loss

Use the following graph to answer questions 8 and 9.

A price control has been set as shown.

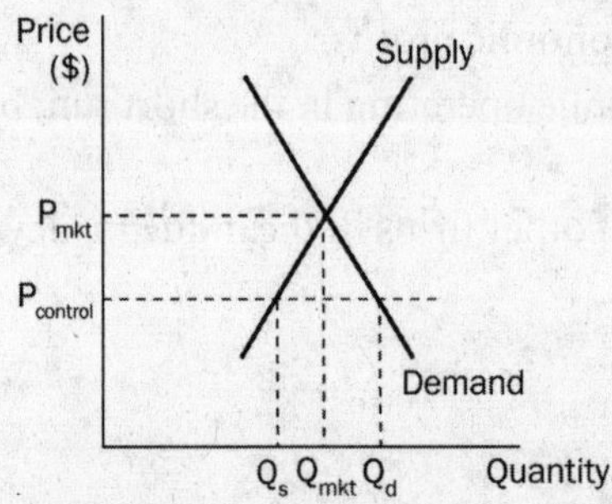

8. What type of price control is shown in the graph?

   (A) Price floor
   (B) Price ceiling
   (C) Minimum wage
   (D) Price surplus
   (E) Price shortage

9. Which function of price has been interrupted by this price control?

   (A) The marginal function
   (B) The storehouse function
   (C) The income function
   (D) The rationing function
   (E) The substitution function

10. If the demand for Good G is price inelastic, a seller of Good G who wants to increase total revenue should

    (A) decrease quantity supplied
    (B) raise price
    (C) target marketing efforts at narrower audiences
    (D) increase quantity supplied
    (E) lower price

11. A 20% rise in Good Z's price creates a 30% decrease in quantity demanded. Demand for Good Z is thus

    (A) price elastic
    (B) price inelastic
    (C) unit elastic
    (D) perfectly elastic
    (E) perfectly inelastic

12. Which of the following factors would tend to make demand for a good price elastic?

    (A) There are no close substitutes for the good.
    (B) There are no cross-price substitutes for the good.
    (C) The good is a necessity.
    (D) Consumers have only a short time to respond to price changes.
    (E) The cost of the good is a large proportion of consumers' budgets.

13. A tax is levied on Good X, as shown. Which of the following describe the tax as it is shown here?

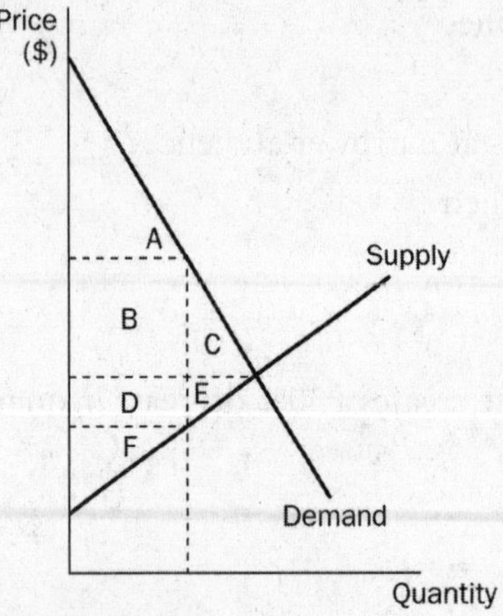

I. Consumers bear most of the tax.
II. Suppliers bear most of the tax.
III. Consumer surplus has risen from A to ABC.
IV. Area CE is deadweight loss as a result of the tax.
V. Producer surplus has fallen from DF to E.

(A) I, II, and III
(B) II and IV
(C) I and IV
(D) III and V
(E) I, III, and V

14. Which of the following demonstrates the law of diminishing marginal utility?

(A) Consuming four hot fudge sundaes is less enjoyable than consuming just one.
(B) Eating more of something that is initially disagreeable makes it taste better.
(C) The fifth new worker hired adds less to output than the first new worker hired.
(D) A producer gets less output per dollar when more money is spent on an input.
(E) Almost all consumers face budget constraints.

15. Which of the following demonstrates the law of diminishing marginal returns?

(A) After Thanksgiving dinner, many people refuse dessert because they are full.
(B) The fifth new worker hired adds less to output than the first new worker hired.
(C) Almost all consumers face budget constraints.
(D) When a producer spends more money on a particular output, fewer inputs are needed.
(E) A perfectly competitive firm will always tend to produce the quantity with the minimum average total cost.

Use the following graph to answer question 16.

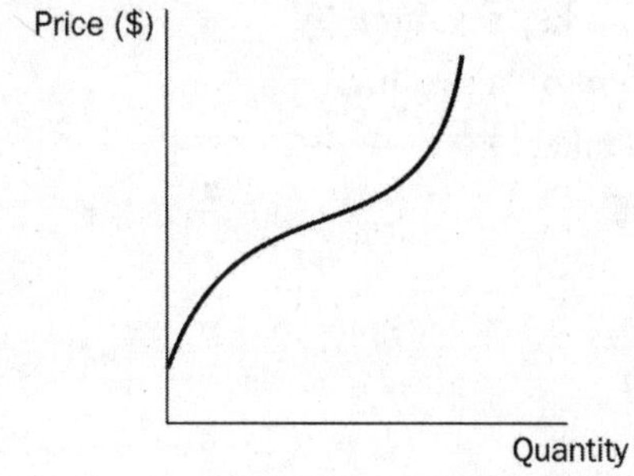

16. Which of the following statements is true of the curve shown in the graph?

I. It is a total cost curve.
II. It is an average variable cost curve.
III. The curve shows that diminishing returns eventually set in.
IV. It is a marginal cost curve.
V. The curve shows that early in production there are increasing returns.

(A) I, III, and V
(B) I and III
(C) II, III, and V
(D) III, IV, and V
(E) III and V

17. Which of the following answer choices states a true fact?

    (A) An increase in the price of Good A will decrease the demand for complementary Good B.
    (B) A decrease in income will decrease the demand for an inferior good.
    (C) An increase in income will reduce the demand for a normal good.
    (D) A decrease in the price of Good C will increase the demand for substitute Good D.
    (E) A decrease in income will decrease the demand for a substitute good.

18. Which of the following might cause a monopoly to exist?

    I. Economies of scale
    II. A single firm owning a key resource
    III. A firm owning a patent on a product
    IV. A firm being a price-taker
    V. Price discrimination

    (A) I, II, and III
    (B) II, III, and V
    (C) I, II, and IV
    (D) III, IV, and V
    (E) II, IV, and V

19. The graph below shows a perfectly competitive firm. Which quantity shown on the graph is the profit-maximizing quantity?

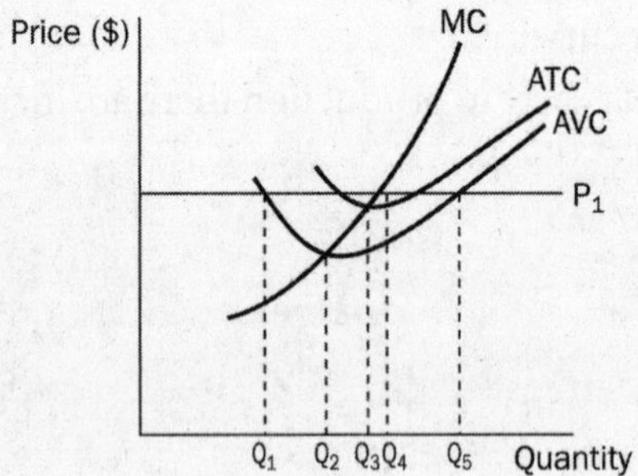

    (A) Q_1
    (B) Q_2
    (C) Q_3
    (D) Q_4
    (E) Q_5

20. In a perfectly competitive industry, market price of the product is $20 per unit. A firm produces at a level of output where average total cost is $18, marginal cost is $20, and average variable cost is $16. Which of the following is true of this firm?

I. It is profit maximizing.
II. It has not yet encountered diminishing returns.
III. It is making economic profits.
IV. Average fixed cost equals $2.
V. The firm will not stay in business in the long run.

(A) I, II, and V
(B) I, III, and IV
(C) I, IV, and V
(D) II, III, and V
(E) III, IV, and V

Free-Response Question

1. Draw a correctly labeled graph for a single-priced monopolist who is earning economic profits. Shade and label the economic profit and deadweight loss.

ANSWERS AND EXPLANATIONS

1. A

A leftward shift in the demand curve is a decrease in demand. When consumer incomes rise, demand for normal goods increases. When incomes fall, demand for normal goods decreases. You can eliminate (B) because for a normal good, this would cause demand to rise. You can eliminate (C) because if the price of chicken rises, quantity demanded of chicken will fall, and people may switch from eating chicken to eating steak. This would cause an increase in the demand for steak, which would be a shift to the right. You can eliminate (D) because a report commending the health benefits of steak would cause steak to rise in popularity, thereby increasing demand and causing a rightward shift of the curve. Finally, you can eliminate (E) because a decrease in cattle prices increase the supply of cattle, and therefore steak, but have no effect on demand.

2. B

Mr. Jones will sell fewer potatoes if fewer fries are being purchased; the decreased demand for potatoes will mean that the potatoes he does sell are sold at a lower price. Because hamburgers and fries are complements, anything that causes a decrease in the number of hamburgers being purchased will entail that fewer fries will be purchased as well. Given the law of demand, an increase in the price of hamburgers will lead to a decrease in demand, and to a corresponding decrease in demand for fries. The price of potatoes will fall, so a rise in the price of hamburger will cause Mr. Jones to sell fewer potatoes at a lower price. You can eliminate (A) because a rise in the price of hamburger will cause the opposite chain of events to happen, increasing (Mr. Jones's) demand for hamburger and increasing the demand for potatoes. You can eliminate (C) because an advance in farming technology will affect potato supply, not demand. You can eliminate (D) for same reason: Changes in farm workers' wages will affect supply, not demand. You can eliminate (E) because this legislation will affect the amount of hamburger used by suppliers, their cost, and therefore, their supply.

3. E

To maximize utility, the consumer should use two units of each good. This is because maximizing utility requires that the consumer use units of the products such that

$$\frac{MU_X}{P_X} = \frac{MU_Y}{P_Y}$$

These two ratios are equal at two units of each good. $\frac{MUX}{PX} = \frac{15}{5} = 3$, and $\frac{MUY}{Y} = \frac{18}{6} = 3$. You can eliminate (A) because at one unit of Good X and three units of Good Y the ratios are $\frac{20}{5} = 4$ and $\frac{13}{6} = \frac{2-1}{6}$. You can eliminate (B) because at three units of Good X the ratio is $\frac{10}{5} = 2$ and at one unit of Good Y the ratio is $\frac{24}{6} = 4$. At (C), the ratios are $\frac{15}{5} = 3$ and $\frac{13}{6} = \frac{2-1}{6}$. Choice (D) is incorrect because at three units of each the ratios are $\frac{10}{5} = 2$ and $\frac{13}{6} = \frac{2-1}{6}$.

4. C

Statement I is correct because the firm could be either a monopoly or a monopolistic competitor. You know this by looking at the demand curve, which is downward-sloping, and the marginal revenue curve, which lies below it. Statement II is also correct because the firm is producing at the output level where marginal revenue equals marginal cost. Statement IV is correct as well, because the price the firm is charging covers average variable cost, but does not cover average total cost. Therefore in the short run the firm will lose less money if it keeps operating than if it shuts down, but in the long run the firm should go out of business. Statement III is incorrect because economic profits require that price be greater than average total cost. In this case, the price the firm is charging does not even cover average total cost at the profit-maximizing level of output, much less exceed it. Statement V is incorrect, too, because economic profits are what attract new firms to an industry. This firm is losing money.

5. B

Economics of scale give a firm the opportunity to lower their average costs as they increase output. The area extending from the left side of the cost curve down to the minimum average cost is the area that reflects economies of scale. In this area, firms are increasing output and lowering average costs. Choice (B) is therefore correct. Choice (A) is the opposite of (B). Choices (C), (D), and (E) are all flawed ideas.

6. D

If the price of Soda A rises, quantity demanded of Soda A will fall. Because Soda B is a substitute, demand for Soda B will rise. An increase in demand causes an increase in price. You can eliminate (A) because if soda was linked with diabetes, it would become less popular, causing a decrease in demand and a drop in price. You can eliminate (B) because aluminum cans are an input in the production of soda, and a decrease in input prices will increase supply, which will cause the price of Soda B to fall. Choice (C) is incorrect because a law pertaining to the recycling of aluminum cans would affect neither the demand nor the supply of soda. Finally, (E) is incorrect because as we discussed, it is an *increase*—not a decrease—in the price of Soda A that will lead to a rise in price of Soda B.

7. C

A drop in input prices causes supply to increase, which means producers will offer more for sale at all prices. Flavorings are an input in the production of flavored coffee, so if their price fell, the supply of flavored coffee would increase. You can eliminate (A) because if a fungus attacked the crop, there would be a decrease in supply. You can eliminate (B) because an increase in input prices will decrease supply. Choice (D) is incorrect because you cannot predict what effect a government seizure of coffee farms would have on the supply of coffee. Choice (E) is incorrect because evidence that coffee consumption helps people lose weight would increase the demand for coffee and would not affect supply.

8. B

The graph shows a price ceiling because price ceilings are set when it is believed that the market price will be too high. You know that the actual market price is higher than the set price, because the price control lies below the market equilibrium. You can eliminate (A) because a price floor would be set *above* the equilibrium. You can eliminate (C) because the minimum wage is a price floor, and the graph depicts a price ceiling. Choice (D) is incorrect because a surplus occurs anytime quantity supplied is greater than quantity demanded, not just when this happens in response to a price control. Choice (E) is not the best answer because you were asked to name a type of price control, not the result of the price control shown, which would be a shortage.

9. D

Price can't perform its rationing function under price controls. Ordinarily, price acts to allocate a market's output; whoever is willing and able to pay the market price can obtain the good. A price ceiling prevents price from rising to its equilibrium level, and therefore causes a shortage because the quantity demanded is greater than the quantity supplied. In this case something else, such as waiting in line, must do the rationing. Choice (A) is not the best answer because this is not a term that economists use. Choice (B) is incorrect because there is no such thing as a storehouse function. You can eliminate (C) because supply and demand register incomes only indirectly. Finally, since there is no substitution involved, you can eliminate (E).

10. B

Total revenue equals price times quantity. If demand for a good is price inelastic, total revenue will follow price changes because price changes are proportionately greater than quantity changes if demand for the good is inelastic. Thus, if the seller wants to raise revenue, she should raise price. You can eliminate (E) because lowering price will lower total revenue. You can eliminate (A) and (D) because price is the variable under the seller's control. Quantity changes follow price changes. Choice (C) is incorrect because narrower marketing is generally more likely to decrease revenues than it is to increase them.

11. A

$$\text{Price elasticity} = \frac{\%\text{ change in quantity demanded}}{\%\text{ change in price}}$$

If this coefficient is greater than one, the percentage change in quantity demanded is greater than the percentage change in price, which means demand is very responsive to price changes (i.e., elastic). You can eliminate (B) because the percentage change in quantity demanded is greater than the percentage change in price, and the reverse would have to be true for the good to be inelastic. Choice (C) is incorrect because if a good is unit elastic, the coefficient equals one, that is, percentage change in price equals percentage change in quantity. Choice (D) is incorrect because for a good to be perfectly elastic, an infinite change in quantity would accompany zero change in price. Choice (E) is incorrect because for a good to be perfectly inelastic, zero change in quantity would accompany an infinite change in price.

12. E

Demand tends to be price elastic for goods that make up large portions of consumers' budgets. An increase in the price of something like housing reduces consumers' purchasing power, and thus importantly reduces the amount of those goods that they are able to purchase. You can eliminate (A) because if there are no close substitutes, consumers will have no choice but to pay the higher price for the good, making it inelastic. You can eliminate (B) because this simply means the good carries no complements, which would have no effect on elasticity. Choice (C) is incorrect because if the good is a necessity, then people will continue to buy it no matter what happens to price, making demand for the good inelastic. Choice (D) is incorrect because if there is only a short time span involved, it is harder to find substitutes, making the good inelastic to price.

13. C

Statement I is correct because demand is less elastic than supply (reflected by the fact that the demand curve is flatter), which means consumers have a hard time leaving the market and therefore must pay the tax. You can also see this by looking at the difference between the market price and the new prices after the tax. The consumer's new price has increased more than the seller's new price has decreased. Statement IV is also correct because the two areas C and E represent surplus lost due to a decrease in transactions. Therefore CE is deadweight loss. Statement II is incorrect for the same reason that statement I is correct. Statement III is incorrect because consumer surplus is the area below the demand curve and above price. Before the tax, consumer surplus equaled ABC; once the tax is imposed, consumer surplus falls to A. Statement V is incorrect because producer surplus is the area below price and above the supply curve. Before the tax, producer surplus equals DEF; after the tax, producer surplus drops to F.

14. A

The law of diminishing marginal utility says that you get less satisfaction from consuming more units of a good. The decreased enjoyment of the fourth hot fudge sundae is a sign of diminishing utility. You can eliminate (B) because it suggests the opposite of the law at issue, i.e., that marginal utility might actually *increase* as a result of consuming more of a good. Choice (C) is incorrect because the law of diminishing marginal utility refers to consumption, not production. Choice (D) also concerns production, and so is also incorrect. Choice (E) can be eliminated because it simply states a fact about limited financial resources, and says nothing about what consumers might get from their resources.

15. B

The law of diminishing marginal returns pertains to the slowing of output increases as more of an input is used. As a producer adds more variable inputs, the output eventually declines. Choice (B) states that as more workers are added to production, the new workers add less to output than those already working, so (B) is correct. Choice (A) is incorrect because it refers to consumption, not production. Choice (C) states a fact about consumers' budgets, and has nothing to do with production. You can eliminate (D) because spending money on output doesn't tell you what the output cost, and therefore doesn't tell you how much output your input is producing relative to its cost. Choice (E) is a true statement, but one unrelated to the law of diminishing returns. Perfectly competitive firms produce at minimum average total cost because economic profits are competed away, not because of diminishing returns.

16. A

Statement I is true; you know it is a total cost curve by its shape. The positive intercept on the vertical axis indicates fixed costs and the rest of the curve shows fixed costs plus variable costs. Statement III is true because the second half of the curve is rising at an increasing rate, indicating that more input is required (and therefore costs are increasing) to produce output. Statement V is true because the first half of the curve is rising at a decreasing rate, indicating that initially more output is produced per additional unit of input. This will cause costs to rise slowly. Statement II is false because an average variable cost curve is U-shaped. Statement IV is false because a marginal cost curve is either U-shaped or slopes upward to the right, depending on when diminishing returns set in.

17. A

When the price of a good like jelly increases, consumers will purchase a lower quantity. If jelly has a complement like peanut butter, consumers will buy these goods together. So when they purchase a lower quantity of jelly, their demand for peanut butter declines. Choice (A) states that concept. Choices (B) and (C) are flawed since the relationship between income, normal and inferior goods is reversed. Choice (D) is eliminated since a decrease in the price of a good that has a substitute will cause a lack of demand for that substitute. Choice (E) is flawed because income and substitute goods are not related.

18. A

Statement I is correct because economies of scale may dictate that a single large firm can supply a market at a lower cost than several smaller firms can. Statement II is also correct because if one firm is the sole owner of a key resource, no other firms can make the product. Statement III is correct as well, because when a firm owns a patent, no other firm can legally produce the good. Statement IV is incorrect; being a price-taker is a condition for perfect competition. Under perfect competition there are so many firms that none can influence price and they are all price takers. Statement V is incorrect because price discrimination (selling the same product to different markets at different prices) is something monopolists like to do, not something that causes monopolies to occur.

19. D

To maximize profit, a firm must produce at the quantity where marginal revenue equals marginal cost. For a perfectly competitive firm, price equals marginal revenue, so Q_4 is the profit-maximizing quantity because it is the quantity at which the price and marginal cost curves intersect. Choice (A), Q_1, is a quantity at which average variable cost and price intersect. Choice (B), Q_2, is the quantity at which average variable cost intersects marginal cost. Choice (C), Q_3, is the quant ity at which average total cost intersects marginal cost. Choice (E), Q_5, is another quantity at which average variable cost intersects marginal cost.

20. B

Statement I is correct because the firm is operating at the point where marginal cost equals price. Because price equals marginal revenue for the perfectly competitive firm, the output level is such that marginal cost equals marginal revenue. MC = MR is the rule for maximizing profit. Statement II is also correct because price is greater than average total cost (i.e., $20 is greater than $18) and when this is the case, economic profits are made. Statement IV is correct as well, because average fixed cost is the difference between average total cost and average variable cost; $18 – $16 = $2. Statement II is incorrect because firms always produce where marginal cost is rising, which indicates diminishing returns. Statement V is incorrect, because a firm making economic profits will almost certainly stay in business.

FREE-RESPONSE QUESTION

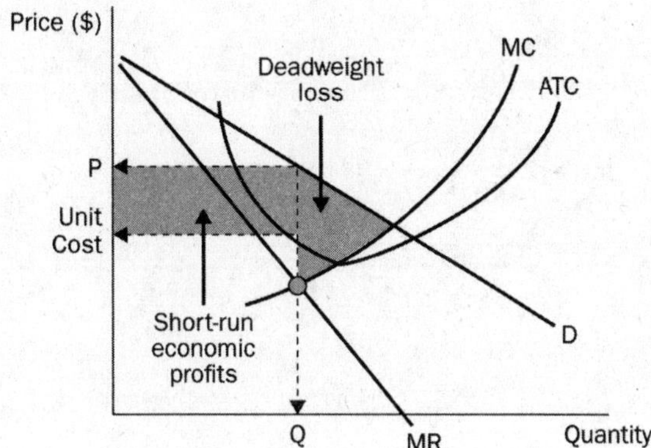

The first action you should take is to label the axes, with dollars on the vertical and quantity on the horizontal. Then you should draw the demand curve, which slopes downward to the left, and the marginal revenue curve, which lies below the demand curve and continues beyond the horizontal axis. The marginal cost curve slopes upward to the right, and the profit-maximizing quantity occurs where marginal revenue and marginal cost intersect. Read from this quantity up to the demand curve and over to the vertical axis to establish price. The average total cost curve, which is U-shaped, should be placed so that the average total cost for the profit-maximizing quantity is below price, thereby showing that the firm is making economic profits. Also, the marginal cost curve should intersect the average total cost curve at the latter's minimum. The economic profit is the difference between price and ATC at the MR = MC level of output. The deadweight loss is the triangle created by three points: MR = MC, P = MC (where the perfect competitor would sell), and P of the monopolist at MR = MC level of output.

Chapter 12: **Factor Markets**

- Derived Factor Demand
- Marginal Revenue Product
- Labor Market and Firms' Hiring of Labor
- Review Questions
- Answers and Explanations

DERIVED FACTOR DEMAND

Firms that were sellers in the product market are now buyers in the factor markets. Households, which were buyers in the product market, are now sellers of resources in the factor markets. The demand for factors of production, such as labor, is a derived demand. This means that the demand for factors of production is derived from the demand for products; this demand is what causes firms to want resources. No one wants to consume an acre of farmland or a tractor; people want to consume the food that is produced using these resources. The demand for farmland and tractors is thus *derived* from the demand for food. In the factor markets, the payment that labor receives is called wages. Natural resources that are completely fixed in total supply receive economic rent. Capital receives interest, and entrepreneurship earns profit.

MARGINAL REVENUE PRODUCT

The **marginal revenue product** of a factor of production is the contribution that using one more unit of the factor makes to the firm's revenue. If the firm is operating under perfect competition, marginal revenue product is calculated by multiplying the factor's marginal product by the price of the product.

$$MRP = MP \times P$$

$$\text{Marginal Revenue Product} = \frac{\text{the change in total revenue}}{\text{unit change in resource quantity}}$$

We will first study the factor markets under the assumption that a firm sells its product in a perfectly competitive market. This means that the firm is a price taker, and can sell all it wants at the market price. We will also assume that the factor markets are perfectly competitive; that is, no buyer or seller is large enough to influence prices of resources. They can buy all they want of the factor at the market price, and if they offer a lower price for the resource they will not be able to obtain any of the factor.

A sample data set appears in the table below. Note that product price stays the same and that diminishing returns set in with the first unit produced.

Units of Resource	Total Product (Output)	Marginal Product	Product Price	Total Revenue	Marginal Revenue Product
0	0		$3	0	
1	8	8	$3	$24	$24
2	15	7	$3	$45	$21
3	21	6	$3	$63	$18
4	26	5	$3	$78	$15
5	30	4	$3	$90	$12
6	33	3	$3	$99	$9
7	35	2	$3	$105	$6

Because marginal product falls, marginal revenue product falls. Therefore, the curve slopes downward. The MRP curve is the demand curve for the market and the firm.

To study firms that sell their product under imperfect competition, recall that if the firm is a monopolist, oligopolist, or monopolistic competitor in the product market, it must lower product price to sell more output. For those firms, marginal revenue product (in the resource or factor market) will fall for two reasons: Marginal product is falling *and* product price is falling. A sample data set appears in the table below.

Units of Resource	Total Product (Output)	Marginal Product	Product Price	Total Revenue	Marginal Revenue Product
0	0		$3.00	0	
1	8	8	$2.90	$23.20	$23.20
2	15	7	$2.80	$42.00	$18.80
3	21	6	$2.70	$56.70	$14.70
4	26	5	$2.60	$67.60	$10.90
5	30	4	$2.50	$75.00	$7.40
6	33	3	$2.40	$79.20	$4.20
7	35	2	$2.30	$80.50	$1.30

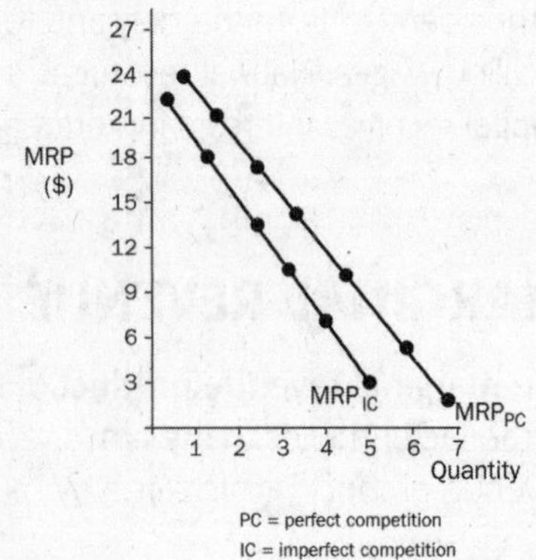

To maximize profit, a firm should hire units of labor (or purchase units of any other resource or factor) up to the point at which the marginal revenue product of the factor equals the resource price. In the case of labor, the firm should hire to the quantity where marginal revenue product equals wage, as shown. The wage is the contribution to cost brought about by using one more unit of labor. To generalize, this is called **marginal resource cost.** Marginal resource cost is the addition to cost brought about by using one more unit of a resource. Up to the profit-maximizing quantity, additional units of labor are contributing more to revenue than to cost. Beyond that quantity, additional units are contributing more to cost than to revenue. For labor, marginal resource cost equals wage.

LABOR MARKET AND FIRMS' HIRING OF LABOR

PERFECTLY COMPETITIVE LABOR MARKET

A purely competitive labor market has a specific set of characteristics:

- A large number of firms hiring a specific type of labor
- Numerous qualified, independent workers with identical skills
- Wage taker behavior (no ability to control wage on either side)
- Market demand is the sum of labor demand curves of the individual firms (their MRP curves)

Market supply slopes upward because as a group, the firms must pay higher wage rates to obtain more workers because workers have some alternatives.

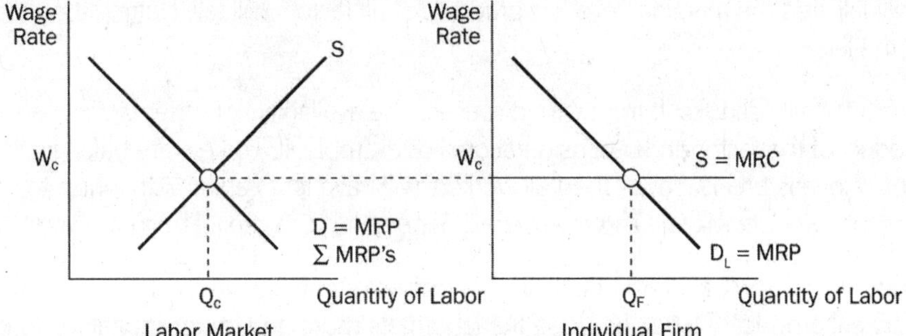

The firms get their wage rate from the market equilibrium of demand and supply of labor. For the firm, the wage rate or MRC (S) is perfectly elastic and MRP is downward-sloping. Each firm will find it profitable to hire labor up to the point at which MRP = MRC.

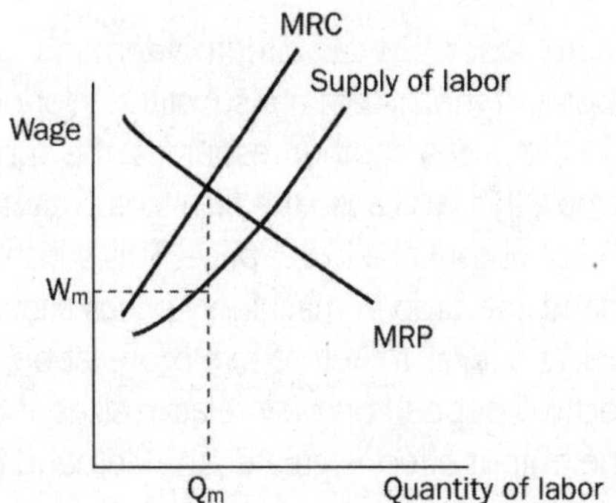

If there is imperfect competition in the labor market, the firm has enough market power to influence wages. A single firm that has market power in the labor market is called a **monopsony**. This firm will face the market supply curve for labor, which slopes upward to the right. In order to hire more units of labor, the firm must offer a higher wage. This higher wage must then also be paid to all previous units of labor hired. Therefore, the marginal resource cost curve slopes upward and to the right and lies above the supply curve. Each additional unit of labor hired adds more to costs than its own wage. The firm will still profit maximize by hiring the quantity of labor where marginal revenue product equals marginal resource cost. The difference betwen monopsony and perfect competition is that marginal resource cost no longer equals wage.

Determinants of Labor Demand

The labor demand curve might shift for a variety of reasons, including changes in:

- Product demand
- Productivity
- Technology
- Worker quality
- The price of other resources

If the demand for the product changes, its price will change, too. In turn, this will change the marginal revenue products of all quantities of all resources. If demand rises, price will rise, and the marginal revenue products will rise, shifting the demand curve for the factors to the right. If product demand falls, price will fall, and the marginal revenue products of all factors will fall, shifting the demand curve for them to the left.

Changes in productivity can result from varied causes. The availability of other factors can affect the marginal product of the factor under consideration. For example, if workers are baking pizzas and one of the pizza ovens breaks down, then all workers will have less capital with which to work. The workers' marginal product will fall. The reverse will happen if more capital becomes available.

A change in productivity will also occur if there is a technological change. Technological advances raise the marginal product of labor, because the labor gets more and better capital to work with. This shifts the marginal product curve—and therefore the marginal revenue product/labor demand curve—to the right. If the pizza ovens are improved so that they bake pizza more quickly, the pizza bakers' productivity will rise. The productivity of the bakers will also rise if there is an improvement in the quality of their work, such as might be created by a training program.

Finally, a change in the prices of other resources can alter the demand for a particular resource, such as labor. Suppose two resources, labor and machinery, are substitutes for one another. In this case, two effects will follow from a change in the prices of other resources: the substitution effect and the output effect. If the price of machinery drops, this will cause the firm to substitute machinery for labor, because it can then produce the same level of output at a lower price. This substitution effect decreases the demand for labor. On the other hand, the drop in machinery prices allows the firm to produce more output at a given expenditure level, and it will therefore hire more labor. These two effects work in opposite directions. Their net effect will depend on their relative sizes. If the substitution effect is greater, the demand for labor will fall. If the output effect is greater, the demand for labor will rise.

Resources can also be complements, that is, they can be used together in the production process. If resources are complements, there is no substitution effect, because the use of one requires the use of the other. There is however, an output effect, as a drop in the price of one resource means that more output can be produced at a given expenditure level.

Determinants of Labor Supply

An upward-sloping supply curve indicates that as wages increase, more labor will be offered for sale. This assumes that the increases in wages are accompanied by an increasing opportunity cost associated with leisure, and that less leisure will be taken as a result. Note, however, that a higher wage may also cause people's incomes to rise to a point at which they will wish to take more leisure, in which case the labor supply curve would be downward-sloping.

The labor supply curve might shift for three reasons:

1. Changes in tastes

   Example: Until the latter half of the 20th century, many married women either chose or were expected to stay home and raise children. Now, tastes have changed and more married women choose to work at paid jobs. This has shifted the labor supply curve outward.

2. Available opportunities in other labor markets

   Example: If pizza bakers can earn more money at another job, say, baking cakes at a bakery, the supply curve for pizza bakers will shift left. If the pay for baking cakes declines, we could expect cake bakers to enter the pizza baking market, shifting the supply curve for pizza bakers to the right.

3. Immigration

   Example: If laborers move into a market from another region or country, the supply curve for labor in the region to which they moved will shift right. In the region from which they came, the supply curve will shift left.

Optimum Allocation of Resources

We have analyzed how much of a resource a firm will use when that resource is the only one that is variable. Next we analyze what combination of resources a firm will use when they are *all* variable, as is the case in the long run.

As a rule, a firm is producing its output using the least-cost combination of resources when the last dollar spent on each resource yields the same marginal product. This means that the ratios of the marginal product of the last unit used of the resources to their respective resource prices are the same. If the resources are labor and capital, this is given by the equation

$$\frac{MP_L}{P_L} = \frac{MP_C}{P_C}$$

For example, suppose the firm is using a combination of resources such that the marginal product of labor equals 20 and the marginal product of capital equals 10. Remember that once diminishing returns set in, marginal product falls with additional units of the resource used; thus fewer units of labor would yield marginal product higher than 20 and more units of labor would yield a lower marginal product. The same is true for capital. For simplicity, assume that the price of both resources is $1 per unit.

We then have

$$\frac{MRP_L}{P_L} = \frac{MRP_C}{P_C} = 1$$

If the firm buys one fewer unit of capital—in other words, if the firm spends $1 less on capital—it will lose 10 units of output. However, if it then spends that same dollar purchasing an additional unit of labor, it will gain 20 units of output. The firm will be producing more output at the same cost. This situation will continue as long as the ratios are unequal. Once they are equal, shifting the dollars spent from one resource to another will not increase output. The ratios must be equal, not just proportionate.

Note that if the firm is producing more output for the same cost, the cost per unit drops. That means that the total cost of any specific level of output is reduced.

A second method to find the optimum allocation of resources is to use the profit maximizing equation. When the MRP per dollar of each resource are equal to one, then the optimum maximization is realized. So,

$$\frac{MP_L = 20}{P_L = \$1} > \frac{MP_C = 10}{P_C = \$1}$$

This is a much easier method because you simply equate the price to the MRP of each resource. If a firm is maximizing profit and producing a given output, the firm is also producing at the least cost.

IF YOU LEARNED ONLY THREE THINGS IN THIS CHAPTER. . .

1. Labor demand factors include changes in: product demand, productivity, technology, worker quality, and/or the price of other resources.
2. Labor supply factors include changes in tastes, available opportunities in other labor markets, and/or immigration.
3. When a society is using the optimum allocation of its resources, it maximizes the net benefits for everybody, regardless of who enjoys the benefits or pays the cost.

REVIEW QUESTIONS

1. Which of the following is indicative of a derived demand?

   (A) The supply of cotton rises because increased demand brings higher prices.
   (B) The price of cotton increases as a result of widespread insect damage to crops.
   (C) Consumers want colorful T-shirts for casual wear, so textile mills hire workers.
   (D) If the salaries of textile workers rise, the quantity of textile workers hired will fall.
   (E) An increase in the price of T-shirts will increase the demand for button-down shirts.

2. Which of the following will yield marginal revenue product of labor when producing Good Z? Assume the firm sells its product under perfect competition.

   (A) $MRC_L \times P_z$
   (B) $MR_L \times P_z$
   (C) $MP_L \times P_z$
   (D) $MP_L \times MC_z$
   (E) $MR_L \times MR_z$

3. To maximize profit, how much labor should a firm hire?

   (A) It should hire until MC = MR.
   (B) It should hire until MP = W.
   (C) It should hire until MC = W.
   (D) It should hire until MRP = W.
   (E) It should hire until MRP = MC.

4. Which of the following would cause the labor supply curve for Industry A to shift left?

   (A) More women seek paying jobs rather than parenting full time.
   (B) The mandatory retirement age is raised.
   (C) Laborers immigrate into the market.
   (D) Another industry, Industry B, raises workers' wages.
   (E) Consumer preference shifts in favor of Industry A's product.

5. Which of the following would cause the labor demand curve for Industry B to shift right?

(A) More people choosing to become full-time parents.

(B) More people choosing to retire early.

(C) A rise in wages in Industry C.

(D) Advances in technology.

(E) A product being produced going out of fashion.

6. Which of the following events could cause an increase in the productivity of labor?

I. Office workers receive faster computers.
II. Wages for textile workers rise.
III. More ladders are given to a construction crew working on a house.
IV. The minimum wage law is repealed.
V. Bank clerks take a training course.

(A) I and III

(B) I, III, and V

(C) I, II, and IV

(D) II, IV, and V

(E) III, IV, and V

Use the following table to answer question 7.

Units Used	MP of Labor	Labor Wage	MP of Capital	Price per Unit of Capital
1	10	$2	16	$3
2	8	$2	13	$3
3	6	$2	9	$3
4	4	$2	5	$3
5	1	$2	3	$3

7. Given the schedule above, how many units of each resource should the firm use to minimize costs?

(A) one unit of labor, two units of capital

(B) two units of each

(C) three units of labor, four units of capital

(D) three units of each

(E) five units of labor, three units of capital

8. If a unit of labor costs $10 per hour, and the price of the product being made is $5 per unit, how much must a worker produce each hour to have a marginal revenue product of $30?

   (A) 3
   (B) 6
   (C) 50
   (D) 150
   (E) 300

9. In a purely competitive industry, a decrease in a firm's MRP could result from

   (A) a decrease in the demand for the product this resource produces
   (B) a decrease in the price of the economic resource
   (C) a decrease in the supply of the resource
   (D) an increase in the marginal productivity of the resource
   (E) an increase in the price of the product this resource produces

10. Which is an example of a change in productivity that increases labor demand?

    (A) Sales via the Internet increase, thus increasing the demand for computer programmers
    (B) SUVs decrease in popularity, thus decreasing the demand for workers who produce SUVs
    (C) An increase in the price of lumber increases the cost of building homes, thus decreasing the demand for construction workers.
    (D) A technological change increases output per worker in the automobile industry, thus increasing the demand for auto workers.
    (E) Income rises so there is an increase in the demand for workers in all industries.

Free-Response Question

(a) Draw a correctly labeled competitive labor market graph showing an increase in demand.

(b) Explain three reasons why the curve might shift as you have shown.

(c) Identify the effect of this shift on wage rates and quantity hired for the market and for individual firms.

ANSWERS AND EXPLANATIONS

1. C

People don't want to consume textile workers, they want to consume T-shirts; their desire for this product is the reason that there is a demand for textile workers, so the demand for textile workers is derived from the demand for T-shirts. Eliminate (A) because it pertains to an increase in price following from increased demand, which will cause economic profits to be made in the industry and will attract new cotton farmers. Eliminate (B) because it concerns a rise in price, which is caused by the decrease in supply, which itself was caused by a pest destroying some of the crop. Eliminate (D) because it concerns how the law of demand operates in the hiring and firing of workers: price rises, quantity demanded falls, and vice versa. Eliminate (E) because it concerns the effect of a price change in a substitute good on the demand of another good. As the price of T-shirts rises, people switch to a substitute.

2. C

Marginal revenue product is the addition to total revenue brought about by using one more unit of a resource. You find marginal revenue product by multiplying the marginal product of the resource times the product price. Only (C) uses the marginal product of the extra worker times the price of the product produced. These are the two factors that create MRP.

3. D

Because we assume perfect competition in the labor market, all units of labor hired earn the same wage. Therefore, wage is the cost added by each unit of labor. Since marginal revenue product decreases (due to the law of diminishing returns), its curve slopes downward. At quantities less than the quantity at which marginal revenue product equals wage, each additional unit of labor used adds more to revenues than to costs, thereby increasing profits. At quantities greater than the quantity where marginal revenue product equals wage, additional units of labor add more to costs than to revenues, thereby decreasing profits. So the profit-maximizing quantity to hire occurs at the point where marginal revenue product equals wage. Only (D) includes that equation.

4. D

A leftward shift of the supply curve is a decrease in supply, so you are looking for factors that will cause a decrease in supply. If Industry B raised wages, workers would leave Industry A to seek jobs in Industry B, causing a decrease in the supply of labor in Industry A. Eliminate (A) because if women are seeking paying jobs, they are entering the labor force, and if this had any effect on Industry A, it would be to *increase* its supply of labor. Reject (B) because raising the mandatory retirement age keeps workers in the labor force longer, increasing the labor force and therefore, if anything, increasing Industry A's supply of labor. Eliminate (C) because immigration into the labor market would cause an increase in labor supply. Eliminate (E) because although this event would increase Industry A's output and thus its demand for workers, it would have no effect on the *supply* of workers.

5. D

When technology advances, the marginal product of labor increases, and therefore its marginal revenue product rises. The marginal revenue product curve is the firm's demand curve for labor, so a shift right in the demand curve is an increase in demand. You can eliminate (A) and (B); both shrink the supply of labor, shifting the supply curve left, but do not affect the demand for labor. You can eliminate (C) because if wages in Industry C rise, workers will leave Industry B to seek jobs in Industry C, decreasing the supply of labor in Industry B. In (E), if the product goes out of fashion, demand for it will decrease and price will decrease as well. A lower price will decrease the marginal revenue product of labor, decreasing demand for labor.

6. B

Statement I is correct because when workers get faster computers, they can do the same amount of work in less time, i.e., their marginal product rises, which equals an increase in productivity. Statement III is correct because a fixed amount of laborers are given additional capital equipment with which to work—which also results in an increase in productivity. Statement V is correct because by taking a training course, workers are improving their quality of work and learning to work more efficiently, which improves their productivity. Other statements are incorrect because the question asks specifically about productivity.

7. D

Recall that the least-cost combination of resources is given by the equation

$$\frac{MP_L}{P_L} = \frac{MP_C}{P_C}$$

The ratio of MPL to PL at three units of labor is $\frac{6}{2}$, or 3. If three units of capital are used, that ratio is $\frac{9}{3}$, or 3, also. At three units each, the ratios are equal. You can eliminate (A) because at one unit of labor, the ratio is $\frac{10}{2}$, or 5. And at two units of capital the ratio is $\frac{13}{3}$, or $4\frac{1}{3}$. You can eliminate (B) because at two units of labor, the ratio is $\frac{8}{2}$, or 4, and at two units of capital the ratio is $\frac{13}{3}$, or $4\frac{1}{3}$ You can eliminate (C) because at three units of labor the ratio equals $\frac{6}{2}$ or 3, and at four units of capital the ratio is $\frac{5}{3}$ or $1\frac{1}{3}$ Choice (E) calls for five units of labor (a ratio of $\frac{1}{2}$) and three units of capital (a ratio of $\frac{9}{3}$ or 3). Therefore, the only combination for which the ratios are equal is three units of each, making (D) the correct choice.

8. B

Marginal revenue product equals marginal product times product price, or

$$MRP_L = MPL \times P_{Prod}$$

So

$$\frac{MRPL}{P_{Prod}} = MP_L$$

Therefore, $\frac{30}{5} = 6$. You can eliminate (A), because it divides marginal revenue product by wage, which is not how marginal revenue product should be calculated. You can eliminate (C), because it multiplies wage by product price. Choice (D) is incorrect because it multiplies marginal revenue product by price, and (E) is incorrect because it multiplies marginal revenue product by wage.

9. A

Decreases in a firm's MRP will be related to a decrease in the marginal product of the workers and/or a decrease in the market price of the product. In (A), a decrease in the demand for the product will lower its price. A lower price will decrease the firm's MRP. Choice (E) is the reverse of the correct answer. Choice (D) causes the MRP to rise. Choices (B) and (C) are supply factors.

10. D

A new technology will increase productivity and increase the demand for labor or the MRP. This is expressed in (D). Choices (A), (B), and (C) are incorrect because they relate to derived demand as a factor in the demand for labor. Choice (E) connects income change to a change in worker demand.

FREE-RESPONSE QUESTION

(a)

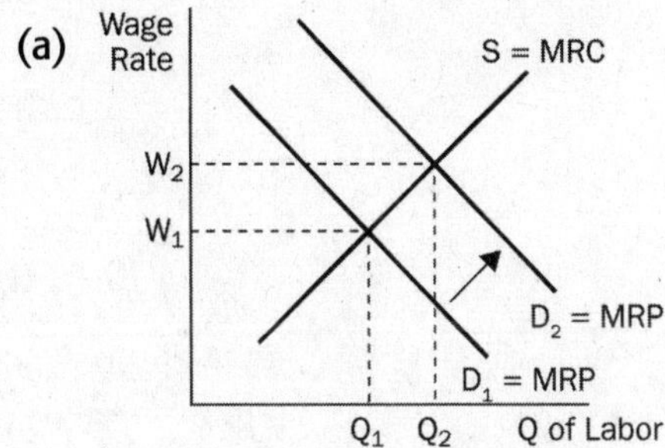

(b) Labor demand might increase for three reasons: an increase in productivity, an increase in demand for the product, or a change in the prices of other resources. If workers' productivity increases, their marginal product will rise. This in turn increases their marginal revenue product, which predicts the firm's demand.

An increase in productivity can occur as a result of a technological advance, an increase in worker quality, or because more capital becomes available. Increase in demand for the product will increase product price. This increase will create an increase in workers' marginal revenue product, because MRP = MP x P. Since marginal revenue product is the firm's demand for labor, an increase in product price will increase that demand.

Demand might also increase due to a change in the prices of other resources. If another resource, say capital, is a substitute for labor, there will be a substitution effect that might decrease the demand for labor. However, there will also be an output effect as firms can produce output more cheaply, and this output effect might be powerful enough to offset the substitution effect and increase demand for labor. If resources are complements, then an increase in the price of the other resource will cause more of that resource to be used, and therefore also more of the labor that goes with it. This will also cause an increase in the demand for labor.

(c) An increase in demand increases wages and the number of workers hired in the market. On the graph, hiring goes from Q_1 to Q_2, and wages go from W_1 to W_2. For the firm, wage rates increase because the firm takes its wage rate from the market wage rate. Therefore, MRC for the firm will rise. However, so will MRP, so the increase in demand will cause more workers to be hired.

Chapter 13: **Market Failure and the Role of Government**

- Externalities
- Public Goods
- Public Policy to Promote Competition
- Income Distribution
- Review Questions
- Answers and Explanations

EXTERNALITIES

MARGINAL SOCIAL BENEFIT AND MARGINAL SOCIAL COST

There are usually clear costs and benefits for producers and consumers when goods are produced or consumed. These are called private costs or benefits. Sometimes, however, when goods are produced or consumed, people *other* than the producer or the consumer benefit or pay costs; these indirect results are called side, or spillover, effects. In these situations, a benefit or cost is incurred by individuals who are not directly involved in the production or consumption of the good. These **externalities** fall on third parties who are not directly involved in the market transaction, and are thus largely ignored by the producer and the consumer.

For example, when someone smokes a cigarette in public, he receives a benefit; people's idea of what the benefit is may vary, but in all cases it is the expectation of a benefit that motivates people to choose one course of action over another. The person smoking in public also incurs a cost: the price of the cigarette and the risk to his health. These are private costs and benefits. However, the people around the smoker also incur a cost: the risk to their health created by secondhand smoke. This is an **external cost**, because costs incurred as a result of this secondhand smoke are not paid by the person consuming the cigarette. The activity of smoking in public thereby produces a **negative externality.** A negative externality is created when a person or firm's actions impose a cost—or adverse side effect—on others.

Production and consumption can also produce external benefits. For example, when your neighbor spends time and money beautifying his front lawn with flowers and trees, he receives a private benefit from his own pleasure and the enhanced value of his home. However, you also receive a benefit whenever you look at the beautiful yard. His beautiful yard also contributes to the value of the neighborhood and may therefore increase the value of your home as well. His yard, then, produces a **positive externality**: a benefit for people who are not directly involved with the good or the market transactions surrounding it.

A specialized vocabulary comes into play when we use marginal analysis to study externalities. Benefits are discussed in terms of marginal private benefit, marginal external benefit, marginal social benefit. Costs are treated in terms of marginal private cost, marginal external cost, and marginal social cost.

Marginal private benefit (MPB) belongs to the producer or consumer of the good. The **marginal external benefit** (MEB) is the spillover. When the two are added together, they equal the **marginal social benefit** (MSB).

$$MSB = MPB + MEB$$

Marginal private cost (MPC) is the cost incurred by the producer or consumer, while **marginal external cost** (MEC) is the spillover, or externality. **Marginal social cost** (MSC) is equal to the sum of these two costs.

$$MSC = MPC + MEC$$

Remember that marginal costs rise as output rises, due to the law of diminishing returns. Also recall that a firm's marginal cost curve, above average variable cost, is the firm's supply curve, and that market supply is simply a summation of individuals' supply curves.

Marginal benefits fall as output, or consumption, increases due to diminishing marginal utility. Remember that demand curves reflect utility; they will therefore mirror this decrease.

Market prices generally reflect only private costs and benefits. Therefore, market supply and demand curves only include private costs and benefits—bystanders are not included because they are not participating in the market. So, graphically, we have:

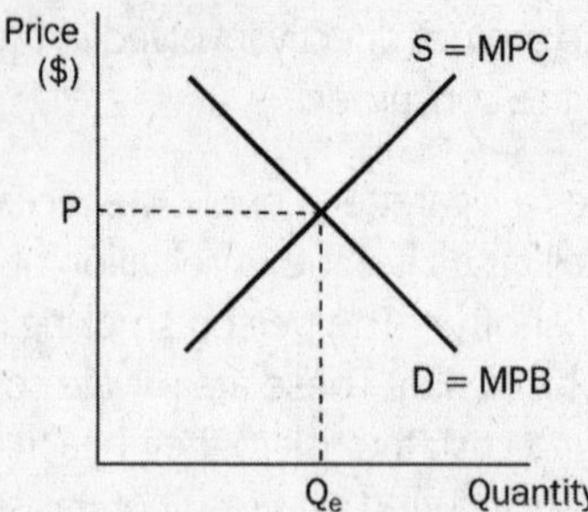

The free market will cause Q_e to be produced. However, if external benefits and costs were to be included, these curves would change.

POSITIVE EXTERNALITIES

Another good that produces positive externalities is education. The person receiving the education obviously receives a variety of benefits, ranging from personal improvement to marketable job skills. However, society also benefits from the fact that educated individuals are better able to look after their own interests in a way that does not harm others, and are less likely to become a burden on society. Productivity gains are also a benefit of education, which raise the overall standard of living for society.

When all of a good's benefits—including positive externalities—are accounted for in evaluating it, utility will rise and the demand (or marginal benefit) curve will shift right.

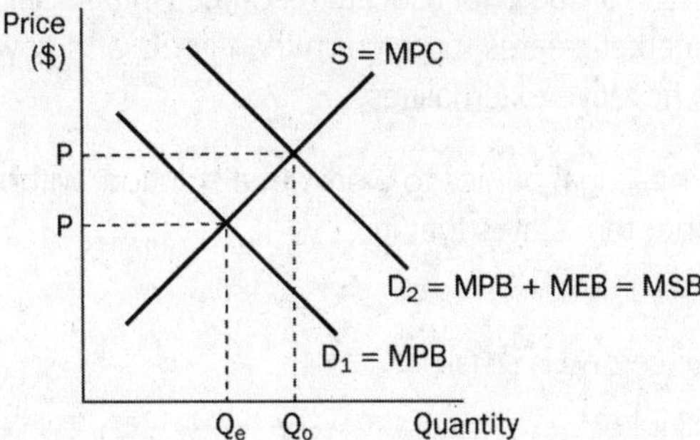

As shown, the quantity of the good produced will rise. The new quantity is the socially optimum level of output—the amount of the good that society would desire if all the good's benefits are taken into account. In the case of a positive externality, society will want *more* resources allocated to the good once all of its benefits have been tallied.

NEGATIVE EXTERNALITIES

As you might expect, the result of including negative externalities in the overall evaluation of a good has the opposite effect. If a good is creating negative externalities, then when all of that good's costs are included in the supply curve, marginal costs will rise, shifting the supply curve to the left.

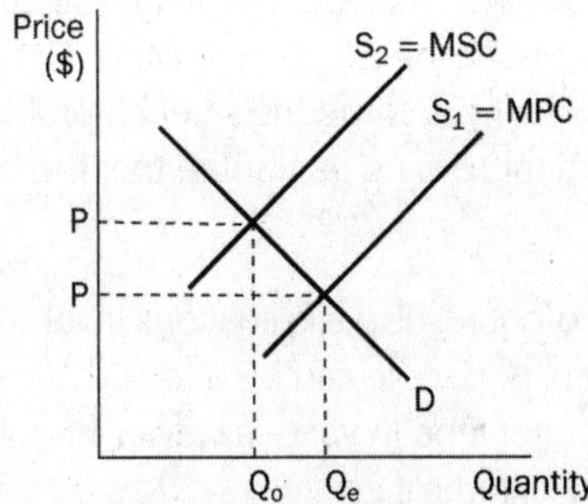

The socially optimum level of output is less than the amount that the market will produce on its own (because the market does not account for these externalized costs). Left to itself, the market will allocate more resources to this product than society would desire if all the costs were accounted for.

Perhaps the most important negative externality of our time is pollution. Serious pollution has been created all over the world as a result of market demand for goods created by processes that create large quantities of pollution. This problem has been created by difficulties in making the market take account of people's right to clean air and water, peace and quiet, and the other resources that are degraded by pollution.

REMEDIES

The difference between a socially optimum level of production and the market level is a **market failure**. The market fails because it does not allocate resources in a socially optimum way. In these situations, the unrestrained market creates more harm than good, and government has a role to play in correcting, or internalizing, negative externalities.

It is sometimes possible for individual parties to work out a solution, without government legislation or intervention. The Coase Theorem states that if

1. property rights are clear
2. the number of people concerned is small
3. bargaining costs are negligible

then parties should be able to negotiate a solution without government intervention.

Suppose your neighbor's dog barks loudly, disturbing you when you are working at home. If there is not a city ordinance prohibiting this kind of noise, you and your neighbor might be able to negotiate an agreement in which your neighbor replaces the income you lost as a result of the disturbance. In this case, the property rights are clear, there are only two people involved, and they can bargain by exchanging words over the back fence.

If private negotiations are unworkable, clear property rights may still help in finding a solution. The U.S. government has erected a framework of laws that protects private property from damage by others; these laws also create a damage recovery system. For example, if you own a farm and a nearby factory pollutes a stream that runs onto your property, you can sue for damages. These lawsuits are often a productive way of dealing with externalities. However, it can be harder to establish liability if the negative externality is someone's health problem. The legal process can be expensive and time-consuming, and there is no guarantee that the company being sued will have the money to pay damages.

The Coase Theorem and lawsuits do not resolve all situations involving externalities. In the case of pollution, for example, large numbers of people can be affected. When private negotiation or litigation is not the answer, government can intervene in various ways. This table summarizes common government approaches to negative externalities.

Problem Resource Allocation

Problem	Resource Allocation Outcome	Ways to Correct
Spillover costs (negative externalities)	Overallocation of resources	1. Individual bargaining 2. Liability rules and lawsuits 3. Tax on producers 4. Direct controls 5. Market for externality rights
Spillover benefits (positive externalities)	Underallocation of resources	1. Individual bargaining 2. Subsidy to consumers 3. Subsidy to producers 4. Government provision

One way that government may intervene to correct externalities is by imposing direct controls. The Clean Air Act of 1990 is an example of a direct control; this legislation required businesses and factories to use the best technology to reduce emissions of 189 toxic chemicals by 90% between 1990 and 2000. It also required a 30-60% reduction in auto emissions and a 50% reduction in the use of chlorofluorocarbons (CFC's, chemicals that deplete the ozone layer). Coal-burning utilities had to cut emissions of sulfur dioxide by 50% to help reduce acid rain.

Direct controls cost businesses money. They increase the marginal cost of a product, shifting the supply curve left and thereby bringing the quantity produced closer to the socially optimum level.

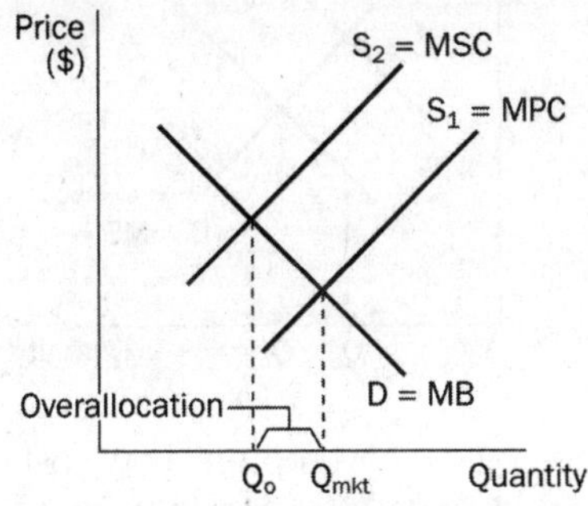

Another policy approach to managing negative externalities is to levy specific taxes. Government has placed an excise tax on the use of CFCs. A firm can choose to use the CFCs and pay the tax, or to alter their technology and avoid using the CFCs. Either way, the firm's marginal cost rises, again shifting the supply curve left as in the graph above. Note that the output shifts to the left (Q_0) corrected the over-allocation of resources.

Where there are spillover benefits, government often uses subsidies to correct the underallocation that the free market would produce. Subsidies can be paid either to buyers or to sellers.

For example, vaccinations produce external, or spillover, benefits, because even those who do not get vaccinated benefit from the lowered risk of getting a particular disease (because of the increase in the vaccinated population). The government might help buyers pay for vaccinations by, say, issuing discount coupons to the parents of small children. Or the government could subsidize sellers by paying either doctors or clinics to administer vaccinations.

If a subsidy is paid to buyers, it will shift the demand curve to the right, raising the output level to something closer to the socially optimum level.

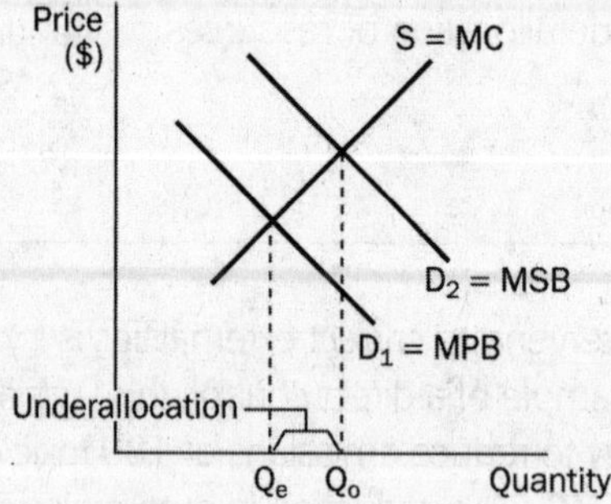

If a subsidy is paid to sellers, it will shift the supply curve to the right, again correcting the underallocation.

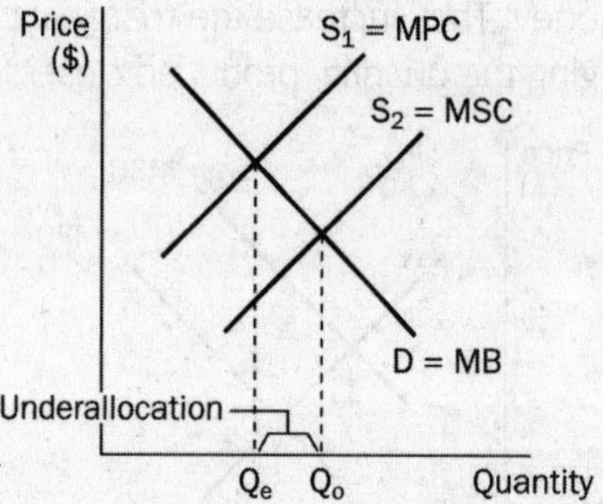

Education is another good subsidized by the government. Low-cost student loans and Pell Grants subsidize the buyers of education (students). Research grants and tax abatements subsidize universities, who are the sellers of education.

Finally, the government can act to provide a good, as it did when it eradicated polio by providing free polio vaccines to all children. It also provides kindergarten, elementary, and secondary schooling free of charge, paying for these services from tax funds.

A more limited government approach involves creating markets for externality rights. To understand this approach, we must first understand that air, bodies of water, and public lands are all targets for pollution because they are held "in common" by the public. People take care of what they own, both to maintain its value for resale and to gain a sense of personal pride. Property rights provide a motive for people to use resources wisely. There is no such incentive with respect to commonly owned property; instead, each user will act in his own self-interest. This **tragedy of the commons** has been recognized since the days when villages had common grazing areas. These areas quickly became overgrazed, as everyone had an incentive to graze as many cows as possible on common land. Today, firms have no incentive to care for air and water, while at the same time they have strong incentive—in the form of reduced costs—to pollute them.

To provide firms with incentives to refrain from polluting public resources, government can create a market for pollution (or any negative externality) rights. To use this approach, a government agency must first decide how much pollution the environment or resource can absorb while remaining healthy and useful. Suppose a large lake can accept 1,000 tons of some pollutant per year. The supply of pollution rights is then fixed at 1,000 tons, and is therefore perfectly inelastic. Demand for pollution rights follows the same pattern as any demand curve: The cheaper it is to pollute, the more pollution will be created and dumped. Suppose that in 2005 the demand curve is D_1 on the graph below. An equilibrium price for pollution rights will be determined by the interaction of demand and supply, as shown.

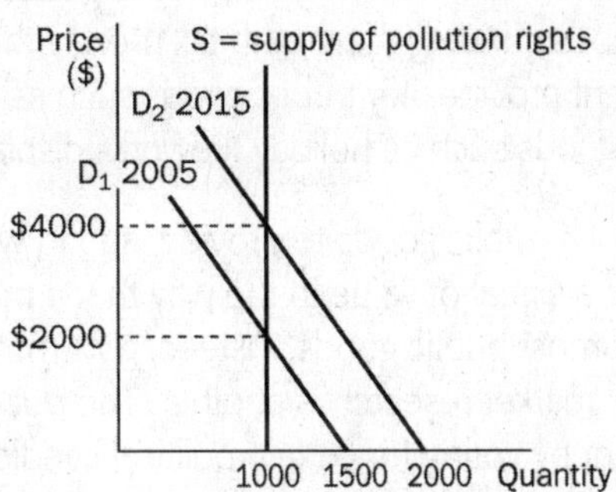

Firms will have to pay $2,000 per ton for pollution rights, and the lake will only have to absorb 1,000 tons of pollution, instead of the 1,500 it would have received if there were no charge for the right to pollute. As human and business populations grow, the demand for pollution rights will grow, as shown by D_2. The price of pollution rights will increase, with the lake still taking the 1,000 tons of pollution that the agency had already decided was feasible.

The government also intervenes in markets where information is difficult to get. For example, government regulation measures ensure that when you buy a gallon of high-octane gasoline, you don't get a quart of low octane. By licensing doctors, the government ensures that patients seeking a doctor are likely to find someone who has at least the minimum amount of required education and training. Market failures would occur if these measures were not enforced.

PUBLIC GOODS

PUBLIC VS. PRIVATE GOODS

Goods can be characterized in terms of how easily they can be used and how much one person's use of a good affects others who might like to use it. If a good is **excludable,** this means that people can be prevented from using it. If a good is **rival**, one person's use of the good decreases another's ability to use it. A private good, such as a slice of pizza, is both excludable and rival. If you don't pay for the pizza the law says you cannot have it, making it excludable (or exclusive); if you eat that slice no one else can eat it, making it rival. A public good, such as national defense, is neither excludable nor rival. If you defend the people of one state against a missile attack, people in other states will also be defended. One person's use of the defense does not lessen another's ability to use it.

PROVISION OF PUBLIC GOODS

The market will not provide public goods because there is no way to make a profit from them. These goods produce many positive externalities, for which the market cannot effectively account. The accessible and desirable nature of public goods inclines people to use these goods, sometimes without paying for the privilege of doing so. This is called the **free-rider problem**, and it is what stands in the way of private firms providing truly public goods. Thus it makes sense for the government to provide public goods, funding them with tax money that is collected from all citizens. This is why the federal government provides for public goods such as national defense, and why municipal governments provide goods such as holiday fireworks displays and parades.

Governments need to decide which public goods to provide, and in what quantities. However, governments cannot use price as a signal of value in the way that a market would, because price does not fully reflect the value of most public goods. Instead, government must use other methods. Public surveys are one approach; market research is another. The public also registers its preferences for public goods to a certain extent by voting for certain political candidates.

The optimal amount of a public good can be shown using supply and demand analysis. The demand curve reflects the collective willingness to pay, as best it can be determined. The supply curve will be upward-sloping, reflecting rising marginal costs. This MB = MC relationship is another way to express allocative efficiency. Society is receiving the goods and services (in this case, public goods) in the quantity it desires.

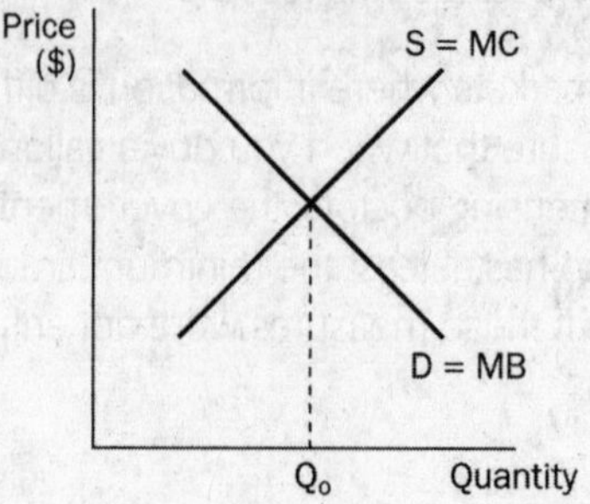

THE ECONOMICS OF TAXATION

When we discuss the quantity of public goods society desires to have, it is difficult to know how much each citizen derives from the use of public goods. Taxpayers across the nation pay the price for making these goods available to society.

Two principles guide the government in apportioning the burden of taxation.

1. The *benefits-received principle* holds that government should tax individuals according to the amount of benefits they receive, regardless of their income. Gasoline taxes are the best example of this approach, because the tax collected goes directly into the fund to finance highway construction and repair.
2. The *ability-to-pay principle* holds that people should be taxed according to their income or wealth regardless of the benefits they receive from government. Those with higher income receive less marginal utility from the goods they buy because their incomes allow them to buy more things to satisfy their wants. A low-income buyer, on the other hand, gets greater utility from each good he purchases because he has less to spend.

Taxes are classified as **progressive**, **proportional**, or **regressive** depending on the relationship between tax rates and taxpayer incomes. A tax is progressive if its average rate increases as income increases; the personal income tax is an example of a progressive tax. A tax is proportional if the average rate remains the same regardless of the size of income; the corporate income tax is an example of a proportional tax. A tax is regressive if the average rate declines as income increases. Regressive taxes generally hurt those in lower income levels; general sales taxes and the FICA (Social Security) tax are examples of regressive taxes.

The discussion of the incidence of taxation in the earlier section on demand and supply showed that the burden of a tax is often borne by people or firms other than those on which the tax was originally levied.

PUBLIC POLICY TO PROMOTE COMPETITION

We have seen that when there is more competition in a market, more total surplus will be provided. Increased competition also means that a market is more likely to provide allocative efficiency by producing the socially optimum amount of a good. However, we have also seen that some markets will organize themselves so as to hinder competition. In these cases, governments can respond in two ways.

ANTITRUST POLICY

One of the government's goals is to make industry more competitive. It does this through a set of laws called antitrust laws that aim to curb monopoly power. The Sherman Antitrust Act was passed by Congress in 1890; it made combinations in restraint of trade illegal, a prohibition that included practices such as collusive price fixing and the separation of markets. The Clayton Act, passed in 1914, strengthened government powers to promote competition, by outlawing tying contracts, interlocking directorates, and price discrimination when it reduces competition. In that same year, the Federal Trade Commission was created. This commission is composed of five members who share joint responsibility with the Department of Justice to enforce antitrust laws.

Over time, both the courts and political administrations have varied widely in how strictly to enforce the antitrust laws. The political climate in which the laws work is important, because although individual parties can file antitrust suits, the litigation is very expensive and often lasts for several years. Government is often in a better position to pursue litigation effectively.

INCOME DISTRIBUTION

EQUITY

Incomes differ for many reasons. Incomes in the U.S. flow in accordance with the maxim "to each according to what he creates." (There are exceptions to this, as we discussed in the preceding chapter.) Whether or not this is a fair or equitable distribution is a hotly debated issue. As a nation, however, our policies reflect the view that certain levels of poverty are unacceptable in a society as well off as our own. Policies to reduce poverty include minimum wage laws, welfare, and Social Security.

SOURCES OF INCOME INEQUALITY

Income is distributed among the various factors of production according to the demand for, and supply of, each one. However, remember that the demand curve for any factor will be its marginal revenue product curve, so the demand for a factor has a great deal to do with the value of the good it produces. For example, a resource that is rare but is used to produce a product no one wants will not command a high price.

The **productivity** of a factor is thus an important determinant of its price. Productivity is the value of the output that one worker produces in one hour. In the U.S., wages have risen over time because as workers' productivity has risen they have gained more and better capital with which to work.

Some jobs pay different wages because of **compensating differentials**. These are the differences in wages that arise from the non-monetary characteristics of jobs. For example, jobs that are easy and safe will pay less than jobs that are difficult and dangerous. This is one reason why a pizza baker will earn less than a coal miner.

Jobs also pay more if they require more human capital. **Human capital** is investment in people, such as education and training. People's opportunity to acquire human capital differs widely, which can lead to problematic inequalities in wages.

However, people's incomes are unequal for reasons that go beyond differences in their jobs. Age, for instance, plays a large role. Union members tend to make more than non-union members in the same trade. Special talents and abilities can also make a big difference, as can inherited wealth. In short, many factors play significant roles in determining income levels.

Income inequality in the United States is normally expressed in fifths, or quintiles, as shown in the table below, which contains figures for the year 2000.

Quintile	Percent of Total Income	Mean Annual Household Income
Lowest	3.6	$10,190
Second	8.9	$25,334
Third	14.9	$42,361
Fourth	23.0	$65,729
Fifth	49.6	$141,620

The table shows the percentage of the nation's total income that each fifth of the population receives, and the mean annual household income of each fifth.

Income inequality in the United States has grown since 1967. One of the commonly used measures of income inequality is the Lorenz curve. It expresses the relationship between the cumulative percentage of households and the cumulative percentage of income. If all households received exactly the same percentage of the total income, the curve would be a straight line at 45° from the origin. The more bowed-out the curve, the more unequal the distribution of income.

The Lorenz curve below corresponds to the data given in the table.

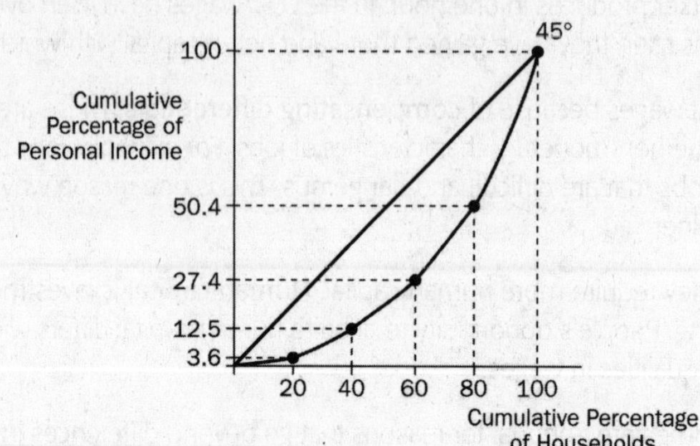

The government acts to mitigate income inequality when it makes transfer payments such as welfare or Social Security, when it subsidizes certain parts of a household's budget (e.g., healthcare) and when it sets the minimum wage.

IF YOU LEARNED ONLY FOUR THINGS IN THIS CHAPTER. . .

1. A positive externality provides a benefit for people who are not directly involved with a good or the market transactions surrounding it, while a negative externality is produced when a person or firm's actions impose a cost or adverse side effect on others.

2. The Coase theorem states that externalities can be efficiently controlled through voluntary negotiations among the affected parties.

3. Taxes are classified as progressive (the average rate increases as income increases), proportional (the average rate remains the same regardless of the size of income), or regressive (the average rate declines as income increases).

4. An antitrust policy aims to curb monopoly power.

REVIEW QUESTIONS

1. In the case of a market in which a negative externality is produced, which of the following is true of marginal social cost?

   (A) MSC = MPC
   (B) MSC = MPB
   (C) Government can intervene to cause MSC = MEC
   (D) Marginal social cost is not reflected in the supply curve
   (E) Bystanders are bearing the marginal social cost

2. In the case of a market in which a positive externality is being produced, which of the following is true of the demand curve?

   (A) It reflects marginal social cost.
   (B) It does not reflect marginal external benefits.
   (C) It reflects marginal social benefits.
   (D) It reflects marginal external benefits.
   (E) It does not reflect marginal private benefits.

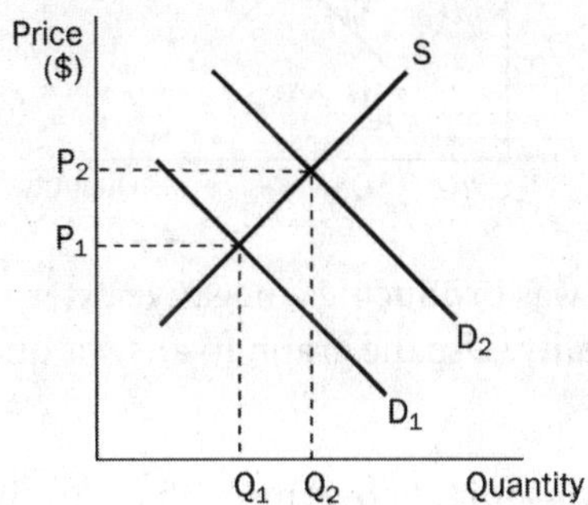

The graph represents a market that produced a positive externality until the government intervened to correct the externality. Use this graph to answer questions 3 and 4.

3. Which of the following actions might the government take to shift the demand curve from D_1 to D_2?

   (A) Providing a subsidy to buyers
   (B) Levying a tax on buyers
   (C) Canceling a contract with a firm that was providing the good
   (D) Using the Coase theorem to include all benefits in the demand curve
   (E) Passing a law clarifying property rights

4. Once the demand curve has been shifted to D_2, which of the following is true?

   I. Marginal social cost is now reflected in the demand curve.
   II. Output has now reached the socially optimum level.
   III. Marginal external benefits are now reflected in the demand curve.
   IV. The overallocation of resources represented by the difference between zero and Q_e has been corrected.
   V. The underallocation of resources represented by the difference between Q_e and Q_o has been corrected.

   (A) II and V
   (B) III and IV
   (C) III and V
   (D) II, III, and IV
   (E) II, III, and V

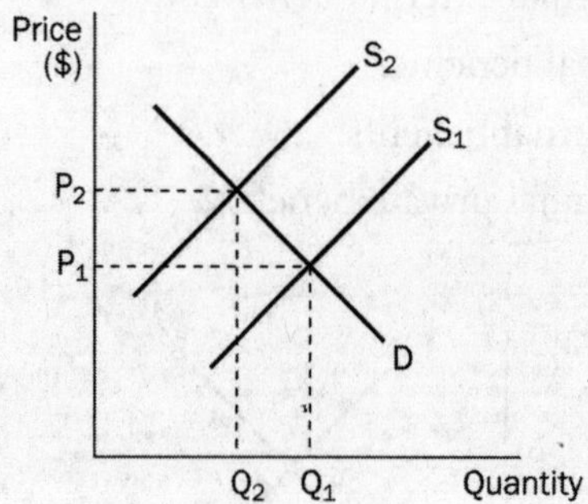

The graph depicts a market that was producing a negative externality until the government intervened to correct the externality. Use the graph to answer questions 5 and 6.

5. Which of the following actions might government take to shift the supply curve from S_1 to S_2?

   I. Taxing buyers
   II. Passing laws to clarify property rights
   III. Setting up a market for externality rights
   IV. Providing a subsidy to sellers
   V. Imposing direct controls on producers

   (A) I and IV
   (B) I, II, and III
   (C) III and IV
   (D) II, III, and V
   (E) III and V

6. Once the supply curve has been shifted to S_2, which of the following is true?

   I. Marginal private benefits are now reflected in the supply curve.
   II. Output has reached the socially optimum level.
   III. Marginal social costs are now reflected in the supply curve.
   IV. The overallocation of resources equal to the difference between Q_e and Q_o has been corrected.
   V. The underallocation of resources equal to the difference between zero and Q_o has been corrected.

   (A) I, II, and IV
   (B) II and III
   (C) II, III, and IV
   (D) III and IV
   (E) III, IV, and V

7. Private firms will not provide such goods as lighthouses or flood-control projects because

   (A) such projects generate harmful spillover effects
   (B) marginal benefits invariably fall short of marginal costs in such projects
   (C) they are major sources of revenue for government
   (D) there is a free-rider problem associated with these products
   (E) it is impossible to earn a profit from these goods

8. The ability-to-pay principle of taxation

   (A) has been declared illegal because people's wealth is taken without due process of law
   (B) implies that one should pay taxes in proportion to the benefits one derives from public goods and services provided
   (C) is the basis of every tax paid by Americans for public goods
   (D) implies that taxes should vary directly with one's income and wealth
   (E) implies that taxes should vary inversely with one's income and wealth

9. A general sales tax is regressive because

   (A) the incidence of the tax is placed upon the seller rather than the buyers
   (B) the incidence of the tax is placed upon the buyers rather than the seller
   (C) tax rates are constant and incomes are variable
   (D) families with lower income save a smaller percentage of their income than do families with higher income
   (E) tax rates decrease as consumer spending increases

10. Which of the following is a compensating differential?

    (A) An attractive person making higher wages than a less attractive individual
    (B) A union member making more than a non-union member
    (C) A job that requires human capital paying more than a job that does not
    (D) A worker who puts out oil fires making more than a schoolteacher
    (E) An older person earning less income than a younger one

FREE-RESPONSE QUESTION

Assume that Product X is produced in a perfectly competitive market and yields costs that are borne by third party individuals.

Using a correctly labeled graph, show the market output and price if the market ignores the externality.

(a) Identify the problem in this market.

(b) Identify and explain a remedy to the problem of misallocation of resources.

(c) Amend the graph to show how your remedy has changed the output to the socially optimum amount.

ANSWERS AND EXPLANATIONS

1. D

When there is a negative externality, the private costs that the firm pays do not cover all of the real costs associated with the good—some of them spill over onto bystanders. Marginal social cost, which is the sum of marginal private cost and marginal external cost, is therefore *not* reflected in the firm's supply curve. Eliminate (A) because MSC = MPC only in a market that is not producing externalities. Eliminate (B) because marginal social costs only equal marginal social benefit in a market that produces no externalities and is in equilibrium. Choice (C) is incorrect because MSC = MEC + MPC. Finally, (E) is incorrect because although bystanders are bearing *part* of the marginal social cost, it is only the part that is equal to marginal external cost. The other part of marginal social costs is marginal private costs, and these are borne by the firm.

2. B

A positive externality confers benefits on a bystander, someone who does not participate in the market either by buying the product or working on producing it. Those benefits are called marginal external benefits. The demand curve does not reflect these unless the government intervenes to internalize them. Eliminate (A) because the demand reflects value and benefits, not costs. Choice (C) is incorrect because it describes the basic economic problem associated with a positive externality: Marginal social benefits are not reflected in the demand curve. Marginal social benefits equal marginal private benefits, which are reflected in the demand curve, plus marginal external benefits, which are not. Choice (D) is incorrect; only until government intervenes and internalizes the external benefits will the demand curve reflect marginal social benefits. Eliminate (E) because in fact, marginal private benefits are the *only* benefits reflected in the demand curve, which is yet another way of describing the economic problem posed by positive externalities.

3. A

When there are positive externalities, government can subsidize either buyers or sellers to correct them. When it subsidizes buyers, the demand curve will then reflect marginal external benefits as well as marginal private benefits. Choice (B) is incorrect because taxes are used to correct negative externalities, not positive ones; they shift the supply curve. Eliminate (C) because one way for government to correct a positive externality is to provide the good itself, which it might accomplish by *paying* private firms to produce it. Choice (D) is incorrect because the Coase Theorem has nothing directly to do with government action or regulation; it involves the possibility of using private negotiations to solve an externality. Choice (E) is incorrect because clear property rights are of more use in resolving negative externalities.

4. E

Once the government intervenes, the shift in the demand curve will cause output level Q_0 to be produced. This output is the socially optimum level, so Statement II is correct. Statement III is also correct because the reason that government intervenes is to include the marginal external benefits in the demand curve. Statement V is correct as well, because until government intervenes to correct the externality, the market underallocates resources to the production of the good in question. The amount of the underallocation is equal to the difference between Q_e and Q_0. Statement I can be eliminated because costs are not included in the demand curve; they are included in the supply curve. They are also unrelated to positive externalities. Statement IV can be eliminated because an overallocation of resources is a problem associated with negative externalities.

5. D

Statement II is correct because clear property rights sometimes enable the parties involved to negotiate a private settlement. When money changes hands, even in a private settlement, this raises marginal cost, which shifts the supply curve left. Statement III is also correct because one way to correct negative externalities is to create a market that allows those creating the externality (e.g., polluters) to bid for a fixed amount of rights to create that externality. In this way, the externality is kept to a government-decreed maximum, and those who are producing it have an incentive to stop doing so. Payment for these rights is an increase in marginal cost, which shifts the supply curve left. Statement V is correct as well, because firms have to pay higher costs when government imposes direct controls, which again shifts the supply curve left. Statement I is incorrect because taxing buyers would not internalize the negative externality, and would shift the demand curve. Statement IV is incorrect because subsidies are used to correct positive externalities, not negative ones.

6. C

Statement II is correct because once the government intervention has shifted the supply curve, less of the good will be produced, correcting the overproduction that the market would accomplish if left alone. Statement III is also correct because the purpose of government intervention is to internalize the costs, or in other words, to bring them into the market by causing marginal social costs, which are equal to marginal private costs plus marginal external costs, to be reflected in the supply curve. Statement IV is correct as well, because prior to government intervention the free market caused an overallocation of resources, represented by the difference between Q_1 and Q_2. Government intervention caused fewer resources to be employed in this market. Statement I is incorrect because marginal social benefits belong in a demand curve, not a supply curve. Statement V is incorrect because when there is a negative externality, resources are *overallocated* to the product, not underallocated.

7. D

Lighthouses and flood control projects share the same problem—a private company cannot collect any revenue for providing these services. Thus, no profit is possible. Choice (B) does not apply in the case since the question argues the need for public goods.

8. D

The ability to pay principle of taxation states that there is equity in the notion that those who are able to pay (higher income groups) should bear the greater burden of taxation. So (D) is correct since as income rises, the tax burden increases. Choice (E) is the opposite of the correct answer. An example of this tax is the progressive income tax. Choice (B) correctly explains the other principle of tax equity—the benefits received principle.

9. D

A tax is regressive if the average rate declines as income increases. So, as spending occurs, the tax rate is applied to all purchases. A family earning a low income uses all of their income for spending and little if any is saved. All their income is exposed to the sales tax. Those with high incomes save a portion of that income, shielding it from the sales tax.

10. D

Compensating differentials are the differences in wages that arise from the non-monetary characteristics of jobs. An oil-fire fighter is doing a dangerous, dirty job, whereas a schoolteacher's work is cleaner and safer by comparison. This is not to say that the oil-fire fighter is more valuable than the schoolteacher, only that the characteristics of the two jobs are different. Choice (A) refers to a characteristic of the worker, not the job, as does (B). Choice (C) is incorrect because we would not consider a wage difference caused by a difference in the human capital required to be a compensating differential. Although it is the job that requires the human capital, it is the *worker* who acquires human capital. Choice (E) is incorrect because, again, it refers to a characteristic of the worker, not the job.

FREE-RESPONSE QUESTION

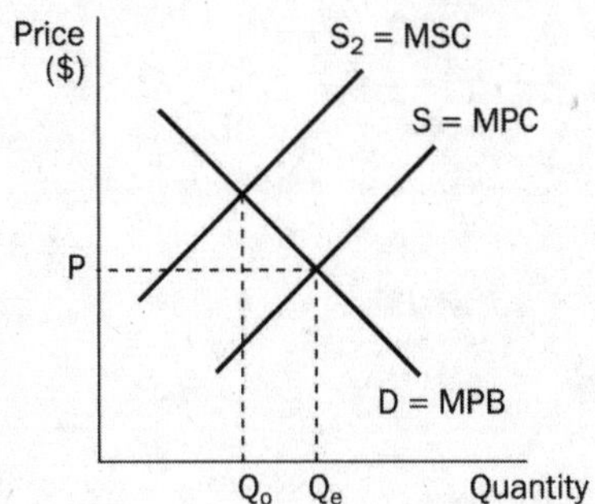

(a) The demand curve is labeled MPB since it represents the benefits to the buyer at various prices. The supply curve is labeled MPC since only the marginal private costs are covered by the seller. At Q_e, the market equilibrium is established as Q_d is equal to Q_s.

(b) The market is ignoring the negative externality caused by Product X. (It might be pollution or harmful effects to the general public.) The buyer and seller are the only participants in the market but others are affected by the production of Product X.

MSB < MSC and there is an overallocation of resources to the production of Product X.

(c) Individual bargaining, ability to sue in court, direct government controls, a tax on each unit produced, and a market for the sale of externality rights are all possible remedies. Each of these solutions will increase the marginal costs and move the supply curve to the left.

(d) On the same graph you can see that the movement of the supply curve to the left has caused the output to move back to Q_o. This is the correction needed to create the socially optimum level of resource allocation so MSB = MSC.

| PART FIVE |

Practice Tests

HOW TO TAKE THE PRACTICE TESTS

The next section of this book consists of two practice tests: one Macroeconomics test and one Microeconomics test. Take both practice tests if you are preparing for both AP exams, or just take the one for the AP exam you plan to take.

Taking a practice AP exam gives you an idea of what it's like to answer test questions for a longer period of time. You'll find out which areas you're strong in, and where additional review may be required. Any mistakes you make now are ones you won't make on the actual exam, as long as you take the time to learn where you went wrong.

Both full-length practice tests in this book include 60 multiple-choice questions and three free-response (essay) questions. You will have 70 minutes to answer the multiple-choice questions, a 10-minute reading period, and 50 minutes to answer the free-response questions. Before taking a practice test, find a quiet place where you can work uninterrupted for two and a half hours. Time yourself according to the time limit at the beginning of each section. It's okay to take a short break between sections, but for the most accurate results you should approximate real test conditions as much as possible. Use the ten-minute reading period to plan your answers for the free-response questions, but don't begin writing your responses until the ten minutes are up.

As you take the practice tests, remember to pace yourself. Train yourself to be aware of the time you are spending on each problem. Try to be aware of the general types of questions you encounter, as well as being alert to certain strategies or approaches that help you to handle the various question types more effectively.

After taking a practice exam, be sure to read the detailed answer explanations that follow. These will help you identify areas that could use additional review. Even when you answered a question correctly, you can learn additional information by looking at the answer explanation.

Finally, it's important to approach the test with the right attitude. You're going to get a great score because you've reviewed the material and learned the strategies in this book.

Good luck!

HOW TO COMPUTE YOUR SCORE

Scoring the Multiple-Choice Questions

To compute your score on the multiple-choice portions of the two Practice Tests, calculate the number of questions you got wrong on each test and then deduct $\frac{1}{4}$ of that number from the number of correct answers you got on each test. For example, on a 100-question exam, if you got six multiple-choice questions wrong, you would deduct 1.5 ($6 \times \frac{1}{4}$) from 94 (the number of questions answered correctly), and your score would then be a 93 (92.5 rounded up), or a 5, for the multiple-choice portion of the exam.

Scoring the Free-Response Questions

The essay reviewers have specific points that they are looking for in each free-response question. Frame your answer in complete, coherent sentences. Make sure that you present the various components of your answer in the right order, and in an order that will be intelligible to your readers. In addition to these basic structural concerns, reviewers will be seeking specific pieces of information in your answer. Each piece of information that they are able to find and check off in your answer is a point toward a better score.

To figure out your approximate score for the free-response questions, look at the key points found in the sample response for each question. For each key point you miss, subtract a point. For each key point you include, add a point. Figure out the number of key points there are in each question, then add up the number of key points you did include out of the total number of key points. Set up a proportion equal to 100 to obtain your approximate numerical score.

Calculating Your Composite Score

Your score on each AP Economics exam is a combination of your score on the multiple-choice portion and the free-response section. While different administrations of the exams give these sections different weights, for all intents and purposes, you can calculate your approximate score on the practice tests in this book.

Add together your score on the multiple-choice portion of the exam and your approximate score on the free-response section of the exam. If your score is a decimal, then round up to a whole number. Divide this sum by two to obtain your approximate score for each full-length exam.

The approximate score range is as follows:

5 = 90–100 (extremely well qualified)
4 = 80–89 (well qualified)
3 = 70–79 (qualified)
2 = 60–69 (possibly qualified)
1 = 0–59 (no recommendation)

If your score falls between 80 and 100, you're doing great; keep up the good work! If your score is lower than 79, there's still hope—Keep studying and you will be able to obtain a much better score on the exam before you know it.

AP Macroeconomics Practice Test
Answer Grid

1. (A)(B)(C)(D)(E)
2. (A)(B)(C)(D)(E)
3. (A)(B)(C)(D)(E)
4. (A)(B)(C)(D)(E)
5. (A)(B)(C)(D)(E)
6. (A)(B)(C)(D)(E)
7. (A)(B)(C)(D)(E)
8. (A)(B)(C)(D)(E)
9. (A)(B)(C)(D)(E)
10. (A)(B)(C)(D)(E)
11. (A)(B)(C)(D)(E)
12. (A)(B)(C)(D)(E)
13. (A)(B)(C)(D)(E)
14. (A)(B)(C)(D)(E)
15. (A)(B)(C)(D)(E)
16. (A)(B)(C)(D)(E)
17. (A)(B)(C)(D)(E)
18. (A)(B)(C)(D)(E)
19. (A)(B)(C)(D)(E)
20. (A)(B)(C)(D)(E)
21. (A)(B)(C)(D)(E)
22. (A)(B)(C)(D)(E)
23. (A)(B)(C)(D)(E)
24. (A)(B)(C)(D)(E)
25. (A)(B)(C)(D)(E)
26. (A)(B)(C)(D)(E)
27. (A)(B)(C)(D)(E)
28. (A)(B)(C)(D)(E)
29. (A)(B)(C)(D)(E)
30. (A)(B)(C)(D)(E)
31. (A)(B)(C)(D)(E)
32. (A)(B)(C)(D)(E)
33. (A)(B)(C)(D)(E)
34. (A)(B)(C)(D)(E)
35. (A)(B)(C)(D)(E)
36. (A)(B)(C)(D)(E)
37. (A)(B)(C)(D)(E)
38. (A)(B)(C)(D)(E)
39. (A)(B)(C)(D)(E)
40. (A)(B)(C)(D)(E)
41. (A)(B)(C)(D)(E)
42. (A)(B)(C)(D)(E)
43. (A)(B)(C)(D)(E)
44. (A)(B)(C)(D)(E)
45. (A)(B)(C)(D)(E)
46. (A)(B)(C)(D)(E)
47. (A)(B)(C)(D)(E)
48. (A)(B)(C)(D)(E)
49. (A)(B)(C)(D)(E)
50. (A)(B)(C)(D)(E)
51. (A)(B)(C)(D)(E)
52. (A)(B)(C)(D)(E)
53. (A)(B)(C)(D)(E)
54. (A)(B)(C)(D)(E)
55. (A)(B)(C)(D)(E)
56. (A)(B)(C)(D)(E)
57. (A)(B)(C)(D)(E)
58. (A)(B)(C)(D)(E)
59. (A)(B)(C)(D)(E)
60. (A)(B)(C)(D)(E)

AP Macroeconomics Practice Test

Section I

Time – 70 minutes
60 Questions

Directions: Each of the questions or incomplete statements below is followed by five suggested answers or completions. Select the best choice in each case.

1. Which one of the following is a *positive* (as opposed to *normative*) economic statement about unemployment?
   (A) The unemployment rate for teenagers has been historically higher than the unemployment rate for adults.
   (B) Unemployment is the most serious economic problem facing this country today.
   (C) If part-time workers were counted as fully employed, the unemployment rate would be a more accurate measure of unemployment.
   (D) Government should be willing to provide incomes for those who are not able to provide for themselves.
   (E) Trade barriers should be eliminated to promote free trade.

2. Assume that a change in government policy results in the increased production of both consumer goods and capital goods. Which statement must necessarily be true?
   (A) There was unemployment and/or inefficient use of resources before the policy change.
   (B) The economy's PPC has been shifted to the left as a result of the policy change.
   (C) The economy's PPC has been shifted to the right as a result of the policy change.
   (D) The economy's PPC curve is bowed inward as viewed from the origin.
   (E) The law of increasing opportunity costs does not apply to this society.

GO ON TO THE NEXT PAGE

3. The demand and the supply curves for a product intersect where

   I. The buying and selling decisions of consumers and producers are consistent with one another
   II. The market is in equilibrium
   III. There is neither a surplus nor a shortage of the product
   IV. Quantity demanded is equal to quantity supplied

   (A) I, II, III, and IV
   (B) I, II, and III
   (C) I and II
   (D) II and III
   (E) IV only

4. How do a nation's citizens benefit from buying imported goods?

   (A) There will be a larger product selection.
   (B) Increased imports help maintain high domestic employment.
   (C) Import competition allows domestic profit levels to increase.
   (D) Imports weaken the value of the dollar.
   (E) Increased imports cause problems for export-producing industries.

5. Discouraged workers are

   (A) counted as unemployed members of the labor force, because they are willing and able to work but have no jobs
   (B) counted as unemployed, because they are dissatisfied with their present jobs and actively looking for other employment
   (C) not counted as members of the labor force, because they are neither employed nor actively looking for work
   (D) double-counted, causing the official unemployment statistics to overstate the actual amount of unemployment
   (E) counted as employed, causing the official unemployment statistics to understate the actual amount of unemployment

6. The short-run Phillips curve is based on the idea that with a constant short-run AS curve, an increase in AD is associated with a

   (A) shift of the short-run Phillips curve to the left
   (B) shift of the short-run Phillips curve to the right
   (C) movement up the short-run Phillips curve
   (D) movement down the short-run Phillips curve
   (E) no change in the short-run Phillips curve

GO ON TO THE NEXT PAGE

7. An increase in AS can

(A) shift the short-run Phillips curve to the left
(B) shift the short-run Phillips curve to the right
(C) cause movement up the short-run Phillips curve
(D) cause movement down the short-run Phillips curve
(E) produce no change in the short-run Phillips curve

8. Which one of the following changes would most likely shift the economy's long-run AS curve to the right?

(A) The economy's currency appreciates.
(B) The economy's currency depreciates.
(C) The price of raw materials decreases.
(D) The economy's money supply increases.
(E) The economy's working-age population increases.

9. An increase in the foreign exchange value of a nation's currency will

(A) increase both AS and AD
(B) increase AD and decrease AS
(C) decrease AD and increase AS
(D) increase AD without affecting AS
(E) increase AS without affecting AD

10. Suppose the spending multiplier is 3. An increase of $50 in investment spending will

(A) increase the RGDP by $3
(B) increase the RGDP by $50
(C) increase the RGDP by $150
(D) increase the RGDP by an indeterminate amount
(E) have no effect on the RGDP

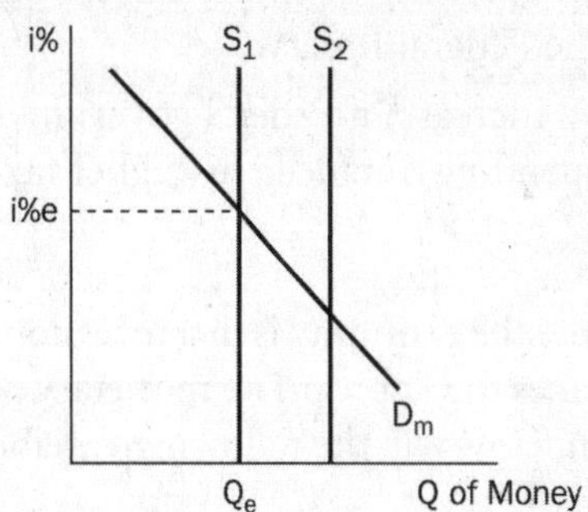

Use this graph to answer questions 11 through 13. The curves S_1 and S_2 represent the supply of money before and after a macroeconomic policy action.

11. The economic model illustrated in the graph shown is known as the

(A) aggregate demand/aggregate supply model
(B) Phillips curve model
(C) money market model
(D) liquidity preference model
(E) loanable funds market model

GO ON TO THE NEXT PAGE

12. The change in the supply of money illustrated above could have resulted from

(A) a decrease in Federal income tax rates
(B) an increase in Federal government spending, financed by borrowing from the public
(C) an open-market sale of bonds by the Federal Reserve
(D) an open-market purchase of bonds by the Federal Reserve
(E) an increase in Federal government spending, financed by higher taxes

13. Assume the economy is in a recession and the Fed takes the appropriate monetary policy action. How will the following variables be affected?

	Consumption spending	Investment spending	RGDP
(A)	Increase	Increase	Decrease
(B)	Decrease	Decrease	Decrease
(C)	Increase	Increase	Increase
(D)	No Change	Increase	Increase
(E)	Increase	No Change	Increase

14. Which of the following changes will cause the U.S. aggregate demand curve to shift to the right?

(A) An increase in the U.S. corporate income tax rate
(B) An increase in U.S workers' productivity
(C) An appreciation of the U.S. dollar against foreign currencies
(D) An increase in U.S. trading partners' national incomes
(E) A decrease in the U.S. money supply

15. Which of the following is best described as a macroeconomic study topic?

(A) An analysis of pricing policies in the electric power industry
(B) Development of an empirical model of the relationship between demand for oil and the automotive industry
(C) A historical study of employment in the 20th century
(D) Development of a theoretical model of the relationship between mortgage interest rates and demand for housing
(E) A comparison of costs of production in two firms producing widgets

16. Applying the theory of comparative advantage, a good should be produced where

(A) the production possibilities curve is further to the right than the trading possibilities line
(B) its cost is least in terms of opportunity costs
(C) its price is highest in terms of profit making
(D) its cost in terms of real resources used is highest
(E) its production method is cutting edge

GO ON TO THE NEXT PAGE

17. A depreciating dollar will tend to
    (A) decrease the prices of both American imports and exports
    (B) increase the prices of both American imports and exports
    (C) decrease the prices of the goods that Americans import, but increase the prices foreigners pay for the goods that Americans export
    (D) increase the prices of the goods that Americans import, but decrease the prices foreigners pay for the goods that Americans export
    (E) have no effect on either exports or imports

18. An increase in the money supply usually
    (A) increases the interest rate, promotes additional investment spending, and increases aggregate demand
    (B) increases the interest rate, discourages investment spending, and decreases aggregate demand
    (C) decreases the interest rate, promotes additional investment spending, and increases aggregate demand
    (D) decreases the interest rate, discourages investment spending, and decreases aggregate demand
    (E) decreases the interest rate with no effect on aggregate demand

19. In the calculation of GDP, transfer payments are
    (A) not counted
    (B) counted as a part of government spending
    (C) counted as a part of investment spending
    (D) counted as a part of consumption spending
    (E) counted as a part of net exports

20. Unemployment compensation and progressive income tax rates are two kinds of
    (A) discretionary fiscal policies
    (B) automatic, or built-in, stabilizers
    (C) discretionary monetary policies
    (D) leakages from the circular flow
    (E) injections into the circular flow

21. The most powerful policy used by the Federal Reserve to implement monetary policy is
    (A) changing reserve requirements
    (B) changing margin requirements for stock purchases
    (C) controlling the number of banks in operation
    (D) controlling the level of bank reserves
    (E) setting the foreign exchange value of the dollar

22. If Jo left her job a month before her baby was born and has been a full-time homemaker and mother ever since, what is her present employment status?
    (A) Unemployed
    (B) Employed but on a leave of absence
    (C) Discouraged worker not counted as unemployed
    (D) Underemployed worker
    (E) Not in the labor force

GO ON TO THE NEXT PAGE

23. If Ana quit her secretarial job two weeks ago for personal reasons, had a job interview last week, but has not heard back from the potential new employer yet, what is her present employment status?

(A) Unemployed
(B) Employed but on a leave of absence
(C) Discouraged worker not counted as unemployed
(D) Underemployed worker
(E) Not in the labor force

24. If William got fired over a year ago, looked for work while he was receiving unemployment compensation, but stopped looking when he moved in with his parents two months ago, what is his present employment status?

(A) Unemployed
(B) Employed but on a leave of absence
(C) Discouraged worker not counted as unemployed
(D) Underemployed worker
(E) Not in the labor force

25. An economy produced $300 billion worth of final goods and services in 2004. Of these, $45 billion were investment goods. During the year, $10 billion of the capital stock in existence at the beginning of 2004 was replaced or repaired. Based on this information, the net domestic product (NDP) for this economy in 2004 was

(A) $265 billion
(B) $290 billion
(C) $300 billion
(D) $310 billion
(E) $335 billion

26. Suppose an economy is at full employment, but is experiencing a high rate of inflation. Which of these policy actions is likely to be most effective in reducing inflation?

I. A temporary reduction in personal income taxes
II. Sale of government bonds on the open market by the Fed
III. An increase in reserve requirements on bank deposits

(A) II and III are likely to be effective, but I is not.
(B) III is likely to be effective, but I and II are not.
(C) I and II are likely to be effective, but III is not.
(D) I, II, and III are all likely to be effective.
(E) None of I, II, or III are likely to be effective.

27. Bank A uses its excess reserves and makes a $50,000 loan to Company XYZ, increasing the balance in XYZ's checking account by $50,000. As a result of these transactions, the economy's money supply

(A) remains unchanged
(B) decreases by $5,000
(C) increases by $5,000
(D) increases by $45,000
(E) increases by $50,000

GO ON TO THE NEXT PAGE

28. The current account section of a nation's Balance of Payments statement includes

    I. Merchandise exports and merchandise imports
    II. Net investment income
    III. Official reserves
    IV. Net foreign investments

    (A) I only
    (B) I and II
    (C) I, II, and III
    (D) I, II, and IV
    (E) II and IV

29. The capital account section of a nation's Balance of Payments statement includes

    I. Capital inflows to the nation
    II. Capital outflows from the nation
    III. Toyota buys an automobile factory in Kentucky
    IV. Net investment income

    (A) I only
    (B) I and II
    (C) I, II, and III
    (D) I, II, and IV
    (E) II and IV

30. Other things being equal, all of the following would cause an increase in a nation's real per capita GDP, EXCEPT

    (A) an increase in the general price level
    (B) a decrease in the population size
    (C) an increase in labor productivity
    (D) a discovery of new resources
    (E) additional funding for job training

31. Economic growth can be shown as a

    (A) rightward shift of the PPC
    (B) leftward shift of the PPC
    (C) movement from a point on the PPC to a point outside it
    (D) movement from a point on the PPC to another point on the curve
    (E) cannot be shown using the PPC model

32. Which statement(s) is (are) true in regard to expansionary fiscal policy?

    I. Government spending increases
    II. Taxes are cut
    III. Consumption increases
    IV. Disposable income increases

    (A) I only
    (B) I and II
    (C) I, II, and III
    (D) I, II, and IV
    (E) I, II, III, and IV

33. The "market basket" of goods used to calculate the Consumer Price Index cost \$200 in 1996 (CPI = 100). The same basket of goods now costs \$250. What is the value of today's CPI?

    (A) 50
    (B) 100
    (C) 125
    (D) 150
    (E) 250

GO ON TO THE NEXT PAGE

34. Components of the U.S. money supply (M1) include

    I. Coins and currency
    II. Credit cards
    III. Checking accounts and other checkable deposits
    IV. Savings accounts

    (A) I and II
    (B) I and III
    (C) I, II, and III
    (D) II, III, and IV
    (E) I, III, and IV

35. Which one of the following policy actions would a supply-side economist recommend to combat "stagflation?"

    (A) A reduction in corporate income tax rates
    (B) A reduction in Federal excise taxes on gasoline
    (C) A decrease in the growth rate of the money supply
    (D) A tax surcharge on the purchase of luxury goods
    (E) An increase in government spending on highway construction

Use the following graph to answer questions 36 and 37.

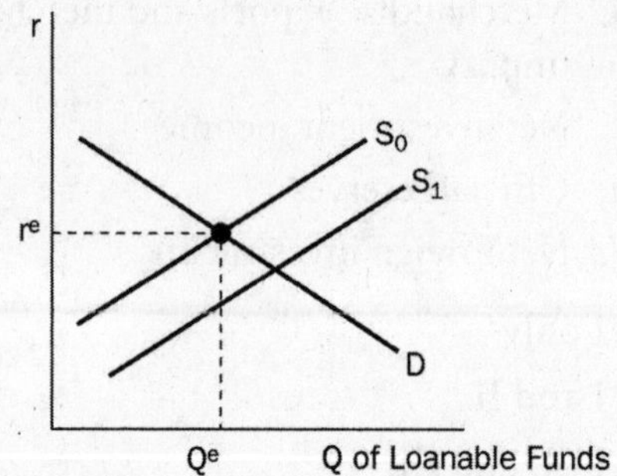

36. Which one of the following changes could cause a shift of the supply of loanable funds curve of the U.S. loanable funds market, such as that shown in the graph?

    (A) An increase in savings by U.S. households
    (B) An open-market sale of bonds by the Federal Reserve
    (C) A decrease investment spending by U.S. firms
    (D) An increase in demand for imports by U.S. households
    (E) An increase in demand for U.S. exports by foreign residents

37. Which of the following variables would be expected to decrease as a consequence of the change illustrated above?

    (A) The U.S. money supply
    (B) U.S. business investment spending
    (C) The price of U.S. government bonds
    (D) Equilibrium real U.S. gross domestic product
    (E) The foreign exchange value of the U.S. dollar

GO ON TO THE NEXT PAGE

38. With the budget initially in balance, suppose that the Federal government increases spending by $20 billion. The increase in spending is financed by a $20 billion tax increase. Which of the following statements best describes what will happen to equilibrium real GDP?

(A) There will be no change in equilibrium real GDP.

(B) Equilibrium real GDP will decrease by $20 billion.

(C) Equilibrium real GDP will increase by some fraction of $20 billion.

(D) Equilibrium real GDP will increase by $20 billion.

(E) The effect of the above changes on equilibrium real GDP cannot be determined without knowing the value of the multiplier.

39. The transition from a barter economy to an economy that uses money would

(A) increase household wealth, and thus increase the number of exchanges which will take place

(B) increase inequality in the distribution of income, making some persons wealthier at the expense of others

(C) increase transaction costs, and thus reduce the number of exchanges which can take place

(D) reduce transaction costs, and thus increase the number of exchanges which can take place

(E) not be expected to have significant effects on the economy

40. The real interest rate is best stated as the

(A) nominal interest rate minus the expected rate of inflation

(B) nominal interest rate plus the expected rate of inflation

(C) expected rate of inflation minus the nominal interest rate

(D) nominal interest rate divided by the expected rate of inflation

(E) expected rate of inflation divided by the nominal interest rate

41. Which of the following effects on an economy's production possibilities curve (PPC) will follow from an increase in the economy's labor supply?

(A) The slope of the curve will increase.

(B) The slope of the curve will decrease.

(C) The curve will shift inward, toward the origin.

(D) The curve will shift outward, away from the origin.

(E) This change will not affect the production possibilities curve.

GO ON TO THE NEXT PAGE

42. Which of the following transactions would be counted as an export of goods and/or services in the U.S. balance of payments accounts?

(A) A British investor buys 1000 shares of stock in a U.S. company.

(B) A U.S. tourist in Hong Kong spends $25 on souvenirs.

(C) A U.S. computer manufacturer buys a Taiwanese company that supplies memory chips.

(D) A French executive in the U.S. on business buys dinner for himself and a client in a New York restaurant.

(E) A Turkish rug dealer sells handmade rugs to a Dallas, Texas, wholesaler.

Use the graph below to answer questions 43 and 44.

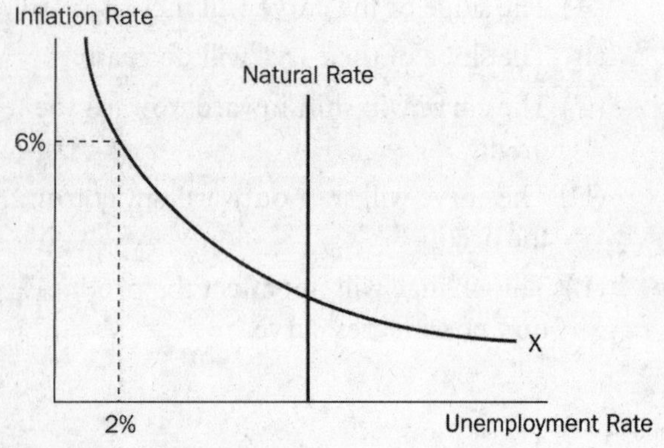

43. In the graph above, Curve X is a(n)

(A) money demand curve

(B) aggregate demand curve

(C) Laffer curve

(D) short-run Phillips curve

(E) production possibilities curve

44. Suppose government policy makers actively pursue supply-side policy actions that move the AS curve to the right. What will be the result in the long run?

(A) Curve X will move to the left as the unemployment rate returns to its original position with a lower inflation rate.

(B) Curve X will shift to the right as the unemployment rate will return to its original position with a higher inflation rate.

(C) The natural rate of unemployment will fall to 2%.

(D) The actual rate of unemployment will fall to 2% and remain at that level.

(E) Both the rate of inflation and the rate of unemployment will return to their original levels.

45. The use of a credit card in a transaction is most like

(A) using a check to make a purchase

(B) using cash to make a purchase

(C) obtaining a short term loan from a commercial bank

(D) increasing the value of money

(E) reducing the value of money

46. If bond prices fall, the

(A) interest rate will increase

(B) interest rate will decrease

(C) interest rate will be constant

(D) transaction demand for money will decrease

(E) transaction demand for money will increase

GO ON TO THE NEXT PAGE

47. The federal funds rate is

I. the interbank lending rate
II. the rate targeted by the FOMC
III. the same as the prime interest rate
IV. the rate that determines all other interest rates

(A) I only
(B) I and II
(C) I, II, and III
(D) I, II, and IV
(E) II and IV

Use the following graph to answer questions 48–50.

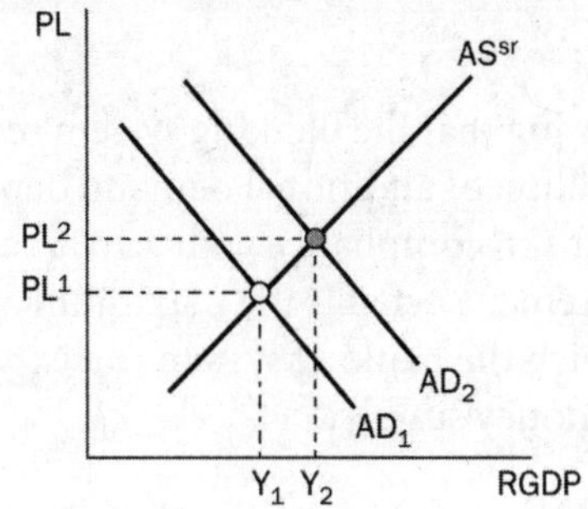

48. Which of the following policy actions is most likely to have caused this economy's aggregate demand curve to shift from AD_1 to AD_2?

(A) An increase in interest rates
(B) An increase in the money supply
(C) An increase in taxes
(D) A decrease in spending by the government
(E) An increase in the foreign exchange value of this economy's currency

49. The policy action depicted in the graph has resulted in

(A) deflation
(B) hyperinflation
(C) cost-push inflation
(D) demand-pull inflation
(E) price level stability

50. Suppose aggregate demand in an economy shifts back from AD_2 to its original level AD_1. However, prices are "sticky downward"; the price level remains at P_2. With aggregate demand having returned to its original level

(A) equilibrium output will remain at its new level, Y_2
(B) equilibrium output will return to its original level, Y_1
(C) equilibrium output will increase further, to some level above Y_2
(D) equilibrium output will decrease to some level below its original level, Y_1
(E) the new level of equilibrium output cannot be predicted

51. Richland, a large, wealthy country, can use its resources to produce 200 widgets per hour or 50 popnuts per hour. Poorland, a small, impoverished country, can produce 30 widgets per hour or 15 popnuts per hour. Which of the following best describes the trading possibilities for these two economies?

(A) Neither economy can benefit from trade with the other.
(B) Richland can benefit by trading popnuts to Poorland for widgets, but there will be no benefit to Richland from such a trade.
(C) Poorland can benefit by trading widgets to Richland for popnuts, but there will be no benefit to Richland from such a trade.
(D) Poorland can benefit by trading popnuts to Richland for widgets, but there will be no benefit to Richland from such a trade.
(E) Both economies will benefit if Poorland trades popnuts to Richland for widgets.

GO ON TO THE NEXT PAGE

52. If velocity is stable, an increase in the money supply will necessarily increase

(A) the demand for money
(B) the supply of money
(C) government spending
(D) nominal GDP
(E) velocity

53. Maria owns and operates a clothing store. She sets the price of a prom dress at $165. This is an example of the use of money as

(A) credit
(B) legal tender
(C) a store of value
(D) a medium of exchange
(E) a unit of account

All Banks	
Assets	**Liabilities**
210 Reserves	2,100 Deposits
400 Bonds	100 Capital
1,590 Loans	

This table represents a "T-account," or simplified balance sheet, for the consolidated U.S. banking system (all banks taken together). All numbers are in billions of dollars. Assume required reserves are 10% of deposits. Answer questions 54 and 55 using this table.

54. Which of the following actions by the Federal Reserve (the "Fed") would prevent the banking system from increasing the money supply?

(A) The Fed does not have to take any action; the banking system is already unable to increase the economy's money supply.
(B) The Fed could sell $10 billion worth of U.S. government bonds to banks.
(C) The Fed could buy $10 billion worth of U.S. government bonds from banks.
(D) The Fed could decrease the discount rate.
(E) The Fed could reduce reserve requirements from 10% to 9%.

55. Assuming that the banking system receives $10 billion of additional demand deposits and remains in compliance with a 10% reserve requirement, what is the maximum amount by which the banking system can expand the U.S. money supply?

(A) Zero
(B) $10 billion
(C) $100 billion
(D) $300 billion
(E) $400 billion

56. Which of the following combinations of fiscal and monetary policy actions would be most appropriate for an economy in recession?

	Fiscal policy	Monetary policy
(A)	Increase government spending	Sell government bonds
(B)	Increase taxes	Sell government bonds
(C)	Decrease government spending	Buy government bonds
(D)	Decrease taxes	Buy government bonds
(E)	Decrease taxes	Sell government bonds

GO ON TO THE NEXT PAGE

57. In an economy, the government has voted to increase spending by $100 million. Which of the following uses of this money would be effective in promoting long-term economic growth?

I. Construction of a medical research laboratory
II. Improved maintenance of national park facilities
III. Widening of two-lane highways to four lanes
IV. Financing research and development for small business development

(A) I and II
(B) II and III
(C) I, II, and III
(D) I, III, and IV
(E) II, III, and IV

58. The principle of comparative advantage suggests that

(A) large, rich nations can exploit small, poor nations in negotiating the terms of international trade
(B) small nations which are rich in natural resources can negotiate favorable trade terms despite their size
(C) rich and poor nations can both benefit by specializing in production and trading with one another
(D) large, rich nations can obtain no economic gain by trading with small, poor nations
(E) in the long run, large, rich nations benefit from trade with small, poor nations as the standard of living in the latter improves

59. An economy wants to increase its rate of economic growth. Which of the following policy actions would be most effective in accomplishing this goal?

I. An increase in business tax rates
II. Government subsidies for research and development
III. An increase in government spending for infrastructure
IV. A cut in government spending for education

(A) I and II
(B) II and III
(C) I, II, and III
(D) II, III, and IV
(E) III and IV

60. Based on the data below, what is the size of the labor force?

Total population = 120 million
Persons of working age (16–65 years) = 75 million
Persons employed = 45 million
Persons actively looking for work = 5 million

(A) 5 million
(B) 45 million
(C) 50 million
(D) 75 million
(E) 120 million

IF YOU FINISH BEFORE TIME IS UP, YOU MAY CHECK YOUR WORK ON THIS SECTION ONLY. DO NOT TURN TO ANY OTHER SECTION IN THE TEST. **STOP**

Ten-Minute Reading Period

Take the next 10 minutes to glance over the three questions that comprise Section II of this test. You can take notes in the margins, but you may not begin answering any of the questions in any way whatsoever.

When the 10-minute period is over, you may begin answering the three free-response questions.

Section II

Writing Time – 50 minutes

Directions: You have 50 minutes to answer all three of the following questions. It is suggested that you spend approximately half your time on the first question and divide the remaining time equally between the next two questions. In answering the questions, you should emphasize the line of reasoning that generated your results; it is not enough to list the results of your analysis. Include correctly labeled diagrams, if useful or required, in your answers. A correctly labeled diagram must have all axes and curves clearly labeled and must show directional changes.

1. Assume an economy is operating at less than full employment.

   (a) Using a correctly labeled aggregate demand and aggregate supply graph, show the following:

   i. Full employment output

   ii. Current output

   iii. Current price level

   (b) Identify an open market operation that could restore full employment in the short run.

   (c) Using a correctly labeled graph of the money market, show how the money market operation you identified affects the interest rate in the short run.

   Explain how this policy action will affect

   i. Bank reserves

   ii. Investment spending in the U.S.

   iii. The price level

   iv. The unemployment rate

   (d) On the graph drawn in part (a), show how the change in the interest rate you determined in
   part (c) affects the price level and the output.

GO ON TO THE NEXT PAGE

2. The Equation of Exchange can be written as MV = PQ, in which

   M = the money supply,
   V = the velocity of money, and
   PQ = nominal gross domestic product.

   (a) Explain what is meant by V, the velocity of money.

   (b) Some theorists believe in the Equation of Exchange, where V is treated as a constant. What reasoning is typically given to justify this assumption?

   (c) Given that V is constant, discuss briefly the mechanism by which each of the following monetary policy actions by the Federal Reserve will impact nominal gross domestic product (assume that banks initially have zero excess reserves):

      i. An open-market sale of bonds

      ii. An increase in reserve requirements

   (d) Given the policy actions in (c) above, will real output and employment necessarily change? Explain.

3. Due to higher interest rates in Country X, capital flows into the country. Explain the effect of that inflow of funds on the following variables:

   i. The international value of the currency of Country X

   ii. Net exports in Country X

   iii. The real interest rate

IF YOU FINISH BEFORE TIME IS UP, YOU MAY CHECK YOUR WORK ON THIS SECTION ONLY. DO NOT TURN TO ANY OTHER SECTION IN THE TEST.

AP Macroeconomics Practice Test: Answer Key

1. A
2. C
3. A
4. A
5. C
6. C
7. A
8. E
9. C
10. C
11. C
12. D
13. C
14. D
15. C
16. B
17. D
18. C
19. A
20. B
21. D
22. E
23. A
24. C
25. B
26. A
27. E
28. B
29. C
30. A
31. A
32. E
33. C
34. B
35. A
36. A
37. E
38. D
39. D
40. A
41. D
42. D
43. D
44. A
45. C
46. A
47. C
48. B
49. C
50. D
51. E
52. D
53. E
54. A
55. C
56. D
57. D
58. C
59. B
60. C

AP MACROECONOMICS PRACTICE TEST CORRELATION CHART

Area of Study	Question Numbers
Basic Economic Concepts	1, 2, 3, 15, 16, 41
Measurement of Economic Performance	5, 19, 22, 23, 24, 25, 33, 60
National Income and Price Determination	7, 10, 14, 19
Financial Sector	11, 12, 18, 21, 27, 34, 36, 37, 39, 40, 45, 46, 47, 53, 54, 55
Inflation, Unemployment,- and Stabilization	6, 13, 20, 26, 35, 38, 43,
Policies	44, 48, 49, 50, 52, 56
Economic Growth and Productivity	8, 30, 31 32, 57, 59
Open Economy: International Trade and Finance	4, 9, 17, 28, 29, 42, 51, 58

ANSWERS AND EXPLANATIONS

SECTION 1

1. A

Positive economic statements are free of value judgments. It is a demonstrable fact that (A) is true. All of the other choices, while they may or may not be true, contain implicit or explicit value judgments, which remain arguable even after all of the facts are in.

2. C

If a nation can produce more capital and consumer goods, the PPC has moved to the right. This makes (C) correct. The government policy that caused this change was related to additional resources made available, a technology gain that boosted productivity, or the nation engaging in international trade. Choice (A) is incorrect because unemployment means that the nation was producing inside the PPC. Choice (B) is incorrect since the PPC has moved to the right, not to the left. Choice (D) states an incorrect and unlikely PPC position. Choice (E) is incorrect because it mentions increasing opportunity costs, which means that the curve is bowed outward since resources are not perfectly able to be shifted between capital and consumer goods.

3. A

Demand and supply curves intersect where the $Q_d = Q_s$. This point is called market equilibrium. Buyers and sellers are in agreement and since the market is in equilibrium, there is no shortage or surplus of the good. Choice (A) is the correct answer as it covers all the statements noted above. All other choices are flawed since they do not include all of these conditions.

4. A

Imports are spending for goods and services produced in foreign countries. When a nation engages in trade, often the increase in imported products provides citizens with a more varied array of products to buy—(A). Choice (B) is incorrect since imports compete with domestic goods so some domestic workers do lose their jobs. Choice (C) is incorrect since imports that compete with a nation's products will often keep domestic prices lower. Choice (D) is incorrect because the sale of more imported goods moves with the value of the currency; an appreciating currency will make imports cheaper since the exchange rate is favorable. Since imports do not compete with firms that produce goods for export, (E) is incorrect.

5. C

The term *discouraged workers* describes people who are unemployed but who are no longer looking for work. They are willing and able to work, and have sought employment in the past. However, they have given up looking, at least temporarily, because they do not think they will be able to find a suitable job. Because the labor force only includes people who are employed and people actively looking for work, discouraged workers are not considered when the unemployment rate is estimated. Choice (C) is the correct answer while (A) and (B) incorrectly consider these discouraged workers as employed. Choice (D) is incorrect as well, since these discouraged workers are not counted twice; rather, they fall out of the count altogether. Choice (E) is incorrect since they are not working and should not be counted as employed.

6. C

The short-run Phillips curve is downward-sloping and shows the trade-off between an inflation rate and the unemployment rate. When the AD increases, RGDP increases and price level rises. This causes the unemployment rate to fall and the inflation rate to rise. This will mean that we move up the short-run Phillips curve—(C). Choices (A) and (B) both incorrectly shift the short-run Phillips curve which is caused by change in aggregate supply. Choice (D) is incorrect since a movement down the curve will indicate a higher unemployment rate and a lower inflation rate. Choice (E) is incorrect since it does not indicate any change.

7. A

An increase in AS will lower the price level and increase RGDP. Unemployment rate declines at the same time the rate of inflation falls. The short-run trade-off is lost. An increase in AS will shift the short-run Phillips curve to the left as both variables decrease. Choice (A) is correct, while Choice (B) incorrectly moves the curve to the right, which would indicate that both variables increased. Choices (C) and (D) are both incorrect since these movements along the short-run Phillips curve result from change in aggregate demand. Choice (E) is incorrect since it does not indicate any change.

8. E

The long-run aggregate supply curve shifts to the right when the economy's productive capacity increases. This occurs as a result of technological progress and/or increases in the availability of productive resources, one of which is labor. This means that (E) is correct, as the working-age population adds more labor. Currency changes as in (A) and (B), as well as the price effect in (C) influence short-run aggregate supply. Choice (E) is incorrect because changes in the money supply affect aggregate demand.

9. C

As the value of the dollar increases, U.S. residents need fewer units of domestic currency to pay for imported goods. They substitute imports for domestically produced goods. At the same time, people in other countries find that U.S. goods become more expensive in terms of these other countries' currencies. Hence, aggregate demand for U.S. goods decreases. On the supply side, imports of resources (factors of production) from foreign countries become cheaper, reducing costs of production for U.S. producers and increasing U.S. aggregate supply. Choice (C) correctly states that AD decreases while AS increases. Other choices do not reflect the statements above.

10. C

The equilibrium level of national income, or RGDP, increases by a multiple (determined by the value of the *multiplier*) of any increase in spending—consumption, investment, or government spending. In general, $\delta Y_e =$ (multiplier) · (new spending) or, for the example, $\delta Y_e = 3 \cdot 50 = 150$. This makes (C) the correct answer. The other choices do reflect the spending multiplier equation.

11. C

As noted in (C), the money market model is a supply/ demand model of the market for determining nominal interest rates. The demand and supply factors of money determine the nominal interest rate. Choice (A) is incorrect because an AD/AS graph shows the relationship between price level and RGDP. Choice (B) is flawed because a Phillips curve in the short run reports the trade-off between unemployment and inflation. Choice (D) is incorrect because this model is a technical tool used by the Fed and the banking system. Choice (E) is incorrect because a loanable funds model employs a supply/demand graph, but determines real interest rates.

12. D

When the Federal Reserve buys bonds on the open market, the proceeds from those bond sales by private sector economic agents are deposited into the agents' bank accounts and become a source of excess reserves for banks. Banks are then able to make loans, expanding the money supply by deposit creation. Choice (B) is incorrect because new money can also be created if the Federal government finances new spending by selling bonds to the Federal Reserve, a process known as monetization of the deficit. However, sale of bonds to the public has no effect on the money supply. Choices (A) and (E) are incorrect since both deal with fiscal policy action rather than monetary action. Choice (C) is incorrect because the sale of bonds would decrease the money supply.

13. C

The reduction in interest rates resulting from the increase in the money supply can be expected to cause higher business investment spending, as well as increased spending by consumers on interest-sensitive consumption goods (such as cars, appliances, home renovations, etc.). As long as the economy is not already at full employment, these higher levels of spending will increase aggregate demand and, in the context of the AD/AS model, shift the AD curve to the right, increasing equilibrium output and RGDP.

14. D

Choice (D) is correct because an increase in U.S. trading partners' national incomes will increase *their* imports, thus increasing the net exports component of U.S. aggregate demand. Choice (A) is incorrect because an increase in corporate income tax will affect investment adversely. Choice (B) is incorrect because it is an aggregate supply determinant. Choice (C) is incorrect because an appreciation of the U.S. dollar, while generally considered to be positive, actually decreases net exports by making U.S. imports cheaper and exports more expensive for foreign buyers. Choice (E) is incorrect because a decrease in the money supply raises interest rates, which decreases investment spending, resulting in a decrease in AD.

15. C

Macroeconomics can be defined as the study of the economy as a whole, or as the study of economic aggregates. Choice (C) is correct because employment statistics are macroeconomic in nature. Choice (A) is incorrect since research, whether theoretical or empirical, that focuses on individual economic agents, markets, industries, or sectors is *not* macroeconomic in character. Choice (B) involves the study of two markets—oil and autos, a microeconomic topic. Choice (D) is incorrect as it deals with two markets—the mortgage industry and housing. Choice (E) is incorrect because it involves costs of production, another microeconomic concept.

16. B

The theory of comparative advantage holds that there is an advantage when you as a producer incur a lower relative cost than another producer. In other words, you suffer the least opportunity cost, giving up the least in allocation of resources. This means that (B) is the correct answer. Choice (A) is incorrect because moving the PPC to the right beyond the trading possibilities is not possible. Choice (C) is incorrect because the highest priced items are not thought to be the best to sell. Choice (D) is incorrect because if the cost is highest, then advantage is lost. Choice (E) is flawed since cutting-edge production is not always the least costly.

17. D

A depreciation of the dollar means a decrease in the international value of the currency relative to another currency. Under these conditions, when Americans want to buy imports, they must give up more of their dollars to obtain the currency needed to buy the imported product. Buyers of American exports are in the opposite position; they give up less of their currency to receive a dollar to buy the American export. So, when the dollar depreciates, imports fall and exports rise, causing net exports and AD to increase. Choices (A) and (B) are incorrect because imports and exports do not move in the same direction with a currency value change. Choice (C) is incorrect because it states the opposite of the correct answer. Choice (E) is flawed since it describes no change.

18. C

The Fed can increase the money supply by purchasing government securities and increasing checking deposits in banks. This action increases bank reserves used to make loans, which increases the money supply. Firms needing capital goods are willing to borrow because the additional funds decrease the interest rate. When investment spending increases, the AD will increase, raising RGDP. Choice (C) is the correct sequence of events following the increase in the money supply. All other choices do not follow the correct sequence of events, technically called the "transition mechanism" described above.

19. A

Transfer payments are government payments made to individuals who fulfill a set of criteria to receive such payments but produce no current production. Unemployment compensation, welfare payments, and Social Security payments are examples of transfer payments. Choice (A) is correct because these items are not added to GDP since these recipients produce no production. All the other choices add transfer payments incorrectly to one of the components of GDP.

20. B

Choice (B) is correct because automatic, or built-in, stabilizers are institutional features of the economic system that "lean against the wind," supporting output and employment in recession and dampening demand during economic booms. As opposed to discretionary fiscal policy measures described in (A), they require no legislative action by Congress. Choice (C) is incorrect because monetary policy is managed by the Fed and not by Congress. Choices (D) and

(E) are incorrect: While (progressive) income taxes are a "leakage" from the circular flow, unemployment compensation is an "injection."

21. D

Choice (D) is correct since both open-market operations and reserve requirements affect bank reserves and hence the capacity of the commercial banking system to make loans and to expand the money supply. Choice (A) is incorrect because reserve requirements *can* be used as a tool of monetary policy, but rarely are. Choice (B) is a Fed tool but it controls the stock market transactions. Choice (C) is not a Fed tool since the Comptroller of the Currency also has power over the banking system. Choice (E) is incorrect because our currency value is determined in a freely floating market subject to the forces of demand and supply for currency. The Fed does not control currency rates.

22. E

Because she chooses not to work, Jo is not a member of the economy's labor force and thus is not counted as either employed or unemployed. Choice (E) is correct. Other choices do not accurately describe Jo's status.

23. A

Ana, a person with readily marketable skills, is probably best regarded as being "between jobs," and hence as being frictionally unemployed. Choice (A) is her status, and the other choices do not accurately describe Ana's situation.

24. C

William is classified as a discouraged worker, one who is not actively seeking work. He is lost in the statistics because he is difficult to count. He is technically out of the labor force. Choice (C) is the correct status for William; other choices do not apply, by definition.

25. B

Net domestic product (NDP) is defined as gross domestic product less the depreciation or the value of the capital stock used in production during the year. For the example, NDP is ($300 - $10) = $290 billion. Other choices are not properly calculated.

26. A

Statement I represents a fiscal policy of reducing taxes, which would increase consumer disposable income and result in increased demand-pull inflation. Statements II and III are contractionary monetary policy actions. Either or both of these would reduce the growth rate of the money supply and (with a time lag) put downward pressure on prices. Choice (A) is the only alternative that describes this position.

27. E

The economy's money supply includes checking account balances. Thus, any increase in a bank customer's checking account balance (which is not offset by a decrease in some other customer's checking account balance) increases the money supply dollar for dollar. In a word, banks create money when they make loans. Choice (E) correctly describes the $50,000 increase in the money supply. Other choices are flawed since they do not include this figure.

28. B

The current account section of a nation's Balance of Payments (BOP) would include trade items like exports and imports.
It would also include net investment income, which is the net difference between interest and dividend payments between one nation and the world. Official reserves are the "balancing tool" to make it a Balance of Payments and are not included in the current account section. Net foreign investments are a capital account item. Choice (B) has those current account items covered; other options do not consider all the items listed in the current account and mistakenly include other Balance of Payments items.

29. C

The capital account section would include both inflows and outflows in a net foreign investment category. The purchase by a foreign company of an automobile factory is included in this capital section because this is new investment in the nation. Net investment income is the return on the investment and is counted in the current section of the BOP. Choice (C) includes only the capital account items covered; other options do not consider all the items listed in the capital account and mistakenly include a current account item.

30. A

Per capita GDP increases when the GDP rises and the population size does not rise faster than the GDP increase. Only (A) is correct because changes in the price level do not affect the level of current GDP. Choice (B) would cause an increase in the per capita GDP, as the GDP "pie" is shared by fewer citizens. Choices (C) and (D) add to the GDP as the "pie" grows larger. Choice (E) allows workers to be more productive, which produces a greater GDP.

31. A

Economic growth relies on the same factors that allow a nation to expand its potential output. The rightward shift of the PPC represents economic growth. Choice (A) is correct. Choice (B) is incorrect because it moves the PPC in the opposite direction and would mean a loss of potential. Choices (C) and (D) are incorrect because movement along the PPC means new choices are implemented with the same resources. Choice (E) is incorrect because economic growth can be modeled with the PPC model.

32. E

Governments enact expansionary fiscal policy to stimulate the economy in the hopes that consumers will buy more. To encourage consumer spending, governments cut taxes, which gives consumers more disposable income, which leads to increased consumption. Government spending must also increase. Choice (E) is correct.

33. C

The Consumer Price Index (CPI) is calculated as the ratio of the cost of the market basket of goods in the given year (in the question, "today"), to the cost of the same goods in the base year (1996), multiplied by 100. Given the information in the question, this is calculated as CPI (today) $= \frac{250}{200} \times 100 = 125$. Choice (C) is correct; the other choices do not calculate the answer properly.

34. B

Choice (B) correctly notes that the M1 money supply in the U.S. includes coins and currency in circulation, checkable deposits sometimes called demand deposits, and travelers' checks. Statement II falsely states that credit cards are money when they are in fact loans. Savings accounts are part of the M2 money supply so statement IV is false.

35. A

Stagflation is a condition characterized by slow or negative economic growth, coupled with a moderate or high rate of inflation. Supply-side economists point out that both problems can be addressed simultaneously by implementing a policy that will increase aggregate supply, i.e., a policy that will shift the short-run AS curve to the right. Tax reductions for businesses (A) accomplish this goal. All of the other choices represent traditional demand-management alternatives.

36. A

Through saving, households are net suppliers of loanable funds. An increase in autonomous saving (the component of saving that is not a function of disposable income or the interest rate) will shift the supply of loanable funds curve to the right, as shown in the graph accompanying this question. The Fed's actions, as in (B), are depicted on a money market graph. Choice (C) is incorrect because a decrease in investment is usually preceded by an increase in interest rates. Choices (D) and (E) incorrectly use imports and exports to explain this model. Neither has an effect on the availability of loanable funds.

37. E

A lower real interest rate, other things equal, will decrease foreign investor demand for assets denominated in U.S. dollars. This will, in turn, reduce demand for U.S. dollars and result in a depreciation of the dollar on foreign exchange markets, shown in (E). Choice (A) is incorrect because the loanable funds market is not linked to the Fed and its control of the money supply. U.S. business investment spending should increase with a lower real interest rate, so (B) is incorrect. Choice (C) is incorrect because the price of bonds is inversely related to the yield of the investment. Choice (D) is incorrect because the RGDP will rise as new investment spending increases AD.

38. D

This question uses the Balanced Budget Multiplier concept to show that the increase in government spending financed by an increase in taxes will increase equilibrium real GDP dollar for dollar. The Balanced Budget Multiplier equals one, so (D) states the correct answer: The GDP grows by the amount of additional spending. Choice (A) is incorrect because it states that there will be no change in equilibrium. Choice (C) is incorrect because the Balanced Budget Multiplier equals one, not a fraction thereof. Choice (E) is incorrect because the value of the spending multiplier is not needed.

39. D

Barter requires a "double coincidence of wants" for mutually beneficial exchanges to take place. By providing a medium of exchange (in addition to a standardized unit of accounting), money facilitates exchange (i.e., reduces transaction costs), increasing general economic welfare as in the correct choice (D). Choice (A) is incorrect because household wealth is the personal wealth of individuals and the general economic welfare is society's shared wealth. Choice (B) is incorrect because inequality of income is not caused by the introduction of money, but rather by factors such as differences in skill and education. Choice (C) is the opposite of the correct response. Choice (E) is incorrect because it states no change would occur.

40. A

The nominal or market rate of interest is the sum of the real interest rate and the expected rate of inflation: i = r + ?[e] . Simple algebraic rearrangement provides the correct answer, (A). The remaining choices do not reflect the formula stated here.

41. D

The production possibilities curve (PPC) is a frontier that shows the limits of an economy's productive capacity. An increase in the labor supply will increase productive capacity, as would an increase in any factor of production. Choice (D) correctly states that this would be illustrated graphically as an outward shift of the PPC, or a shift to the right. Choices (A) and (B) are incorrect because the slope of the curve would not change. The outward move of the PPC means that more of the goods can be produced without sacrifice or opportunity cost. Choice (C) moves the PPC in the wrong direction—which would indicate that a factor of production has been lost or destroyed. Choice (E) is incorrect because it states that there would not be any change to the PPC curve as a result of the parameters set forth in the question stem.

42. D

Foreign visitors' purchases of U.S. goods or services while in the U.S. are treated as exports in the Balance of Payments accounts as stated in (D). Choice (A) is incorrect because a foreigner's purchase of U. S. stocks would be placed in the capital account of the Balance of Payments. Choice (B) is incorrect because a U.S. tourist's purchase of souvenirs in a foreign country would be entered into the accounts as an import. Choice (C) is incorrect because a U.S. firm buying a foreign firm is a capital account item. Choice (E) is incorrect because a rug dealer in a foreign country is selling to a firm in the U.S.—a transaction that is categorized as an import.

43. D

The short-run Phillips curve illustrates an empirical relationship between the rate of unemployment and the rate of inflation. Other choices are all economic models, but they do not reflect the relationship described in the question stem.

44. A

Changes in AS will shift the short-run Phillips curve to the right or left. An increase in AS will lower the Phillips curve (moving it back to the original natural rate of unemployment at a lower rate of inflation), because it lowers inflation and improves the unemployment rate. Choice (B) incorrectly moves the curve to the left which would reflect a decrease in AS. Choices (C) and (D) are incorrect because the natural rate of unemployment remains at the position of the vertical curve, which is the long-run Phillips curve. Choice (E) is incorrect because the government action results in a lower inflation rate.

45. C

Credit cards are not part of the money supply. When a consumer uses a credit card, he is using a line of credit he has established with a bank. He can pay the balance each month without incurring interest or he can make payments over time with interest. Choice (A) is incorrect since funds in a checking account are part of the money supply. Choice (B) is incorrect because cash is part of the money supply. Choices (D) and (E) are incorrect because credit card use does not affect the value of money. The value of money is influenced by the amount of goods and services that are available to be purchased.

46. A

There is an inverse relationship between the interest rate and bond prices. When the demand for bonds declines, the price of bonds decreases. Lower bond prices force higher interest rates as stated in (A). Choice (B) is incorrect because it states the opposite of the correct response. Choice (C) does not recognize the relationship between the interest rate and bond prices at all. In (D) and (E), the main determinant of the transaction demand for money is the level of RGDP.

47. C

The federal funds rate is the rate banks charge each other for overnight loans. Banks borrow in this manner when they need to cover their legal reserves from day to day. The recent focus of the debate at the Federal Open Market Committee (FOMC) has been the federal funds rate. When the FOMC wishes to change interest rates, it sets a target rate for the federal funds rate and then uses open markets operations to affect the change. The rate also is the lowest rate in the banking system (lower than the prime rate) and determines all other interest rates. For all these reasons, (D) is the correct response. The remaining choices do not consider these points.

48. B

Both the money market and loanable funds models imply that a money supply increase will reduce interest rates, increasing interest-sensitive consumption and investment spending, and raising aggregate demand. Choice (B) is the correct response; all the other choices indicate a *decrease* in AD.

49. C

The increase in aggregate demand has resulted in both higher equilibrium output and a higher price level, i.e., demand-pull inflation, as indicated in (D). Choice (A) is incorrect because deflation is a decline in a nation's price level. Choice (B) is incorrect because hyperinflation is a very rapid rise in the price level. Choice (C) is another type of inflation that is driven by higher resource prices. Price level stability, as noted in (E), indicates that there was no change in the price level.

50. D

The so-called "ratchet effect" of increases in aggregate demand which are subsequently reversed predicts that with prices "sticky downward," the final equilibrium level of output will be below the initial level, Y_1. In fact, given the graph as drawn, equilibrium output will fall to the level corresponding to the point where the AD_1 curve intersects the horizontal line drawn at price level P_2.

51. E

Poorland has a *comparative advantage* in production of popnuts, while Richland has a comparative advantage in production of widgets. Hence, *both countries* will benefit if Poorland trades popnuts to Richland for widgets. Choice (E) is the correct response. It is tempting but incorrect to assume that because Richland is a large, rich country and has an *absolute advantage* in production of both goods, that no basis for mutually beneficial trade exists; thus, the remaining choices are incorrect.

52. D

The equation of exchange states that $MV = PQ$, that is, the money supply times the velocity will equal the nominal GDP. When V is stable and M increases, the equation must remain balanced, so the nominal GDP will increase as stated in (D). Choice (A) is incorrect because the demand for money is not the same as the money supply. Choice (B) is incorrect because it repeats the question. Choice (C) is incorrect because government spending is a fiscal policy concept and unrelated to the equation of exchange. Choice (E) is incorrect as it erroneously uses one of the question variables to arrive at its conclusion.

53. E

Choice (E) correctly identifies a unit of account as a standard for measuring or denominating value. By setting the price of the dress in dollars, Maria is using money to denominate its value. Choice (A) is incorrect because using credit is a consumer choice. Choice (B) uses the term legal tender, which means that paper currency must be accepted for all debts public and private or else the creditor forfeits both the privilege of charging interest and the right to sue. Choice (C)'s function of money means that we can transfer value of money from present to future. Choice (D) is incorrect because when a customer actually purchases the dress, she will be using money as a medium of exchange.

54. A

Choice (A) is correct because the table shows that there are no excess reserves to lend. Choice (C) is incorrect because this action would create excess reserves. In (D), the discount rate is a tool used by the Fed and a decrease could have the effect of increasing the money supply, but member banks are not forced or required to borrow funds at the discount window at the Fed. Choice (E) would also create excess reserves. Choice (B) would cause the banks to fall out of compliance with the reserve requirement.

55. C

The banking system has $10 billion in *new deposits*. With a 10% reserve requirement, these reserves can support $100 billion in new lending, which would increase the bank's checking account deposits (a component of the money supply) by $100 billion, as noted in (C). In this case, the money multiplier was 10. All other choices fail to calculate the amount properly.

56. D

Appropriate fiscal and monetary policies to combat recession are expansionary—they work to increase government spending and/or decrease taxes, as well as to increase the money supply and/or decrease interest rates. Choice (D) is correct because a decrease in taxes gives consumers more money to spend, and as the Fed buys bonds, funds will flow into bank reserves to make loans. The other choices do not reflect these combinations that work to stabilize a recessionary economy.

57. D

Economic growth is enhanced by investment in real capital (e.g., small business ventures), human capital (education), infrastructure (highways), and new technology (laboratories). All but statement I are correct so (D) is the correct answer. Since improved services for national park visitors promote consumption, not production, statement II is false. All other choices do not have the correct combinations of the listed statements.

58. C

The principle of comparative advantage states that consumers in both rich and poor countries benefit when each country specializes in the production of those goods that it can produce relatively cheaply, and trades with the other country for the goods that it cannot produce as cheaply. This principle applies to all countries, regardless of relative size and/or wealth. Choice (C) is the correct answer and the other choices do not express these concepts correctly.

59. B

Higher business taxes discourage capital formation, slowing economic growth. Increases in government spending for research, development, and infrastructure will add to long-run growth. Only statements II and III are true which means (B) is the correct response. The other choices include false statements.

60. C

The U.S. Department of Labor defines the labor force as the number of employed individuals (45 million) plus the number of people actively looking for work (5 million), which equals 50 million, (C). The persons of working age include people who are not willing and able to work. Only (C) correctly states the size of the labor force given the parameters set forth in the question stem.

SECTION II

1. (a) The U. S. economy is not at full employment. The *full employment unemployment rate*, also known as the *natural rate of unemployment*, is the rate of unemployment that prevails when there is no cyclical unemployment in the economy—all unemployment is either frictional or structural. On the graph, note the vertical AS^{lr} curve with Qf as the label. The intersection of AD^1 and short-run AS will denote the recessionary state of the economy.

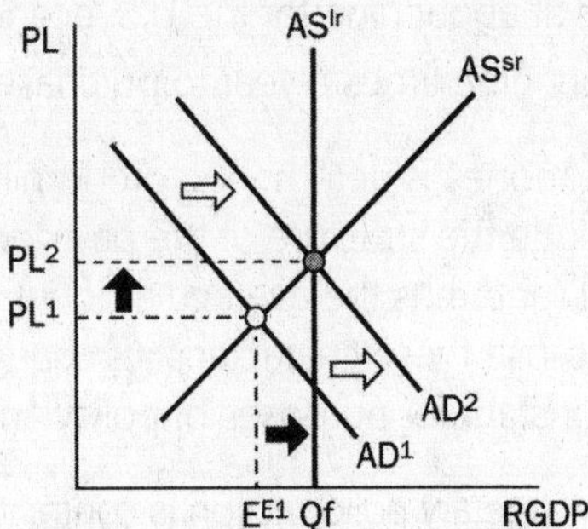

(b) The Fed would buy government securities in order to raise bank reserves. Banks would then have a greater ability to create new money through the loan process.

(c) The money market graph uses the demand and supply of money to determine a nominal interest rate. The graph shows that the supply of money has moved to the right, lowering the nominal interest rate.

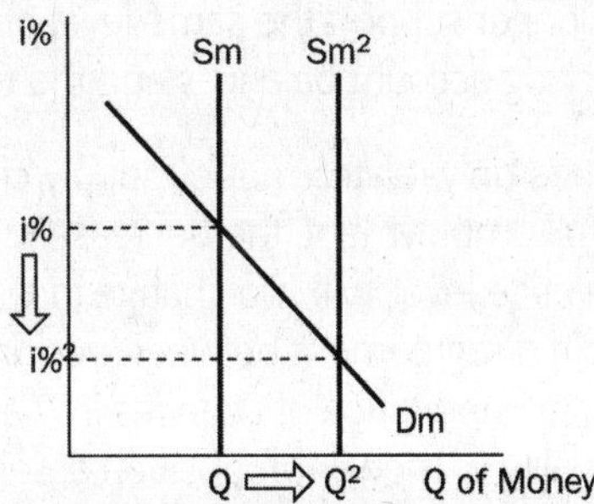

i. Bank reserves will rise as a result of the Fed's purchase of government securities. As bonds are sold back to the Fed, the central bank increases the demand deposits of the former bondholders. This new checking deposit money becomes the source for banks to create loans and new money after their reserve requirement is met.

ii. With a lower interest rate in the market, investment spending will increase. Businesses borrow funds for capital goods when the rate of interest is lower than the expected rate of return.

iii. With the increase in investment spending, the AD moves to the right, increasing the price level.

iv. The increase in the AD also increases the RGDP. The inverse relationship between the RDGP and the unemployment rate determines that the unemployment rate will decline.

(d) On the graph above, the AD curve has moved to the right and now the economy is functioning at the full employment RGDP.

2. (a) The velocity of money is a measure of the number of times each currency unit (dollar) is spent to buy currently produced output. It is a measure of how rapidly money circulates in the economy. Simple algebraic rearrangement of the equation of exchange expresses V as the ratio $\frac{(PQ)}{M}$. Using nominal GDP and M1 as proxies for the (PQ) and M, respectively, V can be roughly estimated at about nine for the U.S. economy. Thus, each dollar of the M1 money supply is spent about nine times a year to purchase output produced in that year.

(b) The value of the velocity of money is determined predominantly by institutional features of the economy. These include the structure of the payments system and the frequency with which people are paid (and thus the average amount of money they desire to hold for transactions purposes). Because these characteristics change very slowly over time, V can generally be regarded as constant for purposes of policy analysis.

(c) In each case, the indicated monetary policy action is contractionary, i.e., designed to decrease the money supply.

i. In an open-market sale of bonds, reserves are removed from the banking system by the sale of bonds. The new, lower level of reserves can support a smaller deposit base, and banks must "call in" loans, reducing their customers' checking account balances.

ii. In an increase in reserve requirements, there is no change in the actual level of reserves in the banking system. However, because of the increase in required reserves, banks' actual reserves can no longer support the same level of deposits. Again, banks must "call in" loans, and checking account balances and the money supply decrease.

(d) No. The equation of exchange only relates money supply changes to changes in nominal GDP. If the economy is at full employment, the decrease in the money supply could result only in a decrease in P, the price level, with no change in Y, real output, or employment. There is, in fact, considerable disagreement between neoclassical and mainstream economists about the relative importance of changes in P and Q in response to changes in M. The neoclassical neutrality of money proposition asserts that changes in M affect only prices, at least in the long run. Keynes and the modern Mainstream economists that follow his lead argue that, to the contrary, output and employment effects are important and persistent.

3. Drawn to the high interest rate, foreign investment flows into Country X. Foreigners will need to have the currency of Country X in order to place their funds in banks or other interest earning investments. The currency of Country X will appreciate since there will be an increase in demand for the currency.

Net exports will fall since exports will decline and imports will rise. The appreciation of the currency means that foreigners will give up more of their currency to get the currency of Country X to buy an export. Citizens of Country X will find that imports are cheaper since they give up less of their currency to get an import.

Additional funds will flow into the loanable funds market of Country X, lowering the real interest rate.

AP Microeconomics Practice Test
Answer Grid

1. Ⓐ Ⓑ Ⓒ Ⓓ Ⓔ	21. Ⓐ Ⓑ Ⓒ Ⓓ Ⓔ	41. Ⓐ Ⓑ Ⓒ Ⓓ Ⓔ
2. Ⓐ Ⓑ Ⓒ Ⓓ Ⓔ	22. Ⓐ Ⓑ Ⓒ Ⓓ Ⓔ	42. Ⓐ Ⓑ Ⓒ Ⓓ Ⓔ
3. Ⓐ Ⓑ Ⓒ Ⓓ Ⓔ	23. Ⓐ Ⓑ Ⓒ Ⓓ Ⓔ	43. Ⓐ Ⓑ Ⓒ Ⓓ Ⓔ
4. Ⓐ Ⓑ Ⓒ Ⓓ Ⓔ	24. Ⓐ Ⓑ Ⓒ Ⓓ Ⓔ	44. Ⓐ Ⓑ Ⓒ Ⓓ Ⓔ
5. Ⓐ Ⓑ Ⓒ Ⓓ Ⓔ	25. Ⓐ Ⓑ Ⓒ Ⓓ Ⓔ	45. Ⓐ Ⓑ Ⓒ Ⓓ Ⓔ
6. Ⓐ Ⓑ Ⓒ Ⓓ Ⓔ	26. Ⓐ Ⓑ Ⓒ Ⓓ Ⓔ	46. Ⓐ Ⓑ Ⓒ Ⓓ Ⓔ
7. Ⓐ Ⓑ Ⓒ Ⓓ Ⓔ	27. Ⓐ Ⓑ Ⓒ Ⓓ Ⓔ	47. Ⓐ Ⓑ Ⓒ Ⓓ Ⓔ
8. Ⓐ Ⓑ Ⓒ Ⓓ Ⓔ	28. Ⓐ Ⓑ Ⓒ Ⓓ Ⓔ	48. Ⓐ Ⓑ Ⓒ Ⓓ Ⓔ
9. Ⓐ Ⓑ Ⓒ Ⓓ Ⓔ	29. Ⓐ Ⓑ Ⓒ Ⓓ Ⓔ	49. Ⓐ Ⓑ Ⓒ Ⓓ Ⓔ
10. Ⓐ Ⓑ Ⓒ Ⓓ Ⓔ	30. Ⓐ Ⓑ Ⓒ Ⓓ Ⓔ	50. Ⓐ Ⓑ Ⓒ Ⓓ Ⓔ
11. Ⓐ Ⓑ Ⓒ Ⓓ Ⓔ	31. Ⓐ Ⓑ Ⓒ Ⓓ Ⓔ	51. Ⓐ Ⓑ Ⓒ Ⓓ Ⓔ
12. Ⓐ Ⓑ Ⓒ Ⓓ Ⓔ	32. Ⓐ Ⓑ Ⓒ Ⓓ Ⓔ	52. Ⓐ Ⓑ Ⓒ Ⓓ Ⓔ
13. Ⓐ Ⓑ Ⓒ Ⓓ Ⓔ	33. Ⓐ Ⓑ Ⓒ Ⓓ Ⓔ	53. Ⓐ Ⓑ Ⓒ Ⓓ Ⓔ
14. Ⓐ Ⓑ Ⓒ Ⓓ Ⓔ	34. Ⓐ Ⓑ Ⓒ Ⓓ Ⓔ	54. Ⓐ Ⓑ Ⓒ Ⓓ Ⓔ
15. Ⓐ Ⓑ Ⓒ Ⓓ Ⓔ	35. Ⓐ Ⓑ Ⓒ Ⓓ Ⓔ	55. Ⓐ Ⓑ Ⓒ Ⓓ Ⓔ
16. Ⓐ Ⓑ Ⓒ Ⓓ Ⓔ	36. Ⓐ Ⓑ Ⓒ Ⓓ Ⓔ	56. Ⓐ Ⓑ Ⓒ Ⓓ Ⓔ
17. Ⓐ Ⓑ Ⓒ Ⓓ Ⓔ	37. Ⓐ Ⓑ Ⓒ Ⓓ Ⓔ	57. Ⓐ Ⓑ Ⓒ Ⓓ Ⓔ
18. Ⓐ Ⓑ Ⓒ Ⓓ Ⓔ	38. Ⓐ Ⓑ Ⓒ Ⓓ Ⓔ	58. Ⓐ Ⓑ Ⓒ Ⓓ Ⓔ
19. Ⓐ Ⓑ Ⓒ Ⓓ Ⓔ	39. Ⓐ Ⓑ Ⓒ Ⓓ Ⓔ	59. Ⓐ Ⓑ Ⓒ Ⓓ Ⓔ
20. Ⓐ Ⓑ Ⓒ Ⓓ Ⓔ	40. Ⓐ Ⓑ Ⓒ Ⓓ Ⓔ	60. Ⓐ Ⓑ Ⓒ Ⓓ Ⓔ

AP Microeconomics Practice Test

Section I

Time – 70 minutes
60 Questions

Directions: Each of the questions or incomplete statements below is followed by five suggested answers or completions. Select the best choice in each case.

1. Most of the choices that people make are not all-or-nothing choices. As a result, economists generally employ
   (A) graphical analysis
   (B) average cost curves
   (C) marginal analysis
   (D) financial analysis
   (E) laboratory analysis

2. Suppose that the number of law school graduates continues to increase. In that case, lawyers' salaries
   (A) must fall
   (B) must increase
   (C) will fall only if demand increases
   (D) will fall only if demand increases more than supply increases
   (E) will fall only if demand increases less than supply increases

3. The marginal revenue product of capital indicates
   (A) the additional output generated by an additional unit of capital, all other things being equal
   (B) the additional cost to the firm when it employs an additional unit of capital, all other things being equal
   (C) the additional profit the firm earns when it employs an additional unit of capital, all other things being equal
   (D) the additional revenue the firm earns when it employs an additional unit of capital, all other things being equal
   (E) the capital required to produce an additional unit of output, all other things being equal

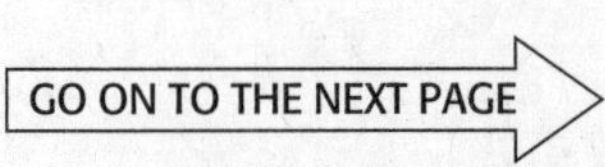

4. Corn is a resource needed to produce tortilla chips. If the demand for tortilla chips increases, then the
   (A) supply of corn will increase
   (B) supply of corn will decrease
   (C) demand for corn will increase
   (D) demand for corn will decrease
   (E) price of corn will decrease

5. If it is too costly to prevent those who refuse to pay from enjoying the benefits of a particular good, we call this
   (A) non-exclusion
   (B) non-rivalry in consumption
   (C) non-feasibility
   (D) the free-rider problem
   (E) a negative externality

6. Ten cases of apple juice can be sold at $10 each in a perfectly competitive product market and the marginal physical product of the last unit of labor is five. In this situation, the marginal revenue product of the last unit of labor is
   (A) $15.00
   (B) $30.00
   (C) $50.00
   (D) $2.00
   (E) $.50

7. The demand curve for any product slopes downward because
   (A) the total utility falls below marginal utility as more of a product is consumed
   (B) the marginal utility lies below the total utility as more of a product is consumed
   (C) marginal utility diminishes as more of a product is consumed
   (D) time becomes less valuable as more of a product is consumed
   (E) the income and substitution effects precisely offset each other

8. Price elasticity of demand is useful because it measures how changes in price affect
   (A) transaction costs
   (B) costs of production
   (C) consumers' behavior
   (D) taxpayers' behavior
   (E) producers' willingness to produce

9. If City B's planners expect that an increase in bus fares will raise mass transit revenues, they must think that the demand for bus travel is
   (A) elastic
   (B) unit elastic
   (C) inelastic
   (D) perfectly inelastic
   (E) perfectly elastic

GO ON TO THE NEXT PAGE

10. A price ceiling in the market means that

(A) there is an excess amount of the product in the market

(B) there is a shortage of the product in the market

(C) government wants to stop a deflationary spiral in the market

(D) government has set a legal price which is less than the market equilibrium price

(E) government has set a legal price which is greater than the market equilibrium price

11. If Arianne claims that "price is no object" when it comes to buying handbags, then her demand curve for handbags is likely to be

(A) horizontal and perfectly elastic

(B) vertical and perfectly inelastic

(C) highly inelastic

(D) upward-sloping

(E) unit elastic

12. As cities thrive and per capita incomes increase, the demand for mass transit diminishes. This suggests that

(A) cities could raise revenue by increasing mass transit fares

(B) the demand for mass transit travel is price elastic

(C) automobile travel is a complement for mass transit travel

(D) mass transit travel is an inferior good

(E) some consumers prefer mass transit travel

13. Cheese increases in price from $2 to $4 per pound, and this change leads to a decrease in the quantity demanded from 120 to 80 pounds. Demand for cheese is therefore

(A) elastic

(B) inelastic

(C) unitary

(D) zero

(E) inferior

14. An increase in the price of gasoline will shift the demand for hybrid cars to the

(A) right and reduce the market price of hybrid cars

(B) left and reduce the market price of hybrid cars

(C) right and increase the market price of hybrid cars

(D) left and increase the market price ofhybrid cars

(E) perfectly inelastic vertical position

15. The demand for paper clips tends to be

(A) inelastic, because there are few substitutes for paper clips and it represents a large percentage of a consumer's budget

(B) inelastic, because there are many substitutes for paper clips and it represents a large percentage of a consumer's budget

(C) inelastic, because there are few substitutes for paper clips and it represents a small percentage of a consumer's budget

(D) elastic, because there are no substitutes for paper clips and it represents a large percentage of a consumer's budget

(E) elastic, because there are many substitutes for paper clips and it represents a large percentage of a consumer's budget

GO ON TO THE NEXT PAGE

16. Which of the following would show that canned spaghetti is a substitute for macaroni and cheese?

(A) Calculating the cross-price elasticity and getting a positive number
(B) Calculating the income elasticity and getting a number less than one
(C) Calculating the income elasticity and getting a positive number
(D) Calculating the price elasticity of demand and getting a number greater than one
(E) Calculating the income elasticity and getting a negative number

17. The most probable reason that Sam drinks two cups of coffee at breakfast instead of four is that

(A) the marginal utility of the coffee eventually diminishes
(B) most people can't afford four cups of coffee
(C) the total utility of coffee increases as one consumes more
(D) the price of coffee increases as one buys more
(E) the marginal satisfaction derived from cups of coffee remains constant

18. Unemployment and/or an inefficient allocation of resources

(A) causes the production possibilities curve to shift outward
(B) causes the production possibilities curve to shift inward
(C) can exist at any point on a production possibilities curve
(D) can be illustrated by a point outside the production possibilities curve
(E) can be illustrated by a point inside the production possibilities curve

19. If the price of a good is zero, a consumer will

(A) consume all units that have positive total utility
(B) consume an infinite amount of the good
(C) consume all units with positive marginal utility
(D) consume the entire amount supplied
(E) consume until total utility reaches zero

20. Suppose Ruben truthfully tells a car salesperson that the most he is willing to pay for a new car is $15,000. The salesperson says, "You're in luck; we have one on the lot for $15,000." Which of the following statements is true?

(A) Ruben will not buy the car.
(B) The car is not worth $15,000.
(C) Ruben gets $15,000 in consumer surplus from this deal.
(D) Ruben gets no consumer surplus from this deal.
(E) The salesperson earns $15,000 in consumer surplus from this deal.

21. Suppose Jones could increase his total utility from consuming cookies and ice cream bars by consuming one more ice cream bar and one fewer cookie. Which of the following is true?

(A) The marginal utility of cookies exceeds the marginal utility of ice cream bars.
(B) The marginal utility of ice cream bars exceeds the marginal utility of cookies.
(C) The marginal utility of cookies is negative.
(D) The marginal utility per dollar spent on ice cream bars exceeds that of cookies.
(E) Jones's total utility is at a maximum.

GO ON TO THE NEXT PAGE

22. Gerry is a psychologist who charges his patients $125 per hour. He leaves his office early to do some shopping for his mother's birthday, spending two hours at the mall and buying her two scarves that cost $20 each. How much did these gifts truly cost Gerry?

    (A) $40
    (B) $240
    (C) $250
    (D) $290
    (E) $330

23. If a retail store earns a normal profit this year, this means that its

    (A) economic profit is equal to its accounting profit
    (B) economic profit is zero
    (C) economic profit is greater than the average accounting profit in other industries
    (D) accounting profit is zero
    (E) accounting profit is less than its economic profit

24. Which of the following is a short-run adjustment?

    (A) A firm closes a processing plant.
    (B) Faced with increasing enrollment, a community college builds a new School of Health Sciences building and hires twelve new professors.
    (C) Because of staggering losses, three tire companies exit the industry.
    (D) A retail store adds clerks during the holiday rush.
    (E) Three new banks enter the regional market.

25. If marginal cost is greater than average cost, then

    (A) average cost is constant
    (B) marginal cost is constant
    (C) average cost is rising
    (D) average cost is falling
    (E) marginal cost must be falling

26. If Company A produces 5,000 harmonicas per year at an average variable cost of $4 and an average fixed cost of $2 per harmonica, then the company's total cost is

    (A) $20,000
    (B) $6,000
    (C) $10,000
    (D) $30,000
    (E) $5,000

27. Suppose a tractor company produces 100,000 tractors per year at its Arizona plant at an average cost of $800. It doubles its production by building an identical plant in Mississippi, which is also capable of producing at an average cost of $800. This firm has thus exhibited

    (A) diminishing marginal returns
    (B) economies of scale
    (C) constant returns to scale
    (D) an upward-sloping planning curve
    (E) price discrimination

GO ON TO THE NEXT PAGE

28. The demand curve in a purely competitive product market is downward-sloping while the demand curve for a single firm in that industry is

(A) perfectly inelastic
(B) upward-sloping
(C) perfectly elastic
(D) vertical
(E) price inelastic

29. Which of the characteristics of perfect competition ensures that economic profit will be zero in the long run?

(A) Each firm is small with respect to the market.
(B) Each firm has access to perfect information.
(C) Goods produced in the market are homogeneous.
(D) Each firm is a price taker.
(E) There is freedom of entry and exit in the market.

30. Businesses aim to make money. Economists reflect this goal in their assumption that firms seek to

(A) maximize accounting profits
(B) maximize economic profits
(C) maximize total revenues
(D) maximize normal profits
(E) minimize total costs

Use the following graph to answer questions 31–33.

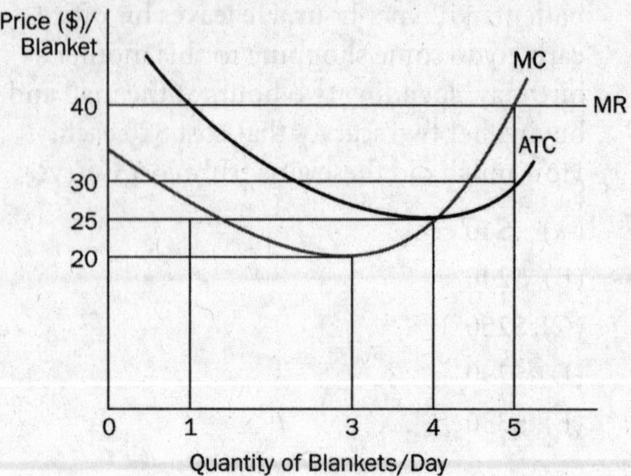

31. Given the information in the graph above, the price of a blanket is

(A) \$20
(B) \$25
(C) \$30
(D) \$40
(E) dependent on the quantity sold

32. Given the information in the graph, what is the profit-maximizing (or loss-minimizing) level of output?

(A) No blankets
(B) One blanket
(C) Three blankets
(D) Four blankets
(E) Five blankets

GO ON TO THE NEXT PAGE

33. According to the graph, how much profit is the firm earning (or how much of a loss is it experiencing) as it attempts to maximize its profits or minimize its losses?

(A) A loss of $15
(B) Profit of $60
(C) Zero profit or loss
(D) Profit of $50
(E) Profit of $10

34. At a 200-unit rate of output, a perfectly competitive firm has total variable costs of $10,000, marginal costs of $50, and charges the market price of $40 per unit. To improve its profit/loss situation, this firm should

(A) increase the output
(B) decrease the output, but not to zero
(C) maintain the present rate of output
(D) shut down production
(E) increase the price

35. If a perfectly competitive firm shuts down, in the short run its owners must pay

(A) all the variable costs, but not the fixed costs
(B) no costs at all
(C) all the variable costs and all the fixed costs
(D) only the variable costs
(E) only the fixed costs

36. If a perfectly competitive firm is operating in long-run equilibrium and market demand suddenly falls, the short-run result will be

(A) increased economic profit
(B) the normal profit
(C) a lower average total cost
(D) a lower average variable cost
(E) an economic loss

37. Perfectly competitive firms achieve production efficiency in the long run by

(A) striving to minimize fixed cost
(B) striving to maximize revenue
(C) producing the MR = MC output at their minimum long-run average cost
(D) producing the MR = MC output at their minimum long-run marginal cost
(E) producing the output consumers want most

38. A firm in an oligopolistic industry

(A) faces a perfectly elastic demand for its product
(B) considers the actions of the other competitors when it determines its pricing and promotion policy
(C) produces a product identical to the products produced by its rivals
(D) produces a product very much the same, but not identical to, the products of its rivals
(E) tries to find a way to market its product that is different from its rivals

GO ON TO THE NEXT PAGE

39. A cartel's profit-maximizing quantity occurs where
    (A) marginal cost equals marginal revenue
    (B) marginal cost equals demand
    (C) a single price monopoly sets its price
    (D) the perfect competitor sets its price
    (E) cost is lowest

40. The downward-sloping demand curve of a monopolistic competitor
    (A) reflects the product differentiation of its products
    (B) becomes perfectly elastic in the long run
    (C) becomes perfectly inelastic in the long run
    (D) indicates the collusion among the members of the product group
    (E) ensures that the firm will produce at the minimum average cost in the long run

41. Barriers to entry
    (A) prevent monopolies from earning profit in the long run
    (B) prevent monopolies from earning profit in the short run
    (C) allow monopolies to earn economic profit
    (D) prevent government from regulating a monopoly
    (E) prevent a natural monopoly from raising its price

42. Compared to firms producing goods in perfect competition, single-price monopolists tend to charge
    (A) lower prices and produce lower quantities of output
    (B) higher prices and produce lower quantities of output
    (C) lower prices and produce higher quantities of output
    (D) higher prices and produce higher quantities of output
    (E) higher prices and produce the same quantities of output

43. Why should we expect to observe airlines engaging in price discrimination?
    I. Airline travel for some is an inelastic good.
    II. Everyone likes to fly.
    III. Airline tickets are not transferable to someone else.
    IV. Airline travel for some is an elastic good.
    (A) I and II
    (B) I and III
    (C) I and IV
    (D) I, III, and IV
    (E) II, III, and IV

GO ON TO THE NEXT PAGE

44. Monopolistic competition describes
    (A) exactly the same market arrangement as the term "monopoly"
    (B) perfect competition that includes strong entry barriers
    (C) an industry in which there is one seller of many differentiated products
    (D) an industry in which there are many sellers of homogeneous products
    (E) an industry in which there are many sellers of differentiated products

45. In the long run, the output of a monopolistically competitive firm
    (A) is greater than the output of a perfectly competitive firm
    (B) is less than the output of a perfectly competitive firm
    (C) will equal the point at which long-run average cost is minimized
    (D) equals the output of a perfectly competitive firm
    (E) is less than the output of a single monopolist

Production Possibilities (per day) for Two Countries, Alpha and Beta

	Boats	Barrels
Alpha	160	80
Beta	100	40

46. According to the table, which of the following is true?
    (A) Alpha has an absolute advantage in producing both goods and a comparative advantage in producing barrels.
    (B) Beta has an absolute advantage in producing both goods and a comparative advantage in producing boats.
    (C) Neither country has an absolute advantage in production.
    (D) Alpha has an absolute advantage in producing both goods and a comparative advantage in producing boats.
    (E) There can be no gains from trade between these two countries.

47. What is Beta's opportunity cost per boat?
    (A) 40 barrels
    (B) 100 boats
    (C) 0.4 barrels
    (D) 2.5 barrels
    (E) 4000 barrels

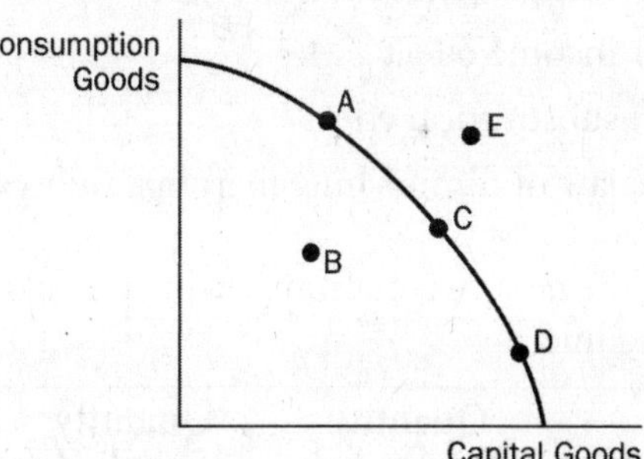

Use this production possibilities frontier for capital goods and consumption goods to answer questions 48 and 49.

48. If chosen today, which point would provide greater economic growth in the future?

(A) Point A
(B) Point B
(C) Point C
(D) Point D
(E) Point E

49. Which point represents an economy in which there is unemployment?

(A) Point A
(B) Point B
(C) Point C
(D) Point D
(E) Point E

50. Consumers' real purchasing power rises as the price of a good falls, and they may demand more of that good. This behavior reflects the

(A) law of increasing marginal costs
(B) complement effect
(C) income effect
(D) substitution effect
(E) law of diminishing marginal utility

Answer the next two questions using the following schedule:

Price	Quantity Demanded	Quantity Supplied
$7	0 units/day	210 units/day
$6	40 units/day	170 units/day
$5	80 units/day	150 units/day
$4	120 units/day	120 units/day

51. According to the information in this table, the total expenditures of consumers at the market price will be

(A) $240
(B) $120
(C) $750
(D) $480
(E) $400

52. If the current price is $6, there would be a

(A) 30-unit shortage
(B) 30-unit surplus
(C) 60-unit shortage
(D) 130-unit shortage
(E) 130-unit surplus

53. Marginal cost

(A) measures the change in the AFC as more units of capital are added to production
(B) is defined as the difference between total cost and total variable costs
(C) rises for a time, but then begins to decline when the point of diminishing returns is reached
(D) declines as long as output increases
(E) intersects both AVC and ATC at their minimum points

GO ON TO THE NEXT PAGE

54. Which of the following is likely to be considered a public good?

(A) A movie theater in a low-income neighborhood
(B) An amusement park built on an empty rural lot
(C) A fireworks display funded by the city
(D) A catfish pond in a gated community
(E) A swimming pool in a condominium development

55. Byproducts of production or consumption that impose costs on individuals other than those who purchase or produce the good are known as

(A) negative externalities
(B) free-rider problems
(C) common pool problems
(D) positive externalities
(E) Coase byproducts

56. At the socially efficient output and price for a good whose production causes pollution, we can expect that

(A) the offending pollution will be eliminated
(B) the marginal social cost of production will exceed the marginal social benefit of production
(C) the private cost of production will equal the private benefit of production
(D) the marginal social benefit of production will equal the marginal social cost of production
(E) too little of the good will be produced

Use the following graph to answer questions 57–59.

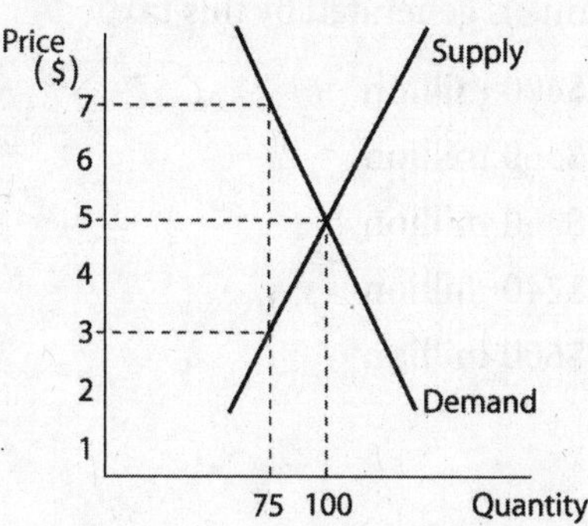

57. This graph shows the effect of a $4 per unit excise tax. What net price will producers receive if the tax is enacted?

(A) $3
(B) $6
(C) $7
(D) $10
(E) $16

58. According to the graph, which of the following is true about how the burden of the tax is distributed?

(A) Consumers bear 75% of the tax burden, while producers bear 25%.
(B) Consumers bear 100% of the tax burden.
(C) Producers bear 100% of the tax burden.
(D) Consumers bear 25% of the tax burden, while producers bear 75%.
(E) Consumers bear 50% of the tax burden, while producers bear 50%.

GO ON TO THE NEXT PAGE

59. According to the graph, how much tax revenue is generated by this tax?

(A) $400 million
(B) $560 million
(C) $300 million
(D) $240 million
(E) $600 million

60. A method economists use to display the degree of income inequality is

(A) a demand curve
(B) a Lorenz curve
(C) an LRAC curve
(D) an income consumption curve
(E) a Keynesian consumption curve

IF YOU FINISH BEFORE TIME IS UP, YOU MAY CHECK YOUR WORK ON THIS SECTION ONLY. DO NOT TURN TO ANY OTHER SECTION IN THE TEST.

Ten-Minute Reading Period

Take the next 10 minutes to glance over the three questions that comprise Section II of this test. You can take notes in the margins, but you may not begin answering any of the questions in any way whatsoever.

When the 10-minute period is over, you may begin answering the three free-response questions.

Section II

Writing Time – 50 minutes

Directions: You have 50 minutes to answer all three of the following questions. It is suggested that you spend approximately half your time on the first question and divide the remaining time equally between the next two questions. In answering the questions, you should emphasize the line of reasoning that generated your results; it is not enough to list the results of your analysis. Include correctly labeled diagrams, if useful or required, in your answers. A correctly labeled diagram must have all axes and curves clearly labeled and must show directional changes.

1. A pharmaceutical firm holds a patent on a drug that provides relief from a life-threatening disease. The firm is a profit-maximizing operation, earning economic profit.

   (a) Define the term "patent."

   (b) Draw a correctly-labeled graph for this firm, showing the profit maximizing level of output and the market price. Shade the economic profit and label the deadweight or efficiency loss.

   (c) Define consumer surplus.

   (d) If the firm wishes to gain more of the consumer surplus, what are three conditions it must meet?

   (e) Explain the effect on economic profit if the firm fulfills the three conditions and is able to become a perfectly discriminating monopolist.

2. Answer this question using the following graph:

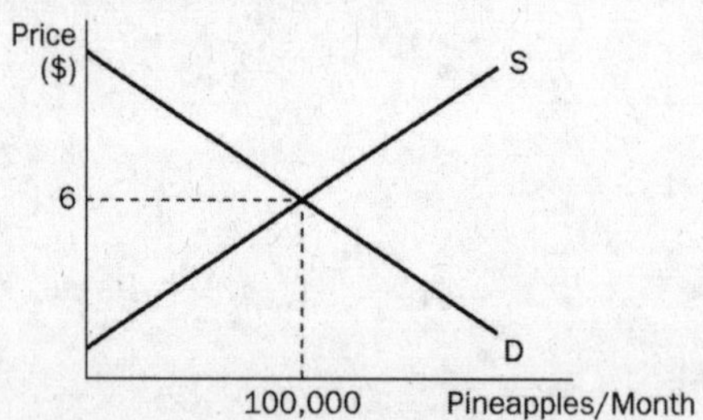

   (a) Assuming a perfectly competitive market for pineapples, with supply curve S and demand curve D, explain how the market price and quantity of pineapples are determined.

   (b) If consumers considered pineapples and cantaloupes to be good substitutes, explain how an increase in the price of cantaloupes would affect the market for pineapples.

   (c) If the government paid a $1 per unit subsidy to pineapple growers, explain how the government subsidy would affect the pineapple market.

   (d) How would the consumer surplus be affected by this government subsidy?

   (e) Explain how an increase in the wages paid to the workers who harvest and process pineapples will affect the pineapple market.

GO ON TO THE NEXT PAGE

3. Microeconomics studies the effect of market structure on market outcomes, such as price, output, profit, and efficiency. Imagine that the government is considering two ways to move a pure monopolist toward a more competitive position:

   (a) a monopolistically competitive market

   (b) a perfectly competitive market

   For each of these two options, describe how the change would affect:

      i. the market price

      ii. the profit maximizing level of output

      iii. economic profit

      iv. allocative and productive efficiency

IF YOU FINISH BEFORE TIME IS UP, YOU MAY CHECK YOUR WORK ON THIS SECTION ONLY. DO NOT TURN TO ANY OTHER SECTION IN THE TEST.

AP Microeconomics Practice Test: **Answer Key**

1. C
2. E
3. D
4. C
5. A
6. C
7. C
8. C
9. C
10. D
11. B
12. D
13. B
14. C
15. C
16. A
17. A
18. E
19. C
20. D
21. D
22. D
23. B
24. D
25. C
26. D
27. C
28. C
29. E
30. B
31. D
32. E
33. D
34. D
35. E
36. E
37. C
38. B
39. A
40. A
41. C
42. B
43. D
44. E
45. B
46. A
47. C
48. D
49. B
50. C
51. D
52. E
53. E
54. C
55. A
56. D
57. A
58. D
59. C
60. B

AP MICROECONOMICS PRACTICE TEST CORRELATION CHART

Area of Study	Question Numbers
Basic Economic Concepts	1, 18, 22
Production Possibilities Curve	48, 49
Comparative Advantage, Specialization, and Trade	46, 47
Supply and Demand	2, 10,12,14, 51, 52, 57, 58, 59
Elasticity	8, 9, 11, 13, 15, 16
Theory of Consumer Choice	7,17,19, 20, 21, 50
Production Functions Short and Long Run	24
Short-Run Costs	25, 26, 53
Long-Run Costs and Economies of Scale	27
Profit	23
Perfect Competition	28, 29, 30, 31, 36, 37
Profit Maximization	32, 33, 34, 35
Monopoly	39, 41, 42, 43
Monopolistic Competition	40, 44, 45
Oligopoly	38, 53
Factor Markets	3, 4, 6
Income Distribution	60
Public Goods	5, 54
Externalities	55, 56

ANSWERS AND EXPLANATIONS

SECTION I

1. C

Economists use marginal analysis to model the benefits and costs of incremental choices, which constitute the majority of choices. Choice (C) is therefore correct.

2. E

Choice (E) is correct because if the supply of lawyers increases, lawyers' salaries will fall only if the supply curve for lawyers shifts to the right (increases) more than the demand curve for lawyers does. Choice (A) does not consider demand as a factor. Choice (B) is incorrect because the supply of new lawyers will move the supply curve as noted. Choice (C) considers demand but not supply. Choice (D) states the opposite of the correct answer.

3. D

The correct choice (D) states that the marginal revenue product (MRP) of capital is defined as the additional revenue a firm earns when it employs an additional unit of capital, all other things being equal. MRP considers both the additional product that the new capital produces and the price of the product made. This makes (A) incorrect. Choice (B) is incorrect because the cost of the additional unit of capital is not used in the calculation of MRP. Choice (C) is incorrect because profit is determined by taking the revenue earned and subtracting the costs. Choice (E) does not use the "additional" capital used.

4. C

If consumers exhibit a demand for an output, a demand for inputs arises. Thus, an increase in demand for tortilla chips (output) generates an increase in demand for corn (an input). Choice (C) defines this derived demand. Choices (A) and (B) note that supply shifts, but a change in the demand for chips will not cause a shift in supply. Choice (D) is incorrect, being the opposite of the correct choice. Choice (E) is incorrect because a higher demand for chips will increase the demand for corn resulting in a higher price for the resource, corn.

5. A

Public goods are not exclusive and they are not rival. Those goods that exhibit non-exclusion are those for which it is too costly to develop a means of preventing those who refuse to pay from enjoying the benefits. Choice (B) is another characteristic of public goods but not the term used to define the question. Choice (C) is not an economic term. Choice (D) is incorrect because it defines the condition of those people who benefit as third party from a market transaction that others have entered. Choice (E) is also incorrect because it defines a market failure where third parties are harmed by a market transaction that others have entered.

6. C

For a firm selling in a perfectly competitive market, the marginal revenue product (MRP) is equal to the marginal physical product (MPP) times the market price. Here, five units per labor input times $10 per unit of output equals $50. Choice (C) is the correct answer while the other choices do not follow the formula, MRP = MPP∞ P.

7. C

Choice (C) expresses the view that the demand curve is downward-sloping because of the law of diminishing marginal utility. After some point, as one consumes more
of a good or service, the marginal or extra utility will decline. Choice (A) is incorrect because total utility cannot fall below the marginal utility. Choice (B) is also incorrect because even if this statement is true it does not define why the demand curve is downward-sloping. Choice (D) is incorrect because time is not related to marginal utility. Choice (E) is incorrect because the income and substitution effects are reasons why the demand curve is downward-sloping, but they do not work together to offset each other.

8. C

Choice (C) is correct because price elasticity of demand measures how consumer demand changes in response to a change in price. Choice (A) is incorrect because transaction costs are the opportunity costs in making a transaction. Choice (B) is incorrect because demand does not involve supply ideas like cost. Choice (D) is incorrect because price elasticity does not factor in taxes, and (E) is incorrect because it is not a supply idea but a demand notion.

9. C

Inelastic demand occurs when the percentage change in quantity demanded is less than the percentage change in price. Total revenue is the price of the product times the quantity demanded. Choice (C) correctly states that a price increase will yield higher total revenues only if the demand curve is inelastic. Choices (A) and (B) are other measures of elasticity but (A) would mean that total revenues would fall, and (B) would mean that total revenues would be constant. Choices (D) and (E) are incorrect because "perfectly" means that either no change or infinite change would result.

10. D

A government imposes a price ceiling when it feels that the price of a good or service is too high. Choice (D) correctly states that the ceiling price is set below the market equilibrium, making it possible for more consumers to afford to buy the good or service. Choice (A) is incorrect because a price floor will create an excess amount, or surplus. Choice (B) is incorrect because a price ceiling *creates* the shortage; it is not the definition of a price ceiling. Choice (C) is incorrect because government price ceilings aim to lower the price for consumers. Choice (E) is incorrect because it defines a price floor set above the market price.

11. B

A vertical demand curve as described in (B) represents a situation where elasticity is zero, that is, where consumers will buy a certain quantity regardless of price—hence the demand curve is vertical and perfectly inelastic. Choice (A) is incorrect because a horizontal and perfectly elastic demand curve would indicate that quantity demanded would be any amount at a particular price. Choice (C) is incorrect because Arianne would not be unwilling at some prices. Choice (D) is incorrect because demand curves are downward-sloping. Choice (E) is incorrect because unit elastic means that the percentage change in quantity demanded is the same as the percentage change in price.

12. D

For an inferior good, consumer income and demand are inversely related. As cities prosper, more citizens switch away from mass transit and prefer to drive themselves, making (D) the correct answer. Choice (A) is incorrect because cities would not be able to raise revenue if the demand for mass transit fell. Eliminate (B) because price elasticity is not connected to income. Choice (C) is incorrect because automobile travel and mass transit travel are generally substitutes for each other, not complements. Choice (E) is a statement of opinion and therefore not an economic factor.

13. B

When the demand for a good is inelastic (B), the percentage change in quantity demanded is less than the percentage change in price. Here, the change in quantity demanded is $\frac{40}{120}$ or 33%; the change in price is $\frac{\$2}{\$2}$ or 100%. Other choices do not apply the correct formula shown above.

14. C

As the price of gasoline increases, hybrid cars will become a cheaper alternative to gasoline-only cars. This substitutability is a non-price determinant for demand. Choice (C) is correct because demand for hybrid cars will increase, and, *ceteris paribus*, raise the market price. Choice (A) is incorrect because it states that the price of hybrid cars will fall. Choices (B) and (D) are incorrect because they propose that the demand curve for hybrid cars would move to the left. Choice (E) is incorrect because it changes the elasticity of the hybrid cars though no change has occurred.

15. C

Price elasticity of demand is less for goods with few substitutes and which constitute a small portion of the consumer's budget. Choice (C) correctly states that paper clips exhibit inelastic demand. Choice (A) wrongly states that paper clips are a large part of most people's budgets. Choice (B) wrongly states that there are many substitutes for paper clips. Choices (D) and (E) are both incorrect because they assert that the demand is elastic.

16. A

If the price of a good rises, and consumers demand more of a substitute, the cross-price elasticity between these goods will be positive–(A). Choices (B), (C), and (E) use income elasticity incorrectly. Choice (D) is incorrect because it uses the price elasticity of demand concept.

17. A

Choice (A) correctly identifies the reason for Sam's coffee intake: The marginal utility of the coffee eventually diminishes. This is a clear definition of the law of diminishing marginal utility. Choice (B) incorrectly mentions budget constraints; (C) incorrectly states that total utility increases as more is consumed. Total utility reaches a peak and then falls as the marginal utility becomes negative. Choice (D) incorrectly brings price into the answer. Choice (E) incorrectly states that marginal utility is constant, in violation of the law of diminishing marginal utility.

18. E

On a production possibilities curve (PPC), efficiency is on the curve. When an economy suffers unemployment or there is a misallocation of resources towards production, the economy lies inside the PPC. Choice (E) is correct because production will be lower than when it sits on the curve. Choices (A) and (B) state that shifts of the PPC are correct; shifts of the curve means that a nation employs new resources like labor, capital or the natural. Choice (C) is incorrect because efficiency, noted on the PPC, cannot exist while there an inefficient use of labor resources caused by unemployment. Choice (D) is incorrect because points outside the PPC are unattainable with the set of current resources.

19. C

To maximize utility, consumers will consume free goods up to the point at which the next unit provides them no additional utility, or zero marginal utility, so (C) is the correct answer. Price is not the only factor that drives consumption. Choice (A) is incorrect because for most of the range where the total utility is rising, the marginal utility is falling. Choices (B) and (D) are incorrect because a consumer's satisfaction falls with additional or marginal units. Choice (E) is incorrect because when total utility is at zero, marginal utility is very negative.

20. D

Consumer surplus is the difference between the maximum a consumer is willing to pay and the amount they actually pay for a good. In (D), by revealing his maximum price, Ruben will get no consumer surplus. Choice (A) is false because Ruben has stated that he would be willing to spend the $15,000. Choice (B) is a value judgment, not a statement of fact. According to the definition above, (C) is incorrect. Choice (E) is incorrect because we have no information as to the wholesale value of the car or what commission rate the salesperson earns. Furthermore, consumer surplus relates to the buyer, not the seller.

21. D

Consumers maximize their utility by directing their expenditures until the marginal utility per dollar is equal across all goods. If this is not true, then rearranging their consumption bundle can yield higher total utility for the same expenditure, as in (D). Choices (A), (B), and (C) are incorrect because they do not use marginal utility per dollar. Choice (E) is incorrect because when the total utility is maximized, the marginal utility is zero.

22. D

The total cost of the items includes the opportunity cost of the time spent purchasing them. Gerry's regular wage (2 hours times $125) provides a good approximation of value for the next best use of his time. Thus, the scarves cost $40 in cash and $250 in time for a total of $290. The other choices contain either math errors or incorrect assumptions about the solution.

23. B

A normal profit is defined as one such that accounting profit is just enough to cover all costs, including the next best rate of return. In other words, economic profit, which includes such opportunity costs, is zero—(B). Choice (A) is incorrect because economic profit differs from accounting profit, since economic profit considers the opportunity cost of an action. Choice (C) is incorrect because it states a false or unrelated idea. In (D), if the firm has no accounting profit, it is likely to be near closure without a normal profit. Choice (E) is incorrect because economic profit is usually greater than accounting profits because it considers opportunity costs.

24. D

In the short run, at least one resource is fixed. In (D), the retail store varies its labor usage with a fixed amount of capital. A short-run adjustment usually means that firms can add labor while they hold constant other factors. Choice (A) is incorrect because the shutdown of a plant is a long-run adjustment to a price less than its average variable costs. Choice (B) adds capital, which signifies long-run change. Choice (C) is incorrect, as it is another long-run change. Firm entry in (E) signifies a long-run adjustment.

25. C

Marginal costs show the additional cost of producing another unit of output. If the marginal unit costs more than the average unit, the average cost must increase. Choice (C) correctly states this concept. In graphs of these costs, marginal cost intersects average cost when it reaches its lowest point. Choice (A) is incorrect because it fails to recognize that marginal cost and average costs are related. Choice (B) is incorrect because changes in marginal cost happen when new resources are employed. Choice (D) is incorrect because it states that the average cost falls, which is opposite to the correct answer. Choice (E) is incorrect because marginal cost only falls briefly when additional units are produced and average cost is falling.

26. D

Total cost is equal to total fixed costs plus total variable costs (TC = TFC + TVC). Total fixed costs are equal to average fixed cost multiplied by quantity (TFC = AFC × Q), or $2 × 5,000 = $10,000. Total variable costs are equal to average variable costs multiplied by quantity (TVC = AVC × Q), or $4 × 5,000 = $20,000. Total cost in this case, then, is $30,000 because $10,000 + $20,000 = $30,000. Choice (D) is correct. All the other choices contain math errors or incorrect applications of the formula stated above.

27. C

Choice (C) correctly states that if a firm doubles inputs and output exactly doubles, the firm is witnessing constant returns to scale and its long-run average costs remains the same. Choices (A) and (E) are incorrect because they state concepts not related to the question. Choice (B) is incorrect because economies of scale define the downward portion of a long-run total average cost curve. Choice (D) is incorrect because it is not an economic term.

28. C

The market is a summation of all suppliers and buyers; the demand curve slopes downward, reflecting the law of diminishing marginal utility. Firms operating in a perfectly competitive industry are price takers who have no influence over their price. The price is taken from the market and is thus perfectly elastic. Choice (C) is correct. Firms must sell at the market price or lose sales to other firms in their industry. Choices (A) and (D) are incorrect because a perfectly inelastic curve is vertical. Choice (B) is incorrect because supply curves are upward-sloping while the demand curve is downward-sloping. Choice (E) is incorrect as well, because price inelasticity would have some slope to the curve.

29. E

Any above-normal profit earned in the short run will attract other businesses to the field, increase supply, and drive down price until just normal profit is earned. Choice (E) is true because open entry and exit give firms freedom to act. Choices (A), (C), and (D) are characteristics of pure competition, but not the answer to the question. Choice (B) is incorrect because firms take their price from the market but do not know the cost structures of the other competitive firms.

30. B

Because economic profit includes all cost of production (including opportunity cost), economists assume that firms aim to maximize economic profit–(B). Choice (A) is incorrect because accounting profits do not consider opportunity costs as a factor. Choice (C) is incorrect because economic profit is revenue minus all costs. Choice (D) is incorrect as well because normal profits are in the absence of economic profits and only keep the owner working with the hope of economic profits in the future. Choice (C) incorrectly states that total cost should be minimized, forgetting that revenues must be maximized.

31. D

In a perfectly competitive market, price equals marginal revenue (P = MR), which in this example is $40. Choice (D) is the correct response; other choices do not reflect the correct formula as stated here.

32. E

Profit is maximized when producing the quantity at which MR = MC; here, MR and MC intersect at an output of five blankets, (E); the other choices do not reflect the correct formula as stated here.

33. D

The firm earns revenues of $40 per unit, incurs costs of $30 per unit, and produces 5 units. Thus, its total profit is $10 per unit times 5 units, or $50, so (D) is the correct answer. It is important to find the ATC directly above the quantity found where MR = MC.

34. D

The market price of $40 is less than the AVC of $50. As a result, the firm's loss exceeds its fixed cost, and it would be better off shutting down and just incurring fixed cost. Choice (D) is correct. Choices (A), (B), and (C) all incorrectly maintain some level of production but price does not cover the average variable costs. Choice (E) is incorrect because perfectly competitive firms cannot change their price since it comes from the market.

35. E

Because variable resources can be reduced to zero in the short run but fixed resources cannot, firms must only pay fixed costs when they shut down, as (E) states. Choice (A) is incorrect, stating that all the variable costs must be paid–these costs are only incurred when production occurs. Choice (B) is incorrect because fixed costs like rent, insurance, or wages of salaried workers must be paid regardless of production. Choices (C) and (D) are incorrect because variable costs are only incurred when production is undertaken.

36. E

In long-run equilibrium, a perfectly competitive firm's price equals average cost. They earn zero economic profit, but they can earn normal profit. A reduction in market demand will drop price below average cost, forcing the firm to suffer an economic loss. Choice (E) is correct. Choice (A) is incorrect because with a lower price, the firm cannot earn an economic profit. Choice (B) is incorrect because in the long-run position, normal profit is earned. Choices (C) and (D) are incorrect because price changes do not change cost.

37. C

In the long run, perfectly competitive firms remain in business by choosing the most efficient combination of resources that yields minimum long-run average costs–(C). Minimizing fixed cost (A) is incorrect because it will not be able to minimize long-run average costs. Choice (B) is incorrect because maximizing revenue does not affect costs or efficiency. Choice (D) is incorrect because minimum marginal cost does not occur at the MR = MC output. Choice (E) is incorrect because it defines allocative efficiency.

38. B

Because there are so few firms in oligopolies, each firm's actions can significantly affect price, and thus, the other firms. These firms must take into account their rivals' responses when making pricing, marketing, and production decisions–(B). Only firms in perfectly competitive markets face perfectly elastic demand curves, so (A) is incorrect. Choices (C) and (D) are incorrect because firms in oligopolies can either sell differentiated or homogeneous products.

39. A

Cartels, like all firms, will maximize industry profits by pricing and producing where MR = MC. Choice (B) is incorrect because the marginal revenue curve in a graph for an oligopoly acting as a cartel will lie below its demand curve. Choice (C) is incorrect because a single-price monopoly finds its profit-maximizing level of output where MR = MC, and then finds the price directly above that output on the demand curve. Choice (D) is incorrect because perfect competitors get their price from the market equilibrium. Choice (E) is incorrect because the type of cost is not specified.

40. A

The demand curve for a monopolistically competitive firm is relatively elastic because of the product differences that distinguish their product from another firm's product. Choices (B) and (C) are incorrect because elasticity does not change for these firms in the long run. Choice (D) is incorrect because there are too many competitors in a monopolistically competitive industry for collusion to be effective. Choice (E) is incorrect because these firms do not produce at the minimum average cost in the long run.

41. C

Only when new firms cannot easily enter a market in which above normal profits are being earned will these profits persist in the long run. Often monopoly is formed because they gain the advantage in some way with barriers to entry. This makes (C) the correct response. Choices (A) and (B) are incorrect because barriers to entry allow monopoly firms to make profits. Choice (D) is incorrect because government regulation is enacted to prevent monopoly power from taking the advantage. Choice (E) is incorrect because natural monopolies are usually regulated with prices determined by a public service authority.

42. B

While both perfect competitors and single-price monopolists find their output at MR = MC, a monopolist can charge a higher price because a monopolist's demand curve lies above its marginal revenue curve. The slope or elasticity of the monopolist also means that it will produce a lower output than the perfect competitor. Choice (B) is therefore correct. Choice (A) is incorrect because the price is higher for monopoly firms. Choice (C) is incorrect because price and output statements are both incorrect. Choices (D) and (E) are incorrect because quantity for the monopoly firm is lower.

43. D

An airline that is price discriminating must be able to differentiate between its customers' demand elasticity to charge different prices. Furthermore, it must possess some degree of monopoly power, while its customers cannot resell their tickets. Choice (D) is the correct answer. The other choices all have flaws in that they do not account for the correct conditions of a price-discriminating firm.

44. E

Choice (E) correctly states that monopolistic competition differs from perfect competition only in that its firms sell a differentiated product. It is this differentiation that gives the demand curve a slope. Choice (A) is incorrect because monopoly is another distinct form of market structure. Choice (B) is incorrect because entry barriers are not a part of monopolistic competition. Barriers are open and this fosters the competition. The error in (C) lies in its stipulation that there is only one seller. In (D), there is a fallacy in its mention of homogeneous products.

45. B

Because firms in monopolistic competition face demand curves that are not perfectly elastic, they maximize profits by selling less output at a higher price. The marginal revenue curve lies below the sloped demand curve. This means that (B) is correct because the output is determined by the MR = MC point. Choice (A) is incorrect because it states the opposite of the correct answer. Choice (D) is incorrect because even though both monopolistically and perfectly competitive firms use the same MR = MC equation, the perfectly competitive firm has an inelastic demand curve. Choice (E) is incorrect because a single-price monopoly will offer the lowest output of all the market structures.

46. A

With a day's resources, Alpha can produce more of each good and thus has an absolute advantage in producing both goods. However, producing one barrel costs Alpha two boats $\left(\frac{160}{80}\right)$, whereas producing a barrel costs Beta 2.5 boats $\left(\frac{100}{40}\right)$. Alpha therefore has a comparative advantage in producing barrels. Choice (A) is the correct response. Choices (B) and (D) are incorrect because producing one boat costs Alpha $\frac{1}{2}$ barrel, but if Beta produces one boat it costs them only $\frac{2}{5}$ of a barrel. Choice (C) is incorrect because Alpha has the absolute advantage in both products. Choice (E) is incorrect because both nations can gain by specializing in the good in which they incur the least opportunity cost and then trade for the good they no longer make.

47. C

Producing 100 boats uses up resources with which Beta could produce 40 barrels, so each boat costs Beta 0.4 barrels. Choice (C) is correct because $\frac{110}{40} = 0.4$. Other choices do not employ the correct logic.

48. D

Because capital goods produce goods in the future, point D will yield the greatest future production possibilities. Choice (D) is the correct response. Point A will yield slower growth because the current allocation is for more consumer goods. Point B is inefficient; resources are underemployed. Point C could be termed a neutral position—not too slow, not too fast. Point E may be a future goal, but it is not attainable with current resources.

49. B

From point B, the economy could move to points that produce more of both goods. Thus, point B represents some underemployment of resources relative to what is possible when resources are being used efficiently, choice (B). (Refer to the answer for question 48 for the description of the other points on the graph.)

50. C

There are three reasons why the demand curve slopes downward: the law of diminishing marginal utility, the income effect, and the substitution effect. The income effect shows the change in consumption attributable to the change in real income that is due to the price change—(C). Choices (A) and (B) are incorrect because there are no such economic concepts. Choice (D) is incorrect because the substitution effect would mean that as prices increase, consumers look for lower-priced substitutes to purchase. Choice (E) is incorrect as well, because this law is one of the reasons why the demand curve is downward-sloping.

51. D

Because equilibrium occurs where $Q_s = Q_d$, the market price will be $4 and the market quantity will be 120. Total expenditures will be $4 · 120, or $480. The other choices reflect incorrect calculations.

52. E

At a price of $6, the quantity supplied will be 170 units; the quantity demanded will be 40 units. Therefore, the market will yield a surplus of 130 units. The other choices misidentify the surplus.

53. E

The nature of marginal cost means that as the variable costs are added, the marginal cost increases. When the average variable costs and the average total cost reach their minimum, they intersect with the marginal cost—(E). Choice (A) is incorrect because the change in AVC is what changes the marginal cost. Choice (B) is incorrect because it presents the wrong equation. Choice (C) incorrectly mixes the "rises and falls." Choice (D) is incorrect because the marginal cost cannot decline as costs increase.

54. C

Goods from which it is difficult to exclude people and which many can consume at the same time (i.e., goods that are neither exclusive nor rival) exhibit the character of public goods. A fireworks display (C) is an event that many people can watch at the same time with no rivalry. However, it is difficult to prevent anyone from watching simply because he or she did not pay for the display. Choice (A) is incorrect because you cannot enter the theater without paying.

Choice (B) is incorrect because again, you must pay to go to an amusement park. Choices (D) and (E) are incorrect because placing the pond or the pool in a restricted community will mean it is exclusive.

55. A

Negative externalities are defined as byproducts of production or consumption that impose costs on other consumers or on other firms which we call third parties. Choice (A) is the correct answer. Choice (B) is incorrect because the free-rider problem means that some people enjoy the benefits of a product without paying for it. Choice (C) is incorrect because common pool goods are used once but no one can be excluded from using what is available. Choice (D) is incorrect because a positive externality gives benefits beyond the benefits derived by the buyer. Choice (E) is incorrect because the Coase theorem tries to solve negative externalities with negotiation.

56. D

For the output of a good to match the level that maximizes society's welfare, the marginal social cost must equal the marginal social benefit. Otherwise, opportunities to increase welfare would exist. Thus, (D) is correct. It is never economically efficient to clean up pollution completely, so (A) is incorrect. Choice (B) is incorrect because it is the opposite of the correct answer. Choice (C) is incorrect because social benefit and social cost are the important terms. Choice (E) is incorrect because a negative externality means that too much of the good is produced.

57. A

The market price is $7, and suppliers must remit the tax to the government. The producers' net price is the market price minus the tax, or $3, making (A) the correct answer.

58. D

As a result of the tax, suppliers see their net price fall by $2, while consumers see price rise by $2. Recall that the tax is $4. This tells us that consumers bear 50% (½) of the tax burden, while producers bear 50% (½). Choice (D) is the correct answer.

59. C

Tax revenue equals the tax rate multiplied by the quantity of the good sold, or, in this case, $4 x 75 million units. This gives us a total tax revenue of $300 million.

60. B

The Lorenz curve (B) shows the percentage of income earned by the corresponding percentage of families when they are ranked from low income to high income. A Lorenz curve on or close to the diagonal indicates an equal distribution of income across families. Choice (A) is incorrect because a demand curve is part of a model that shows the market. Choice (C) is incorrect because an LRAC curve is part of the market structure model. Choices (D) and (E) are incorrect because they use terms that are not microeconomic in nature.

SECTION II

1. This question tests your knowledge of single price monopoly and price discrimination. You are asked to draw the single price monopoly graph showing economic profit and deadweight loss; the comparison to the price discriminating model is tested as well. Here's what a sample response might look like:

(a) A patent is the exclusive right given by government to produce and sell a product for 20 years from the time of the patent application. It gives the inventor the opportunity to gain a profit from his idea or invention.

(b)

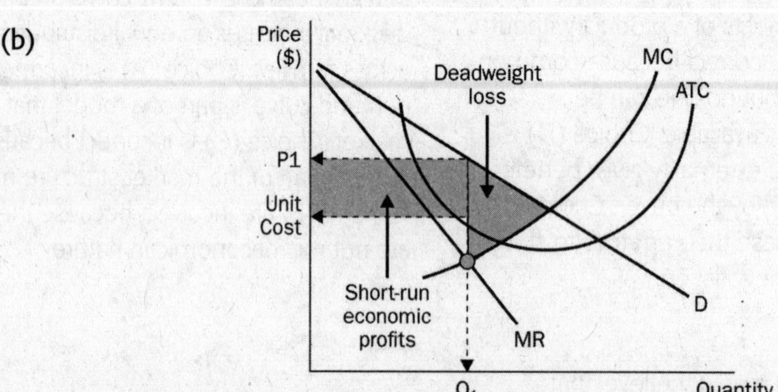

(c) Consumer surplus is the difference between what the consumer was willing to pay for a good or service and what was actually paid; it is the triangle below the demand curve but above the market equilibirum price.

(d) If the firm wants to gain more of the consumer surplus, it can try to become a price discriminating monopoly. It must have market power which it gets from the patent it holds. The firm will just be able to segment the market based on the demand elasticitities of the consumers. Some will be willing to pay a high price for the good or service while others will not. The firm must be able to keep these groupings separated so no resale of the good or service is possible.

(e) If the firm can fulfill these conditions, it can sell its product all along the demand curve to the point where the demand curve becomes inelastic. If the costs are lower than these prices, the firm can earn a greater profit than a single price monopoly.

2. This question tests knowledge of supply and demand curves as well as efficiency. To predict market outcomes and show the efficiency aspects of changes in markets, you must understand the theoretical basis of supply and demand. Here's what a sample response might look like:

   (a) The market price and quantity is an equilibrium in which the quantity demanded exactly equals the quantity supplied, holding all other things constant. In this case, quantity demanded equals quantity supplied at a price of $6 and a quantity of 100,000 pineapples per month. Consumers are buying the quantity they are willing and able to buy at that price, and sellers are selling the quantity they are willing and able to sell at that price. As such, there is no incentive for consumers to bid up the price of pineapples in an effort to acquire more, nor is there an incentive for firms to cut price in an attempt to sell more. (Note: A superior answer will show how surpluses or shortages that occur at other prices are eliminated through adjustments in the price.)

   (b) An increase in the price of a substitute means that a smaller quantity of the substitute will be demanded. This shifts the demand curve for pineapples to the right, resulting in an increase in the market price and quantity of pineapples.

   (c) The subsidy would induce suppliers to offer more pineapples at a lower price, thus shifting the supply curve to the right. As a result, the market equilibrium price of pineapples would decrease and the quantity produced and consumed would increase.

   (d) Consumer surplus is the difference between what consumers are *willing* to pay for a good and what they *actually* pay. The subsidy reduces the price of pineapples and consumers will benefit from the price reduction. Receiving additional consumer surplus on the pineapples they would have consumed at the old price, and the opportunity to earn consumer surplus on their added consumption are beneficial to them.

   (e) An increase in the wages paid to workers harvesting pineapples increases the costs of production and will shift the supply curve of pineapples to the left. This movement of supply will increase the price and reduce the quantity of pineapples.

3. This question tests knowledge of market structures and efficiency. Predicting market outcomes and showing how changes in markets affect efficiency requires an understanding of the theoretical basis behind the different types of market structures. Here's what a sample response might look like:

(a) If the outcome is a monopolistically competitive market, price will fall, as each firm will have less market power than the original pure monopolist. However, price will not fall to the perfectly competitive level, because firms will attempt to maximize their profits by restricting output and raising prices based on the amount of product differentiation they can offer to consumers. Free entry will force long-run economic profits to zero—only normal profits will be earned. Because price will be above marginal cost, there will be allocative inefficiency, as markets allocate too few resources to this good; production inefficiency will result from a lack of pressure to minimize long-run average cost and insufficient incentive to take full advantage of economies of scale.

(b) If the outcome is a perfectly competitive market, price will fall to the minimum of long-run average costs. Output will be greater than in any other market structure as firms expand to the point where price equals marginal cost. Free entry will force long-run economic profits to zero—only normal profits will be earned. At the long-run equilibrium output, price will equal marginal cost, ensuring allocative efficiency, in which markets allocate the amount of resources to this good that maximizes consumer welfare. There will also be production efficiency, because the output will be produced at minimum long-run average cost as firms expand to take advantage of all economies of scale.

AP Economics Glossary

A

absolute advantage
the ability to produce more goods using fewer resources than another producer

aggregate demand curve
curve depicting the relationship between real GDP demanded (i.e., expenditures) and the price level in the economy; the aggregate demand curve slopes downward from left to right

aggregate supply curve
curve defining the relationship between real production and price level

allocative efficiency
allocating resources among production techniques in such a way as to produce those goods and services that maximize society's well-being; part of economic efficiency, along with productive efficiency

appreciation
when the price of one currency rises relative to another currency, the first currency has appreciated relative to the second

B

balance of payments
a summary record of a country's international economic transactions during a given period of time, divided into two accounts: the current account balance (reflecting the trade balance) and the capital account balance or net capital inflows (the difference between foreign purchases of U.S. assets and U.S. purchases of foreign assets)

barrier to entry
a technological, governmental, institutional, or economic restriction that keeps firms from entering a market or industry, such as resource ownership, patents, or start-up costs

boom
period in which the economy moves from a trough to a peak and real GDP is increasing; also called an expansion

broad money
also called M2, consists of M1 + savings deposits + money market funds

business cycles
fluctuations in real GDP around the trend value; also called economic fluctuations

C

cartel
a group of colluding firms acting in unison to set price and output

circular flow
the economic concept that one person's spending is another person's income

Coase theorem a policy claim that negative externalities can be managed through voluntary negotiation, provided that certain minimal conditions are met (and in which clearly defined ownership rights play an important role)

collusion oligopolists' coordinated efforts to set output and price

commodity money
money that is also some sort of commodity that traders can either use themselves or trade to someone else (items such as corn, tobacco, and salt have all served as commodity money)

comparative advantage
the ability to produce one good at a comparatively lower opportunity cost than another good

compensating differentials
the differences in wages that arise from non-monetary job characteristics

complements
goods that are used together; two goods are complements if a decrease in the price of one good increases demand for the other good

constant returns to scale
when long-run average cost stabilizes relative to output in the range of constant returns to scale; the returns occur when inputs increase by a factor of X and output increases by that same amount

consumer surplus
the difference between the maximum price a consumer is (or would be) willing to pay and the price he actually pays

contractionary fiscal policy
policy enacted when the government deliberately reduces its deficit to slow the economy down (usually with the goal of reducing inflation or of reducing the deficit for its own sake); when the government cuts spending (decreases G), raises taxes (increases T), or both, and slows the economy by contracting AD

contractionary monetary policy
monetary policy methods by which the Federal Reserve ("the Fed") aims to decrease the money supply and raise interest; contractionary policy goals are achieved by increasing the required reserve ratio, increasing the discount rate, and selling government securities on the open market

cost-push inflation
inflation created when an increase in the costs of production (wages or raw materials) shifts the short-run AS curve to the left; tends to push prices up while reducing the level of real GDP at the same time (stagflation)

countercyclical
changes that move in a different direction than real GDP, such as unemployment

cross-price elasticity of demand
a measure of how responsive the demand for one good is to changes in the price of another good

cyclical unemployment
unemployment that reflects changes in the business cycle; in a recession period, firms need less of all resources, including labor, whereas in expansion periods increased demand reduces cyclical unemployment

D

deadweight loss
surplus lost due to a drop in transactions, such as that which follows the imposition of a tax

demand for dollars
demand for U.S. currency created by foreign demand for U.S. exports, foreign demand for U.S. investments, and speculation

demand-pull inflation
inflation that follows from an increase in aggregate demand, which will cause equilibrium real GDP (Y) to increase and the equilibrium price level (P) to increase

depreciation
when the price of one currency falls relative to another currency, the first currency has depreciated relative to the other one

depression
period in which a recession becomes prolonged and deep, involving high unemployment

derived demand
a demand that is derived from the demand for finished products, such as the demand for labor and other factors of production

diminishing marginal product
if other inputs are held constant, adding more of one input will initially increase output, but at some point it will increase at a decreasing rate, and will finally decrease; this property is called diminishing marginal product

diminishing marginal utility
if other inputs are held constant, adding more of one good will increase utility initially, but at some point it will increase at a decreasing rate, and will finally decrease; this property is called diminishing marginal utility

discount loans
banks can borrow from the Fed when they have a temporary shortfall; this is the Fed's role as the "lender of last resort"

discount rate
interest rate that the Fed charges to banks for borrowing

discouraged workers
people who are willing and able to work, but whose lack of success in finding a job has caused them to stop actively looking for jobs; these people are not counted as part of the labor force and thus are not included in unemployment figures

diseconomies of scale
costs that occur when long-run average cost increases as output increases; an increased quantity of inputs are needed to get the same or smaller changes in level of output

double counting
counting the value of a good twice when figuring the GDP; the effort to avoid double counting is the reason that the GDP counts only final goods and does not include intermediate goods

E

economic fluctuations
fluctuations in real GDP around the trend value; also called business cycles

economic growth
an increase in the real GDP of an economy

economic profit
a firm makes economic profit when its revenues cover both implicit and explicit costs with money to spare

economic rent
the factor market payment for natural resources that are completely fixed in total supply

economies of scale
economies that occur when inputs are increased by a factor of X and output increases by *more* than a factor of X; these economies happen because increasing size allows for increasingly specialized equipment and increasingly specialized labor, both of which increase output beyond the level of the increased inputs

elastic
significantly responsive to a change in price

embargo
a prohibition against trading particular goods

equilibrium price
the price at which everything offered for sale is purchased, so that there is no pressure on the price to move either up or down; the equilibrium price is also called the market-clearing price

equilibrium quantity
the amount of a good supplied that matches the amount demanded by consumers

exchange rate
the price of a domestic currency in terms of a foreign currency

excludable
if a good is excludable, this means that people can be prevented from using it

expansion
period in which the economy moves from a trough to a peak and real GDP is increasing; also called a **boom**

expansionary fiscal policy
enacted when the government deliberately increases its deficit to stimulate the economy; the government increases its spending (increases G), cuts taxes (decreases T), or both, and stimulates the economy by expanding aggregate demand (AD)

expansionary monetary policy
monetary policy methods by which the Fed aims to increase the money supply and lower interest rates, thereby creating an increase in output; in pursuit of expansionary policy goals, the Fed can lower the required reserve ratio, lower the discount rate, or purchase government securities on the open market

expenditure approach
a way of measuring the GDP by adding up all spending on final goods and services during a given year

explicit costs
costs that a business has to pay out

external cost
a cost that does not fall on the person who is consuming a good or service, but falls instead on some other party not involved in the transaction

externalities
costs or benefits that accrue to people other than those who produce or consume goods and services (contrasted with private costs and benefits); externalities can be negative or positive

F

Federal Reserve System
("the Fed") the centralized banking and monetary authority in the U.S.

fiscal policy
changes, adjustments, and strategies that dictate government spending and taxes; in the U.S., these decisions are in the hands of the President and the Congress

fixed costs
the costs of those inputs that cannot change in the short run, such as rent on buildings and payments on machinery; because these costs are inflexible in this way, they are independent of the amount of output

fixed exchange rates
exchange rates that are set and maintained by government actions; this approach requires continuous fine-tuning by central banks and monetary officials often must sell foreign exchange to keep the fixed rate in place, increasing their risk of running out of foreign exchange reserves

fixed inputs
in the short run, at least one input (usually factory size or farm size) is constant and not changeable; these are called fixed inputs

free-rider problem
the reason that public goods are not provided by the free market; public goods create broad positive externalities, and the accessible and desirable nature of public goods inclines people to use these goods, often without paying for the privilege of doing so

frictional unemployment
unemployment associated with the normal workings of an economy; it takes time for workers to find producers who will pay for their labor and it takes producers time to find appropriate workers

full-employment equilibrium
the intersection of the downward-sloping AD curve, the short-run AS curve, and the vertical long-run AS, which occurs at the full-employment output

G

gross domestic product (GDP)
market value of all the final goods and services produced by a country's economy in a given time period, generally a year

gross national product (GNP)

a measure of the market value of all goods and services produced with resources provided by firms and residents of a nation, even if the resources are not located in that nation and the production does not occur there

H

human capital
investment in people, such as education and training

hyperinflation
a very high rate of inflation; under hyperinflation, prices go up very rapidly—often more than 1,000%—in a single year and money becomes a poor store of value

I

implicit costs
opportunity costs of not pursuing another course of action; these costs are recognized by economists, but not by accountants

import quotas
restrictions on the quantity of the good that can be imported

income approach
a way of measuring the GDP as an aggregate of all of the income derived from production

inelastic
not significantly responsive to changes in price

inferior good
a good for which there is *less* demand as income rises

inflation
a sustained increase in an economy's average price level

inflationary gap
a type of disequilibrium in which demand outstrips production and firms will sell off much of the inventory that they had been planning to sell later; high demand means that the prices of those goods will go up, generating inflation. Firms will expand their production to meet the higher-than-expected demand, and eventually a new equilibrium will emerge at a higher level.

interest
the payment that capital receives in the factor market

interlocking directorates an arrangement in which the director of one firm is also the director of another and the result is reduced competition

K

Keynesian multipliers
expressions of the ratio of a change in aggregate output to a change in tax or spending policy; they describe increases and decreases in the effectiveness of fiscal policy

L

labor force
the group of individuals who are either working or actively looking for work; the labor force includes the unemployed: labor force = number of individuals who are employed + number of individuals who are unemployed

labor force participation rate
a measure of the percentage of the adult population that is part of the labor force, i.e., labor force participation rate = number of individuals in the labor force / number of individuals in the adult population (expressed as a percentage)

law of demand
states that as prices rise, people are willing and able to buy less of a good and hence the quantity demanded decreases; as prices fall, people are willing and able to buy more and so the quantity demanded increases and the demand curve therefore slopes downwards

law of supply
states that as prices increase, sellers are willing and able to sell more of a good so the quantity supplied increases; as prices fall, the sellers are not able or willing to sell as much—the quantity supplied decreases and the supply curve therefore slopes upwards

liquidity
the ease with which an asset can be converted into spending

LRAS curve
long-run aggregate supply curve

M

marginal analysis
economic analysis of decisions about small, incremental changes to an existing course of action (as opposed to assessing more dramatic, all-or-nothing decisions)

marginal cost
the cost of producing one more unit of output

marginal external benefit
the benefit that spills over to parties not involved in the transaction

marginal external cost
costs that spill over to those not involved in the transaction

marginal social cost
the sum of marginal private cost and marginal external cost

marginal private benefit
the benefit that accrues to the producer or consumer of the good

marginal private cost
cost incurred by the producer or consumer

marginal product
the marginal product of any input used in the production process is the increase in total output obtained from using one more unit of that resource

marginal propensity to consume
the proportion of each additional dollar of income that will go toward consumption expenditures

marginal propensity to save
the proportion of each additional dollar of income that is saved

marginal resource cost
the addition to cost brought about by using one more unit of a resource

marginal revenue product
the contribution that using one more unit of a factor of production makes to a firm's revenue; it is calculated by multiplying the factor's marginal product by the price of the product

marginal revenue
the addition to total revenue created by selling one additional unit of output

marginal social benefit
the total of marginal private benefit and marginal external benefit

marginal utility
the change in utility from obtaining one more unit of a good; marginal utility decreases as more units of Good X are acquired, which is indicated by its decreasing slope

market demand curve
the sum of each individual consumer's demand curves for a certain good in a market (e.g., all the individual quantities of Good B demanded at each price)

market equilibrium
occurs when supply and demand are balanced such that the market price and the quantity exchanged are under no market pressure to change

market equilibrium price
the price at which the quantity supplied (Qs) and the quantity demanded (Qd) are equal, so that there is no shortage or surplus that pushes toward a change in price

market failure
a situation in which the market does not allocate resources in a socially optimum way

market supply curve
the sum of all the quantities of a good supplied by all producers at each price

market-clearing price
the price at which everything offered for sale is purchased, so that there is no pressure on the price to move either up or down; also called the equilibrium price

monetary policy
changes, adjustments, and strategies related to the money supply; in the U.S, these decisions are in the hands of the Federal Reserve

monetizing the deficit
increases in the money supply that keeps the interest rate from getting too high and basically reduces the amount of debt on the market as a result of the change in the money supply; monetizing the deficit comes at a significant cost: it is apt to cause inflation and lower long-run growth of the GDP

money multiplier
economic tool used to determine exactly the amount of the new demand deposits that can be created from an initial deposit

monopoly
an industry structure in which there is only one seller for a product

movement along a demand curve
movement up or down a single demand curve, contrasted with movement of the demand curve itself

N

narrow money consists of currency + checking accounts + travelers checks + other checking deposits; the most liquid forms of money; also called M1

natural monopoly
a situation that exists when economies of scale are such that a single firm can supply an entire market at a lower unit cost than could several firms; many public utilities are of this type

natural rate of unemployment
the rate of unemployment at which cyclical unemployment is zero; this rate reflects the unemployment that arises from natural features of a market society

nominal GDP
the gross domestic product calculated using current-year prices; for example, the nominal GDP for 2001 would calculate the value of production using 2001 prices for goods and services. Nominal GDP can vary widely from year to year, due to forces such as inflation.

normal good
a good for which there is *more* demand as income rises

normal profits
a firm makes normal profits when its revenue covers both its explicit and implicit costs

O

oligopoly
a market with only a few sellers, each offering a product that is largely the same as the others' products; in an oligopoly, there is always a tension between cooperation and competition

open-market operations (OMOs)
the Fed's most powerful tool for adjusting bank reserves; the Fed engages in open-market operations when it buys and sells government securities (such as Treasury bills, Treasury bonds, and other federal agency securities) in the open market

opportunity cost
the cost of something in terms of what you must give up to get it

P

peak
the highest point of a business cycle

perfectly elastic
demand for a good is said to be perfectly elastic if the absolute value of price elasticity of demand equals infinity; demand is strongly responsive to price in this case

perfectly inelastic
demand is perfectly inelastic when the absolute value of price elasticity of demand equals zero; in this case, demand is unresponsive to price; because demand is price insensitive, and any price change will leave the quantity demanded unchanged

Phillips curve
graphic representation of an inverse relationship between wage growth (percentage change in price level, such as inflation) and unemployment

positive supply shock
a rightward shift in the AS curve means that the supply of all goods and services is increasing

precautionary motive
the inclination to hold onto money for unexpected cash expenses, such as medical bills or car repairs; one motive behind money demand

price ceiling
price control set when the market price is believed to be too high

price discrimination
the practice of selling at different prices in different markets

price floor
price control set when the market price is believed to be too low

private benefits
benefits that accrue to the individuals who consume or produce goods and services (contrasted with externalities)

private costs
costs that accrue directly to the individuals who consume or produce goods and services (contrasted with externalities)

private good
a good that is both excludable and rival

procyclical
changes that move in the same direction as the real GDP, such as investment spending, consumption spending, and stock prices

producer surplus
the difference between the price a producer actually gets for her product and the price she is willing to take

product differentiation
the difference between products, or the effort to distinguish them from one another

production function
the relationship between the quantity of inputs (resources) a firm uses and the output produced with them

productive efficiency
using resources in the least costly way; part of economic efficiency, along with allocative efficiency

productivity
value of the output that one worker produces in one hour; the productivity of a factor is thus an important determinant of its price

profit
the payment that entrepreneurship receives in the factor market

public good
a good that is neither excludable nor rival

Q

quantity exchanged
the amount of a good actually sold

quantity theory of money
a theory which states that the nominal quantity of money determines the level of nominal income; one of the theoretical commitments of monetarists

R

rationing function
role price plays in allocating scarce goods; the main alternative to market rationing is government rationing

real GDP
nominal GDP corrected for inflation; real GDP is calculated using prices from a given base year, which may not be the same as the year being measured or the year in which the calculations are made. Real GDP allows economists to realistically compare changes in production across years, creating a stable price index so that rising prices in general do not increase real GDP.

recession
period in which the economy moves from a peak to a trough and real GDP falls

recessionary gap
a type of disequilibrium in which aggregate demand is low and goods are piling up on shelves (unintended inventory accumulation); as a result, firms will cut back on production and try to sell off those inventories. Eventually, a new equilibrium will emerge at a *lower* level.

required reserve ratio
a specific percentage of checking account deposits that each bank must keep in liquid, zero-interest reserves; this amount is set by the Fed

rival
if a good is rival, one person's use of the good decreases another's ability to use it

rule of 70
mathematical approximation used to measure the effect of economic growth; this rule tells us the approximate number of years it will take for some measure (real GDP, price level, savings account, etc.) to double, given a known annual percentage increase

S

scarcity
the conflict between limited resources and unlimited human wants; the basic economic problem facing all societies

simple money multiplier
1/RRR, where RRR is the required reserve ratio expressed as a decimal; if the required reserve ratio is 10% (=.1), the money multiplier is 1/.1 = 10

specialization
to emphasize production of the good(s) and/or services at which one is best, rather than trying to be fully self-sufficient

speculative motive
the desire to hold cash in order to be prepared for cash-based investment opportunities; one motive behind money demand

SRAS curve
short-run aggregate supply curve

stagflation
a type of inflation that occurs when an economy's output (real GDP) decreases and its price level rises; production stagnates (as during a recession) while prices (and unemployment) go up

statistical discrepancy
a special account used to ensure that the two sides of the balance of payments actually do balance

structural unemployment
the unemployment that results when there is a mismatch between the kinds of jobs available and the skills of those who are unemployed, or between the location of jobs and the location of unemployed individuals

substitutes
goods that can be used instead of one another; two goods are substitutes if an increase in the price of one good increases demand for the other good, or if a decrease in the price of one good decreases demand for the other good

supply elastic
when the quantity supplied of a good is responsive to changes in price, that good is said to be supply elastic

supply inelastic
when the quantity supplied of a good is not responsive to changes in price, that good is said to be supply inelastic

supply of dollars
supply of U.S. currency in foreign markets, created by American demand for imports, American investments in foreign countries, and speculation

T

tariff
a special tax imposed on imported goods

token money
money that serves as a representation of value; its value is greater than its cost of production would suggest

trade deficit
a country has a trade deficit if the value of its commodity imports exceeds the value of its commodity exports

trade surplus
a country has a trade surplus if the value of its commodity exports exceeds the value of its commodity imports

tragedy of the commons
destruction of public resources resulting from individuals' collective tendency each to use common resources in the way that best serves his or her private self-interest, without considering how that affects the resource or, more specifically, how this approach affects others who also need or want to use the resource

transactions demand for money
money needed for transactions, one kind of demand for money

transactions motive
the desire to hold onto money for cash-based transactions; one motive behind money demand

trough
the lowest point of a business cycle

tying contracts
contracts that require consumers to buy two products when they only want one

U

underemployment
sub-optimal employment situation which occurs when people can find only part-time work or can only find jobs for which they are over-educated or over-trained

unemployed
a civilian, non-institutionalized adult is considered to be unemployed when he or she does not have a job but is actively looking for one; unemployment figures reflect the number of individuals meeting this definition who are part of the labor force

unemployment rate
a measure of the percentage of the labor force that is not working; unemployment rate = number of individuals who are unemployed / number of individuals in the labor force (expressed as a percentage)

unit elasticity
unit elasticity occurs when the absolute value of price elasticity of demand is equal to one and the percentage changes in price and demand are the same; when demand is unit elastic, any change in price will create a directly proportional change in demand

utility
a person's measure of well-being or satisfaction

V

variable costs
the costs of those inputs that vary with the amount of output produced, such as wages

variable inputs
inputs that can be changed in the short run, such as labor; adding more variable inputs to a fixed input will eventually result in diminishing marginal product

W

wages
the payment that labor receives in the factor market

NOTES

NOTES